CECIL COUNTY PUBLIC LIBRARY
301 NEWARK AVENUE
ELKTON. MARYLAND 21921

JUN 1 2 2000

P9-CSZ-857

EASTERN SHORE

INDIANS OF

Virginia and Maryland

EASTERN SHORE
INDIANS OF
Virginia and Maryland

Helen C. Rountree and Thomas E. Davidson

University Press of Virginia
Charlottesville and London

The University Press of Virginia
© 1997 by the Rector and Visitors of the University of Virginia
Maps © 1997 by Helen C. Rountree
All rights reserved
Printed in the United States of America

Second printing 1999

⊗ The paper used in this publication meets the minimum
requirements of the American National Standard for
Information Sciences—Permanence of Paper for
Printed Library Materials, ANSI Z39.48-1984.

Library of Congress Cataloging-in-Publication Data

Rountree, Helen C., 1944–
    Eastern Shore Indians of Virginia and Maryland / Helen C. Rountree
and Thomas E. Davidson.
        p. cm.
    Includes bibliographical references and index.
    ISBN 0-8139-1734-4 (cloth : alk. paper). ISBN 0-8139-1801-4 (paper)
    1. Indians of North American—Virginia—History. 2. Indians of
North America—Maryland—History. 3. Indians of North America—
Eastern Shore (Md. and Va.)—Antiquities. 4. Human ecology—
Eastern Shore (Md. and Va.) 5. Eastern Shore (Md. and Va.)—Social
life and customs. 6. Eastern Shore (Md. and Va.)—Antiquities.
I. Davidson, Thomas E. II. Title.
E78.V7R68   1997
975.2′100497—dc21   97-2651
                                                              CIP

For a teacher,
Carol E. Ballingall,

and

for a mother,
Rhubetta Whitener Davidson

Contents

Illustrations

Tables

Preface

THIS BOOK DEALS WITH the Eastern Shore Indian tribes of Virginia and Maryland. We have not included Delaware because the native population of that state has been examined by other scholars, notably Jay Custer, William Marye, and C. A. Weslager. The natives of the Virginia Eastern Shore appear in Rountree's *Pocahontas's People*, but in less detail than in this volume. And the Maryland Eastern Shore natives other than the Wicomiss and the Nanticokes have been sadly neglected up to now. This is therefore a detailed account of the Delmarva tribes in both Virginia and Maryland.

Our cutoff date is not a recent point in time. Our primary interest is in native *tribes* rather than detribalized *individuals*. Formally organized Indian tribes ceased to exist on the Maryland Eastern Shore in the late eighteenth century and in the Virginia sector in the early nineteenth century. We have traced the remnants of those tribes for only a short time, more or less as an addendum to our text. Tracing all the descendants who remained on the Eastern Shore would be a horrendous task, unilluminated by records stating them to be publicly Indian and requiring several more years of full-time research. We have not made such an attempt, especially since present-day organizations such as the Occohannock Tribal Association are active in doing it. Consequently, we cannot and do not comment on the "authenticity" of any of the "Indian" organizations currently existing on the Eastern Shore.

The Eastern Shore of Maryland and Virginia is a treasure trove of documents for historians because it has unbroken county records over a very long period (since 1632 in Northampton County, Virginia). The history displayed in those records and in the colonial records of Virginia and Maryland is an unusual one when it comes to Indians: the native tribes of the region lost their land, as was typical across the United States, but they lost it without ever participating in a major war with the whites. In Virginia they also lost it without being actual signatories to any treaties, local or colonial. And yet the Eastern Shore saw a proportionately greater survival of Indian communities past 1750 than any other part of Maryland or most parts of Virginia. Thus we felt that a description of the tribes' histories was needed, along with hypotheses explaining those histories.

In this book we explore Indian history, Indian culture, and Indian ecology. All three, after all, are intertwined in real life, so that we must comprehend them in order to understand the native people of the region. (Since we are both anthropologists, we have had to lean upon the expertise of people in other fields; we acknowledge their help below.) We found as we went along with the project that the varying topography and econiches around the Delmarva Peninsula had some serious effects on the lives of Indian people. We therefore were not surprised to find that the Eastern Shore tribes near the southern tip of the peninsula differed culturally in some respects from both the other Eastern Shore tribes and the tribes of the western shore with whom they were allied.

We further found that for ecological reasons (in the seventeenth century) and also geographical reasons (throughout), the colonies of Virginia and Maryland had quite different policies toward Indians living within the territory they claimed. Those policies in turn affected the nature and detail of the Indian-related records left by the two colonies. Virginia's settlement was earlier, with the Indians continuing to farm and fish as they always had, but with many more people around them. Maryland's settlement was later, with that colony starting up later and the land rush being postponed further in the richly forested interior by a very active fur trade in beaver skins. These differences set the stage for different responses of native people to the invasion of their regions. The Accomacs (later Gingaskins) wound up on a postage-stamp-sized reservation and had to begin anglicizing early in order to survive. The Occohannocks joined the Maryland tribes, who held onto large tracts of farming and foraging land until the mid-eighteenth century and thus could retain their traditional language and culture much longer. Colonial policies toward Indians followed from those Indian responses. Virginia aimed at protecting individual Indian people on that isolated reservation and incorporating them into the colony's population, resulting early on in many Indian appearances in county-level records. Maryland, on the other hand, responded primarily to major unrest among native communities that seemed monolithically "foreign" and ready to ally with the geographically closer Iroquois, which has left us with records that are fewer and mainly colonial-level. Thus the Virginia chapters of this volume deal with civil rights issues and many individuals, while the Maryland chapters paint a broader picture. The Gingaskins were finally detribalized in situ in circumstances made more uneasy by the isolation of the south end of the Delmarva Peninsula. The Maryland tribes finally faced losing the land base supporting their traditional culture, and most chose to move away, many joining the Iroquois. Ultimately, then, ecology and geography were major underlying factors in the Indians' varying fates.

Thomas Davidson's interest in the region began when, after taking a doctorate at Edinburgh University and doing archaeological fieldwork in Europe and the Near East, he took the position of regional archaeologist for the southern part of the Maryland Eastern Shore (1980–86), while teaching part-time at Salisbury State University in Salisbury, Maryland, and the University of Maryland–Eastern Shore. To immerse himself in the area around him, he began surveying both archaeological sites and any historical documents he could find. That engendered an enduring interest in both the Indians and the African Americans of the region, even though fieldwork largely fell by the way when he became the chief curator at the Jamestown-Yorktown Foundation, a Virginia state museum.

Helen Rountree's interest in the Virginia Eastern Shore arose out of her fascination with the Virginia Algonquian-speaking Indians generally, an interest she began to pursue in 1969 while teaching cultural anthropology at Old Dominion University in Norfolk, Virginia. She scoured the Northampton and Accomack County records for Indian references in the summer of 1971 and again in 1975. She first went to Northampton with the additional hope of meeting Susie Ames, whose meticulous work in the court records had excited her admiration; she met Ames's sister and learned to her regret that Ames had died two years before. Rountree wrote up her findings about the Virginia Eastern Shore Indians both in her doctoral dissertation (Rountree 1973) and in her book *Pocahontas's People: The Powhatan Indians of Virginia through Four Centuries* (Norman, Okla., 1990).

Rountree met Davidson after he came to Jamestown Settlement. Finding that he had collected Maryland Eastern Shore Indian data in much the same way she had collected Powhatan data, she invited him to join the contributors to her edited volume, *Powhatan Foreign Relations, 1500–1722* (Charlottesville, Va., 1993). That chapter of his by no means exhausted what he knew, so together we hatched the plot of doing a book specifically about the Eastern Shore Indians. Rountree has added to her previously collected data her recently compiled ecological material and also more on the non-Indians with whom the Gingaskins interacted.

In many ways we wrote this book together, for our interests and knowledge overlapped enough that we added to each other's work. However, the approximate division of responsibility was: ecology by Rountree; prehistory by Davidson and traditional Indian culture by Rountree; history in Virginia by Rountree and history in Maryland by Davidson; fate of detribalized Indians mainly by Davidson; summary by both of us. Rountree did the maps, and both of us took the various photographs. We are grateful to the graphics gang in the Publications Department at Old Dominion University for their assistance in computerizing Rountree's maps and making the necessary internegatives. Rountree received small grants from Old Dominion University, as a 1994 and 1995 finalist in the State Council on Higher Education in Virginia's Outstanding Faculty Award Program (she won in the latter year), which covered some of the graphics costs; she received another grant from the College of Arts and Letters at the university to cover the costs of doing new research at the Library of Virginia in Richmond. In addition, Rountree's employer gave her some time to write during ordinary semesters and a one-semester sabbatical to study medicinal plants.

We wish to thank a number of people who have helped us in the researching and writing process. Mel Ely of Yale University coached Rountree, while doing his own research at the Library of Virginia, on using government documents to prove comparative amounts of racism in early nineteenth-century Virginia; Michael Huccles of Old Dominion University's History Department commented on the resulting text. Miles Barnes of the (Virginia) Eastern Shore Public Library, a professional historian, and local historians Doris Adler and Frances Bibbins Latimer (a Gingaskin Indian descendant) kindly read a preliminary version of chapter 6. Two botanists, Lytton Musselman of Old Dominion University and Donna M. E. Ware of the College of William and Mary, critiqued Appendix C on wild plants. Additional help was rendered by a physical anthropologist, Donna Boyd of Radford University, and by a nutritionist (Rountree's sister), Mary C. Rountree, Ph.D., of Riverside Hospital in Newport News, Va. The staff at the Maryland Historic Trust, especially Richard Hughes, was also a great help in getting Rountree oriented to the Late Woodland scene in Maryland before writing chapter 1. And Keith Smith, a member of the Nansemond Indian Tribal Association, also reviewed chapter 1 for readability by laymen.

In all of his Maryland Eastern Shore work, Davidson benefited from the help and support of the Maryland Historical Trust and its parent organization, the Maryland Department of Housing and Community Development, which funded the Lower Delmarva Regional Center for Archaeology. Special thanks should go to Richard Hughes, who worked with him on various Regional Center archaeology projects and who conducted an aerial photographic survey of Eastern Shore Indian towns with him, and also Professor Peter Lade of Salisbury State University, who directed the Lower Delmarva Regional Center. Another Maryland archaeologist who made valuable contributions to the research for this book is Joe McNamara, formerly of the state archaeologist's office. Chuck Fithian of the Delaware State Museums also offered important insights on the Contact period history and archaeology of the Eastern Shore region. Virginia archaeologist Keith Egloff read and commented on various portions of an earlier draft of the manuscript. Finally, Davidson would like to thank collectively the many avocational archaeologists and historians of the Maryland Eastern Shore, who have taught him most of what he knows about that region's past.

EASTERN SHORE

INDIANS OF

Virginia and Maryland

One

The Native People's World

WHEN EUROPEAN EXPLORERS first penetrated the Chesapeake Bay region in the sixteenth century, they encountered a rich land with several already-existing Native American societies there. Although divided by politics and to some extent by language, the Indian tribes of the region lived lives that were more alike than different, and they relied on many of the same tools, both technological and social, to deal with the natural world and with each other. In particular, the solutions that individual Indian groups found to the basic problems of getting food, clothing, and shelter were rooted in a shared cultural tradition that had been evolving in the Chesapeake Bay region for several millennia. A critical factor shaping this tradition was the specific environmental conditions that existed in the Chesapeake world, which then as now offered people a rich and diverse set of natural resources to exploit.

All peoples are in some measure dependent upon the natural environment in which they live. But when people lack elaborate transport systems, and when they aim more at sustaining their families than at producing surpluses to trade, then they focus upon their own locality with an intensity entirely alien to modern Americans. Their environment becomes their grocery and department store, full of riches for those who know its intricacies, but also a store that with its limitations and dangers must be treated with respect.

The Indians of the Eastern Shore, especially in the south, were farmers. But their meat supply came entirely from wild sources: fish, fowl, and land animals. The larger land animals additionally provided people with hides for clothing and bones for toolmaking. The people's vegetable diet came partly from wild sources, especially in summer before the corn crop came in. Wild plants further produced medicines, fibers for cordage, and wood for tools, house building, and fuel. In sum, most

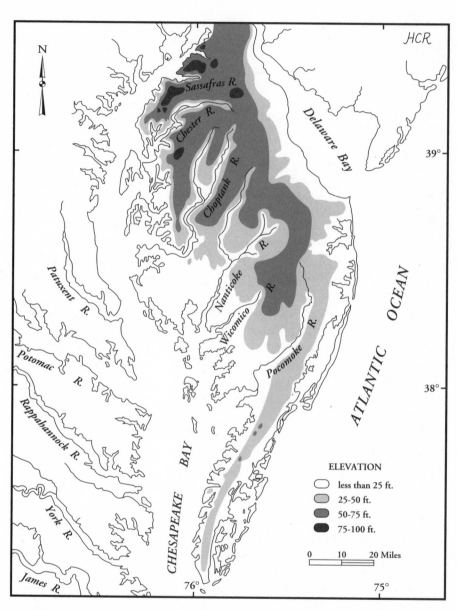

Fig. 1.1 Eastern Shore topography

of the things that Indian people ate or used came from the natural world immediately surrounding them. The native people thus had every incentive to know their country intimately.

The historical sources say enough about the closely related western shore Indians that by adding modern scientists' studies we can estimate how the Eastern Shore's people would have viewed it as a region to exploit. Of course, that was only part of the picture in Indian minds. The early English observers tell us nothing of the rich religious, historical, and mythological associations that places, people, plants, and animals had for the native people. All of those things were passed down orally among the nonliterate Indians, but no English people were interested enough to record them. So we must be satisfied with an ecological reconstruction that is primarily economic in nature.

The Land and Its Resources

The Eastern Shore is a lowish peninsula surrounded by large expanses of water—the Chesapeake Bay to the west and the Atlantic Ocean and Delaware Bay to the east—and indented by a great many streams and their tributaries (fig. 1.1). The peninsula's length from north to south is about 115 miles (185 kilometers) as the crow flies; its maximum breadth in the narrow Virginia part is about 14½ miles (23 kilometers), while in the Maryland-Delaware sector it is about 45 miles (71 kilometers). The major ecological zones the Indians used were waterways, marshes and swamps, and the dry land. Anglo-Virginians and Anglo-Marylanders have historically used the first and last, preferably where they exist side-by-side and the waterways are deep enough for transport ships to put in. Indian people wanted that combination, too, but they also wanted ready access to extensive marshes. Deep water was not of interest to them; shallow water, preferably fresh, was, because of the emergent plants with edible roots growing there. Hence the concentration of aboriginal Indian populations well up the rivers and creeks of the Eastern Shore (fig. 1.2).

Because no place on the peninsula is very far from a major body of water, the climate is somewhat milder than on the western shore away from the Chesapeake. The average winter temperature is 35 degrees Fahrenheit in the north, 40 degrees in the south; the average summer temperature is 75 in the north, 76 in the south. Annual rainfall averages 40 to 45 inches, usually spread throughout the year, and most years see

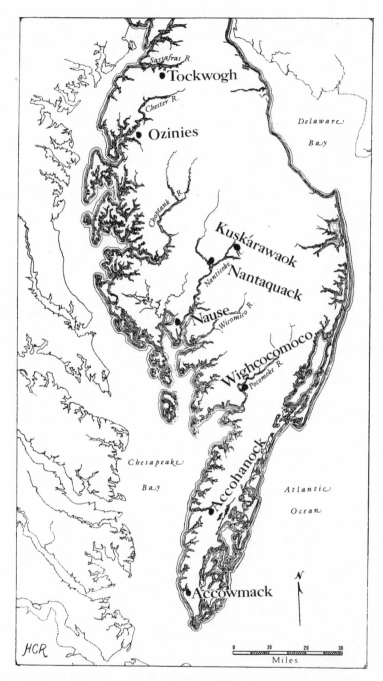

Fig. 1.2 Map of Eastern Shore Indian settlements known to Captain John Smith (1608)

190 frost-free days in the north and 210–20 in the south, depending upon closeness to the waterfront.[1] The waters in and around the Eastern Shore occasionally freeze hard, especially in the northern part of Chesapeake Bay where the water is fresher. At the time the Europeans arrived, there was a cold spell in progress, called the Little Ice Age, which went on in the Northern Hemisphere from about 1450 to 1850; it made itself felt primarily in harsher winters.[2]

There is a low spine running along the shore's length; for the Indians this higher ground was foraging territory, and for the Europeans it was the last farmland to be settled. In addition to its spine, the Eastern Shore tilts gently toward the east and south. Higher ground with more contours is generally found in the north, where the landmass is also considerably wider, and the whole eastern edge of the peninsula is low and lined with salt marshes and barrier islands.[3] Thus near Chesapeake Bay from the Chester River up, the land is high, gently rolling, and deeply indented by rain-fed rivers that meander little and have minimal marshes. Those marshes are fresh or nearly fresh, being so far from the ocean-fed mouth of Chesapeake Bay, so that they produce some edible plant foods (see Appendix C). The high ground south of the Chester River is less high, but thanks to the shore's spine it still has sufficient altitude, above the level of invading salty water from the Atlantic by way of the bay, that the upper reaches of the Choptank, Nanticoke, and Pocomoke Rivers are fresh rather than brackish. The valleys of these streams are wider, often being lined with flat farmland that does not erode readily. There are also extensive marshes on these streams, saltwater ones nearer the Chesapeake Bay and freshwater ones up the longer Maryland rivers, especially inside stream meanders. However, the headwaters of the rivers are usually forested rather than marshy, so the best edible aquatic plants do not grow there. Forested swamp was only useful to the Indians when it had cypress trees for canoe making. On the Virginia Eastern Shore, the creeks tributary to the Chesapeake Bay are all short estuaries (figs. 1.3 and 1.4) containing salty or salty-brackish water. In aboriginal times they were rich in oysters, and their farthest headwaters may have contained a few nearly freshwater emergent plants to eat.[4]

Waterways have multiple ecological zones in them, based upon the depth and salinity of the water and the nature of the bottom. Fish and marsh plants have preferences about salinity; fish also have depth preferences at different times in their lives (see Appendix D). Those preferences determined where Indians looked for the marine foods they

Fig. 1.3 A bayside tidal estuary, Accomack County

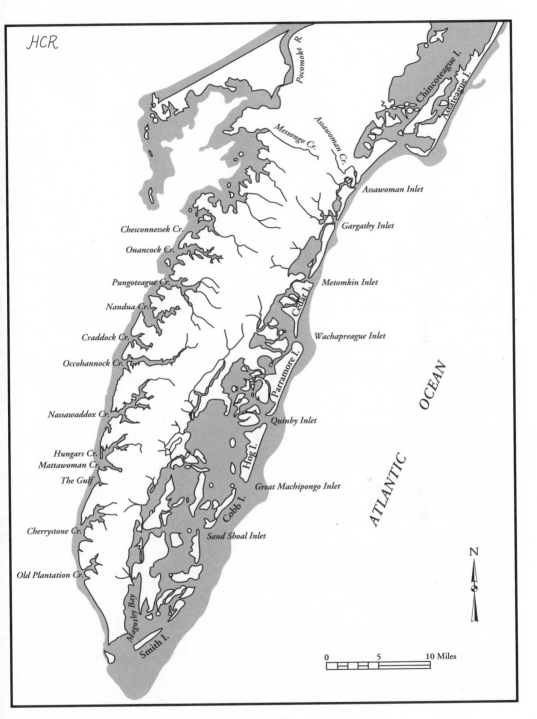

Fig. 1.4 Map of the Virginia Eastern Shore

wanted on a given day. Some zones, though, were more useful than others to the Indians, who traveled in dugout canoes and used fairly basic implements in their fishing and shellfishing. People lacking long-handled tongs could not go oystering in deep water. Fishing weirs (pounds) were the most steadily productive way to catch fish, but people with only stone axes to cut down trees and hand-paddled dugouts to transport them in probably would not have built their weirs in the deeper water that made longer, bulkier poles necessary. So depth of water was a seriously limiting factor in Indian fishing. Most of the really large fish with which a man could have fed all his relatives from one specimen were deep fresher-water ones like the channel catfish (available year-round) or the deep saltier-water ones like cobia and bonito that visit the bay in the warm months (see Appendix D). Deepwater fishing for Indians meant sitting in a canoe and angling until a fish bit, a storm rolled in, or dusk fell. So most fish taken were the smaller but still abundant ones in the shallower waters.

Canoeing could be dangerous on any waterway wide enough for the wind to whip it up on a blustery day. Log canoes are heavy and cumbersome to maneuver and tended to slew around perpendicular to the wind, where waves can wash over their sides.[5] Squalls can blow up quickly in the Chesapeake region, so Indian people probably made religious offerings before setting out. We know that the priests on the Virginia western shore could perform rituals to quell storms,[6] an ability that would have seemed well worthwhile when northeasters lasted five days or so.

The stream valleys of the Eastern Shore are continually losing land to the rising sea. It is likely that the most productive level, alluvial farmlands in the river valleys, were flooded and taken out of human use by the Late Woodland period, A.D. 900–1600; sea level has risen another three feet since 1600. There are still many patches of good corn-growing land on the Shore, but their soils are not the richer alluvial ones. Most of the soils available to Eastern Shore farmers, both in A.D. 1600 and in the present, are not naturally fertile.[7] They must be artificially fertilized, which the Indians did not do; or the crops on them must include nitrogen-returning plants such as soybeans, which the Indians did not have; or the garden plots must be allowed a long fallow period while cultivation goes on elsewhere. This last was the Indian method, and it was feasible because many fewer people were living on the land in Indian times. Even then, prime soils for Indian corn growing were still somewhat limited in extent. The farmers, who were the women, wanted not only flat riverside land but also loamy soil (such as Matapeake and Sassafras loam, silt loam, and fine sandy loam) that was easy to cultivate with digging sticks and that also had a low water table so that it warmed up quickly in the spring for early planting. Along the banks of the Chesapeake's tributaries, most such soil is found well up the Choptank, Nanticoke, and Pocomoke Rivers. The Virginia Eastern Shore has other level, warm, easily tilled soils, but their sandiness makes them less productive of corn.

Correlations between better soils and prehistoric Indian settlements are chancy at present. The archaeological surveying of the Eastern Shore remains in its infancy, so many more Late Woodland sites will certainly turn up. The areas for which we feel some confidence are the Pocomoke River above Dividing Creek and the Nanticoke River in the Marshyhope Creek vicinity. A preliminary comparison (by Rountree in 1993) of the occurrences of the Matapeake and Sassafras loamy soils with known Late Woodland Indian sites along the Maryland waterfronts showed a reasonable correlation between the two. But that correlation may not hold up as more surveying and recording are done. There is, however, a good correlation between historic period Indian village sites and the occurrence of Matapeake and/or Sassafras soils, especially the loamy ones.[8] Village sites and Matapeake/Sassafras soils in turn generally correlate with the fresh-brackish and freshwater portions of the rivers, which provide spawning grounds for anadromous fish (shad, herring, alewife, sturgeon, spot, croaker, and white perch) in the spring and produce the edible marsh plants (arrow arum, wild rice, duck potato, and others) favored by the Indians (figs. 1.5 and 1.6; for details on the correlation, see note).[9] Ironically, Sassafras sandy loam is also the best tobacco-growing soil,[10] which created conflict with invading Europeans later. That conflict was delayed, however, because the freshwater portions of the streams were often lined with trees and shrubs (birch, alder, red maple, beech, oak, witch hazel, cherry, willow, and serviceberry, among others)[11] that supported large beaver populations. The fur trade, flourishing in the Maryland but not the Virginia portion of the Eastern Shore, led colonial officials to delay English settlement in some areas until the beaver population had been decimated.

The forest that covered the Eastern Shore in Indian times was probably a predominantly hardwood one, though increasingly mixed with pines to the southward. There are large patches of pine-dominated

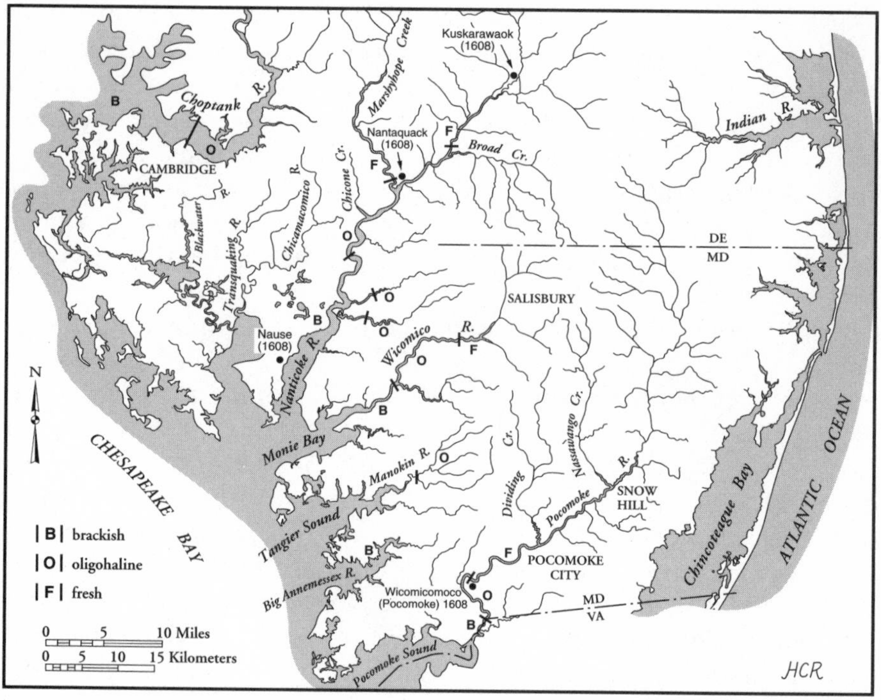

Fig. 1.5 Map of southern Maryland Eastern Shore Indian towns, with water salinities

woods today, but except in the eastern and southernmost parts of the peninsula they are second-growth woods, the result of extensive clearing in historic times. In aboriginal times the woods of the Eastern Shore were likely to be oak-hickory, oak-gum, or oak-pine types, all of which still exist there in second-growth form.[12] Oak-hickory forests usually grow on the higher grounds north of the Choptank River, preferably along the spine of the shore. Oak-gum forests grow on the high and moderately high grounds both on and around the spine; they are found southward a little way into Virginia.[13] Oak-pine forests prefer lower ground that is not actually marshy, and this kind of forest is found today from the Choptank River south to the tip of the peninsula and up the low-lying eastward flank of the spine. The amount of acorns, nuts, and seeds (gumballs and pinecones have these) produced by each of these forests is varied, the richest zone being oak-hickory, the poorest being oak-pine.

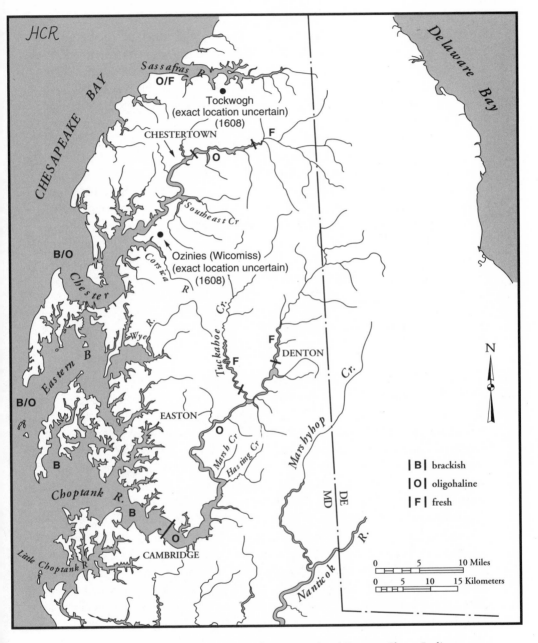

Fig. 1.6 Map of early seventeenth-century northern Maryland Eastern Shore Indian towns

Before European farmers cleared much of the forest, this variation in mast production had a distinct effect upon the amount of nuts that people could gather for the winter and also the number of nut- and seed-eating game animals available to human hunters. The two premier game animals in Indian eyes, deer and wild turkeys, are both heavy consumers of nuts and seeds. Both are also territorial, with deer occupying constricted areas of about one mile in radius.[14] People needed to know where deer could easily be found. The "abundance of Fish and Fowle" in the area, as John Smith phrased it, provided them with ample dietary protein, but deer had larger skins for human clothing and larger bones for toolmaking than any other animal available (except elk, which may never have been common in the region). In Early Contact times the human population on the narrow Virginia part of the shore was dense enough that the Indians themselves perceived that "there is not many Deere."[15] So Accomac and Occohannock men intent upon bringing in a deer on a given day had to know where the limited herds were likely to be. Since the wild plants used for both food and medicine also are confined to certain ecological zones and not others, and useful at some seasons but not others (see Appendix C), it made sense for women as well as men in Indian society to have an extensive knowledge of terrain and plants within their territory.

Indian clearing of land for gardens increased the variety of ecological zones in the region. Altogether there were fifteen major zones (exclusive of beaches and dunes, where wild foods are very limited), each of them capable of further division by depth of water, gradient of streambed or slope of land surface, type of bottom or soil, etc. The major zones produced varying amounts and kinds of sustenance for the native people at various seasons, which in turn meant that people visited these zones at various times of year. Anyone running out of stored corn and nuts and wanting starchy food in winter went into the deciduous forest; in late spring and early summer before the new corn came in, the freshwater marshes were the place to go. Overgrown fields in the thicket stage had the greatest variety of fruit to tempt one's palate, especially in the fall (rather than the summer). Fresh vegetables were few in the wintertime, but sprouts from cattail roots in the fresher marshes were available (for details, see part 1 of Appendix C). The zones are briefly summarized here.

Aquatic zones of decreasing saltiness occur as one moves farther from the ocean or the mouth of the Chesapeake Bay.[16] Each zone has fish, shellfish (fig. 1.7), plants, and other animals that are usable by human

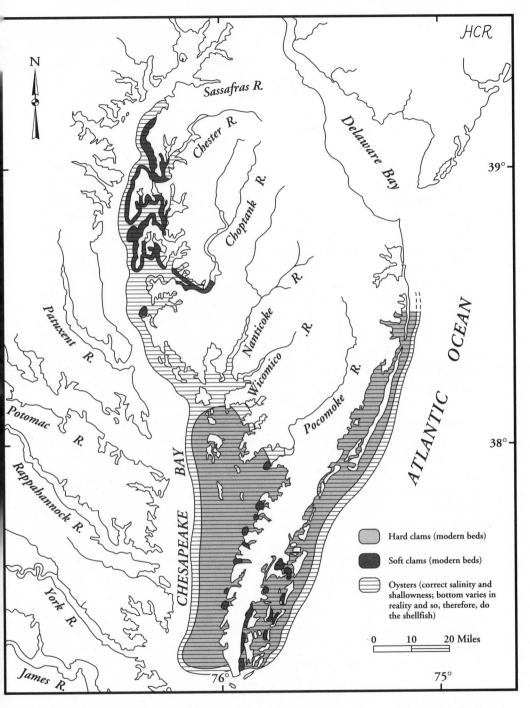

Fig. 1.7 Distribution of modern shellfish resources in Chesapeake waters adjacent to the Eastern Shore

beings. Waters of all salinities attract migratory ducks and geese in spring and fall, the Chesapeake and its tributaries being on the great eastern flyway. *Salty water*, found in the Atlantic Ocean and the lower reaches of the bay, is home to the American oyster, hard clam (quahog), and soft clam (manninose) as well as channeled and knobbed whelk in the shallower areas (fig. 1.7); the blue crab inhabits all depths year-round, retreating to deep areas in the colder months. Shellfish used to be abundant in the creeks of the Virginia Eastern Shore, but by the mid-nineteenth century the oysters, at least, had been completely depleted in many of the creeks by overharvesting.[17] The warm months see visits by really big fish such as bluefish in deep salty water; Indian fishermen would have had to angle for them there. Juveniles of those fish grow up in shallower depths where Indian weirs could catch them. On the tidal flats are smaller crustaceans, prey to foraging raccoons.[18] *Salty-brackish water* has the same shellfish but fewer warm-weather and more cold-weather fish. *Fresh-brackish (oligohaline) waters* harbor channel catfish in deeper areas and a variety of large fish in shallower areas year-round. They also serve, along with truly fresh waters, as spawning grounds for shad, herring, alewife, perch, and striped bass. The shellfish available in fresh-brackish water are the blue crab, the burrowing crayfish, and the coastal plains river crayfish. *Fresh water*, with no salt in it at all, is found in the upper reaches of the bay (except in the fall) and in the longer river tributaries. In addition to its varied fish population, this is the only zone in which the Chesapeake's biggest fish, the sturgeon, spawns. The shellfish are the blue crab, burrowing crayfish, coastal plains river crayfish, and two genera of freshwater mussels. Smaller freshwater streams attract beaver if they have a low gradient (so that the beavers' dams do not wash away) and margins forested with the trees and shrubs the beavers eat.

Saltwater marsh, located along the Atlantic littoral, is not particularly productive of food for humans. The shellfish in this marsh, which are edible but not used commercially today, are the Atlantic ribbed mussel and the marsh periwinkle. *Salty-brackish marsh* is found in the lower reaches of the bay, occurring in tremendous expanses around the mouths of the Wicomico and Nanticoke Rivers and sheltering hundreds of thousands of migratory waterfowl. The shellfish of this zone are like those in salt marshes. In the less salty parts of this zone, Phragmites reeds produce starchy seeds and rootstocks, while most of the parts of cattail plants are edible. The major kind of food that salty-brackish marsh produces for people is animals: muskrats, otters, and raccoons forage here,[19] various birds such as rails live here year-round, in addition to the seasonal ducks, geese, and swans. The major Indian household material provided by the marsh was Phragmites reeds, which were woven into mats. Higher up the bay and its tributaries, or out in the wide marshes where topography impedes the invasion of salty water a little bit, lie *fresh-brackish marshes*. In the freshest part of this kind of marsh and also in the true *freshwater marsh* occur the large-tuber-producing emergent plants the Powhatan Indians collectively called *tuckahoe* (arrow arum, arrowheads that include duck potato, and golden club), along with wild rice and various lilies. These plants grow best in constantly flooded, open, sunny locations and in greatest expanses on the inside of river meanders. The native people could gather vegetable foods in these marshes from one species or another practically all year long. One emergent plant, sweetflag, has roots that are not only edible but may also have medicinal properties. Another wet-loving but not emergent species found in both marshes and swamps is cowbane (*Cicuta maculata*), an extremely poisonous plant that may have figured in an anti-English plot in 1621. Marshes also harbor various small animals preyed upon year-round by muskrats, otters, and raccoons.

The emergent plants above-named do not grow in salty-brackish marshes, which means that the Virginia Eastern Shore lacked them before Anglo-Virginian farmers began damming streams to create ponds. On the other hand, the Maryland Eastern Shore probably produced even more emergents in A.D. 1600 than it does today. The Nanticoke and Pocomoke Rivers both have large meanders with marshes inside them. Today's higher sea level puts the Nanticoke's meanders in the upper salty-brackish and lower fresh-brackish zones, with Phragmites and cattails growing there and arrow arum, arrowheads, wild rice, etc., occurring only upriver. The Pocomoke's meanders are in the lower fresh-brackish zone today, and only a little more salt-tolerant arrow arum grows there, along with cattails and Phragmites. Four centuries ago salt water would not have intruded so far up both rivers,[20] and more of the marshes inside their meanders would have been fresh-brackish or even nearly fresh. Consequently those marshes would have produced more of the emergent plants the Indians found desirable.

The extent of freshwater or fresh-brackish streams (for anadromous fish runs) and marshes (for emergent plants) had a definite impact on how many Indians lived in various sectors of the Eastern Shore. (The same is true for the western shore as well.)[21] Human populations whose diet includes a substantial amount of wild foods are dependent upon the availability of those foods, especially in the late spring and early summer, the hungriest season of the year, when stored foods such as corn and last fall's nuts have run out, the new crop is not yet ripe, and the people have to forage. Indian tribes whose territories had more wild foods available at that time lost fewer people, for there was less danger of malnutrition intensifying the effects of other diseases. Over time those tribes grew. The only Englishman to record Eastern Shore population figures was John Smith, who estimated the numbers of warriors. The Kuskarawaoks (Nanticokes) on the Nanticoke River, rich in fish-spawning areas and richest in emergent plants, had 200 fighting men, while the Wiccocomicos (Pocomokes) on the Pocomoke River and the Tockwoghs on the Sassafras River had 100, and the Ozinies (Wicomiss) on the Choptank had only 60. Smith estimated the fighting power of the Accomacs at 80 and that of the Occohannocks (most of whose towns he missed) at a too-low figure of 40.[22] John Pory wrote in 1621 that the Virginia Eastern Shore Indian people produced more corn than the western shore natives did. He did not specify if they produced a year-round supply, but John Smith indicated that the James and York River people produced less than six months' worth.[23] Pory's account fits the Accomacs and Occohannocks but probably not the people of the Maryland Eastern Shore, if the skeletal evidence from the Thomas site is any indication. The Accomacs and Occohannocks probably had to raise more corn and beans, given their greatly reduced access to tuckahoe and spawning fish, to see themselves through the lean months of spring and early summer. But these crops were originally Mesoamerican species, and even after centuries of hybridization they would have proved unreliable in the droughts that plague the Chesapeake region about one year in three. Thus there was a somewhat lower human population on the Virginia Eastern Shore.

Before we turn to the terrestrial ecological zones, we must note one more thing. Close examination of a modern botanical study[24] shows that the Maryland Eastern Shore is deficient, compared with the western shore, in several emergent plants, some of them components of tuckahoe: water lily, arrow arum, and scythe-fruited and long-nosed arrowhead. These are all species more common in the south, at the same time that they require freshwater flooding; on the Eastern Shore freshwater marsh occurs more frequently in the north (up to the Choptank

River valley). The Eastern Shore also has a deficiency, compared with the western shore, in arrowhead plants for reasons that are unclear. Duck potato (broad-leaved arrowhead) occurs in many more Shore locations than the other arrowheads. Yet ironically, the duck potato grows only in fully freshwater marsh, which is very limited in extent in many of the peninsula's rivers, while several of the other arrowheads would grow—but do not—in the more extensive fresh-brackish marshes. Latitude and altitude combined seem to be limiting the extent of arrowhead plants on the Shore.

Swamp or low woods is an ecological zone that Native Americans found good for foraging, while Europeans tended to avoid it because it could not be farmed extensively without the labor of draining it. Standing water in swamps allows emergent plants to grow, if they get enough sunlight; areas that are merely wetted frequently produce other plants. The smooth alder bushes (*Alnus serrulata*) that grow in such wet places have inner bark that people can eat in emergencies; the bark also may have medicinal properties. The swamp forest along the Pocomoke River produces the rot-resisting bald cypress trees so useful in making dugout canoes. Higher places in the swamp support various nut-bearing trees, along with a variety of plants with edible berries, shoots, and roots. The animals that like berries occasionally would seek them in the swamp: raccoons, deer, foxes, opossums, and sometimes squirrels[25] today and black bears, too, in Indian times. The oak trees' acorns attract the same animals in the fall, plus deer[26] and wild turkey. And beavers, otters, and snapping turtles up to two feet long[27] live in the swamps' pools.

Terrestrial zones are usually in a state of flux, unless they are mature forests or meadows growing on soils favorable to grasslands. When Indian women abandoned old fields, these bits of disturbed ground went through several stages of overgrowth until mature forest appeared. While the ideal time for leaving a field fallow before reclearing was at least twenty-five years (it takes over a century and a half in eastern Virginia for mature deciduous forest to form),[28] it is the first seven years that produces the greatest variation in wild edible plant communities.

Disturbed or nearly cleared ground, whatever the reason for its clearing, is a major producer of useful plants. Modern Americans consider most of these species to be weeds, yet many of them can provide people with greens in the spring. Another weed is the passionflower (*Passiflora incarnata*, known as *maracock* to the Powhatan Indians), which invades cultivated fields and produces edible fruits in the late summer; its roots may also be medicinal. *Old fields* that have lain fallow for one to two years will grow weeds usable as greens in the spring or fruits in summer and fall, like blackberries (*Rubus argutus* and *cuneifolius*, shoots and berries both edible). Common milkweed (*Asclepias syriaca*) has leaves that can be used as greens when young, fibrous stems for cordage, and roots that may be medicinal. Indian hemp (*Apocynum cannabinum*), which grows in old fields and also in the next stage, thickets, was probably the plant the English colonists called silkgrass because of its soft fibers for twining and braiding; it too has roots that may be medicinal. And the flavoring of the roots of sassafras, a shrub common to old fields and woodland borders, is well known to modern Americans in root beer; tea made from the roots is a very old herbal remedy. Because old fields have berry bushes starting to grow in them, squirrels, wood-chucks,[29] deer, foxes, raccoons, and bears come to visit; so do rabbits, which eat the greens.

Thickets grow where fields have lain fallow for three to seven years and woody plants are beginning to establish themselves at the expense of lower-growing vegetation. Thickets are very productive in fruits from early summer through fall, with a resultant increase in fruit-loving ani-mals for humans to prey upon. Several fruit-bearing species, such as black cherry (*Prunus serotina*) and several wild grapes (*Vitis* spp.), have other parts that may be medicinal. The two major colonizing trees of Eastern Shore old fields and thickets, pines (*Pinus* spp.) and sweetgum (*Liquidambar styraciflua*), also are useful to humans. Gum sap can serve as chewing gum, and tea made of its bark is said to be medicinal (traditional Cherokees use it today). New pine needles can be boiled into a tea rich in vitamins A and C in the early spring, while the inner bark can be made into a nutritious emergency flour. The smaller roots of pine trees are also usable as cordage. However, mature *pine woods* are not especially rich in the nuts, berries, and herbs that are highly attractive to either people or animals. That may be another reason why the Virginia Eastern Shore, where pines are more common, had lower warrior counts (which probably meant fewer people) than the Mary-land portion. *Mixed deciduous forest* is the ecological zone that pro-duces the greatest variety of plant foods for people in the spring through fall. It is also home to the greatest number of species useful in herbal remedies, the best known being ginseng (*Panax quinquefolius*). The bloodroot (*Sanguinaria canadense*, or *musquaspenne* to the Powhatan Indians) that the native people used for red pigment and possibly for medicine also grows only in that kind of forest. Mature forest has an understory of trees, like the red mulberry (*Morus rubra*) whose berries were savored by the Indians, but it has little underbrush. John Smith said of it in the early seventeenth century, "a man may gallop a horse amongst these woods any waie, but where the creekes or Rivers shall hinder"; Father Andrew White wrote that the woods around St. Mary's were so free of underbrush that "a coach and fower horses" could be driven through them.[30] (The reason we see so little of such parklike woods today is that nearly all the forest in Virginia and Maryland is second growth, being either old overgrown farms or actively producing tree farms.) Deciduous forest is ordinarily exceedingly rich in nut-producing trees, which attracts all the terrestrial nut-eating animals in the fall and winter. However, the Eastern Shore of both Maryland and Virginia is deficient, compared to the western shore, in the chestnut trees that used to be so widespread elsewhere in the two states.[31] The large pawpaws that are frequently found in the fall on the western shore are also far less common on the Eastern Shore. And the Virginia Eastern Shore lacks bitternut and shagbark hickory, chinquapin, and blackjack oak altogether.

Open woods is a mixture of woodland and small clearings, made by streams or humans or forest fires. Aside from the useful field and thicket plants growing at the edges, the young saplings at those edges were a major source of materials for the Indians' house frameworks. Another tree hugging the forest's perimeter is witch hazel (*Hamamelis virginiana*), whose wood served for bows and whose bark makes a herbal medicine even today. The bigger trees' fallen branches, of a size to drag easily, became fuel for Indian cooking. Open woods, when containing large stands of deciduous, nut-bearing trees, must have been the most desirable ecological zone to have near an Indian town. Aside from all the food and other things it has for people, this zone is extremely attractive to browsers like deer and elk (extinct in eastern Virginia and Maryland by about the eighteenth century). These cervids not only eat nuts and acorns but also like the reachable leaves and twigs at the woodland's edges and the cover that the underbrush there provides.[32] The native people had good reason, then, to hunt deer by the fire-surround method in the fall:[33] it not only brought in plenty of venison for the winter, but it also preserved clearings and made new ones that would attract deer to the vicinity the next year.

The Eastern Shore has a tremendous variety of natural resources upon which people can live directly—if, that is, there are not too many people. In Late Woodland times only a few thousand people were living in the region, and there was enough for all. The resources, however, would have been somewhat different in quantity from what they are today. There would have been far more mature deciduous forest with nut-producing trees, for Indian clearing of garden plots was very limited in extent. With a lower sea level, more of the meanders in the middle Nanticoke and lower Pocomoke Rivers would have contained tucka-hoe. The beds of oysters and clams would have been located farther southwest in what is now deeper water; they and the crabs and fish living around them would have been exceedingly plentiful because they were being harvested by a much smaller human population that was not armed with elaborate deepwater technology. On the other hand, there would have been fewer deer and other herbivorous prey animals available to Indian hunters, because the large native predators like bears, cougars, and bobcats [34] had not been hunted to extinction by Europeans. Timber wolves were once abundant throughout the region, and they catch and eat everything from mice to elk.[35] (When European farmers arrived, the wolves found new targets in the farm animals.) Gray foxes were also more common—it is the open-country-loving red foxes that have increased since European farmers arrived—and these competed with humans for gamebirds, turtles, fruit and berries, nuts and grain.[36] Nevertheless, on the whole, the Eastern Shore must have been seen by the native people as a place to live prosperously, probably with the women doing a bit more foraging to the north and more farming to the south.

The Archaeological Record

From the time of the first peopling of the Eastern Shore more than ten thousand years ago Indian groups living there were linked to contemporary western shore Indian groups by shared elements of material culture and by similar strategies for extracting natural resources from the Chesapeake Bay and coastal plain. Since none of the peoples of the Chesapeake kept written records before the coming of the English, we cannot be certain about just how different Eastern Shore and western shore groups were from each other in social and political organization prior to contact. Archaeology does tell us, however, that Eastern Shore Indians had moved through much the same sequence of changes in material culture that is evidenced for other groups in the larger region, and we know that the Indian societies European explorers eventually did encounter on the Eastern Shore shared many elements of nonmaterial culture with Indian societies on the western shore.

The story of the Eastern Shore Indians whom we know of from early historical accounts, as opposed to other Indian groups who lived in the area during the more distant prehistoric past, is probably best begun about a thousand years ago. Sometime around A.D. 800 to 1000, major changes occurred to Indian cultures on both the eastern and western shores of the Chesapeake. These changes marked the beginning of what archaeologists call the Late Woodland period. The most important new element of the Late Woodland in the Chesapeake was the introduction of maize agriculture. Indian groups in the southeastern United States had been farming for centuries, with maize or Indian corn as the principal crop. For reasons that are not entirely understood by archaeologists, maize agriculture spread rather slowly up the Atlantic coastal plain.[37] Once this new technology did arrive in the Chesapeake, however, the stage finally was set for the emergence of the kinds of Indian societies that were present in the region at the time of contact.

Maize was not the only crop that Late Woodland Indians grew in Virginia and Maryland. Other cultigens included the beans and squash we are familiar with today, as well as certain plants that our farmers no longer produce, such as little barley (*Hordeum pusillum*) and *Chenopodium*.[38] Some of these other plants may well have been grown in the Chesapeake area even before maize arrived, but it was maize agriculture that apparently triggered the most significant social and economic changes associated with the Late Woodland period.

On the Eastern Shore the appearance of maize agriculture coincided with the introduction of a new kind of pottery called Townsend ware (fig. 1.8). Like the Middle Woodland Mockley ware that preceded it, Townsend ware is shell-tempered, and again like Mockley, it turns up all over the Eastern Shore of Maryland and Virginia and on the western shore as well. Townsend is the main pottery type found in Late Woodland archaeological sites in nearly all areas of the Eastern Shore. Only in some parts of Maryland's upper Eastern Shore, notably near the head of the Chesapeake Bay and along the upper drainage of the Choptank River, is Townsend pottery not completely dominant. In these two areas Minguanan pottery generally resembles Townsend ware but has mineral temper rather than shell temper. It was the most commonly used

Fig. 1.8 Late Woodland and Contact period artifacts from the Chicone site, Dorchester County, Maryland

variety of pottery in northern Delaware during the Late Woodland period.

Most of the archaeological research that has been done on Delmarva Peninsula Townsend sites has taken place in southern Delaware rather than in Maryland or Virginia. In fact, Townsend ceramics were first recognized in Delaware, and Daniel R. Griffith's Townsend ceramic sequence, which charts the development of the ware, was worked out on the basis of the Delaware data.[39] The Delaware Late Woodland period sites where Townsend ware predominates are referred to as Slaughter Creek Complex sites.[40] In terms of material culture at least, the Slaughter Creek Complex in Delaware and the Townsend sites on the Maryland and Virginia Eastern Shore appear to be practically indistinguishable. However, the Slaughter Creek sites show a good deal of regional variation in size, complexity, and economic orientation, so that the strong similarities in material culture between all of these sites where Townsend pottery is the principal ceramic type may mask a considerable amount of underlying variation in other aspects of culture.

While southern Delaware provides the closest parallels for the Late

Woodland archaeological evidence from the Virginia and Maryland Eastern Shore, it also seems clear that Eastern Shore Indian cultures were following the same general pattern of development as did Indian cultures on the western shore of the Chesapeake. On both sides of the bay, it is possible to recognize an earlier and a later phase within the Late Woodland period.[41] The most obvious distinction between these phases is a change in the style of decoration exhibited by Townsend pottery, with corded decoration replacing incised decoration around A.D. 1300. As far as the Eastern Shore is concerned, this change in pottery styles seems to have been part of a broader cultural phenomenon that brought the Eastern Shore region into closer economic and social contact with Indian societies on the western shore. This is particularly true for the central Eastern Shore region between the Nanticoke and Pocomoke River drainages and the lower Potomac River drainage on the western shore. Ceramics in both regions were strongly influenced by the Potomac Creek ceramic tradition, which probably spread west-to-east down the Potomac drainage, entering the coastal plain about A.D. 1300–1400.[42] Potomac Creek pottery appears in some quantity on the central Eastern Shore, and it is probably evidence of close east-west trading links in the latter part of the Late Woodland period.[43] Interestingly, there is limited archaeological evidence for a similar trade-driven linkage between Townsend ceramic-using peoples on the Virginia Eastern Shore and Late Woodland groups living on the coastal plain of southeastern Virginia, where Roanoke simple-stamped pottery is the dominant ceramic ware.[44]

Other changes observable on both the eastern and western shores of the Chesapeake during the Late Woodland period concern the number, geographical distribution, and internal structure of village sites. Maize agriculture apparently encouraged people to become more sedentary, to concentrate more on the storage of food, and to establish new settlements in areas like river floodplains where agriculture was especially productive.[45] Because of the limited amount of archaeological excavation that has been done so far on the Eastern Shore, it is easier to discuss the overall distribution of Late Woodland sites there than it is to describe the features present at individual sites. However, limited excavations done at the Chicone site, a Late Woodland-to-Contact-period site along the Nanticoke River in Maryland, revealed large numbers of storage pits, a characteristic that is shared by Slaughter Creek sites in Delaware.[46] The Chicone storage pits seem to date both to the earlier part of the Late Woodland period, which is marked by the presence of Townsend incised ceramics, and to the later phase of the Late Woodland, a phase during which corded decoration was typical.[47] One of the Chicone pit features that produced corded Townsend pottery but no incised Townsend pottery also contained part of a Potomac Creek vessel, an occurrence that supports the idea of trade links between the Potomac Creek area and the central Eastern Shore during the latter part of the Late Woodland period.[48]

Another feature present at Chicone that has parallels on the western shore is what appears to have been a defensive palisade around part of the site. During an aerial photographic survey of the Chicone vicinity, a large circular soil mark was recognized (fig. 1.9) in a field adjacent to the excavated part of the site that contained the pit features.[49] When examined on the ground, this soil mark turned out to be a shallow ditch that defined a circular area over two hundred feet across. The most likely explanation for this feature is that it is a ditch associated with the construction of a palisade.[50] A similar feature was found at the Potomac Creek site on the western shore.[51] There are several other examples of

Fig. 1.9 Aerial view of the Chicone site showing circular ditch feature

palisades at sites on the western shore, and all seem to date to the Late Woodland or Contact periods. They may have been connected with the formation of the political structure known to anthropologists as chiefdoms,[52] which was fully in place by the time Europeans began settling in the region (see below).

Ossuary burials are an additional Late Woodland trait that was shared by cultures on the eastern and western shores. A recently excavated Eastern Shore ossuary called the Thomas site, located within the drainage of the upper Choptank River in Caroline County, Maryland, shows a strong resemblance to some excavated ossuaries in the Potomac River drainage in particular.[53] At the Thomas site thirty-seven individuals, ranging in age from newborns to persons over forty-five years old, were buried together in a single pit during the latter part of the Late Woodland period. The skeletons interred there were secondary burials,[54] and no burial goods were associated with them. This appears to be a classic late prehistoric or protohistoric ossuary burial, where the remains of all the members of a tribe who have died within a certain period are brought together and reburied in a single location.[55]

The people buried at the Thomas site were generally healthy, although dental evidence suggests that they may have gone through intermittent periods of nutritional stress.[56] The source of this stress is uncertain. Subsistence data are quite limited for Eastern Shore Late Woodland occupation sites, but deer clearly were the most important mammal species hunted, while the widespread occurrence of oyster and other shells at these sites indicates that shellfish were still an important food. The discovery of nut hulls and fragments at archaeological sites in Delaware and Maryland suggests that wild plant foods were still being gathered in quantity,[57] a proposition borne out by the historical accounts of Indian lifeways. At the present time there is no direct archaeological evidence that Indian people on the Eastern Shore raised maize, but little systematic attempt has been made to recover plant remains from archaeological sites there.

Nevertheless, it seems clear that the Late Woodland societies of the region continued their intensive hunting and foraging activities even after agriculture appeared on the Eastern Shore. The ability to grow maize increased the efficiency of their overall subsistence strategies and encouraged greater sedentism and population growth, but knowledge of agriculture did not transform the Eastern Shore Indians into peasant farmers. The extent to which different Late Woodland Indian groups there depended on cultivated crops probably varied a great deal. The teeth of the skeletons found at the Thomas site, for example, have only a small incidence of dental cavities,[58] so they do not show the characteristic dental pathology of people who depend on maize for a large part of their diet. Indian societies located at the northern end of the Eastern Shore were probably less agriculturally dependent than societies farther south, in large measure because the naturally available food resources are not the same throughout the region.[59]

The limited amount of controlled archaeological excavation that has been done on Late Woodland sites on the Eastern Shore still leaves many questions unanswered about this critical period of prehistory. Everything points to the conclusion that the Indians who lived there during the Late Woodland period were the ancestors of the Indians occupying the region when the English arrived at the beginning of the seventeenth century. In terms of material culture, Indian groups like the Nanticokes and Accomacs seem to have been direct heirs of the Townsend pottery–using Indians who lived throughout the central and southern Eastern Shore during the Late Woodland period. For the time being, however, archaeological data cannot tell us when the tribes described by the English actually came into being as tribes. An Indian tribe, like any human society, is defined less by tangible things than by shared beliefs, customs, and social institutions. It is easier to learn about these nonmaterial aspects of culture from historical than from archaeological evidence. Archaeology does have the potential to answer questions about the nonmaterial as well as the material culture of the Late Woodland period, but both the quality and quantity of the archaeological evidence presently available from the Maryland and Virginia Eastern Shore are still relatively poor, so that only limited inferences can be made from the data.

Among the central questions that still need to be answered about the Late Woodland period on the Eastern Shore is how and when ranked societies, especially chiefdom-level societies, evolved there. The first English historical accounts of the region's Indians describe them as living in complex societies headed by hereditary chiefs or "emperors" and paying tribute (almost but not quite taxes) to these leaders. Understanding the process by which the basically egalitarian, subsistence-oriented Eastern Shore societies of earlier prehistory were transformed into hierarchical, tribute-producing societies with hereditary authority structures is the key to linking Eastern Shore history with Eastern Shore prehistory.

It is reasonably clear that complex societies directed by hereditary chiefs had appeared on the western shore by the latter part of the Late Woodland period.[60] However, some archaeologists have questioned whether the Eastern Shore chiefdoms known from the seventeenth-century historical accounts had their origins in the prehistoric period at all. Drawing mainly on the Delaware evidence, Jay Custer and Daniel Griffith argue that even the larger Slaughter Creek Complex sites represent "villages of relatively egalitarian social group composition," and that in southern Delaware at least, "the necessary social environments for the development of more complex ranked societies" were not present.[61] The key archaeological evidence that they cite in support of this position is basically negative: that is, a lack of ossuary burials containing large numbers of individuals, little evidence of maize agriculture, and the absence of "extensive trade and exchange and mortuary complexes" of the kind associated with the earlier Delmarva Adena Complex. Custer and Griffith hold the position that prehistoric Eastern Shore chiefdoms, if they existed at all, were not on the same level of complexity as the western shore chiefdoms, and they may have developed only in response to pressures from the western shore.[62]

Probably the best way to approach the question of when and how chiefdoms appeared on the Eastern Shore is to look at both the archaeological and ethnohistorical evidence from the region and then to compare that evidence with what archaeologists and historians know about the evolution of chiefdoms on the western shore. The historical record demonstrates that the Powhatan Indians of Virginia and the Piscataway/Conoys of southern Maryland possessed not only chiefs but also paramount chiefs or "emperors" when the English began settling in the Chesapeake region. If there are in fact clear-cut material-culture indicators for the development of chiefdoms in the Chesapeake, as Custer and Griffith claim, then some of the terminal Late Woodland sites in the Virginia tidewater and in the lower Potomac/Patuxent River region of Maryland should exhibit these traits.

As it happens, though, archaeologists have yet to recognize a material-culture pattern that signals the emergence of chiefdom-level societies on the western shore. As Randolph Turner points out, it is difficult, if not impossible, to prove with archaeological evidence alone that even the Powhatans, with the largest and most complex polity in the whole region, had the kind of personal status differentiation that Custer and Griffith see as the most important criterion for marking ranked societies.[63] Wealth in the form of exotic goods (copper, puccoon, pearls, and shell beads) was certainly accumulated by high-status individuals among the Powhatans and the Piscataways, but the practice of "burying" chiefs' bodies aboveground in mortuary houses did not leave much of a trace in the archaeological record.[64] Copper artifacts have been found in several post-Contact Indian burials on the western shore, and the amount and kind of copper artifacts present in the burials are apparently status-related, but this evidence all dates to the period after large-scale trading had begun between the English and the native people. Burials from the western shore that are clearly prehistoric contain little evidence of status differentiation.

The size of ossuary burials, another criterion that Custer and Griffith use to detect the presence of ranked societies in the Chesapeake, does not seem to mean very much, either. The southern Maryland ossuaries associated with the Piscataway/Conoy chiefdoms, some of which contained the remains of hundreds of individuals, and the similarly large ossuaries associated with the Patawomeke site in northern Virginia show that ossuaries created by chiefdom-level societies in the Chesapeake can be very large. However, significantly smaller ossuaries are also present in these same areas, and most ossuaries discovered within the geographical limits of the Powhatan paramount chiefdom in the coastal plain of Virginia are smaller still, containing less than twenty individuals.[65] The wide variation in the size of Late Woodland ossuaries on the western shore and the general variability in burial practices there during the latter part of the Late Woodland period[66] demonstrate that the burial customs that led to the formation of very large ossuaries were not common to all chiefdom-level societies in the region.

Finally, Custer and Griffith imply that chiefdom-level societies in the Chesapeake must have been dependent upon maize agriculture, and they suggest that if archaeological sites in a given region do not produce good evidence of heavy reliance on maize, then a ranked society probably did not exist there. Maize agriculture does appear to be intimately linked with the emergence of complex societies in the Chesapeake, but the form of that linkage is not clear as yet. So few good studies of archaeological plant remains have been done to date on Late Woodland sites from either the western shore or the Eastern Shore of the bay that any attempt to correlate a specific level of maize usage with the presence of a ranked society there is futile. Such evidence as exists from the Virginia coastal plain sites suggests that the degree to which different Indian communities relied on maize may have varied significantly from place to place, depending on what other resources were available in the surrounding environment.[67] We have already seen that the wild plant resources in the Chesapeake region were plentiful. Without systematic recovery of both large- and small-sized plant remains through flotation and detailed studies of human skeletal material from archaeological sites, we do not know how important maize was, in absolute terms, to the Late Woodland Indian diet in the Chesapeake.

The archaeological evidence for the Late Woodland period on the Eastern Shore is insufficient to tell us how and when groups like the Accomacs/Occohannocks, Choptanks, Nanticokes, and Pocomokes came to be ruled by chiefs, but what evidence we do have from the Eastern Shore is generally consistent with what we know of early chiefdoms on the western shore. Late Woodland sites on the Eastern Shore closely resemble Late Woodland sites across the bay, showing parallel traits like defensive palisades and ossuary burials. There are no conclusive archaeological data that prove that Eastern Shore chiefdoms date back to prehistoric times, but by the same token nothing in the known archaeological record suggests that the chiefdoms do not predate English contact.

When we view the archaeological evidence in conjunction with the historical data, the case for a prehistoric origin for Eastern Shore chiefdoms becomes significantly stronger. Most of the historical evidence dates to a somewhat later period (1608 and after) than the equivalent evidence from the western shore (which begins in the 1560s), but that is basically a result of the fact that Europeans tried to colonize the western shore earlier. When John Smith first visited the Eastern Shore in 1608, he described Indian societies there that were basically like the ones he had already encountered to the west. The Accomacs and Occohannocks of the Virginia Eastern Shore appear to have been part of the Powhatan paramount chiefdom, while the Kuskarawaoks (Nanticokes) of Maryland were clearly a large tribe who inhabited multiple-village sites and maintained a long-distance trading network that extended to the western shore. Furthermore, an unidentified Eastern Shore tribe, probably the Nanticokes, was acknowledged by the Piscataway/Conoys in 1660 to have had an "emperor" long before, and in Piscataway tradition, at least, this Eastern Shore paramount chiefdom actually predated their own.[68] In brief, there seems to be no reason to suspect that the Eastern Shore chiefdoms did not originate during the Late Woodland period, and some fairly solid ethnohistorical data indicate that the Eastern Shore chiefdoms, like the western shore ones, dated back to at least the early to middle sixteenth century.

It may well be that not all of the Indian groups existing on the Eastern Shore in the Late Woodland period developed chiefdom-level societies. Cultures evolve to meet conditions in the real world around them, and change in the direction of greater sociopolitical complexity is not necessarily advantageous in all circumstances. As Custer points out, there is little to suggest that the way of life pursued by the inhabitants of Minguanan sites like Arrowhead Farm, a large Late Woodland-to-Contact-period base camp on the upper Eastern Shore of Maryland, was much different from the way of life pursued by people occupying the same area before the Late Woodland period.[69] On the other hand, other upper Eastern Shore Indian sites like Tockwogh, described by John Smith during his 1608 exploration of the Chesapeake, probably were more like the Indian villages or towns that existed at the end of the Late Woodland period on the central and southern Eastern Shore. It is wrong to seek a single pattern for all Late Woodland Eastern Shore societies. By the time the first English colonists reached the Chesapeake, the Eastern Shore region probably exhibited a mosaic of different native societies whose political structures and economic orientations varied with local conditions.[70]

Historical Evidence

For the Late Woodland period, especially the latter part of it, archaeology can be vastly supplemented by the written observations of visiting Europeans. Most of these accounts were, as it happens, written about the Algonquian-speaking peoples of the western shore of Virginia and Maryland. But English explorers and early settlers visited the Eastern Shore and saw enough that the wording of their descriptions indicates that Indian lifeways were very similar—though not identical—on both sides of the Chesapeake Bay.[71]

Indian people preferred to live along the waterways, both in camps and in larger and more permanently occupied settlements. The latter included moderate-sized "capital" towns and one or more satellite hamlets. Even the larger Indian towns were not always visible from the water. Thus in 1608 John Smith explored the creeks of the Virginia Eastern Shore without realizing that any towns other than Accomac and Occohannock existed (fig. 1.10).[72] The "hidden" towns were probably not de-

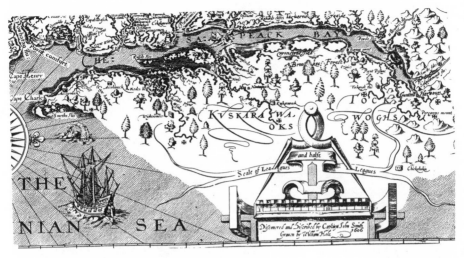

Fig. 1.10 Detail from the John Smith map of 1608

liberately secreted away. They usually consisted of a collection of sapling-and-mat/bark houses scattered among small overgrown-looking fields interspersed with groves of trees.

The native towns of the Eastern Shore in 1608 have usually given their names to the stream drainages in which they were located. They were, moving from south to north: [73]

Accomac, capital of both the Accomac district and of the "kingdom" (technically, the paramount chiefdom) [74] that comprised the Virginia Eastern Shore, was located on the south shore of Old Plantation Creek. The only satellite town recorded for the district was *Mattoones*, located either on Hungars Creek or Mattawoman Creek; this town appears only in records of the 1630s. The Accomacs had eighty fighting men, according to John Smith; this figure would have been a considerably reduced one from late prehistoric times, for Smith heard that many of the Accomacs had died before his visit. [75]

Nassawaddox was a chiefdom that could have belonged to either the Accomacs or the Occohannocks; by the 1640s its chief Tapatiapon (Debbedeavon) was more closely allied to the latter.

Occohannock, capital of the paramount chiefdom that was in turn subject to the Accomac chief, was located near the head of the creek of the same name. Later in the seventeenth century, the capital would shift. The subject districts, documented from the 1640s onward, were either

CECIL COUNTY PUBLIC LIBRARY
301 NEWARK AVENUE
ELKTON, MARYLAND 21921

on bayside creeks north of Occohannock Creek—*Craddock* (probably originally Currituck), *Nandua, Pungoteague, Onancock, Chesconnessex*—or else on small oceanside bays in upper Accomack County—*Machipongo, Metomkin, Kegotank*. The Indian people of *Assawoman* and *Chincoteague* farther north appear occasionally in the late seventeenth-century Virginia records but were usually closer to the Pocomokes of Maryland than to the Virginia groups.

Pocomoke (*Wighcocomico* of John Smith), whose "chief's house" was somewhere in the middle reaches of the Pocomoke River. No satellite towns were recorded for this group.

Nanticoke (*Kuskarawaok* of John Smith), capital of a district that comprised all of the Nanticoke River drainage and possibly also those of the Wicomico, Manokin and Annemessex Rivers as well, was located on the Nanticoke River near the present-day border between Maryland and Virginia. Two satellite towns appear on John Smith's map: *Nause* down in the marshy mouth of the Nanticoke River and *Nantaquack* farther up; two more, *Sarapinagh* and *Arsek*, are mentioned in Smith's *Generall Historie*.[76]

Wicomiss (*Ozinies* of John Smith), a district apparently near the Chester River. No satellite towns were recorded for this tribe.

Tockwogh, capital of a district that encompassed the Sassafras River and probably more, was located fairly far up the south bank of the river. No satellite towns were recorded for this tribe.

The native people in the north spoke a language that was sufficiently different from the Powhatan language of the James River basin that John Smith noticed it; he said he had to use an interpreter at northernmost Tockwogh.[77] The language difference could have been one of language family, i.e., the Pocomokes and people farther north may have spoken an Iroquoian language. But more likely they were Algonquian-speakers who were so far away geographically that their dialect and the James River ones Smith knew simply were not mutually intelligible. The Nanticoke words that were recorded later are Algonquian.[78]

The placing of towns along the waterfront on creeks and rivers[79] made sense, given the people's need to watch for enemies and the extremely varied Indian diet in the Late Woodland period. The ideal habitation sites had workable farmland nearly at the water's edge, with a minimum of marsh to cross for launching canoes and an extensive freshwater marsh not far away up- or downstream. Water for drinking and cooking came from springs if the river or creek nearby was too salty; bathing was done—daily—in the river or creek no matter how salty.[80] Woodland Indian people did not expect, as we do, to take baths in drinking-quality water.

Most of the Indian towns of the Eastern Shore were not concentrated settlements. The palisaded Tockwogh town was the sole exception mentioned by English visitors of 1608, and the palisade at Chicone is the only one found archaeologically so far. The other towns were usually settlements only in a loose sense, "like Countrey Villages in England." They consisted of a scatter of houses interspersed with cultivated gardens and overlooked by groves of trees that partially protected them from bad weather; there were no streets as such.[81] Archaeological excavations on the western shore show that there was also no tradition of orienting all the houses in a certain direction. English accounts do not indicate that there was any special orientation or permanence even for the houses of chiefs, which were simply longer than other people's. All Indian towns were small by European standards: a hundred people made a large town, and most people lived in hamlets.[82] It was not uncommon for people belonging to the same town to live on both sides of a stream. People were accustomed to moving about so often on the waterways, for food getting and communications, that streams formed the center of political units, not the boundaries as among the English.[83] The inhabitants of each town kept the underbrush in its vicinity cleared away, partially through using it for fuel and partially to make it harder for enemies to approach without being seen.

Indian houses on the Eastern Shore, as in the rest of the Chesapeake region, were moderately substantial and made of local, perishable materials.[84] Consequently all we find of them archaeologically are posthole patterns, if that. The preferred house shape was that of a loaf with rounded ends (oval floor plan, barrel roof); the two doors might be placed anywhere. Ordinary houses had one large room, in which "six to twenty" people slept at night; only chiefs' houses and temples had separate rooms in them. Saplings fifteen or so feet long were cut, debranched, and set into holes several inches deep and a foot or so apart around the periphery of the intended building. Wooden crosspieces were then lashed on, parallel to the ground and a foot or so apart. The builders stood on the completed crosspieces to reach the higher levels, and eventually the weight of people working several feet up bent the sides and ends inward until they met, where they were lashed tight to make the roof of the framework. Then either reed mats or large strips of bark were lashed onto the framework, overlapping so as to shed rain. A smokehole was left in the center of the roof over the hearth, and low doors were left in the frame and its sheathing; both openings had their own movable coverings. (Modern museum exhibits have tall doors made for unlimber tourists; Indians had to crawl through their doorways.) It required at least two people working simultaneously to complete the top of the framework, and the building of a house was probably a group effort. All of this work was sufficiently light that it could be done by active members of either sex, and there is evidence from the western shore of Virginia that women performed it.

The built-in furnishings of Indian houses consisted of platforms ranged along the sides for beds; individual sleeping places were separated by mat partitions. Bedding consisted of mats and/or deerskins and furs. Some people also slept on the floor, presumably nearer the fire in cold weather. Among the Kegotank Indians and probably others, the five-foot spaces between the two-yard-long platform beds served for storage or as foul-weather work areas. The hearth had a fire kept alight in it all the time, to keep the house warm in cold weather and to repel insects with smoke in the warmer seasons.[85] Equipment for farming, gathering, hunting, and cooking and serving meals might be stored indoors when it was not in use or when the weather was bad. But cooking and the making and repair of tools and utensils went on outdoors whenever possible, since houses with only a smokehole and a low door had little light to see by. Much of the lives of the houses' inhabitants therefore went on in public view. Daily bathing and probably most kinds of work except deer stalking were done in sociable groups; certainly house building and anything that involved traveling in a sizable dugout canoe would require at least two people. Therefore we may surmise that in the Indian world, personal privacy was hard to get, and it was probably not much valued.

Indian towns were not occupied all year long, except by very old or disabled people who could not move about. The components of the Indian diet changed with the seasons, so whole families would move between towns and campsites during the year. John Smith described much of the annual cycle; with archaeological evidence and botanical knowledge, we can reconstruct the rest.

Spring was one of the hungriest times of the year for most native people in the Chesapeake region. The last year's crops were running out (except perhaps among the Accomacs and Occohannocks), new field

crops were only being planted, and most wild plants other than tuckahoe became edible later. So many Eastern Shore Indian people went to
live in camps and ate mainly whatever greens and fish and meat they
could get. The fishing was done primarily in weirs at that season; angling and the spearfishing recorded for the Accomacs were done in less
severe weather.[86] Hunting was by stalking for most of the year; drives
and surround hunts were reserved for late fall and early winter when
quantity mattered, and the meat was dried for the cold months.[87] The
Kegotank Indians, and probably others, set snares for deer in the wintertime.[88] The main problems in getting proper nutrition in the early
spring would have been getting enough calories and vitamin C and various B vitamins.[89] The available land animals are lean in the early spring;
aside from the shellfish available year-round, the late March arrival of
anadromous fish such as shad must have been very welcome. The Chesapeake region's natives had few or no sugar maples to tap in the early
spring, as did peoples to the north. So it is likely that contrary to John
Smith's account, they ate some of last fall's nut harvest before summer
arrived, for high-fat nuts have both calories and B vitamins. What the
Indians did for vitamin C to prevent scurvy is unknown; water boiled
with new pine needles would have served.

All the Eastern Shore Indians foraged through April, May, and June,
as berries and wild greens became available. People also went back to
their towns at intervals to plant garden crops (women) and begin clearing next year's fields (men). The clearing, done with stone axes, was
small-scale[90] and aimed merely at allowing the sun to reach the crops
that would grow on the ground; digging-stick agriculture does not require the removal of stumps. Since the native people used no fertilizer,
older (more than three years old),[91] less productive fields were left fallow, and some new ones were cleared each year. Planting took place in
several plots per family, some in late April, some in May, and some in
early June, so that a moderate but continual supply of fresh farm produce would be available in August through October.

While doing their farmwork in the towns, people got the protein they
needed largely from the last nuts and acorns from the previous fall,
coupled with fish from the weirs. Starchy foods may have come from
tuckahoe (John Smith does not mention it at that season, but it is easy
to find from April onward) or from little barley (*mattoume*), which
grows well in newly fallow fields and ripens in April through June.[92]
Given the practice of shifting cultivation, the less-than-overgrown fal-

low fields ideal for mattoume would have changed somewhat from year to year, so Indian people probably kept some of the harvest back each year for planting, as with corn.[93] In between planting and clearing sessions, people foraged for meat, fish, berries, and greens, which took men and women out into the woods and onto the waterways.

Early summer was another potentially lean time. In June, July, and August the planted fields needed the most attention, which kept the women and children running back and forth between farming in the towns and foraging farther afield. Men, as usual, came and went on their hunting and fishing business. The people's practice of intercropping, or planting beans and squash between the equally spaced corn plants, probably cut down on the growth of weeds, but some weeding was required nonetheless in the lush climate of the Chesapeake. The small fields and the near proximity of woods would have made even more necessary the protection of the growing plants from greens-loving animals like rabbits, beavers, deer, and woodchucks; once the corn and beans began to ripen, raccoons, squirrels, and bears also would come calling.[94] Fencing of fields against such raiders was not feasible, given Indian technology and already existing demands on people's time. But children could be used as scarecrows, especially boys who could get target practice and add food to the stewpot at the same time.[95] Other items on the Indian menu during those months were fish and shellfish, groundnuts, wild greens if boiled several times, green corn, and bread made from starchy tuckahoe tubers that had first been baked in an earth oven or sliced and sun-dried to neutralize the stinging oxalic acid in them.[96] Once last fall's nuts ran out, the major source of the calories to keep up all the work must have been tuckahoe.

Late summer and early fall were the time of plenty in field crops. Much of the corn was dried and shelled for use later in the winter as bread. People of both sexes and all ages were able to stay for longer periods in the towns. Late fall was a time of serious, specialized foraging for nuts and venison, so that nearly the whole population of a district might move out for a time into the more distant woods where the deer population was less depleted. Once real winter set in, people returned to their towns to hold ceremonies and live off the food they had stored until it ran out, usually in the early spring. (When Englishmen wrote of being feasted on cornbread in February or March, their hosts were rich people like chiefs, who had such supplies year-round.)

Towns that were fully occupied only for part of the year misled Europeans. The Jesuit missionaries on the Maryland western shore remarked upon "so unrestrained and wandering a mode of life," while John Smith felt that the James and York River people improvidently lived "from hand to mouth."[97] What these outsiders did not notice was that the people's movements were regular and seasonal within well-known territories. The newcomers also failed to appreciate that the Indian diet, with its heavy reliance upon native wild sources, was both more varied than their own and less vulnerable to droughts. Further, it had fruits and greens in it for much more of the year than the English one did, either in England or in early seventeenth-century America.

However, in one respect the English were partially right about "nomadism": Indian towns, those collections of dispersed houses and fields, did not have the permanence of European towns. Indian houses were eminently biodegradable and would not last longer than about five years. Houses were built near fields that were under cultivation, and shifting cultivation meant that each year some new fields—farther away—were cleared and older ones left fallow. Eventually the commute to the current fields would become onerous, and just as important, the firewood available nearby would be depleted. So Indian families moved their houses every few years, and whole towns would appear to be in flux if visited over a couple of decades.[98] Across several centuries most of any river's waterfront land suitable for farming would have had Indians occupying it, and thus we find shallow archaeological evidence of Woodland Indian habitation all up and down such riverbanks throughout the Chesapeake region.

Indian people of both sexes and all ages went in and out of the towns on a regular basis. Hunting and fishing obviously required the men to go where the wild animals or fish were. Women and girls were working women and were by no means confined to a domestic sphere[99] at home: they had to go into the marshes to gather tuckahoe for eating and reeds for weaving mats, while gathering nuts and firewood sent them into the woods as well. New garden plots were some distance from the houses, and once new houses were built to reduce the distance to the farms, the old fields producing mattoume, greens, and berries were some distance away. A stay-at-home woman would have been considered lazy, for she produced no food, house-building materials, or fuel for the family.

Thus both men and women frequently used both the major methods of travel: canoes and footpaths. Dugout canoes were made from single cypress logs, at least three feet in diameter for up to fifty feet long; the

Pocomoke River is rich in cypress trees, though after the logging operations of the nineteenth century few such huge logs can be found today.
Dugouts are heavy and cumbersome to paddle, but several people can
move them along very well. John Lawson remarked of the Indians of the
eastern Carolinas in 1709 that "many of the Women are very handy in
Canoes, and will manage them with great Dexterity and Skill, which
they become accustomed to in this watry Country." Colonel Henry
Norwood noted that the Eastern Shore Indians who rescued him and
his companions in 1649 propelled their canoes with long "booms"
(poles), which they pushed while standing with a foot on each gunwale
of the canoe.[100] Footpaths connected towns and hamlets, both along the
rivers and across peninsulas. They were used for travel when the loads
being transported were not huge, the weather was too severe for water
travel, or truly rapid communication was needed across a peninsula.
Women as well as men used the paths. Both sexes had food-getting business away from the towns, and both sexes visited relatives and friends
in other towns. Both sexes were accustomed to hauling heavy loads
from one place to another on foot: men brought back animals (especially deer) for the pot, and women brought back stacks of firewood
and net bags full of gathered plant foods. Men and women alike were
expected to be strong and physically fit.

Indian people of both sexes were healthier than early seventeenth-
century English people, though not necessarily longer-lived.[101] Many Indians had at least one bout of infectious disease, with its concomitant
decrease in food intake, that was of a length and seriousness to leave
marks on their bones. The diseases are hard to identify when we have
only bones from archaeological sites, but these ailments would have
been more common in the larger Indian settlements, especially the palisaded ones that concentrated people into small areas. Nearly all Indian
people, especially those whose diet contained more corn and beans, had
dental cavities because of a fairly starchy diet and a lack of tooth-
brushes. As people aged, their cavities became more frequent and more
likely to cause abscesses and tooth loss, which eventually caused malnutrition from being unable to chew food. That process alone shortened
Indian life expectancy.

Arthritis afflicted older Indians (in those days, 30 years old or
more),[102] but many people did not live long enough to develop it. Less
than 5 percent of the population, mostly males, reached the age of 50,
and after a hard and active life, they would have looked like our 70-

year-olds. In 1607 an English expedition on the James River met an active, very fit "olde man" who claimed to be 110; by the Powhatan custom of counting each half year separately, he would have been 55, but the white hair on his head and arms and his toothlessness convinced them that he was a centenarian.[103] The ages of greatest mortality among Late Woodland Indians in the Chesapeake region were the first five years (30 percent died then) and the twenties and thirties, when women died in childbirth and men died in war and hunting accidents.

Eastern Shore Indian people were standard Amerinds in appearance. Their skin was sallow white until the sun tanned it and paint reddened it. The faces of these Algonquian-speakers were usually broad with prominent cheekbones, and their eyes were dark. Hair was black and coarse; women wore theirs long, while men wore the left side long and knotted up, the right side shaven, and a roach or stand-up ridge along the crown from front to back. Although the "Wighcocomicoes" (Poco-mokes) were "short" in English eyes, other Chesapeake region Indians were taller than English people of that day. Men averaged 5 feet 7½ inches (versus 5 feet 6½ inches for male Londoners), and women averaged 5 feet 3½ inches (versus 5 feet 1 inch for female Londoners).[104]

The native people went through most of the year wearing very few clothes.[105] That must have added to the impression of their surefooted-ness; it was hard for Englishmen to be graceful in their heavy woolen clothing and leather boots. The only real cold-weather garment was a deerskin cloak (matchcoat), the forerunner of the "Indian blanket." It was warm but ill-adapted for active work. People found it simpler to acclimatize themselves as far as possible, with oil and grease smeared on the skin for a little extra warmth after each morning's cold-water bath.[106] Thus for much of the year and for some activities even in frigid weather, all adults wore only deerskin loincloths, and children wore nothing at all. Leggings and moccasins were added when moving through the woods, to protect against briers. "Dressing up" meant add-ing red puccoon paint and shell-bead jewelry; richer people also donned fringed deerskin garments that left one arm and shoulder bare.

Eastern Shore Indian society was based upon kinship. Kinship deter-mined whether one could become a chief or (probably) a priest. Kinship determined whom one could and could not marry: acceptable people were either distant by blood or marriage or not related at all, although that may have applied only to people related through women. We do not know exactly how common folk calculated their kinship.[107] Their inheritance of things (rather than social positions) dictated that personal valuables were buried with the deceased and the house and furnishings went to the widow. Chiefly families buried their valuables with the dead, too, but their social positions were passed down matrilineally, focusing only on connections through female ancestors.

Smaller villages and hamlets tended to be comprised entirely of kinsmen, usually people linked through men.[108] Young people courted and came to an agreement, after which their parents negotiated a bride-wealth payment, made by the groom's family to the bride's family (she was valued as a worker and a producer of children). The groom and his family prepared a house complete with utensils, and then the bride was brought to it by her family, after which there was a feast. The couple then resided near the groom's parents. That meant that Indian men tended to remain in the villages where they grew up, along with their brothers and the cousins related to them through other males. Any conflicts with a kin-reckoning system emphasizing either female connections or both sides of the family were resolved by a lot of visiting back and forth. For people who are not chained to eight-hours-a-day, five-days-a-week jobs in one location, and who are moving about getting various kinds of foodstuffs anyway, frequent visiting is an ordinary part of life.

Husbands and wives were primarily partners in creating and supporting a family; very few early seventeenth-century accounts mention romantic attachments (indeed, these were not common in English marriages of the time, either). Spouses treated each other with gravity and respect; younger people treated older people in the same fashion.[109] Yet there was little authoritarianism in all that deference. Men and women led lives that were separate in many ways: women farming and gathering firewood and plant materials, men fishing and hunting and warring.[110] On the western shore of Virginia, the English felt that the men "scorned to be seene" in any female work, but real scorn may not have been involved. The corn and tanned deerskins that women produced were high-status items paid as tribute to the chiefs, so women's work was respected. The fact that both sexes ate ordinary meals and performed welcome dances together indicates relative social equality. It is also likely that men and women cooperated informally when the need arose: fields cultivated specifically for chiefs were planted and harvested by men and women working together.[111] Children in the toddling stage would have been watched by whoever was home, and both men and women had tool making and repairing that they did near the house.

Children imitated their parents' work but were free to learn it at their own speed, without corporal punishment.[112] There was, however, heavy pressure on boys to learn and perform as hunters at fairly early ages. People were given personal names when they were young, but as they moved through life they were given new names that reflected personal characteristics or things they had done. Boys and men were expected to earn ever better names to celebrate ever greater deeds.[113]

On the western shore of Virginia and also apparently of Maryland, teenage boys went through a grueling months-long endurance test called the *huskanaw*, after which they were considered "real men."[114] They had to earn the privilege of being put through that rite of passage by proving themselves adult-level hunters of animals, particularly deer. However, John Pory reported in 1621 that the Eastern Shore Indians, at least those of Virginia, did not have the huskanaw.[115] The most likely reason, if Pory was talking only about the Virginia sector, is that adult men there did not have to perform as much in hunting and war as men did on the western shore, so there was less need for allotting time to keep up a "male mystique." The deer population of the Virginia Eastern Shore was not high; the men would have been going after smaller, less dangerous prey and also doing it on more of a daily basis, with fewer overnight, all-male hunting trips into the woods. The southern Eastern Shore was also more isolated from other people, including enemies wishing to attack them; the men of that part of the peninsula did not need to show continually that they were ready for war. Thus there would have been less need for a ritual process that emphasized males as extremely focused, supertough killers.

The Indian priesthood in either Virginia or Maryland was not well described, and what little we know applies to the western shore but not necessarily the Eastern Shore.[116] Priests were male and persons of importance. Their closer relationship with the *quiocosock* (minor deities) not only established them as intermediaries to prevent misfortune and cure disease, but it also enabled them to see into the future and predict the outcome of various undertakings. The latter was extremely important to the warlike people of the western shore; the Accomacs and Occohannocks may not have had the same emphases in their minds concerning priests. The curing of disease, however, was important to everybody, so it is a pity that the English observers did not record much about it. Any thorough study of Indian use of medicinal plants in Virginia or Maryland has to be a reconstructive one.

Native religious beliefs in the Chesapeake region were closely allied to everyday life. Considerable personal autonomy was allowed in personal beliefs, which echoed the family-oriented, weakly taxed economy the people practiced. Most people agreed that there had been a creator deity (called Ahone in the James River valley and the Great Hare by the Patawomecks) who did the job and then retired.[117] People paid more attention to the many spirits that were still active in the world (called *quiocosock*, anglicized to "okee" or "okeus"). These had to be shown veneration when encountered in their many forms, usually through offerings of food, deer suet, tobacco, and the like.[118] Not making offerings invited misfortune: for example, skimping on this year's first-fruits celebration (apparently held when the corn first became ripe) presaged a poor crop in the next year. Most religious rituals, unless involved with curing someone, took place outdoors and whenever they were needed or appropriate; weekly indoor services were foreign to the Indian mind.[119]

Indian temples were places for seclusion and security, not places of public worship. They were built like dwelling houses, but longer, and they contained space for priestly rituals, plus the storage of chiefs' valuables and sometimes also chiefs' bones after death (recorded for the Pocomokes and Assateagues).[120] Ordinary people were buried in the ground,[121] and it is their bones that archaeologists find, not the chiefs'. Ideas about the afterlife, recorded on the western shore of Virginia, varied depending on whom the English colonists interviewed. But they agreed that only chiefs and priests had souls, and these traveled to a place that really was a "happy hunting ground," with good food and lots of singing and dancing.[122]

All the people in the Indian towns of the Eastern Shore lived active, productive lives from day to day. But when strangers came to call or the time came for a ceremony, then the important people in town—chiefs, councillors, and priests—assumed other duties and physical trappings that made them stand out. Even the most important, powerful chiefs in the Chesapeake region worked on most days like ordinary men and women; they took pride in being able to do so. However, they were contributing to families that were already wealthy.[123]

Chiefs received tribute in corn raised especially for them, deerskins, and luxury goods such as copper pieces and shell beads. The Eastern Shore people, especially the Nanticokes, produced great quantities of these beads.[124] Chiefs had multiple spouses—wives for the males, perhaps husbands for females—so that more food was coming into their households, to be used later in entertaining. They had larger dwellings to house the greater number of people both living there and coming to call; a really powerful chief like Powhatan had several such houses scattered in his dominions. Within a chief's house, the ruler's bed was longer and had finer fur bedding on it.[125] In dressing up, chiefs had finer garments of deerskin and other furs, with elaborate shell-bead embroidery. They and their families could paint themselves lavishly with puccoon, which had to be imported from non-Algonquian-speaking Indians.

When important visitors arrived, they would be met formally by all the townspeople and conducted into the chief's presence. The chief's spouses, bodyguards, and councillors would all be on show, in lavish dress, and after a grave and formal greeting the guests would be presented with much more food than they could possibly eat, in an aggressive display of hospitality. After oratory and dancing by the townspeople, the guests would be put up for the night, either in the chief's own house (Maryland) or in another house (Virginia), and often they would be lent sleeping partners for the night. The partners, who may have been volunteers for the honor, would be women from out in the town; Indian wives had a great deal of sexual freedom unless they were married to a chief, who then claimed them exclusively. Sentinels watched over the chief's house each night and, by extension, also over visitors under his protection.[126]

The Pocomokes had district chiefs who were simply allied with one another; the Accomacs/Occohannocks and the Nanticokes had district chiefs who were subject to paramount chiefs, and the Accomac/Occohannock paramount chief was semisubject to Powhatan over on the western shore. All of these chiefs became the focus of English interest as soon as the first ships arrived. English observers got the impression that Indian chiefs were very powerful and important people, but that was because most of them saw these leaders only on state occasions. The reality was less spectacular. Indian leaders were chiefs but they were not real kings or queens or emperors. Their status had official terminology—*weroance* or *weroansqua* for district chiefs, male and female respectively; *mamanatowick* (Powhatan word) or *talleck* (Nanticoke word, equivalent to Piscataway *tayak*) for paramount chiefs, in Virginia and Maryland respectively—but even the commonest people addressed them to their faces by their personal names.[127] Chiefs could give orders in matters that concerned themselves directly, such as hospitality to visitors, warfare against other Indian groups, or offenses against their own persons, and expect to have those orders obeyed, even if it meant putting someone to death. But apparently they had little control over quarrels that occurred between their subjects. The major crimes in Indian society were killing or stealing from one's own people; priests were involved in naming culprits, but chiefs seem to have been only peripherally involved in their execution.[128]

The children of chiefs were not equivalent to European princes and princesses, either. Chiefs inherited their status matrilineally. The inheritance ran from a mother to her sons (in order of age), then her daughters (in order of age), then to the sons of the eldest daughter (in order of age), then to the daughters of the eldest daughter (in order of age), etc.[129] Children of male chiefs were prominent (sons were called *tawzin* on the Maryland western shore), but only as long as their fathers lived; after that, their eminence faded. This matrilineal rule went against the patrilineal English one, and later in the seventeenth century some Indian groups would begin to change over. Close relatives of a chief remained important during his or her lifetime and not uncommonly would be given a satellite town to rule.[130] In 1621 John Pory found the easygoing Accomac "Laughing King," Esmy Shichans, was titular head of his domain, and his energetic younger brother Kiptopeke, district chief of Occohannock, was de facto ruler of the whole Virginia Eastern Shore with his brother's permission.[131]

Chiefs had to consult with councils of priests and outstanding warriors (appointed from certain families, at least among the Piscataways) before they could give orders, especially military ones. Council sessions were always orderly and decorous, each person being listened to in silence until finished; even chiefs had to observe this rule of politeness. Councillors were called *crotemen*, at least by the Kegotanks; perhaps also *wiso* (Piscataway term) or *mangoy* (Powhatan term, later used in both Virginia and Maryland colonies). The Nanticokes may, like the Piscataways, have had a hierarchy of councils parallel to that of the chiefs: district tribal council and paramount-level *matchacomico* or council comprised of the paramount chief's personal council plus the district chiefs and their councils. The Piscataways also had a special position called a speaker, or official announcer, which the Nanticokes with their Piscataway ties may also have had.[132]

The Eastern Shore Indians had extensive contacts with other peoples, especially in the north where the Chesapeake Bay is narrower and easier to cross. Only some of these contacts were friendly. Generally speaking, archaeology and history indicate friendly trading relations with the Algonquian-speakers directly to the west: the Nanticokes and Pocomokes with the Patuxents and Piscataways, and the Occohannocks and Accomacs with the Powhatans. (The latter two were also militarily allied with—and, according to the man Powhatan, subjects of—the paramount chiefdom on the Virginia western shore.) The goods traded apparently were mainly luxury goods. Powhatan told John Smith he received tribute from the Accomacs/Occohannocks on a regular basis in the form of shell beads. These beads were the major high-status item other than surplus corn (there is no record before 1622 of exporting corn to Indians across the bay) that the Accomacs and Occohannocks produced.[133] The beads were probably not the common *roanoke*, thin disks made from broken mussel shells; mussels are common on both sides of the Chesapeake. Instead they were likely to be *peak*, or *wampumpeak*, which was harder to manufacture, being short, drilled tubes of clam shell (the purple part) or whelk shell (the column, which is white). Clams are common in the salty parts of the Chesapeake system, but whelks need very salty water, so they wash up on the beaches only in the southernmost parts of the bay and along the ocean beaches. Only Eastern Shore people would have had access to large quantities of them. The beads were used for embroidery and jewelry in aboriginal times; their use as money came after the arrival of the English. The Eastern Shore people, especially the Nanticokes, are known from later records to have been trading with western shore people to get puccoon; in 1681 they bought it from Nanzaticos, who had traveled from the Rappahannock River.[134]

Relations with other peoples were strained or hostile. By 1621 the Accomacs were at loggerheads with the Powhatans after being "too friendly" to the English for several years. The Accomacs had long been at odds with the Patuxents, for causes unspecified. The Ozinies (Wicomiss) and the people of the Patuxent River were all at war with the Iroquoian-speaking Susquehannocks, who were trying to extend their territory southward. That effort was successful, and it created anti-Susquehannock feelings among the mid-seventeenth-century Nanticokes. And everybody was afraid of the Massawomecks, Iroquoian-speakers from far to the northwest (their identity is uncertain) who could make lightning raids because of the lightness and speed of the birchbark canoes in which they traveled.[135]

Indian people who were often threatened by enemies responded by being warlike themselves; when the threat was very frequent, they also lived in palisaded towns.[136] John Smith felt that all Eastern Shore people were at least fairly warlike, and the Tockwoghs lived inside a very sturdy palisade. Our information on warfare otherwise comes from the western shore. Most Indian fighting took the form of small-scale raids; among the more politically complex Powhatans and Piscataways, at least, these were led by war captains called *cockarouses*. Individual bravery was emphasized, but not at the risk of unnecessary exposure of oneself; Indian men thought that the English practice of open-field fighting was suicidal (and so it was). Weapons consisted of bows and arrows to wound enemies and tomahawks to finish them off. The bows that Virginia Indian men carried would shoot level for forty yards, those of Maryland Indian men for only twenty yards. Warriors wore little or no protective clothing (a few Virginia tribes used bark shields); they relied on speed and effective use of natural cover to stay alive. Any man captured alive by the enemy could expect to be tortured to death—an "honor" that most Eastern Woodland people paid each other reciprocally. The victim who died bravely would show no pain; on the contrary, he would sing a death song that derided his torturers as weaklings who could not hurt him. Trophy taking from dead enemies was recorded on the Virginia western shore: it took the form of scalps, hands that were dried and worn as decorations, etc.[137]

We can now understand better why the western shore people, and probably the Maryland Eastern Shore people as well, trained their boys to be effective warriors. Only the Virginia Eastern Shore groups, with their relative isolation, seem not to have lived under a constant threat. That may go far to explain why those people in the south generally behaved so peacefully, even while their area was being inundated by English settlers in the mid-seventeenth century. It is to the post-Contact history of these southerly, more settled people that we now turn.

Two

The First Century with Virginia

THE ACCOMAC AND OCCOHANNOCK INDIANS' dealings with the colony (later the commonwealth) of Virginia ran the gamut of Indian-white relations elsewhere in North America: early friendliness, loss of the Indians' land, and reservations kept and then relinquished. Only one element, so common elsewhere, was missing on the Virginia Eastern Shore: the Accomacs and Occohannocks never went to war with the whites. Yet they went through the same historical process—at a faster pace—that more warlike people did. If nothing else, their history shows that in essence, Native American people on this continent were flooded out of their territories by larger European populations. The warfare that makes such dramatic historical accounts delayed the process but was not central to it.[1] The Indians' earliest contacts with Europeans, however, would not have warned them of what was coming, for such visitors were few in number and most were either on their way somewhere else or dropping in because they were famished.

The first Europeans that the Virginia Eastern Shore people could have seen—and then only if they happened to be fishing or oystering along the Atlantic littoral that day—would have been Giovanni da Verrazano and his crew, who in 1524 sailed past the Virginia Capes without stopping. In 1546 an English ship was forced by a storm into a large bay; the account is vague, but the latitude given (37°) matches the Chesapeake. We have only the cabin boy's version, recorded by a Spaniard in 1559, but that brief account mentions "over thirty canoes in each of which were fifteen to twenty persons" meeting the ship for purposes of friendly trade. The Indians traded over a thousand marten skins for English "knives, fishhooks, and shirts." However, martens are arboreal weasels living in cool-climate spruce and fir forests; those forests are uncommon even in the Virginia and Maryland Appalachians.

Therefore the boy was remembering either the wrong animal or the wrong latitude.[2]

In 1570–72 Accomac fishermen very probably saw the Spanish ships that came to the lower Chesapeake Bay bringing Spanish Jesuit missionaries. The tribe and its Occohannock neighbors certainly would have heard through the "moccasin telegraph" about the setting up of the mission, as well as the Spanish military's looking in vain for it the next year and punishing the killers the year after that. Indians in the James River basin were left with a distaste for the Spanish, which may have spread to other tribes like the Accomacs. Subsequent Spanish visits must have done little to erase the taste. The king of Spain regarded what is now Virginia as part of La Florida within his dominions, so Spanish ships came up the coast several times in the 1580s. In 1588 a ship went all the way to the Potomac River, where its crew forcibly seized a boy; it then visited somewhere on the Eastern Shore and kidnapped another boy there. Their captors expected both boys to learn Spanish, convert to Catholicism, and become mediators in the planned conversion of their people. However, the Potomac River boy died of grief, while the Eastern Shore boy went to Santo Domingo and converted but then died of smallpox.[3]

The native people of the Virginia and perhaps Maryland Eastern Shore also would have been aware of the three early English attempts to settle in what is now North Carolina. The first colony sailed briefly into Chesapeake Bay in 1584 and got a hostile reception from persons unknown. A party from the second colony spent part of the winter of 1585–86 with the Chesapeake Indians (in what is now Virginia Beach); Accomacs may have comprised some of the Indian visitors who came to see the foreigners during that time. Later on, refugees from the third, or "lost," colony of 1587 may well have come to live among the Chesapeakes, giving the southern Eastern Shore people more chances to pick up information.[4]

In the 1590s the Accomacs and Occohannocks had to begin to deal with a new, powerful native leader on the western shore. Powhatan had inherited six small tribes near what is now Richmond, and he had been expanding his domains eastward for some time. In 1596–97 he forcibly took over the Kecoughtans, in what is now Hampton; sometime around 1607 he would also conquer the Chesapeakes.[5] Between those two coups, he moved his capital eastward to Werowocomoco on the York River, a location central for a territory that he meant to include the

Virginia Eastern Shore. The handwriting was on the wall: fourteen miles' width of bay water would no longer isolate the Accomacs and Occohannocks. They would either have to fight Powhatan's forces, which outnumbered theirs, or pay him tribute and take his orders to a certain extent. They elected to do the latter—a policy that echoed their later passive accommodation to the influx of English settlers. Thereafter, until the final break with the western shore chiefdom in 1621, the Accomacs and Occohannocks sent over beads[6] made of the shells that were so common in their territory but not elsewhere in Powhatan's realm.

In 1603 or thereabouts, the southern Eastern Shore people may have had further encounters with Europeans. An English ship captained by Bartholomew Gilbert was driven by a storm into a bay that may have been the Chesapeake in July 1603, and a party putting ashore near the bay's mouth in search of fresh water was shot at by hostile local people. The other ship, possibly an English ship captained by Samuel Mace, arrived a few years before Jamestown was founded (year uncertain). First its captain met with Powhatan himself, after which the ship proceeded northward. Meeting a delegation of Rappahannock Indians, the visitors took offense about something, killed the tribe's chief, and took prisoners away with them. When the Jamestown colony was founded in 1607, Powhatan and his people were still fuming.[7] The Accomacs may have been involved in the first incident; they surely would have known about the second.

There was only one epidemic ever recorded among the Indians of the Virginia Eastern Shore. Around 1607 a large number of Accomac tribesmen viewed the bodies of two children who had died, presumably of some infectious malady, and shortly afterward they all died.[8] Without details of the symptoms, we cannot say what the disease was or whether it came from Europeans.

Relations with the Early Jamestown English

In early June 1608 Captain John Smith led two exploratory expeditions up the Chesapeake Bay and its tributaries. On the first of these he met Accomacs and Occohannocks, and communication was hindered by the lack of a good interpreter. Two "grimme and stout Salvages" who were fishing at Cape Charles directed the English to the chief's town once they were convinced that the visitors came in peace. The chief, who at that time may or may not have been the same man as the later "Laughing King," gave the English a friendly reception and willingly described the geography of the region to the north. John Smith gathered, incorrectly, that there was only one district chief in what is now Accomack County. His written accounts do not make it clear whether or not he explored the creeks there to learn differently.[9]

The Accomacs, and even more so the Occohannocks, had little contact with English people except for trading for over a decade afterward. Not being threatened by the English colony's expansion after 1610, they remained friendly during the First Anglo-Powhatan War (1610–13). People from Jamestown began regular fishing operations near the southern tip of the Eastern Shore in 1612, and in 1613 Samuel Argall began exploring the adjoining mainland, finding the native people friendly. By 1616 the English had established a saltworks on Smith Island and a residential base for it nearby. Although the project had failed by 1619, that year saw a regular trade between the Accomacs and the English— in corn, not furs. The corn trade was not always stress-free, however. Captain John Martin was charged with taking corn by force from an unnamed tribe. The tribe was either the Accomacs or the Occohannocks, since the original complaint was made first through an "Eastern Shore" chief and then through Opechancanough, younger brother of Otiotan (formerly called Opitchapam), who had become the new paramount chief of eastern Virginia after Powhatan's death in 1618.[10]

The surviving records are not clear about when Ensign Thomas Savage went to live on the Eastern Shore, but in the 1620s and early 1630s he became a crucial factor in the peaceful invasion of the peninsula by the English. Savage had acquired fluency as a youth in Powhatan's own language, a dialect closely related to the Accomac and Occohannock dialects; he may have served as an interpreter in the saltmaking enterprise. In any case, Savage somehow became acquainted with the Accomac chief Esmy Shichans, who appears in the records as the "Laughing King." This easygoing man, the titular ruler of both the Accomacs and the Occohannocks, would be the major conduit in the transfer of land from his Accomac people to the English. Thomas Savage's linguistic abilities must have helped immensely when the English decided to settle on the Eastern Shore.

Relations between the Accomacs and the western shore Indians were sour by the early 1620s. Not long before, some "Westerly Runnagados" (perhaps renegade Chickahominies who had previously killed some English people and raided their own people's temple) "conspired against the laughing King" apparently with the intention of taking over his territory. They failed and went elsewhere, becoming reconciled with Otiotan by 1621.[11] In that year, however, a real break occurred between Otiotan and the Accomacs. The famous "massacre of 1622" was originally planned for 1621, and Otiotan and Opechancanough sent word to Esmy Shichans that they wanted a supply of a herb with which to poison the English at a meeting. The herb was probably cowbane (*Cicuta maculata*), an extremely poisonous plant which grows much more plentifully on the eastern side than the western side of the Chesapeake Bay in Virginia. Esmy Shichans refused the request and (perhaps clandestinely) alerted the English. The English took up arms, and the great Indian assault had to be postponed for a year.[12] Sometime that same year John Pory visited Esmy Shichans and Kiptopeke, with Thomas Savage acting as interpreter. Pory found the Accomacs at loggerheads with the Patuxents in what is now Maryland and also with Opechancanough himself. Not long before, Thomas Savage not only had diverted the English trade to the friendlier Eastern Shore but also had rescued a compatriot, Thomas Graves, from Opechancanough's son and thirteen Pamunkeys while a hundred Accomacs looked on. After that, "all those Easterlings so derided them, that they came there no more."[13] It is hard to know, from the wording of the records, which came first, the rescue or the betrayal. But the break was genuine: when hundreds of warriors attacked the English in 1622, no Eastern Shore men participated. Thereafter the Accomacs and Occohannocks had to remain firmly in the English camp.

The English settlement that eventually would all but dispossess the natives began in about 1620.[14] The best evidence is that the Accomacs gave up their land peacefully, while the English, intent upon expansion and economic power in their own world, overran them. As with so many people who expect to take over the territory and rights of others, the English expected the Indians to resist, at least covertly, even when there was no direct evidence of such resistance except clashes over marauding livestock. Although the English leadership in Jamestown and London tried to keep the peace, the grassroots English settlers in Accomack (now Northampton and Accomack) County distrusted Indian people no matter what and kept on pushing them.[15] That would even be true of Thomas Savage's descendants, who became neighbors of the last Indian settlement in Northampton County. The Accomacs did not seem to recognize the English refusal to coexist—perhaps because of the mitigating influence of Thomas Savage—until all but a few hundred acres of their lands were gone and it was too late.

Before May 1620 Sir Thomas Dale bought land from the Accomac chief for the Virginia Company. In 1620 the English also tried to reestablish a salt-making operation on Smith's Island, but it folded again after three years. One of the first private English settlers was Thomas Savage, though the date of his taking up land is uncertain. The Laughing King gave him a very large tract running from the bay to the seaside, from Wiscaponson Creek (now The Gulf) south to Accomac (now Cherrystone) Creek; it included modern Savage Neck and also the later site of the Gingaskin (Accomac) Indian reservation on the seaside south of Indiantown Creek (fig. 2.1). Sir George Yeardley got a bayside-to-seaside tract to the north of it, up to Hungars Creek. After that, other English people claimed Eastern Shore land as payment for bringing new colonists to Virginia according to the headright system that had been set up in 1618.[16]

In the summer of 1622, following the great assault in March, the English colony bought its corn from the friendlier Indians of the Potomac River and the Eastern Shore. Accomacs and Occohannocks, especially the Machipongos, sold corn, and Esmy Shichans gave rather than sold a quantity of it to the English governor, through the mediation of Thomas Savage. However, the battered English distrusted all Indians, and there was a danger of inflated prices if trade by private individuals was allowed. So in September 1623 the Virginia colony's governor outlawed unlicensed trade with all Indians, including those on the Eastern Shore. Thomas Savage, who was genuinely friendly with both sides, got caught in the middle. In March 1625 he was ordered to act as interpreter at Accomac under the supervision of Captain William Epps, but he also had to give bond "not to have any Conference at all or familiaritie with the Indians of those partes."[17] The extent to which he obeyed is unknown; he continued to live on his holdings until his death in 1635.

The first English patents for Eastern Shore land were taken out in 1626 for plots on Old Plantation Creek. Other English people (including a few women)[18] had settled on the "peaceful" frontier without any such formality; by October of that year enough English farms existed that the Accomacs were killing English hogs that were allowed to roam freely. Even though the Indians agreed to pay damages (in corn), Captain Epps warned that further hog killing would constitute a breach of the peace.[19]

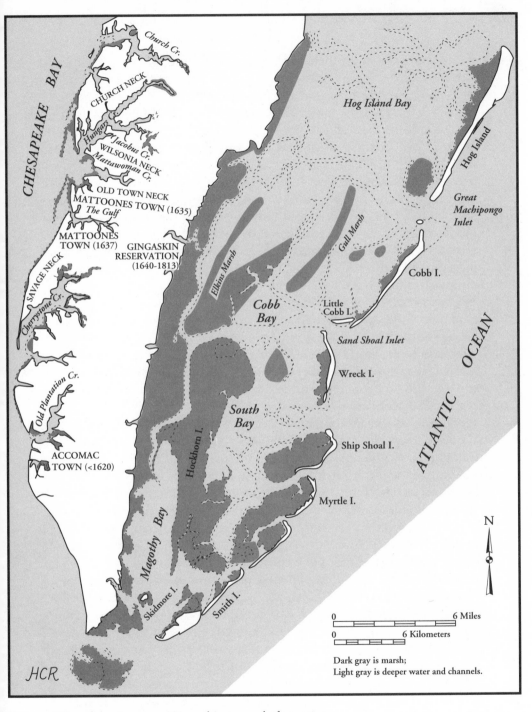

Fig. 2.1 Map of the Accomac/Gingaskin towns before 1645

The following labels appear on the map:

CHESAPEAKE BAY

Church Cr.

CHURCH NECK

Hungars Cr.

Jacobus Cr.

WILSONIA NECK

Mattawoman Cr.

OLD TOWN NECK

MATTOONES TOWN (1635)

The Gulf

MATTOONES TOWN (1637)

GINGASKIN RESERVATION (1640-1813)

SAVAGE NECK

Cherrystone Cr.

Old Plantation Cr.

ACCOMAC TOWN (<1620)

Elkins Marsh

Hog Island Bay

Hog Island

Gull Marsh

Great Machipongo Inlet

Cobb I.

Cobb Bay

Little Cobb I.

Sand Shoal Inlet

Wreck I.

South Bay

Hockhorn I.

Ship Shoal I.

Myrtle I.

ATLANTIC OCEAN

Magothy Bay

Skidmore I.

Smith I.

N

0 _____ 6 Miles

0 _____ 6 Kilometers

Dark gray is marsh;
Light gray is deeper water and channels.

HCR

Captain Epps and others were repeatedly commissioned for the Indian trade through the late 1620s, Epps for corn to feed incoming settlers until their crops came in and others for corn, Maryland furs,[20] and other things. English goods for trade did not include glass bottles, which could be made into arrowheads; these were prohibited in trade in 1628. The distrustful English also forbade their people in 1631 to "parley" with Indians except on the Eastern Shore, where Indians, "especially the Mattawombes," could be conversed with but not allowed into English houses. The Mattawombes were the Accomacs, who had given up much of their land and moved north to the town of that name (modern Mattawoman Creek probably preserves the name, as modern Old Town Neck preserves the location). The English occupied most of the bayside land south of Hungars Creek; in 1635 they began to claim seaside land on Magothy Bay.[21]

By 1633 the Laughing King had given away all his land, though his great men still had some they could sell. Far from feeling dispossessed, the untroubled chief made annual friendly visits to Colonel Obedience Robbins's house in those years. His people also went out of their way on occasion to avoid causing the English concern, even offering in 1635 to pay roanoke for the killing of some traders at Kent Island that the Accomac English had not yet heard about.[22]

By 1635 all the Accomacs were concentrated in Mattoones, at the southern lip of the mouth of Hungars Creek—but not for long. The neck opposite, Wilsonia Neck, was patented by William Stone that year without any mention of Indians in the area. Two years later the "old [deserted] Indian town named Mattoones" was patented, and the Indians were living south-southeast of it across a creek, probably The Gulf. That move (voluntary or not) put them on the land claimed by George Yeardley's son Argall; in fact, he claimed Stone's land as well in a patent of 1638. Yeardley and Stone went to court in 1640, and the Accomacs got caught in the crossfire. For their protection the council of colonial Virginia promised them 1,500 acres.[23] That acreage, located on the less-settled seaside north of Taylor Creek and taken out of Thomas Savage's land, was neighbor to and predecessor of the reservation that survived until 1813. Its land was as good for corn growing as Mattoones and the original Accomac town had been,[24] and it had equally easy access to marine resources. The Accomacs were known thenceforward as Gingaskins. Savage's descendants, remembering the origin of the reservation, would generally be hostile in the future.

The Gingaskin reservation came under threat of attrition immedi-

ately. The order assigning the land to the Indians said that their southern neighbor Philip Taylor's right to 200 acres was not to be infringed;
no infringement did occur, since his patent stated that his northern
boundary was "the broad creek" (now Taylor Creek).[25] But Taylor was
an aggressive man on the make. He immediately began harassing the Indians, who complained to the Northampton County court. The court-
ordered commissioners concluded in January 1641 that Taylor's land
was properly south of the creek, and also "that if the Indians be displaced of[f] the two hundred acres of land . . . they in noe wise can
subsist." Taylor appears to have lost.[26] But Taylor was not a good man
for the Indians to have crossed: by the summer of 1643 he had become
a justice of the peace for the county, commander of a military force
aimed at the Maryland English, burgess in the Grand Assembly in
Jamestown, and high sheriff of Northampton County. Douglas Deal
compares him to Edmund Scarburgh, his fellow burgess at the time, in
his ruthless attitude toward Indians.[27] Taylor did not give up his land
claim, and his quarrel with the Gingaskins escalated. In January 1643
the Northampton County court sent an armed force to the Gingaskin
town, the commander being Philip Taylor. Understandably, that did not
help matters, and the court ordered the county militia to mobilize in the
spring of 1643.[28] After that show of force, things seem to have simmered
down again slowly.

Esmy Shichans, the Laughing King of Accomac, was last mentioned in
a land patent of 1637; his date of death is uncertain. His successors
(whose relationship to him is unknown) were "King Tom" in 1649 and
"Mister Peter" in 1660.[29] After that, no one leader we could call a chief
appears in records concerning the tribe. The paramount chiefdom of
"the Eastern Shore" shifted northward to Occohannock territory after
1640, and no records clearly link the Gingaskins to it. Robert Beverley
wrote in 1705 that "the Empress" at Nandua "hath all the Nations of
this Shore under Tribute," but then he mentioned the Gingaskins separately.[30] However, the Gingaskins' welfare must still have interested the
Occohannocks. In July 1643 the county court ordered three Englishmen
to pay roanoke to Wackawamp, then chief of the Onancocks, for "the
quiet & peaceably enjoyeing of their land wch they now possess." The
Onancocks apparently had not made any complaints themselves. Douglas Deal feels the payment was a sop thrown to the Onancocks after the
pressures put on the Gingaskins in 1640–41 and the unrest of 1643.[31]

Indian-English relations not concerning land were complex in the
1630s and 1640s. Trade continued, for in 1638 a deceased Englishman's

estate included roanoke, peak, and green beads to sell to Indians, and a 1642 estate included an Indian mat and seven Indian bowls. Thomas Savage enlisted some of the native people to help him round up wild cattle, intending to reimburse them for their time. And the Indian world appealed to runaway English servants as a refuge: in 1638 a servant planning a getaway had a book on the "Indyan tongue" (probably not a local language). There was a darker side, of course. In 1647 an Englishman stole corn belonging to an Indian named Johnaboy, who promptly went to court about it.[32] Indians taking Englishmen to court later became a standard feature of life on the Virginia Eastern Shore.

The Occohannocks began to have intensive contacts—and therefore problems—with English settlers along Nassawaddox Creek in the late 1630s. They suffered their major loss of land after 1645 as the tide of Englishmen washed northward. Accomack County split off from Northampton County in 1663, by which time settlers (many of them religious nonconformists) had invaded what is now Maryland; Somerset County, Maryland, was formed in 1666. By that year, the Occohannocks had parted with most of their land.

The nature of the Occohannocks' dealings with the invaders in the mid-seventeenth century varied with their geographical closeness to English settlements. In 1647 an Englishman on Nassawaddox Creek took an Indian's gun away and held onto it by court order. Yet in 1649, when Henry Norwood was shipwrecked somewhere north of Kegotank territory, the hospitable natives who rescued him (Kegotanks or others) were unacquainted with European firearms. Norwood showed the chief how to fire a gun, and when the man stood on his bedstead in the house and let off a shot through the smokehole, he set the house on fire. Some northern chiefdoms within the Occohannock paramount chiefdom found themselves dealing with both Virginia and Maryland in the early 1660s.[33] And they continued to do so after the colonies' boundary dispute was settled, because they themselves were moving to and fro across it. Henry Norwood's rescuers were pushed northward by settlers in spite of their hospitality.

The Occohannocks had several paramount chiefs after the Gingaskins left the picture; the kinship relations between some of them, and between them and Esmy Shichans and Kiptopeke, are unknown. Wackawamp appears, along with his second-in-command Norris, in the court records between 1643 and 1657, when he died leaving a written will.[34] He was originally based at Onancock, with sovereignty over Pungoteague (see fig. 2.2; modern creek names show where tribes were lo-

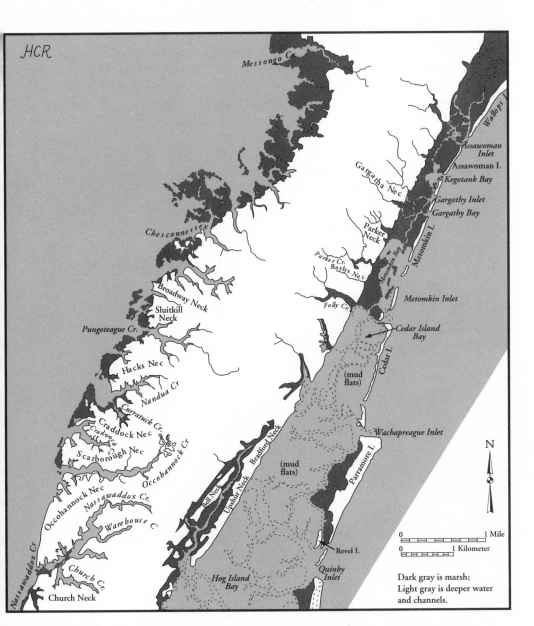

Fig. 2.2 Map of the Occohannock Indians' area in the seventeenth century

cated, although precise locations of later, constricted Indian towns are hard to pinpoint). In 1650 Wackawamp appeared as "king" (*weroance*) of Occohannock, after which his title was "Great King of the Eastern Shore." He specified that his heirs be his young daughter (name not recorded), then his brother's son Akomepen, and then his deceased brother's son Quiemacketo. His daughter apparently did not live long. His actual successor was Tapatiapon (Debbedeavon), who may have been one of the nephews under a new "throne" name.[35] Tapatiapon appears in the records as the ruler of Nandua and adjacent chiefdoms in 1648–49, ruler of Nassawaddox in 1652–53, and "King of the Eastern Shore" in 1663. He was dead by 1672, leaving a daughter named Mary as his heir; in the fall of that year she had to get the English to arbitrate a dispute over her right to succeed. Her rival, an Indian man named Johnson, asked Governor Sir William Berkeley's help in keeping his position, but his claim was proved fraudulent in November 1673 when Berkeley had the county court investigate it.[36] The date of Mary's death is not known; she appears under that name in a court record of 1703,[37] so she was probably the "Empress" based at Nandua that Robert Beverley wrote about in 1705.

Other Indian leaders appear in the Northampton and Accomack County records, since the district chiefs and also their councillors ("great men") could sell land and prosecute court cases on behalf of their people. Thus we find Andiaman, great man of Craddock and Nandua (1651–54); Nowchetrawen, apparently chief of Chesconnessex (1663); Ekeeks, great man of Onancock and Chesconnessex (1663); Piney, chief of Machipongo (1661); and Matahocus, chief of Onancock (1663, 1670), all appearing in court independently of either Wackawamp or Tapatiapon. In 1658 the son and heir of one such man (Choratyswince) sold the land he had inherited at the mouth of Onancock Creek; perhaps significantly, he himself had taken the name William in addition to his Indian name of Parahokes.[38] Many leaders' appearances concerned Indian lands; at other times they were protesting against the actions of English neighbors. The one thing that neither the paramount chiefs nor their subordinates ever got mixed up in was a war against the English.

No Indians on the Virginia Eastern Shore participated in Opechancanough's last major assault in April 1644. In 1645 some "Achomack" (Gingaskin?) Indians aided the English as spies in the war that followed. The Indians who stayed home appear to have been completely peaceful, but that did not help their English neighbors trust them. In September 1644 William Andrews was haled into court to answer for trading with "Indians," considered a suspicious undertaking.[39] No Eastern Shore Indians were signers of the treaty made in October 1646; only the new Powhatan paramount chief, Necotowance, signed it. That left the Accomacs' and Occohannocks' status somewhat vague. In the years to follow, they were generally treated as though they had treaty rights, but their protection came primarily from a proclamation that Governor Berkeley issued about the Gingaskins in 1650. No Eastern Shore Indians were involved in the unrest surrounding Bacon's Rebellion, either; on the contrary, a Gingaskin Indian whose broken gun was kept by a gunsmith during the rebellion succeeded in getting a court order for the gun's return. Thus there were no Eastern Shore signers of the Treaty of Middle Plantation in 1677.[40] Once again, the Gingaskins and Occohannocks were treated as though they had been signers, a custom that would become significant in Gingaskin history in the late eighteenth century. Armed with their equal-to-English civil rights—at least until the late seventeenth century—they went to court on an equal basis with their English neighbors. But in their eyes, converting to the English way of life was another matter.

English Neighbors at Mid-Century

English people regarded their culture as the "right" one and hoped to assimilate the neighboring Indians, whose conversion to "superior" English culture would help justify English expansion onto Indian lands. However, the native people did not feel English culture in general was superior, nor was the English way of life, as they observed it, attractive. Some aspects of that lifestyle paralleled Indian culture, so that the natives would have seen nothing to "convert" to; other aspects of it differed from traditional Native American ways in a manner that Indian people found alien or even repellent. Let us examine the English in Virginia, as far as possible through Indian eyes.

Most English householders in seventeenth-century Virginia and Maryland were farmers, only one in seven being a craftsman. These farmers either made things for themselves or more often imported what they needed: there were few stores, or, for that matter, taverns or ordinaries, until the next century. The imports were paid for by the variable income earned from raising tobacco.[41] The Indians made nearly everything themselves out of local materials and did not have to rely on oceangoing transport for "necessities."

English settlement patterns on the Eastern Shore contrasted with the Indian one. The English lived on their scattered farms, in spite of their government's urging them to concentrate, while the Indians were town dwellers. That situation probably added to the settlers' feelings of vulnerability to Indian attack, even when the Indians were peaceful. And the Indians may have felt that the settlers were relatively unsociable.

The colonial Eastern Shore was not a place of large plantations with big houses surrounded by velvety fields of crops. Rather the opposite. Most colonists after 1640 had farms of about 250 acres, on which they raised tobacco, corn, and livestock. The laborers on these farms were the landowners' families and also English indentured servants; the number of enslaved Africans rose steeply only at the end of the century. Some human labor on the farms went to build houses, storage buildings, and fences, but the bulk of it had to go into raising tobacco, which was a labor-intensive activity. Tobacco exhausted soil as well as humans, so before long a garden had to be left fallow and another one cleared, i.e., shifting cultivation, learned from the Indians. Given the short life of a field and the fact that tobacco did not require the plow, it made sense not to remove tree stumps from fields; there was not enough labor to perform the job anyway. Thus extensive, manicured-looking fields were rare, and instead English tobacco fields resembled Indian food-producing ones: messy while being tilled and soon abandoned and overgrown.[42]

The labor shortage coupled with shifting cultivation had an effect upon the construction of buildings, including dwelling houses: these tended to be small, ill-wrought, and worse-tended. Gloria Main has phrased it nicely: "For the first century of settlement, the planters lived in straggling wooden boxes dribbled over the landscape without apparent design." In fact, English houses and their furnishings were only marginally more substantial and elaborate than Indian ones; only the top third of society had houses with more than three rooms. Other colonists had frame houses of one or two rooms with a loft, an earthen or wooden floor, and sparse, roughly made furnishings.[43] Many colonists had pallets instead of beds, and most people slept in their clothes. Cooking and serving of food was usually rudimentary, consisting of boiled, often meatless one-dish meals, eaten with a spoon (forks had not come into fashion yet, even among the elite) and a cornbread "pusher." These limited amenities would have been congenial to Indian visitors, except that the families of Indian fishermen had more meat in their stews. Indian spoons also held half a pint at a time, which the Indians regarded as more sensible than the European version.[44]

Most English buildings were made from green wood, becoming "virtually uninhabitable after a decade unless they were substantially reconstructed. Since they were inexpensive to build in the first place, it may often have been preferable to build anew rather than repair the old, with the additional advantage that one could relocate closer to fields under current cultivation. A process such as this eventually left a scattering of abandoned houses in various stages of decay for shocked visitors [English ones, that is] to moralize about. Throwaway houses became a new American tradition."[45] No, throwaway houses were an old tradition borrowed from the Indians along with the technique of shifting cultivation.

There were other ways for English colonists to cut corners. Except for the richer planters who could hire labor to clear pastures for sheep and build fences to keep them in, most farm animals were those that could reasonably well run free year-round in the woods and marshes. Thus most English livestock consisted of cattle, horses, and hogs, which were fetched or hunted when wanted—Indian-style. These foraging animals suffered attrition by disease and starvation and also reduction in size; there are indications in the seventeenth-century Maryland records that hogs averaged under one hundred pounds at that time.[46] They were also decidedly vulnerable to being shot, especially when they raided neighbors' cornfields, which brought Indians and Englishmen alike into the courts.

Limited time and labor away from the tobacco fields further meant that female colonists made next to no cloth or soap, and these items were imported as the profits from tobacco allowed. Thus many seventeenth-century farm families had little more than the clothes on their backs, and those were not frequently washed. Neither, by English custom, were people's bodies, in contrast to the Indian practice of daily bathing. The native people wore fewer clothes but had a far higher standard of personal hygiene, which must have made the idea of living among the "impractical" English olfactorily distasteful.

English and Indian households alike were often large by modern American standards. However, the English ones were apt to be a hodgepodge of relatives, with unrelated servants added in the case of the older establishments. Older farmers, often former indentured servants who had been unable to marry until set free, would manage to produce one or two children before fatal local "bugs" such as malaria, dysentery, and typhoid killed them. Many parents died before their children were grown.[47] Stepparents, later spouses of stepparents, and uncles and aunts by blood and marriage were all enlisted to rear the children from the various unions. The result was a *ménage* family, an economic and child-rearing unit potentially held together by kin ties of any type, with constantly fluctuating members due to the high mortality rate.[48] Only in the eighteenth century, when most Anglo-Virginians were native-born, did life expectancy increase, creating smaller and more stable—and more patriarchal—families.[49] Meanwhile, the *ménage* families and their servants, even married ones, all slept in the main house, however small and ill-constructed it was. Indian visitors would have been familiar with such large, unprivate households. Theirs were similar, except that the people in them were all related in standard ways and had a longer life expectancy. It is likely that Indians considered English people, in spite of their large numbers that were continually increasing through immigration, to be rather frail as individuals.

Some of the work assignments on the colonists' farms must have seemed alien to Indian visitors. In the seventeenth century most English planters worked the ground along with their servants or, in poor families, their wives; not until well into the eighteenth century were the elite, and then only the elite, freed from such labor. Men doing most of the farming would have repelled Indian men, who regarded cultivation as predominantly women's work. Corn grinding on English farms was done by servants, usually male ones, and was thought to be ignoble drudgery; among the Indians it was women's work, inappropriate to men but not necessarily degrading.[50]

English servants were considered socially inferior during the time of their indenture, and they had to follow orders or else endure corporal punishment, which they were expected to accept in a properly servile, even abject, manner. Many masters mistreated English servants as readily as nonwhite ones, for the court records are full of abuse cases.[51] The possibility of being physically as well as psychologically abused would have been very off-putting to any Indian considering employment on an English farm.

Lastly, there was little leisure for anyone in the English families determined to get ahead by raising ever more tobacco. That also would have put off Indian people, whose men's work was in bursts interspersed with days of rest and whose women's work was continual but slowly paced. Indian families subsisted, rather than trying to get rich, and they allowed time for socializing, music, and dancing, all of which earned them the epithet "lazy" among the English. It is no wonder that until late in the seventeenth century the only adult Indian employees recorded were men hired to hunt out in the forest.

Among colonists and Indians alike, the networks of kin and neighbors made for strong if informal social control upon people. But it was an English tradition to reprimand wrongdoers publicly,[52] and public arguments were fairly common, especially when people had been drinking. Indians would have been offended by the loud, face-to-face nature of the English altercations, especially the drunken ones. Native society stressed personal autonomy with grave politeness prevailing between disagreeing parties. Departures from that rule were rare among the Virginia Indians until the use of alcohol became more common in the 1680s.[53]

Thus at mid-century the Gingaskins on their reservation and the Occohannocks on their shrinking lands would have had deep-seated objections to converting to English ways. Aside from English firearms, few distinctively English traits seemed worth adopting. English people as individuals could be made into friends; but the English in the aggregate were definitely aliens. The Occohannocks eventually withdrew rather than convert, while the Gingaskins hung onto their waterfront reservation and changed enough that they could manage to coexist with the English for over a century and a half.

Native People under Pressure

The Gingaskins continued to have trouble with encroaching English farmers. Their reservation, supposedly protected by a patent of 1641 (now lost), was surrounded by Englishmen, and in October 1660 they complained to the Grand Assembly in Jamestown that "the English seat so neare them, that they receive very much damage to their corne," presumably from free-roaming livestock. The assembly ordered their land surveyed and made inalienable; the order did not mention a prior patent or the acreage involved. Seven years later the Indians complained to the Northampton County court that Thomas Savage's son John and other Englishmen were taking away their land. The commissioners appointed to investigate reported in March 1668 that most of the reservation lay within Savage's patent, a fact the colonial council had not noticed until now.[54] Yet the court gave no order about how much acreage the Gingaskins were entitled to, or what was to be done about the conflict with Savage's patent. Perhaps the justices counted upon the Gingaskins to give up eventually and move north, in which case the English patentees would take possession.[55] The Gingaskins stayed, and the conflict continued.

In October 1673 the Virginia council, apparently in response to the aggravated Gingaskins, ordered that 650 acres were to be surveyed for the tribe and that neighbor Thomas Harmanson was to be "turned out" if he had encroached upon their land. Nothing was said about the original 1640 promise of 1,500 acres. The following April the council had to inquire into the still-existing boundary conflict with John Savage and told Harmanson to come to the General Court and answer the "Indians' suit." The resulting report, in September 1674, was that Harmanson was excused; both the Indians' and Savage's titles were doubtful; and John Kendall, Savage's son-in-law who managed part of Savage's land, was also now occupying part of the Gingaskins' land and harassing them about it. The council's solution to this messy situation was to set apart another part of Savage's lands, this time on the south bank of Angood's (eventually renamed Indiantown) Creek, thereby reducing the conflict to a two-sided one. Kendall had to post a bond for good behavior in the future. The Indian title was subordinate to Savage's by implication: the Gingaskins were to pay him an ear of corn annually for "their" land. In the survey made the next September, the acreage set aside was wrong, in favor of the Indians: the reservation in 1813 consisted of 690 acres.[56] But no patent was issued until nearly five years later, in July 1680, after the Gingaskins went to court several times complaining that Susanna Savage Kendall was cutting trees on their land. The next October an agreement was stuck: the Indians were to keep the fallen timber and the remaining trees on their reservation; they were also to keep up the boundary fence between themselves and their English neighbors.[57] The reservation fence, if repaired at all, did not remain up for long. In January 1683 the county court heard that an Englishman's "bull stagg" was pursued into the Indian fields and killed by two other Englishmen. One of those two, Henry Warren, had publicly requested in 1681 that all persons going to the Gingaskin town proceed by way of the gate near his house rather than "pullinge downe my pasture Fence."[58] Fences, even English ones in the neighborhood of the reservation, do not seem to have been much regarded by the general populace.

The Occohannock tribes lost their land later than the Gingaskins, some by deserting land that Englishmen had previously claimed and many of them by selling out. The English custom in what is now Accomack County seems to have been to compensate the local Indians, or promise to do so, and then get an official record made in the form of a patent. An acknowledgment in court from the Indians was required by law after 1654, but few of these appear, indicating private transactions or simple takeovers or both. The existing acknowledgments of sales by Indian leaders show the northward spread of English settlements reaching the Occohannock district chiefdoms, one by one: English planters had been allowed to settle at Nandua in 1648–49 (by Tapatiapon), Craddock in 1649 (by Tapatiapon), the town of Occohannock in 1650 (by Wackawamp), Onancock in 1652, Pungoteague in 1651–53, and Chesconnessex in 1663 (by Nowchetrawen and Ekeeks).[59] Desertions did not leave records, so that we cannot be sure when the seaside Metomkins and Kegotanks lost their land. And since there were far fewer sales than English patentees on the bayside creeks, Indian "desertion" must have played a major role there, too.

All the surviving Virginia Indian tribes lost land at an alarming rate in the 1650s, leaving them angry and on the verge of starvation. A law of 1652 limited sales to individual Englishmen unless the parties came to the quarter courts, which required the permission of local justices. But Indian lands continued to evaporate, so in 1654 the Grand Assembly made all sales by individual Indians illegal, except on the Eastern Shore. Two years later a new law made Indian lands throughout Virginia "inalienable . . . to any man," and a law of 1658 further confirmed the lands the Indians retained and required that only the governor could approve transfers. Yet Eastern Shore planters went on buying Indian lands anyway. Douglas Deal sees this as evidence that Eastern Shore English people believed they were autonomous from the western shore, especially in 1647–52 before the colony made its peace with the English Commonwealth at home. He also sees the strong influence of militantly anti-Indian planters like Edmund Scarburgh in the Eastern Shore colonists' insistence on acquiring Indian land for themselves in spite of the law.[60]

The Occohannock tribes were not very happy about accommodating so many foreigners, many of whom disregarded Indian rights. English people took up so much of Onancock Creek by 1652 that the Indians there complained about the settlers who took their hunting grounds and laid out farms "even unto ye very Towne of Oanancocke." The court ordered that no Englishmen were to move north of Pungoteague Creek pending an agreement with the Indians. Two years later the Onancocks protested that the English people seating their land at Pungoteague were refusing to pay for it. In the same year Andiaman and his people from Craddock to the south made the same complaint. The dispute with the Onancocks was resolved the next year by a county court order that all tracts on Onancock and Pungoteague Creeks received from the Indians were to be recorded after being properly surveyed. Yet no Indian acknowledgments resulted, in spite of the newly passed law. The original surveyor had been Edmund Scarburgh.⁶¹

The sales on Onancock Creek continued, in spite of Northampton County's efforts to block them. An Englishman buying Indian land with a (legal) gun in 1660 was fined. The Onancocks promised to sell land to two individual Englishmen and invited them to settle on it, but the county court ruled that the Indians had acted illegally.⁶² When Accomack County was formed in 1663, its territory included Onancock Creek, and Indian sales to individual English settlers resumed without hindrance. Tapatiapon as paramount chief continued selling tracts along the creek and he also sold off Wachapreague in 1664; his Onancock district chief, Matahocus, sold land as well. Some English titles remained unclear, perhaps because they lacked Indian acknowledgments. A 1672 transfer between two Englishmen specified that the seller guaranteed the buyer "against the Clayme or claimes of mee my heyres (Indyans excepted)."⁶³

No further references to Occohannock Indian land appear in the records after 1672. The people appear to have held onto small, already claimed tracts, whose location is untraceable; if these tracts lacked access to creeks and the Chesapeake Bay or Atlantic Ocean beyond, they would have had less incentive to hang onto them than the Gingaskins had with their waterfront reservation. There is evidence that in the late seventeenth century the Occohannock tribes intensified their contacts with the still-strong Indian groups in Maryland. Some people probably moved there permanently, reducing the size of the populations who stayed. Robert Beverley wrote in 1705 that seven tribes (chiefdoms) were left in Accomack County, all under the "Empress" of Nandua: Metomkin ("very much decreased of late by the Small Pox"), Kegotank ("reduc'd to a very few Men"), Machipongo ("had a small number yet living"), Occohannock ("had a small number yet living"), Pungoteague ("Govern'd by a Queen, but a small Nation"), Onancock ("has but four or five Families"), Chesconnessex ("has very few, who just keep the name"), and Nandua ("Not above 20 Families, but she [the weroan-squa] hath all the Nations of this Shore under Tribute"). Other Occohannocks moved back and forth, as noted in 1697 by Maryland's governor: "The Eastern Shore Indians remove very often into Virginia and Pennsylvania, so that it is almost impossible to ascertain their numbers. But the Indians of these parts decrease very much, partly owing to smallpox, but the great cause of all is their being so devilishly given to drink."[64] Indian-made goods (trays, bowls, ladles, mats, baskets, shell beads, even a tomahawk) continued appearing in the Accomack County inventories of English people who were not traders well into the eighteenth century, indicating some Indian presence within the previous few years.[65] As late as 1724 a local Anglican minister reported that a "very few" Indians were still living in his parish. A "Charles Indian" (no tribal designation) was exonerated in a murder case in 1712, and "George Rawmush Indian" was sought in a forgery case in 1723. The last person in the Accomack records with an "Indian" label was "Indian John," who was a runaway servant in 1725 and got sued for debt in 1731.[66] Unless scattered Indian families remained behind—which is difficult to trace, since the court records use only English names and mention no ethnic identity—it seems that most if not all of the members of the Occohannock paramount chiefdom eventually joined the Indians of Maryland.

When large numbers of English settlers ensconced themselves near native communities, difficulties were bound to arise, especially since the newcomers were convinced that all Indians were potentially in league against them. The Gingaskins and Occohannocks probably did keep in touch both with one another and with their linguistic relatives in Maryland and on the Virginia western shore. They may have talked about trying to push the invaders back, for talking would have been a good emotional release for people who were getting flooded out by aliens. But they never engaged in active resistance. Nonetheless, for much of the seventeenth century the English on the Virginia Eastern Shore assumed that trouble with local Indians, abetted by allies from Maryland, was just around the corner, and sometimes they acted accordingly.[67]

English fears often were exacerbated by English settlers who dealt directly with the still-strong native people of the Maryland Eastern Shore. In 1651 William Andrews lost his license to trade with "the Indyans in ye Baye," and the Northampton County court also outlawed fur trading by the Dutch in the northern part of the county (probably in the Pocomoke River area). William Clawson (Lawson) was another example. In 1649 he defended himself against charges of murdering another Indian trader and stirring up Indians (in general) against the English. By 1655 he had gone to live permanently with the Nanticokes, marrying their paramount chief's daughter and acting as a tribal leader himself; his English wife divorced him for it.[68]

The policies of local governments and the colonial government sometimes diverged. In May 1650 Governor Berkeley issued a proclamation ordering that the Gingaskins were not to be disturbed. However, two months later the Northampton County court issued its own proclamation: English citizens of the county were to be on their guard against Indians who plotted their downfall. The defensiveness was a response to reports that were apparently little more than rumors. Philip Mongram, a free black resident, had deposed that the Gingaskin man King Tom had carried tribute roanoke to the Nanticoke paramount chief, which constituted a breaking of the "League formerly concluded betweene us" (perhaps a reference to the 1646 treaty). Mongram also claimed that a general poisoning of English wells was planned (with cowbane?), after which the Nanticokes would attack the English. Another deposition alleged that the district chiefs òf Chincoteague and Wachapreague planned an assault, though the Kegotanks would remain uninvolved. Yet another deposition corroborated the poisoning plan and added that the bayside Indians in Virginia had sold all their corn to pay Indians that "were to come over the Baye" and help in the assault.[69]

No Indian attack on wells or people ever materialized, possibly because Edmund Scarburgh and fifty men short-circuited it in April 1650 by staging a raid not on the Nanticokes but on the Pocomokes, shooting at people, destroying property, and taking prisoners. The Pocomokes gathered themselves up for revenge, leading the Northampton County court to order in May 1651 that Scarburgh be arrested. Indian trader William Andrews sent reparations: the Pocomoke weroansqua was to have a hundred arm's lengths of roanoke, the Metomkin king two weeding hoes, the Indians who were taken prisoner were to have a coat (matchcoat) each, and the Indian shot by Toby Selby's wife and attended by an English physician the previous year was to have twenty arm's lengths of roanoke. Nonetheless, alarms apparently continued. In the summer and fall of 1651 the county court ordered a party of horse raised at Nassawaddox, believing a massacre was coming. The horsemen, who included Edmund Scarburgh, were allowed to make inquiries and press equipment as needed.[70]

Nothing more was heard about plots from Indians until 1655, when rumors spread that unspecified Indians had "of late growne very bould & insolent." The militia of what later became Accomack County was therefore ordered to begin training and be constantly ready. After that there were no more outbursts until August 1659, when Edmund Scarburgh got Governor Berkeley to ask the Maryland governor to attack the Nanticokes and Wicomicos while Virginia forces attacked the Assateagues and their allies. No specific reason was given for the request, so the Maryland governor demurred. Scarburgh and his people attacked anyway, with both Eastern Shore and western shore Englishmen involved according to the payments ordered later by the Grand Assembly. Late in 1661 militia officers (one being Scarburgh) went north to investigate a complaint from the Nanticokes, Manokins, Wiccocomicos, Transquakings, and Annemessexes that the presents they had sent to Governor Berkeley had not been delivered by the Onancocks and Occohannocks (the district chiefdom).[71] Late in 1663 Scarburgh and a large party of militia went to the Annemessexes and Manokins to check on rumors of Quakers moving in and also on the welfare of Virginia colonists caught in the boundary dispute then going on between Maryland and Virginia. The Indians at the two towns were hostile, at least to Scarburgh, who had not always proved to be any friend of theirs.[72]

The boundary dispute between the two colonies enabled the Pocomokes and others to play both sides against the middle; it made the situation of the Occohannocks uneasy, and it also occasionally created divisions within tribes. At the time Scarburgh had gone north, the Pocomokes had split: the chief favored Virginia and had asked Governor Berkeley for aid, while his great men disagreed violently and were supposedly trying to kill him. He asked for and received military aid from the newly formed Accomack County. Conditions for the English settlers in the disputed area were not much more stable. Early in 1664 Scarburgh issued a proclamation saying Virginia offered protection to the settlers against the Indians, whom he described as "very Insolent Robbers + driuers away both of Cattle + hoggs breaking houses and acting many other Injuries." He neglected to mention the Pocomokes, who wanted to be allies. The Accomack court backed him up, ordering him to inform the settlers that they were living under English law in spite of the boundary dispute.[73] In a frontier environment, however, such orders may or may not carry much weight.

The following February the Assateagues helped in the capture—at their town—of two English fugitives, an Englishman and another man's wife; they were paid for it in roanoke. But late in 1667 the Virginia English disputed about whether Indians who lived on the north side of the Pocomoke River could be arrested for rebelling against the king of England's commands. The next year some militiamen were ordered to man a fort at Gargatha to guard against unspecified Indians. Several Accomack County men raided the "Aquintankee" (Acquintica, on the Pocomoke River) Indians and took some of their property. The Accomack County court prosecuted the raiders in 1668 and ordered that the Indians be reimbursed for the corn stolen from them.[74]

With the alarms of Bacon's Rebellion on the western shore, there came more rumors of Indian plots on the Virginia Eastern Shore, although ultimately none of them were verified. It is unlikely that the local Indians could have done much damage to the English militarily by the 1670s; their populations were probably too small, although no reliable figures exist in the records. Yet late in 1675 two Indian men, Ned and Paul, were whipped for spreading false rumors that had unsettled the colonists. The last rumors of Indian plots circulated in 1691, when a Northampton militia colonel checked and found false a report that a large force of Indians had come down the Eastern Shore of Maryland, along with white men who were said to be French.[75]

As long as the English on the Virginia Eastern Shore feared the local Indians for military reasons, their unease affected their day-to-day relations with Indian people. The Indians' continued cultural differentness had similar effects even after the military issue had faded; the Gingaskins were to find out that it created hostility all the way into the nineteenth century.

Many appearances that Indians made in the Northampton and Accomack County records resulted from things going wrong. People are more willing to speak out when they feel negative; the result is a bias toward conflict rather than cooperation in historical records, whether the parties involved were neighbors of different ethnicities or not. That bias can lead historians and their readers into seeing the past mainly in terms of conflict, disasters, etc. Indeed, Barbara Tuchman formulated what she called Tuchman's law: "The fact of being reported multiplies the apparent extent of any deplorable development by five- to tenfold (or any figure the reader would care to supply)."[76] In the following pages we do a good deal of negative reporting, but we also show as far as possible the positive interactions that the Gingaskins and Occohannocks still had with their English neighbors.

In the seventeenth and eighteenth centuries, Indians on the Virginia Eastern Shore had full rights to take their grievances to court and, if they did wrong, to be tried by a jury. A substantial number of Indians, given their declining populations, went or were taken to court in both centuries, indicating that their coexistence with their English neighbors was not an easy one. Sometimes the disputes were so vaguely mentioned we cannot be sure what the problem was or who was being accused. Often the wording was vague because one or both parties did not appear in court to resolve the issue. Sometimes the disputes were so minor that they were dismissed without ever being described.[77] At other times some Englishmen were being prosecuted for some undefined harassment of Indians, as happened with the Gingaskins in 1663. In still other cases, an Indian summoned to court on unspecified charges "condemned the warrant," i.e., refused to cooperate and risked getting into deeper trouble.[78]

Aside from retaining their land, bearing arms was the hardest right for Indian people to have respected by the English. By a Virginia law of 1659, Indian men were allowed to carry and use guns "within theire owne limitts," i.e., on their own lands. For people who had lost nearly all of their hunting territory, hunting anywhere except the marshes meant going outside "theire limitts," so they got the county court's written sanction, as "Mr. Peter Indian Comander of the Gingaskin Indians" did in 1660. He promised to obey all English laws, and in return he not only got the permission to hunt, but because he lacked a gun of his own, the court ordered a militia colonel to furnish him with one. The Machipongo chief had a gun of his own when he approached the county court for permission to carry it.[79] Other Indian men carried guns when they were hired to hunt for English settlers. A Virginia law of 1654 (repassed in 1658) required these employers to get license first, meaning that they took responsibility both for the character of the Indian hired and for any accidental damage he did. A very few Eastern Shore Englishmen followed this procedure; others ignored it, and they and the men they hired got into trouble.[80]

Many of the unpleasant incidents that occurred between the Indians and the English stemmed from Indian possession of guns. Such incidents, often involving an Englishman taking away an Indian's gun, occurred whether or not a scare was going on locally. English settlers were ordered to return such guns in 1647 and 1649.[81] In the 1650s and 1660s, when Edmund Scarburgh was so active against Indians, there was no legal regulation about Indians carrying guns; and there were also, strangely enough, almost no incidents of Indians being dispossessed of their guns. Instead most of the problems were with the hiring of Indians. Either the Indians were hired without licenses, or else they got into trouble, or both, like the man in 1663 whose illegal employment by Philip Mongram came to light when he assaulted an Englishman. Another illegally hired Indian was trying in 1667 to earn a coat with which to pay off a debt to Edmund Scarburgh. The employer claimed that if he could not get a license from a Virginia authority, he knew he could get one from a county clerk in Maryland. Perhaps that is why Edmund Scarburgh persuaded Governor Berkeley to grant licensing power to the Accomack County court; otherwise, at the time, applicants had to go to Berkeley in Jamestown. In 1678 and 1681 Indians went to court after having guns taken away from them; each time, the seizure was ruled improper.[82]

Other difficulties arose over livestock running loose; the animals in most cases were hogs. Indians who killed English livestock paid damages in roanoke; the payments were often made by tribal chiefs, sometimes before the deadline.[83] Indian crops and livestock also suffered, and the redress sought by Indian owners showed considerable knowledge of English ways.[84] One of Wackawamp's councillors got a court order for his neighbors on Nassawaddox Creek to pen up their cattle every night, while a Metomkin woman had marked her hog's ears, English fashion, so that its killer was easily found.

Indians and English alike were perpetrators and victims of wrongs. Some Indian people remained strong, even violent actors in their own self-interest as their land and populations drained away. As with the other kinds of interethnic difficulties, the incidents of robbery or violence were not concentrated in times of military tension; they were spread throughout the second half of the century, only diminishing at the century's end when the Occohannocks were spending less and less time within the colony.

Many of the imbroglios between Indians and Englishmen involved property. Both took things from each other, and on two occasions the

Indian victims were beaten as well. Andiaman, a great man from Craddock, lost his English wherry and rigging to an English thief in 1651.
Two years later a Nandua man complained in court that when he returned a canoe to its English owners, they paid him with unfinished
("never footed") stockings. In a quarrel in 1682 over a fish weir, the
Indian builder had sold a half interest and then refused to let his English
co-owner fish with it. Other incidents involved debt, possible trespass,
burning of Indian cabins, hindered hunting, and Indians driving away
English hogs.[85] Most culprits received their punishment and resumed
their lives in the community. An exception was the Indian aptly named
Pickpocket, who in 1664 confessed to "divers felonies cheats and housebreakings" over several years. He lived in one of the Occohannock Indian groups, within reach of the Maryland border, and he had tried to
stir up trouble by telling an Englishman that the Indians were planning
something that would make even Edmund Scarburgh afraid, which his
Indian compatriots denied. For all these offenses, Pickpocket was transported and sold as a servant in the West Indies—the only Eastern Shore
Indian from Virginia to be so treated.[86]

Other squabbles involved bodily harm or the threat thereof. One Indian man got drunk in 1683 and violently broke into an English house,
scaring the family inside half to death. Several Englishmen were punished at various times for beating Indians, though on one occasion the
Indians had asked for it. In 1677 Misseteage and his wife, people from
Occoconson on Occohannock Creek, proved in court that a settler had
beaten them. They seemed to be winning until the Englishman proved
that they had killed his hogs, so the case was dismissed. On another
occasion some Indians took an Englishman to court for threatening to
cut their throats when they came to his door. Indian beatings of Englishmen also occurred. Early in 1664 the chief and the great men of Metomkin were hauled into court for beating one John Die. They and over a
dozen other Metomkin men had talked with Die and then tried to take
away an ax he held; they wrestled him to the ground and held him there
"almost an hower by the haire of the head, and put Durt in his mouth
& eares." Die, according to witnesses, had struggled but not struck anyone. Meanwhile, some Indian men had pulled down his house (which
cannot have been very substantial), after which at the chief's order he
was let go. An investigation was ordered, but no report was ever made.
One Englishman's punishment was fifteen lashes on the bare back, an
ordeal reserved in the next century only for nonwhites. Actual killings

of or by Indians were rare. The only recorded case dates to 1680, when an Indian servant was killed by another Indian; the killer had to pay the servant's master fifteen deerskins.[87]

In addition to the tensions that cropped up from time to time, the relations between Indian and English people had pleasanter sides. A certain amount of friendly visiting went on. At least two Indians went to England, for the settlers who paid their passage home again collected headrights on them (in 1652 and 1670). Some Indians attended drinking parties at English houses, sleeping it off afterward in the chimney corner (analogous to their sleeping at home near the fire). One such party landed in the county records in 1648, for an English wife had held the party in her husband's absence and had gone to bed with one of the Englishmen present. She worried afterward that the four Indian guests had informed her husband, though in fact the guests could not speak enough English and it was another Englishman who went public in a scandalous court case.[88]

Sometimes the interethnic visits ripened into intimacy. The native people involved were of both sexes, but the representation of social statuses is uneven. Liaisons appear in the records only when some Englishman was wronged. English males, as well as Indian men and nonservant Indian women, owned themselves and therefore had considerable latitude in conducting affairs (among the native people, any resulting children stayed with the mother).[89] But English husbands claimed full proprietary rights over the bodies of their wives, and English masters felt themselves out-of-pocket when female servants (including Indian ones) became debilitated by pregnancy and preoccupied with child care. Thus the liaisons in the records concern only Indian men as seducers (like the unnamed men rumored to be sleeping with English wives in 1646–47 and the one who fathered a child by an English widow in 1697) and impregnated female Indian servants. One such servant was tried for killing her illegitimate child and was acquitted.[90]

William Custis had to deal with an Indian in each position within a ten-year span. In 1671 his English servant Elizabeth Lang was delivered of an illegitimate child and named an Indian called Kitt as the father. Kitt initially could not be found; when he was run to earth in mid-1672, he condemned the warrant that was served on him for neglecting to pay child support. Perhaps because of this, Lang had turned against him and the Indians in general. By English law the child had to be indentured as a servant until age twenty-four, to pay for its own keep, but the mother added (loudly) that she wanted her child reared among the English, and not "by a Pagan." It all sounds like an affair gone wrong. In 1681 Custis asked for and received damages from two Englishmen because of a child born to a female Indian servant of his.[91]

The Virginia Grand Assembly ordered in 1678 that all Indian trading be confined to certain "marts" at specified places and times: the one for the Eastern Shore was to be held September 10 at Onancock "within one hundred yards of Matahocks [Matahocus's] Cabbin."[92] However, relations were so generally peaceful that it is unlikely that Indian and English people confined their trading so narrowly. Occasionally Indians got into debt and had to be prosecuted.[93] The English goods are not mentioned in the records, but they must have included guns, ammunition, and trade cloth. The goods sold by the Gingaskins and Occohannocks seem to have had nothing to do with the fur trade; instead the items involved were fishnets, canoes, and household furnishings (which appear in estate inventories).

The only Indian goods recorded in English households in the 1640s and 1650s are mats, probably reed ones to put on the floor; there must have been other things traded as well. In the early 1660s one estate had forty Indian pipes, and another contained baskets. Inventories in the 1670s included mats (probably Occohannock-made), wooden trays (probably Gingaskin-made), and bowls that were probably ceramic and were made by both peoples. In the 1680s, as Indian populations declined, the only Indian-related goods recorded in English possession were trade beads, probably for use among the Indian people of Maryland; the traders were from Northampton County. Then in the 1690s through 1730s, baskets, bowls, and occasional trays and mats again appeared.[94]

Canoes and fishnets are to be expected among a native people who had become even more dependent upon marine foods since losing most of their territory. In 1678 a Gingaskin man agreed to make a dugout canoe for a price of two matchcoats; his work was hindered by a quarrel between Englishmen over the ownership of the tree he was working on. Fifteen years earlier an English master had sent his English servant to mend nets "to [at] the Indian," probably meaning the place near where an Occohannock man had built a weir for him and was catching fish on his behalf. In 1667 the Accomack County court stated that fishing was the "chiefest" thing that Indians were hired to do, and it set standard prices to avoid controversy. Two small sheepsheads equaled one large sheepshead, one large drumfish equaled two sheepsheads, and three mature sheepsheads were worth one matchcoat or forty arm's lengths of roanoke.[95]

Increasing poverty induced more Indian people to become employees of Englishmen as the century wore on. Native men had shot food for settlers' tables for a long time. Some who needed money also hunted and collected bounties on wolves, which nobody ate but which English farmers wanted exterminated. The Virginia Grand Assembly had promoted the idea in 1650 and again in 1669, when an assessment of a certain number of wolves for every five bowmen resulted in a sort of census of Indians in all of the colony except the Eastern Shore. Soon thereafter, the Accomack County court ordered people to kill wolves, bears, and "wildcats" (cougars and bobcats), with Edmund Scarburgh receiving the heads as proof and disbursing the legal reward, which was a matchcoat or three shots of powder per animal. That order was altered in 1677: only Indians were to receive bounties, and the recompense was reduced. Bounties were still being paid in Northampton County as late as 1704, when "Jeffrey the Indian" proved that he had killed seven wolves.[96]

A somewhat better gauge of native poverty is the increase in Indian indentured servants. Such servitude—slavery came later—became a more visible feature of life on the Virginia Eastern Shore in the 1660s, when a depression in tobacco prices and a manpower shortage due to the Dutch wars made English indentured servants too expensive for many labor-hungry farmers. But Indian servitude, and even occasional slavery, dated back to the 1640s, with most of the early cases being young people in their teens.[97]

The laws governing servitude were codified in the early 1660s and modified thereafter. For most of the century young servants who had begun their indentures in Virginia became free at age twenty-five (later thirty) and were supposed to receive clothes and corn (seed corn) as a start in life. Virginia, unlike Maryland, did not provide land for ex-servants.[98] In the absence of birth certificates, county courts had to see such servants, preferably at the beginning of the indenture, and estimate their ages for the record. That, along with the tithes (taxes) paid on them, is all we know about most Indian servants of the 1660s and 1670s. If a young person did not get adjudged, then it was the servant's word against the master's, as an Indian named Bess found out in 1673, when she applied to the court for her freedom and was ordered to serve four more years. One Indian made a somewhat better short-term bargain in 1678: "Dick the Indian" agreed—before a witness, on the English master's advice—that he would live with the Englishman, getting food and lodging; in exchange, he would pay two hundred pounds of tobacco when the crop came in, he would plant three barrels of corn during his time there, and he would do his own washing. The deal was sealed with a bottle of brandy.[99]

In the late 1660s (but not earlier or later) a substantial number of Occohannock children were bound out as servants; most of them were boys, and their ages ranged from seven to fourteen.[100] The first wave of children was brought to court by great men from Metomkin, Kegotank, and Onancock, and the clerk recorded their Indian names as well as their new English names (English masters did not care to learn to pronounce polysyllabic Indian names). The clerk only noted tribal origin and new English names in the second wave, and in the third wave of children only the English name of each child was considered significant, making the records so impersonal as to indicate a change for the worse in English attitudes toward the local Indians. (English trade with the Carolina piedmont became regular around 1670, and the trade in captured Indians from distant southern tribes came somewhat later.)[101]

Poverty may have caused parents and leaders to place their children with English settlers in order to feed them. Service may equally have been a means for the children to learn English and English ways, so that later they could serve as "cultural brokers" between their elders and the Europeans who had obviously come to stay. We differ with Deal's opinion that the Occohannocks wanted to tap the English people's "clear technological superiority for the purpose of surviving in their midst." English superiority is hard to prove. Before the switch to plow farming of wheat and other cereals around the turn of the eighteenth century, Anglo-Virginian tobacco farming strongly resembled Indian farming. It is also doubtful that English ships of that period were superior to Indian paddle-propelled dugouts except in their capacity to hold more people and goods. English guns by the late seventeenth century were superior to bows and arrows for hunting, but all male Indians had access to these weapons whether they became servants or not. We also differ with Deal's suggestion that a smallpox outbreak and a hurricane in 1667 led the Indian parents to "sacrifice" their children to a non-Indian power, analogous to Henry Spelman's early seventeenth-century account of Indians' "sacrificing" children to Okee. Although smallpox was at large in October 1667, there is no direct evidence of Indian people contracting it. Sacrifice was also improbable; indeed, what Spelman actually saw and described was the first stage of the huskanaw ritual that the Virginia Eastern Shore Indians lacked.[102] More likely, an inability to feed their children on their vanishing land base drove these Accomack County Indians to bind out their children.

The English desire for child labor drawn from Indian communities escalated. In mid-1670 several Accomack citizens petitioned the county court for permission to acquire "fatherless children" for servants. That the children were to be Indian ones is shown by the court's order that "John the Indian bee imployed to procure the said Children," with a bounty of fifteen arm's lengths of roanoke per child; the court said it would "dispose of them according to priority of petition." Presumably John and others went into business thereafter with a vengeance, for in September 1670 Governor Berkeley condemned Edmund Scarburgh's wholesale oppression of Indian families in order to get hold of their children. Scarburgh was disgraced, and he died the next year.[103]

That seems to have ended the dealings in local Indian children. Instead, a decade later, we see a spate of Indian children who very probably came from southwest of the Virginia colony. English people in both Northampton and Accomack County presented twelve children for age adjudging in the 1680s; their average age was considerably younger than that of the native children who preceded them, five of them being only three to five years old. Some of these children, if not all, were slaves rather than servants. In the following four decades the importation of African slaves swelled tremendously, as the Virginia colony's economy shifted over to dependence upon slave labor.[104]

Presumably the enslaved children lived out their lives in that condition. However, in 1687 one Englishman executed a document stating that two Indian women of his were to become servants instead, with six more years to serve—if they behaved themselves. Less freedom was decreed for their descendants: the daughter that one of the women already had by a black slave was to serve until the age of thirty, and her children (the woman's grandchildren) were to be slaves.[105] It all sounds like a master who acted less from generosity than from having been worn down.

Servitude was not a happy experience for anyone, Indian or non-Indian, who underwent it in the seventeenth century, but some individuals bore it better than others. Those who could not abide the labor and/or the ever-decreasing social status either lashed out against authority or, more commonly, ran away. Runaways who got caught usually were required to serve additional time at least equal to the time they had been away. Some English servants ran away "to the Indians," probably the still-strong communities in Maryland. John Devorax did it twice in the 1660s. During his first sojourn across the border in 1660, he picked up the language, making him useful thereafter. When the Nanticokes' complaints were being investigated late the next year, Devorax was sent along as an interpreter. After another brush with the law for taking and selling a local Indian's gun, he ran away again in 1665. Edmund Scarburgh had to pay roanoke, matchcoats, and tobacco to the Indians who brought Devorax back.[106] Indian people thus participated both as servant catchers who expected a reward and as runaways themselves. Indian leaders were active as either catchers or protectors of runaways for as long as they themselves were powerful.[107]

In Accomack County in the 1660s through 1680s, the varying experiences with English people of several Indian men, most if not all of them acquainted with one another, are well enough documented to give us a picture of just how complex the county's Indian situation was. Two were Metomkins: a youth named Wincewough and a great man named Amongos.[108] The third was a young Metomkin man renamed James Revell when he entered indentured service,[109] and the fourth man was named Dick Shoes.[110] The two with English names never appear in the records with any tribal affiliation (Shoes may have been a Metomkin), but their actions indicate that they were by no means fully integrated into English society.

Wincewough became a servant to Robert Hutchinson in August 1667; he was presented in court by a great man from his tribe, possibly Amongos. He was twelve years old, which meant that if he behaved himself he could expect to be free in 1679. But he did not behave himself: his service record was spotty and prone to extensions on account of absence from work. He took off from Hutchinson's farm in November 1670 and succeeded in staying away, living with the Nanticokes, until July 1672, when Amongos brought him in. He was ordered to serve double the away time (e.g., over three years) in addition to his contracted time. Amongos, meanwhile, had gone to jail. He had promised to bring in not only Wincewough but also two runaway Indian servants from Edmund Scarburgh's estate, an endeavor in which he had failed. The Accomack justices had further discovered that Amongos had been active first in inciting Wincewough to run away and then in concealing his whereabouts; he may have been concealing the hiding place of the two Scarburgh servants as well. We are not told what circumstances induced Amongos to turn against Wincewough and bring him in, but we do know that Amongos was put in irons until the remaining two servants were returned.

Wincewough and Amongos played the same scene again a few years later. In 1675 Robert Hutchinson complained in court that Amongos had helped Wincewough take off again. The youth was gone ninety-eight days this time, and Amongos was detained pending his return. Wincewough's reasons for departure are not hard to guess from the court records. For one thing, by 1675 the English were pronouncing his Indian name "Willywags," and he was sufficiently fluent in English that he probably would have sensed the fun-making tone of the name. The other reason is that Wincewough was getting into serious conflicts with English people other than his master, indicating that he was becoming fed up with English society. A deposition of 1677 described his behavior when he was attending the April 1676 court (for reasons unknown), after his second term of running away. He asked George Boyce to give him credit for drink in exchange for some pipes; when Boyce refused, saying the last ones he had had from him were "rotten," the two got into a slanging match. Wincewough's proficiency in derogatory English was good, and Boyce soon became violent and "beate [Wincewough] and ki[c]ked him about the house and pulled him by the haire of his head." The deponent (an Englishman) was cheering on the Indian, who fought with Boyce "a good while." In 1678 "James Winseweack" ran away yet again and was caught fifteen miles from his master's house.

James Revell, on the other hand, was someone who adapted well to English farm life from the beginning of his indenture in 1667. The limited records about his short life—he scarcely lived past 1680, when he would have gotten his freedom—indicate that he became an owner of hogs and also rose to the position of overseer on his master Edward Revell's plantation. However, the position of Indians in English society went downhill during Revell's lifetime. His position as overseer was tenuous, for working under him was an English youth who hated his authority and fought him physically on several occasions. The incendiary term the underling called Revell was "Indian Dogg," the same epithet that George Boyce had used on Wincewough. Either before or after his death, Revell went into debt to another Englishman for three hundred pounds of pork and twelve days' work; his creditor went to court in late 1681, after Revell's death. His greatest creditor, though, was his former master, who became the administrator of his estate, which appears to have consisted mainly of the hogs.

Dick Shoes was neither a servant nor a great man; he seems instead to have been a hanger-on lodged between Indian and English culture. His name in the records is always the English one, but he required an interpreter when he went to court. Shoes was involved in retrieving Wincewough from his second jaunt to Maryland in 1675 and was paid in roanoke. In 1681 he laid claim to some of the hogs of the recently deceased James Revell (he may have been a kinsman); when three Englishmen killed six of the Revell hogs, Shoes took them to court. The case was continued for lack of an interpreter that day, and when it was renewed early in 1682, Shoes could not prove his claim. One of the sows Shoes wanted lived "about the Cabbins in Great Metompkin Neck," i.e., near James Revell's natal town; Shoes apparently lived near the sow and knew Revell. In the winter of 1680–81, while Revell was still alive, Shoes and several Indians (probably Metomkins) had been approached by the man Kitt (Elizabeth Lang's lover), who wanted to buy the sow or one of her barrows. Shoes told Kitt that the hogs could not be sold, for it was possible that Revell "would come presently to Kill it for his owne use." Revell apparently had gotten his freedom at that time and was living in or near his hometown.

Some Gingaskin and Occohannock people, possibly including the Indians named Robert Atkinson, Argoll Angood, and Peter Mongram, decided to leave their tribes and join English society, presumably because they found it relatively congenial and saw little future for the small islands of Indian territory. A good example of such people was Edward Bagwell, who came from one of the Occohannock enclaves. He was a boy in 1669 when the will of Littell Mannattark, presumably his father, was proved in court. Edward was to serve Thomas Bagwell; another boy, presumably his brother, served another Englishman and took his surname. As a grown man, Edward Bagwell appears in the records again in 1698, in debt and being prosecuted by two different Englishmen and an Englishwoman (probably his former master's wife). The two men collected. The next spring Bagwell and several other citizens were prosecuted for not handing in lists of tithables (taxable persons) on their farms. He was able to prove that he had turned his in after all. In 1709 he died, leaving a will indicating that he was a Christian convert and saying nothing whatever about his Indian background; the ethnic origin of his wife and executrix Mary is unknown.[111]

The Gingaskins still had at least visiting connections with the Occohannocks. In 1697 "Mary Indian Empress" of Occohannock joined with the woman Tonganaquato in complaining to the Northampton County court that the latter's son Assabe was being held in servitude by an Englishman for supposedly killing a cow. The court declared the indenture illegal and had the boy released. The boy probably was captured in Northampton County while going hunting during a visit to the Gingaskins. The Occohannock "empress" still had some political power. The same was not true for the Gingaskin man called "King Tom," who in 1698 was whipped for stealing a silver spoon; the lack of deference shown him indicates that he was an ordinary Indian in all but name.[112]

By 1700 all of the native groups on Virginia's Eastern Shore had shrunk to small numbers, except possibly the Nanduas with "not above 20 Families" according to Robert Beverley. They had lost nearly all of their land and most of their population. They had not, however, given up most of their traditional lifeways. They used English metal tools and wore mantles in winter made of English trade cloth. But their ordinary clothing probably was still skimpy and made of buckskin, which better withstands an active working life, and their houses and furnishings were still the old Indian ones. More native people were learning English, and there may have been monolingual English-speakers among them as there were among the youths on the western shore of Virginia.[113] There is no evidence about the traditional religion's status. Indian men were still fishermen and hunters while the women farmed; the English still hand-raised tobacco, so there was no well-established plow-agriculture model to present to Indians as yet.

The Occohannocks vanished as recognizable tribal entities in Virginia after Beverley wrote about them in 1705; the Gingaskins hung onto their reservation. Douglas Deal has postulated that the Gingaskins' survival into the eighteenth century was due to a combination of adapting to cramped life on the reservation and the distance they lived from "vigilantes" like Edmund Scarburgh.[114] We doubt that either of these reasons is tenable. The Gingaskins probably were not short of space at that time. If the reservation of 690 acres held about thirty families, then there was enough land for the women to farm the traditional shifting plots of a fraction of an acre each, provided they shortened the fallowing period, without clearing the reservation's remaining woodlot.

And as long as the tribe had access to the extensive marshes and channels east of their reservation, its men could bring in plenty of fish, shellfish, and wildfowl for their families. As for the "vigilantes," there is not
good evidence for them anywhere on the seventeenth-century Eastern
Shore after Scarburgh's demise. What probably made most of the Occohannocks willing to move was the continuing strength, in population
and landholdings, of their linguistic (and probably actual) relatives in
Maryland. The Maryland Algonquian-speakers on the Eastern Shore
held some large tracts far removed from English settlements until well
into the eighteenth century.

The marital partners of the Accomacs and Occohannocks in the
seventeenth century probably were mainly Indians and whites; some
Anglo-Virginian families on Chincoteague Island still preserve a tradition of being descended from unions with local Indians that began in
the seventeenth century and continued (after the locals joined the Indian River Indians in Delaware) through the mid-nineteenth century.[115]
Heavy intermarriage with blacks was an eighteenth-century phenomenon. There were a few Indian-African associations, such as Philip Mongram's employing a Gingaskin hunter, which may have led to the birth
of Peter Mongram in the next generation (although there is no proof).
Only one black slave, a runaway, was ever recorded as being connected
with the local Indians, and then it was an Indian and two Englishmen
who caught him. Given the small number of native Indian employees on
English farms at any time in the century, Indian associations with Africans probably were extremely limited. There were definitely some free
African–descended families on the Virginia Eastern Shore for much of
the seventeenth century, and not all of them left for Maryland when
Virginia became legally more racist in the 1690s.[116] But the free black
connections that would undermine the Gingaskins' hold on their reservation do not appear in the records until the latter part of the eighteenth
century.

Three

The First Century with Maryland

THE NATIVE PEOPLE of the Maryland part of the Eastern Shore first met Englishmen as explorers and then as traders, as was true in Virginia. However, their region's potential for fur trading was much greater than that of the narrow peninsula to the south, so English settlement was delayed for several decades while the fur trade prospered. Thus the Maryland Eastern Shore Indians began to be exposed to English settlers and their cultural evangelism considerably later than was the case in Virginia. The Englishmen they met in the meantime were primarily traders, who had good reason to respect the native culture and language and, later, to try to protect the native people from being overrun.

The Fur-Trading Years

After John Smith's brief exploration of the Maryland Eastern Shore in 1608, there were no more recorded accounts of the Indians there until the 1620s, when English traders from the Virginia colony began to visit the region in order to barter for corn and furs. The Eastern Shore Indian trade appears to have been initiated by Samuel Argall, who began buying corn from the Accomacs as early as 1613.[1] For the first decade or so after the initial founding of Jamestown in 1607, the Virginia colonists were interested in getting corn rather than furs from the Indians, since the fledgling Virginia colony suffered from a chronic food shortage. Thus the English traded primarily with the nearby, surplus-producing Accomacs; trade with the Pocomokes and their neighbors to the north came later.

About 1620 English interest in the Chesapeake Bay region as a source of furs for export began to rise. By this time the French were heavily involved in the fur trade in Canada, and the Dutch were creating their own fur-trading network with Indian groups living along Delaware Bay. Between 1620 and 1630 various Englishmen decided that the Chesapeake Bay could become an important fur-trading center, since the Chesapeake and its tributaries offered ready access to a considerable number of Indian groups with furs, especially beaver pelts, to sell. Also, near the head of the bay was the territory of the powerful Susquehannock Indians, whose trade network extended all the way to the Great Lakes. If the Susquehannocks could be persuaded to bring their furs southward down the Susquehanna River to the Chesapeake, then English merchants could capture a part of the fur trade that was then mainly benefiting the Dutch.

During the 1620s several English individuals and groups independently attempted to open up the Chesapeake Bay for fur trading. The full extent of the activities of these traders and the total value of the furs they managed to obtain from the Indians are hard to estimate. Certainly furs never came close to rivaling tobacco as a source for wealth in the region. The profits of the fur trade, however, were shared among a much smaller number of people than were the profits from tobacco. Fortunes would be built on Chesapeake Bay beaver pelts, and keen competition arose both between individuals and between the Maryland and Virginia colonial governments for control of what came to be called the bay trade.

Even though fur trading had the potential for being a very profitable business, the number of English colonists who actually participated in the trade at any given time always remained relatively small. In large measure this was because most of the Englishmen who lived in the Chesapeake region during the seventeenth century never acquired even a superficial knowledge of Indian languages or cultures. Such knowledge was the key to successful trading, for anyone who did not have it was unlikely to be able to develop or maintain a network of trading partners among the Indians.

The first English trader we know of who regularly dealt with Maryland Eastern Shore Indians was John Westlock, who was trading with the Manokin Indians of what is now Somerset County, Maryland, as early as 1620. In court testimony recorded in 1670, Westlock told how "fifty years agoe" he began sailing up the Manokin River to a place called the Trading Branch, which was the site of an Indian village that the English later came to call Manokin town.[2] Westlock is a good example of a small-scale Indian trader who did not have the resources to compete for the big prize in the Chesapeake Bay fur trade, which was at the head of the bay with the Susquehannocks. Besides, when Westlock began his trading activities in the early 1620s, the Virginia colony was still controlled by the Virginia Company of London, a private joint-stock company that sharply restricted trading voyages up the Chesapeake.[3]

The Virginia Company's attempts to capture the fur trade never succeeded, and by 1624 the company had gone out of business. This left the bay trade open for exploitation by others. In the late 1620s a Virginia colonist named William Claibourne obtained English financial backing to set up a trading post on the upper Eastern Shore at Kent Island. Claibourne's main aim was to establish trade relations with the Susquehannocks and to divert their lucrative fur trade south into the Chesapeake.

While some colonists like Claibourne sought outside investment to mount large-scale ventures far up the Chesapeake, other men like Westlock used their own resources to develop smaller and more localized Indian trading networks. Entrepreneurs from the Virginia Eastern Shore seem to have initiated the earliest contacts with the Maryland Eastern Shore natives to their north, particularly those living below the Choptank River. In the 1620s only a handful of English colonists lived on the Eastern Shore, their settlements being restricted to a small area near the end of the peninsula. These colonists had experience in dealing with the local Accomacs, with whom they maintained peaceful relations.

The period of unrestricted competition for business with the Indians of the Chesapeake did not last very long. In 1631 William Claibourne set up a permanent trading post and settlement on Kent Island, thereby attempting to monopolize the head-of-the-bay trade. Claibourne had some initial success in his dealings with the Susquehannocks, although the Kent Island post apparently did not attract as many pelts as the other investors in the venture had hoped. In 1632, however, George Calvert, Lord Baltimore, obtained a royal charter to a large block of territory north and east of the Potomac River. This territory would become the new colony of Maryland, and Kent Island was part of it. Lord Baltimore and his son Cecil Calvert appreciated from the very beginning the potential value of the Chesapeake fur trade and were not about to let Claibourne and other Virginians operate in their territory without hindrance. After a struggle that was both political and military, Claibourne was dislodged from Kent Island.

The Calverts sought to turn a profit from furs by licensing private traders in return for 10 percent of the gains from each trading voyage.[4] The financial accounts of some voyages by licensed traders survive in the Maryland records. These give us an idea of the economics of the Chesapeake Indian trade in the late 1630s and early 1640s. For example, in 1637 Henry Fleet was licensed to trade in the vessel *Deborah*, whose cargo consisted of seventy-four trading axes, twenty-six hoes, nineteen yards of Dutch cloth, sixteen pairs of Irish stockings, two yards of peak, and a chest containing beads, knives, combs, fishhooks, Jew's harps, and looking glasses. On this voyage Fleet apparently sold only the cloth, for which he got thirty beaver skins.[5]

Fleet's list of trade goods compares closely with those of other traders of the period, the main difference being that other trading vessels usually shipped more cloth. Overall, cloth seems to have been the single most important trade item. The kind of cloth in question is usually referred to as Dutch cloth or blue truck or trucking cloth. This is probably the same kind of trading cloth that is described in a 1648 reference as "Dutch or Welsh rugged cloth, a violet blew or red, at four or five shillings a yard."[6] In 1633 Virginia's colonial government became so concerned about the large amounts of cloth being traded to the Indians that the colony actually banned this trade for a time on the grounds that it was causing the English colonists in Virginia to suffer "great want and need" of this essential product.[7]

After cloth, the next most important English trade goods were metal tools, especially axes and hoes. Naturally the Indians also wanted guns, but both Maryland and Virginia tried to prevent the sale of guns and gunpowder at that time. The attempts usually failed, though, since Indians who could not get guns from the English would buy them from the Dutch or Swedish traders on Delaware Bay.[8] In 1659 Virginia simply gave up trying to control the sale of guns, stating that "it is manifest that the neighbouring plantations both of English and fforeigners do plentifully furnish the Indians with gunns, and do thereby drawe from us the trade of beaver to our greate losse and their profitt."[9] By and large all efforts to deny the Indians the goods they really wanted were doomed to failure. It is clear that by the 1640s, at least, the native people were sophisticated consumers who knew what they wanted and would not settle for second best. If one set of European traders would not offer a particular category of goods, the furs would simply be sold elsewhere.

Table 3.1. Beaver prices (per pound) in seventeenth-century Maryland

Year	In tobacco	In currency	In roanoke
1637	30 lbs.	8s.	—
1638	32 lbs.	8s.	—
1639	30–32 lbs.	7.5–8s.	—
1642	40 lbs.	14s.	—
1643	72–100 lbs.	10–15s.	10 arms' length
1644	75 lbs.	14s.	10 arms' length
1661	40 lbs.	5s.	—
1667	("mean" beaver) 25 lbs.	2s.	—
"	("good" beaver) 35 lbs.	3s.	—
1668	—	5s.	10 arms' length

In return for European manufactured goods, bay traders bought skins of all kinds—and also corn—from the Indians. However, it was beaver pelts that the traders really wanted, because beaver brought the most profit. The price that Chesapeake traders could get for beaver was from seven to eight shillings a pound in the 1630s and rose to fifteen shillings a pound by 1643 (table 3.1). The price of beaver fell to about six or seven shillings a pound in the later 1640s and dropped again to five shillings or below after 1660. Profits from the trade were very substantial, particularly in the early 1640s when beaver prices peaked. In trading with a western shore Indian group in 1643, John Hollis sold metal axes worth from five to eight pounds of tobacco each to the Indians at the rate of five arms' length of roanoke per axe. Ten arms' length of roanoke bought one pound of beaver, and in that year the Maryland government valued beaver at a hundred pounds of tobacco per pound, which gave Hollis a very neat profit of between 600 and 1,000 percent on the transaction.[10]

In the 1640s the Chesapeake Bay fur trade reached its fully developed form. The hoped-for diversion of vast numbers of beaver pelts down the Susquehanna River never occurred, but the head of the bay was still a prime trading location, and a number of substantial traders were regularly going there and to the upper Eastern Shore for furs. Between the Maryland traders based on the western shore and the mainly Eastern

Shore–based Virginia traders, all of the Maryland Eastern Shore tribes had been contacted by 1640. The Choptanks appear to have been the last Eastern Shore Indian tribe to establish regular trade relations with the English, probably because of the relatively isolated location of their villages, situated several miles up the Choptank River estuary.[11]

Accounts of the Maryland Eastern Shore Indians themselves are very scanty during the 1630s and 1640s. Maryland's Lord Proprietor discouraged actual settlement by English colonists on the Eastern Shore at this time, so almost the only Englishmen who had any firsthand knowledge of the Indians there were the fur traders who visited the region; these men have left us almost nothing in the way of written records of their encounters. For a long time the Kent Island settlement remained the only permanent English enclave on the whole of the Maryland Eastern Shore. The Indians trading there were both Susquehannocks and the indigenous Indian inhabitants of the region, who were usually referred to as the Wicomiss. Another local Indian tribe called the Monoponsons was also mentioned.[12]

The upper Eastern Shore was going through a period of dramatic ethnic and political change in the 1630s and 1640s. The Susquehannock Indians, who in 1608 had only just begun to spread south into the head of the bay region, by the 1630s had expanded their territory to take in a sizable part of the upper Eastern Shore as well. By about 1650 they appear to have been in control of the whole of the Maryland Eastern Shore north of the Choptank River. That displaced the Wicomiss from all of their lands on the upper Eastern Shore. This expansion also apparently brought the Susquehannocks into conflict with the English, who by the early 1640s were at odds with the Wicomiss as well.

The fur trade undoubtedly played a pivotal role in triggering these events. In expanding southward down the Eastern Shore, the Susquehannocks may have been making a deliberate attempt to control the hinterland from which the English traders at Kent Island drew their furs. The Susquehannocks also were involved in a complex economic and military rivalry with the League of the Iroquois to the north. Access to European trade goods was a key element in this rivalry, and for the Susquehannocks, control of the upper Eastern Shore would have meant control of all the trade with the two English colonies on the Chesapeake Bay.

It appears that the Wicomiss resisted the Susquehannock expansion during the 1630s, but by 1648 they had been subordinated and were compelled to fight for the Susquehannocks in time of war.[13] After 1650, the only documentary references to the Wicomiss describe them as living south of the Choptank River in the territory of the Nanticoke Indians or in southern Delaware among the Chicconese, a Delaware tribe. By 1668 the Wicomiss had placed themselves under the protection of the Nanticokes.[14]

In 1642 Maryland's colonial government simultaneously declared war on the Wicomiss, the Susquehannocks, and the Nanticokes. The immediate cause of this war was an attack on some Englishmen living at Kent Island. Maryland's reason for lumping the Nanticokes, who did not even live near Kent Island, with the Susquehannocks and Wicomiss is not clear. In 1639 Rowland Williams, an English trader from Accomack, had been killed on the Maryland Eastern Shore, and the "Wichocomocos," a tribe that may have been either the Pocomokes or a tributary to the Nanticokes, were blamed.[15] Perhaps Maryland decided to punish the Eastern Shore Indians as a whole for these or other transgressions, and then declared war on the Wicomiss, Susquehannocks, and Nanticokes simply because they were the three strongest Maryland Eastern Shore tribes. Another possibility is that the colony was uncomfortable about the fact that the Eastern Shore was under the control of Indian groups who did not acknowledge the authority of Maryland's Lord Proprietor, even though by English law the Indians' territory was part of the Maryland colony. War was one way to assert control and to remind not just the Indians but also the Dutch to the north and the Virginia English to the south that the upper Eastern Shore was Maryland territory.

Whatever specific incident or incidents may have triggered the 1642 war, a major root cause of this and later English-Indian conflicts on the Eastern Shore was the fact that Indians and Englishmen were the products of very different cultures and did not understand each other. Mutually incomprehensible languages were only a part of the problem. Radically different patterns of social, political, and economic organization were equally important contributors to the generalized misunderstanding of Indians by Englishmen and of Englishmen by Indians. The trader-interpreters of the Chesapeake could go some distance toward bridging this gap, but even their comprehension of Indian cultures was limited.

One serious problem that arose again and again in the seventeenth-century Chesapeake was that both Indian and English people underestimated the amount of political and cultural variability existing within the others' ranks. The English had a great deal of difficulty understanding that all Chesapeake Bay Indians were not alike, and that these Indians had no unified government in the European sense of the term. When Maryland declared war on the Eastern Shore Indians in 1642, the English authorities probably did not realize that the Susquehannocks and the Nanticokes were almost as alien to each other as each tribe was to the English. The Susquehannocks were an intrusive Iroquoian-speaking group who must have been perceived by the Algonquian-speaking Nanticokes as a serious threat. It is unlikely that the Nanticokes would have supported the Susquehannocks in their efforts to control the upper Eastern Shore by allying with them against the English. There is circumstantial evidence to suggest that the Maryland authorities eventually grasped this point, since Maryland canceled the declaration of war against the Nanticokes, but not the Susquehannocks and Wicomiss, soon after it was made.[16]

The Susquehannocks made peace with the English in 1652, and for the next two decades the English of Maryland were the Susquehannocks' chief allies in their long-drawn-out war against the Iroquois. As part of the terms of this peace, the Susquehannocks yielded their claim to the lands of the upper Eastern Shore, though they continued to trade at the head of the bay. A Dutch trader named Jacob Clawson appears to have been their main contact there; Clawson later changed his surname to Young and became an English subject. Another important head-of-the-bay trader was Englishman John Bateman, who established himself near Palmers Island at the mouth of the Susquehanna River. The economic importance of the upper Chesapeake trade is revealed by the inventory of Bateman's wealth taken after his death in 1658. Bateman owned goods worth over seventy thousand pounds of tobacco, making him one of the richest Marylanders of his day.[17]

After the Maryland colony's abortive declaration of war against the Nanticokes in 1642, trading between the two peoples quickly resumed. In fact, English fur traders were so anxious to get back to their Eastern Shore sources that they had to be restrained from resuming operations before the war was over.[18] In 1647, however, the Nanticokes and the Wicomiss were once again in trouble with the Maryland authorities, this time over some attacks made on English colonists on the western shore.[19] Maryland organized a military expedition to punish them, but it accomplished very little. A similar incident occurred in 1651 but had no long-term consequences for the Nanticokes. These little "wars" against the Nanticokes do not appear to have been prosecuted very diligently; each time peaceful trade resumed in short order.

In the 1650s the Nanticokes and their neighbors were still doing business mainly with the Virginians of Northampton County. Virginia Eastern Shore interpreter-traders still tended to operate on a small scale, compared to the traders at the head of the bay. For most Northampton Englishmen, the Indian trade was supplementary to their main economic activity, which was raising tobacco. Such men might mount only one small-scale trading voyage a year and deal with only one Indian tribe year after year.

For a few men on Virginia's Eastern Shore, trading with Indians to the north was more than a part-time activity in the mid-seventeenth century. John Nuttall is a particularly interesting example. Nuttall, or Nutwell, first appears in the Virginia records as a young indentured servant who ran away from his master and went to live with an unnamed Eastern Shore Indian tribe. He was bought back from the Indians for the price of a hoe and carried back to his master "well strapped with Halyards," presumably so that he would not escape again.[20] As a young adult Nuttall worked for the trader John Hollis.[21] Despite his humble beginnings, Nuttall went on to become one of the most successful fur traders in the Chesapeake Bay region. Over the years he developed very strong ties to the Wicomico Indians in what was to become Somerset County, Maryland. In fact, he identified himself so closely with these people that his fellow Englishmen questioned where his loyalties lay; he was once accused of encouraging the Wicomicos to oppose further English penetration of their territory.[22] By the time of his death in 1664, the former indentured servant was a rich man. The inventory of Nuttall's estate testifies to his preoccupation with the Indian trade. Unlike other rich men of his day, the major part of Nuttall's wealth was not in land, tobacco, and servants. The most valuable single commodity he owned was 570 pounds of "neat beaver," which was worth over £140. Additionally he owned a "great sloop" with rigging and nearly a thousand arm's lengths of roanoke.[23]

At the same time that Nuttall was emerging as major figure in the Chesapeake Bay Indian trade, another Northampton colonist, Jenkin Price, became the most important trader who dealt with the Assateagues and other Indian groups who lived on the eastern or Atlantic Ocean side of the Delmarva Peninsula. In the 1650s Price provided virtually the only point of contact between these coastal tribes and the Virginia colonial government. Price was principally a trader, but he also served on occasion as the colony's representative in dealings with the

Indians. For example, in 1649 a group of Englishmen including Henry Norwood who had been shipwrecked on Assateague Island in what is now Worcester County, Maryland, were rescued by the nearby Kegotanks. Jenkin Price was asked by the Virginia government to search for and bring back the lost English travelers. At the same time the Kegotanks concluded that Price was the appropriate man with whom to negotiate the peaceful return of the Englishmen they had found. The Kegotank chief sent an envoy to Price, who came north to fetch the castaways.[24]

Men like John Nuttall and Jenkin Price were soon to fade from the scene, however. By 1660 the great era of the Chesapeake fur trade was coming to an end, and with it ended the dominance of the Northampton trader-interpreters as the main agents for contact between the Maryland Eastern Shore Indians and the English of the Maryland and Virginia colonies. During the 1650s the political barriers that had restrained English settlement on the Eastern Shore north of the Pocomoke River gradually disappeared; colonists began to move in. Soon the Indians, who up to this point had had very little contact with the English except through trade, were confronted with several small but rapidly growing English settlements sited on prime land that the Indians considered to be theirs.

Indian Lands and Polities at Mid-century

In the middle of the seventeenth century, the main Indian groups still inhabiting the Maryland Eastern Shore were the Wicomiss, the Choptanks, the Nanticokes, the Pocomokes, and the Assateagues. The location of the Wicomiss in the 1650s is uncertain, although they were no longer occupying their former lands on the Chester River. In 1668 they were living within Nanticoke territory near the town of Chicone, but they seem to have moved freely within a wide territory between the upper Choptank River and the Lewes Creek area in Delaware. The loss of their upper Eastern Shore lands to the Susquehannocks and then the English seems to have turned them into a wandering group without a well-defined tribal territory of their own.

The Choptank Indians occupied the south side of the Choptank River from about the modern town of Cambridge northward to Secretary Creek, with a territory extending back from the river frontage to take in the headwaters of the Little Blackwater and Transquaking Rivers

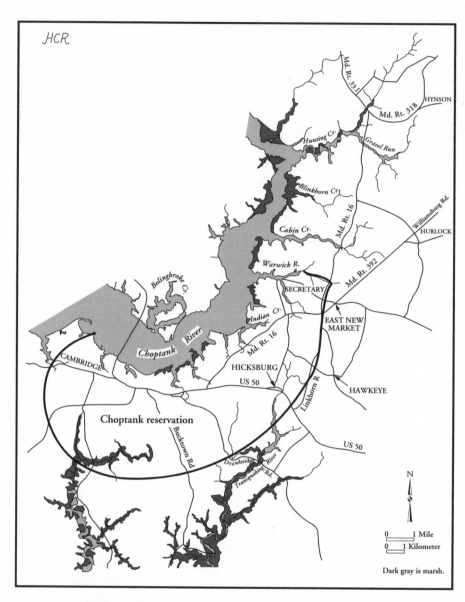

Fig. 3.1 Map of the Choptank reservation

(fig. 3.1). They occupied three or four separate towns at this time, all on creeks flowing into the Choptank.[25]

The next group to the south were the Nanticokes, whose main geographical focus was the Nanticoke River, but whose political authority extended southward to the Wicomico River and probably as far as the Manokin River. The Nanticokes had at least four towns when John Smith visited them in 1608; they claimed to have ten towns in 1697.[26] Their territory certainly extended as far north as the modern town of Laurel, Delaware, and as far south as modern Salisbury, Maryland. The "emperor" of the Nanticokes, whose principal town was Chicone, had authority over other chiefs, some of whom probably were not Nanticokes. The Wicomico Indians, who have already been mentioned as John Nuttall's trading partners, were almost certainly under the suzerainty of the Nanticoke paramount chief. Their own chief resided at the town of Tundotank on the Wicomico River near Salisbury. Tundotank was considered a Nanticoke town by both the Nanticokes and the English, and the English continued to recognize the Nanticoke claim to Tundotank well into the eighteenth century.[27]

There is good reason to suspect that the authority of the Nanticoke "emperor" also extended into the Manokin River drainage. When the English first settled in that region, they showed no concern at all about offending the local ruler, who lived at Manokin town. However, the colonists went to some lengths to placate the Nanticoke paramount chief, whom they referred to as their "neighbor" and to whom they paid a fee of six matchcoats for every plantation that they established in the region.[28] It may well be that the chief of Manokin recognized the paramount chief of the Nanticokes as his overlord, so that it was only the "emperor" who had the right to alienate land.

Nanticoke authority over the Wicomicos and Manokins was not absolute, however, since the chiefs and great men of those two groups seem to have dealt with the English independently on trade matters. In the Indian world, political authority often did not mean economic control of one's "subjects."[29] The Manokin chief in particular appears to have been in full charge when it came to his people's dealings with the English. A brief account of an English trading voyage up the Manokin River in 1656 describes how all trade with the Indians there had to take place at the Trading Branch, which was the site of the Manokin chief's town. The standard practice was to send a messenger to Manokin town when traders arrived at the mouth of the river and then wait for permission to sail upriver to the town.[30]

The Pocomoke Indians occupied the lower Pocomoke River drainage, and they probably lived within the later political boundaries of both Maryland and Virginia. In 1608 Wighcocomico, the main Indian town found there by John Smith, was on the south side of the Pocomoke River and lay within territory claimed by both Virginia and Maryland before the colonial boundary was set in 1667. The use of Pocomoke as a name for the Indians in this region dates only to about 1650 in the Virginia records, and they do not appear as Pocomokes in the Maryland records until 1678, when the chief of the Pocomokes was listed along with the chiefs of six other groups who established treaty relations with the Maryland colony. Four of these other tribes had names that appear as seventeenth-century geographical place-names in the Pocomoke and Annemessex River drainages of Somerset County;[31] at this time they were all living at Askiminikansen on the north bank of the Pocomoke River near the present-day town of Snow Hill (fig. 3.2). The Pocomoke chief stated in 1686 that because of "the Incroachments of the English" they had "already been driven from Pocomoke, to Aquintica, from thence to Askiminokonson."[32] This fact suggests that by the late seventeenth century the Pocomokes had become an amalgamation of several Pocomoke and Annemessex River tribes who had been living along the lower reaches of those rivers before English settlement.

One other Maryland Eastern Shore Indian group, the Assateagues, lived on the Atlantic side of the Delmarva Peninsula. They were not mentioned in the Maryland colonial records before 1659, so the Maryland government seems to have had no relations with them during the first half of the seventeenth century. When in 1659 the Virginia authorities invited Maryland to contribute troops to a punitive expedition against the Assateagues, as well as the Nanticokes and Wicomicos, Maryland's leaders declined to participate on the grounds that they did not know enough about the situation to determine whether an attack on the Assateagues was justified.[33]

The Assateagues may originally have been just one of several poorly documented Indian groups who lived along the Atlantic coast of the Delmarva. By 1686 several of these groups had joined together and occupied a part of the Askiminikansen reservation, in a town north of the Pocomoke Indians' settlement.[34] Beginning in 1677 the Maryland records contain repeated references to an Assateague "emperor," who apparently had authority over several other tribes as well as his own people.[35]

Of all of these Eastern Shore Indian groups, the ones that concerned

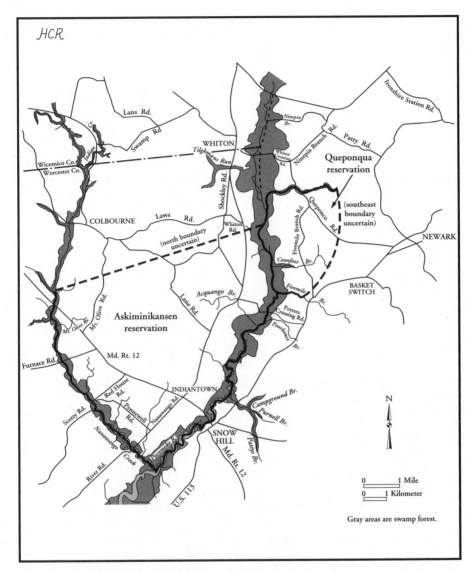

Fig. 3.2 Map of the Askiminikansen and Queponqua reservations

the Maryland colonial authorities the most were the Nanticokes and the Wicomiss. The Choptanks seem to have been firmly allied to the Maryland colony, from the signing of the first treaty in 1659 until well into the eighteenth century. The Pocomokes and the Assateagues both came into conflict with colonists on the Virginia Eastern Shore in the 1650s, but they never were viewed as a threat by the Maryland authorities. Pocomoke and Assateague interaction with English colonists on the Maryland Eastern Shore remained peaceful throughout the seventeenth century.

The Nanticokes and the Wicomiss, however, stood in a different relationship to the Maryland colony. Both tribes had been declared enemies of the province upon occasion, and the Wicomiss continued to be hostile to the Marylanders. The peace made between Maryland and the Susquehannocks in 1652 apparently did not end conflict with the Wicomiss, who probably had been the Susquehannocks' clients or allies before that date. The Nanticokes were at peace with Maryland by the time large-scale English settlement began south of the Choptank River, but Maryland government officials remained wary of them. The Nanticokes undoubtedly were the largest and most powerful Indian group on the Maryland Eastern Shore at that time, and they were also the most important of the Maryland tribes to be still involved in the fur trade.

The main reasons that the English were uneasy about the Nanticokes, however, stemmed from the geographical location and cultural affinities of the tribe. Nanticoke territory stood between the Maryland colony and the Delaware or Lenape Indians who lived along Delaware Bay. Farther north still were the Five Nations of the Iroquois, who by the mid-seventeenth century had compelled some Delaware groups to accept tributary status.[36] The Iroquois League was the most powerful Indian polity in the Middle Atlantic region in those days. It was heavily involved in the fur trade in competition with the Susquehannocks, who were the Maryland colony's chief Indian allies. In 1661 Maryland and the Susquehannock nation established a formal military alliance against the Iroquois.

Because of their indirect link with the Iroquois, the Nanticokes' relations with the southern or Unami Delaware in particular must have aroused the concern of Maryland officials. The Unami spoke an Algonquian language related to Nanticoke, and in legend at least the Unami were the Nanticokes' distant relatives.[37] The Unami town nearest to the Nanticokes was Chicconese, located along Delaware Bay only about 50 miles from the northern Nanticoke town at Broad Creek.[38] The Nanticokes were certainly in regular contact with the Chicconeses of southern Delaware, who were called by the Dutch the *Grote* or Big Chicconeses. The Nanticokes traded not only with the English on the Chesapeake Bay side of the Delmarva Peninsula but also with the

Swedes and the Dutch on Delaware Bay, which meant that Nanticoke furs had to pass through Chicconese territory. In fact, an important Indian trail called the Wicomiss or Whorekill path ran through Nanticoke territory from the upper Choptank River to a Chicconese town near Lewes, Delaware.[39] The Nanticokes were therefore closely involved with a "foreign" Indian tribe which was on peaceful terms with the Iroquois, Maryland's enemies, and they were also trading with the Maryland colony's commercial rivals along Delaware Bay. Maryland's Lord Proprietor regarded the Whorekill region as part of his territory, so that the establishment of a Dutch trading post there seemed an illegal usurpation of his rights.[40]

The Maryland authorities apparently thought that the Nanticokes had the power to function as the gatekeepers for Maryland's northeastern border. In their view Nanticoke leaders could either prevent hostile Indians from entering Maryland from this direction or allow the Delawares or the Iroquois through to attack Maryland settlements. In reality, of course, the Nanticoke "emperors" probably did not have either the level of political authority or the military might to prevent other Indian groups from passing through their territory. Maryland's governor and council did not understand this, though, and repeated the standard English error of assuming that Indian nations had rigid geographical boundaries that could be controlled and defended like the boundaries of European nation-states. Indian "territories" became an even more important issue once English settlers were allowed to take up land in the region.

English Settlers Move In

Before 1660 and the influx of English settlers, conflicts between the Eastern Shore Indians and the English stemmed from trade disputes and small-scale raids by Indians on English plantations. Such conflicts were infrequent and typically blew over quickly. After the lower Eastern Shore was thrown open to settlement by the English, however, a new and much more serious category of disputes emerged: competition for land rights. English newcomers not only could claim the lands that the Indians had traditionally used for hunting and gathering, but they could also patent the ground on which Indian villages stood. This unrestricted right to patent Indian lands caused a great number of disputes between Englishmen and Indians, and sometimes even between Englishmen and Englishmen.

In order to understand the native-settler land disputes that arose on the Maryland Eastern Shore after 1659, it is necessary to keep in mind that the English did not acknowledge native claims to the land based on prior millennia-long occupation. They only recognized titles issued by their own authorities, the ultimate one in Maryland being the Lord Proprietor. The proprietor typically granted land to colonists under an English legal formula called common socage, by which the grantee had full rights to the land as long as he paid an annual fee (a quitrent) to the proprietor or his heirs.[41] Holders of land by common socage could rent, lease, mortgage, sell, or bequeath that land without restriction as long as the quitrents were paid. The Choptank Indians eventually were granted their reservation lands on that basis, so that in English eyes they "really" owned their land as long as they paid their quitrent of six beaver skins per year.[42] The other tribes, however, never did "receive" their lands in so secure a manner. When the other reservations were created, lands were set aside for the Indians through the personal proclamation of the Lord Proprietor of Maryland. But without the protection of a land patent, the tribes did not "own" the land as far as the English populace was concerned, and any Englishman could legally patent the land out from under them. The new owner was supposed to wait for the Indians to leave voluntarily before occupying "his" tract. Many patentees would be too impatient to wait.

Maryland's concerns about the Nanticokes clearly influenced the pattern of English settlement on the Eastern Shore in the 1660s. Settlements spread very rapidly up all of the peninsula's rivers that flow into the Chesapeake with the exception of the Nanticoke River, where the colonists did not begin taking up land in any significant quantity until the 1670s (table 3.2). The first area of the lower Eastern Shore to be

Table 3.2. Acreages that had been patented in Somerset county, by river drainage

	By 1665	By 1670	By 1675	By 1680	By 1685	By 1690
Annemessex/ Manokin	14,610	19,910	24,320	41,570	47,240	54,870
Pocomoke	16,350	24,050	27,770	44,040	53,320	58,040
Wicomico	10,250	13,250	17,100	34,060	40,240	48,700
Nanticoke	1,100	2,600	13,500	24,450	35,880	49,370

Source: Somerset County Rent Rolls.

made available for English colonization was the Choptank River drainage. Colonists began claiming land grants on the south side of the river in 1659, the same year that the Maryland governor and the chiefs of the Choptank Indians signed their first treaty of friendship. The same treaty that defined relations with the Choptank Indians also covered the Monoponson Indians, who by this time may well have been the only native people living on the Maryland Eastern Shore north of the Choptank River.

The area south of the Nanticoke River began to be settled by English people in 1661, when Maryland's Lord Proprietor invited English settlers on the Virginia Eastern Shore to come north and take up lands in his colony. One other inducement used to attract Virginia colonists to Somerset County was the closing off of the Lower Eastern Shore Indian trade to non-Marylanders.[43] This action resulted in the movement of several Virginia trader-interpreters to Maryland, including John Nuttall, Jenkin Price, and John Westlock.

The English colonists in Somerset County were very careful not to offend the Nanticoke paramount chief during the early years of settlement. This attitude persisted into the 1670s, when Somerset County officials were still insisting that the Nanticokes be paid matchcoats for each plantation established within territories claimed by their "emperor."[44] However, the Somerset colonists quickly overwhelmed the non-Nanticoke Indian communities of the southern part of the county, including Manokin Indian town, which ceased by exist by about 1670.[45] This takeover appears to have been accomplished peacefully, with the Manokins and other Indian tribes in the area retreating in a piecemeal fashion as new English plantations were established near them. The Manokins, the Pocomokes, and the other southern Somerset County tribes were not included in any treaty with Maryland until 1678, and before this date their tribal lands were not protected in any fashion by the proprietary government.[46]

Apart from the Indians themselves, the other group of people directly threatened by unrestricted patenting were the English fur traders. These individuals certainly did not want the Eastern Shore Indian towns turned into English tobacco plantations that would profit no one but the plantation owners. The major strategy English traders adopted to protect their Indian customers was to patent Indian village sites themselves and then simply refrain from occupying the land. The land patent stopped anyone else from claiming the Indian village or town, and the English trader who was the nominal owner of the town presumably had no desire to remove the Indians from "his" land because he profited through trade with them.

This strategy began to be used very early in the lower Maryland Eastern Shore settlement process. In 1665 John Edmondson, a licensed Maryland Indian trader, patented the "upper Indian town" on the Choptank River.[47] This was one of the villages then occupied by the Choptanks, and in the eighteenth century it was called the Locust Neck Indian Town. It is clear that Edmondson never occupied or developed this land grant, since four years later, when the Choptank Indians' reservation was created, Edmondson was not compensated for any improvements to the property that he was losing. Other Englishmen who patented land within the Choptank reservation area before 1669 were paid compensation for the houses and agricultural improvements that they lost when their plantations were turned over to the Choptanks, but Edmondson apparently lost nothing by the creation of the reservation.[48]

Indian traders seem to have tried a similar strategy when southern Somerset County was opened to settlement in 1661, but there the settlement of the land proceeded so rapidly that the Indian towns were overwhelmed anyway. Jenkin Price claimed land at Acquintica on the lower Pocomoke River, on or near a Pocomoke Indian town that was probably abandoned early in the settlement process.[49] Another trader, Nehemiah Covington, established his plantation next to an Indian town called Great Monie on Monie Creek.[50] Nothing is known of the cultural affinities of the Indians inhabiting Great Monie or of their subsequent history. It seems likely, however, that the Monie Indians were soon displaced from their lands, just like the other southern Somerset County tribes. The site of the Manokin Indian town at Trading Branch was a much-sought-after piece of property early in the colonization process. John Westlock, the veteran Virginia Indian trader from Northampton County, established his plantation called Brownstone immediately adjacent to the Manokin Indian town. He probably would have claimed the town site itself had not someone else gotten there before him. Westlock's patent for Brownstone is dated just three days later than a 500-acre patent for "Glanville's Lot," which was right on top of the Manokins' town.[51] William Glanville, the patentee, was a nonresident merchant who made no effort to remove the Indians from Manokin town or to develop his grant as a tobacco plantation. His interest in the Indian town at Trading Branch can only have been because of its important role in the fur trade.

However, the short, unhappy life of Manokin town after 1661 illustrates that a strategy based on protecting an Indian dwelling site by itself was insufficient. The native people of the Eastern Shore were dependent on the large undeveloped hinterlands that surrounded their villages. Even if the Indian houses and agricultural plots interspersed among them were protected from encroachment, the inhabitants of the houses still could not support themselves without being able to harvest an extensive range of wild animal and plant resources that were found farther afield. In the case of the Choptank Indian town patented by John Edmondson, a large territory surrounding the village remained open for Indian use from 1669 onward because of the creation of the huge Choptank reservation. The Manokin Indian town stood alone, however (fig. 3.3). Its populace could not survive on a 500-acre private reservation within an area of relatively dense English settlement, and the town certainly could not continue to function as a trading center for furs, which could only

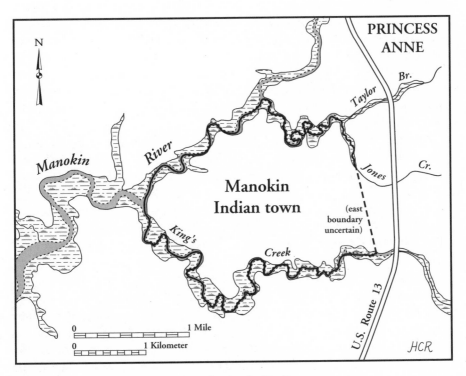

Fig. 3.3 Map showing the location of Manokin Indian town

be gotten in any significant numbers through large-scale hunting. Even if the Manokin Indians' relationship with the English settlers in Somerset had been completely amicable, which it was not (some settlers harassed the Indians and stole their corn),[52] their community at Trading Branch still would have faced economic collapse through the destruction of its natural resource base. The Indians were faced with a choice: change their age-old economy or move. They moved.

Although the Indian towns of southern Somerset County were overwhelmed relatively quickly, Indian communities in the northern part of the county survived the early years of the lower Eastern Shore land rush that began in 1661. Indians living north of the Wicomico River and along the upper reaches of the Pocomoke River were not under serious threat from English settlement until after about 1675. The area north of the Wicomico was probably protected by the fact that it was viewed as Nanticoke territory. English colonists did take up lands in this area during the 1670s, but the Indian towns there were left undisturbed. The upper Pocomoke area was not initially attractive to English settlers, who were mainly interested in the Chesapeake Bay side of the peninsula. Relatively soon after the settlement of the lower Pocomoke began, the upper Pocomoke became a refuge area for displaced Indians. Archaeological evidence demonstrates that the upper Pocomoke region already had a resident Indian population, but by 1678 it had received a substantial influx of other Indian groups, both from the Manokin and Annemessex regions and from the seaside.

The events of the 1660s demonstrated very clearly that Indian-English relations needed to be regulated by formal treaties if Maryland's proprietary government wished to avoid conflict and the destruction of the Eastern Shore fur trade. Land-hungry planters simply pushed the Indians out of the Manokin-Annemessex area entirely, a result that trader-interpreter John Nuttall had predicted when settlement first began there.[53] In the Choptank River area, by contrast, the Choptank Indians lost some land to the English, but their town sites were not threatened and trade was not disrupted.

The most powerful of the Eastern Shore tribes, the Nanticokes, had no treaty with the provincial government of Maryland, either, but they negotiated an agreement with the Somerset County government. This agreement allowed English settlement to proceed in a controlled fashion on the southern periphery of the Nanticokes' territory, so long as the native people were compensated for any land they lost. The Nanticokes agreed to deal exclusively with Maryland traders, provided that they supplied the kinds of goods the Indians wanted.[54]

The lack of a treaty between Maryland and the Nanticokes created problems on another front, however. In the 1660s the Wicomiss Indians continued to harass the English, and the Nanticokes continued to allow the Wicomiss unrestricted passage through their territory. Finally, after the 1667 murder of a Maryland official, Captain John Odber, the provincial government decided to end the Wicomiss problem once and for all.[55] Maryland military forces were sent to destroy the Wicomiss, and since those people were then living in Nanticoke territory, this action raised the possibility of a wider Eastern Shore Indian war. Instead the Maryland government decided to restrict the war to the Wicomiss alone and to enlist the help of the Nanticokes and other Eastern Shore tribes against them. The Choptank Indians were the most enthusiastic supporters of the English in their war against the Wicomiss, perhaps because they had also suffered at the hands of that tribe. In the end it was Ababco, chief of the Transquaking band of the Choptanks, who found the Wicomiss man who had killed Captain Odber and turned him over to the English. Unnarocassimmon, the Nanticoke paramount chief, also agreed not to shelter the Wicomiss people living among the Nanticokes anymore and to give them all up.[56] The Wicomiss were almost completely destroyed by 1669, and at least some members of the defeated tribe were sold as slaves in Barbados.[57]

One result of the Wicomiss war was that on May 1, 1668, the Nanticokes signed a treaty for the first time with Maryland's provincial government.[58] The Choptanks renewed their treaty with Maryland at the same time, and they also received title under Maryland law to their territory along the Choptank River as a reward for their cooperation in the war as well as their consistently peaceful stance toward the English. This was the first of the "Indian towns" or reservations to be created on the Maryland Eastern Shore.[59]

The Nanticoke treaty established the general rules and principles that were to govern Nanticoke-English relations. These include peace between the Lord Proprietor and the Nanticoke "emperor," forgiveness of past acts of hostility on both sides, provisions that Indians who commit crimes against the English should be punished under English law, provisions making the Nanticokes' paramount chief responsible for the behavior of the Indians of other nations who might come into his territory, and confirmation of the Nanticokes' foraging rights. These same clauses

appear in subsequent treaties between Maryland and the various Eastern Shore Indian groups, and even the specific wording of the treaties
was little changed. New treaties were signed whenever a new Nanticoke
leader came to power, whenever the Maryland government underwent
a major change in policy toward "foreign" or Maryland Indians, and
whenever important disputes between the Eastern Shore Indians and
the English arose. Treaties were signed with all or most of the Eastern
Shore tribes in the years 1678, 1705, and 1742. Additionally, the Nanticokes alone signed or renewed treaties in 1687 and 1693, and the Pocomokes signed a treaty in 1692. The Pocomokes were not included
in any treaties before 1678, probably because they were not involved in
the Wicomiss war and because until the mid-1660s they had been regarded as a Virginia tribe.

Eastern Shore Indians were always very concerned about maintaining
their right to use lands for hunting and gathering even after English
settlers had claimed possession of those lands. Maryland treaties always
contained a "Hunting, Crabbing, Fowling and Fishing" clause, and it is
clear that the Indians interpreted that clause to mean that they could
extract wild resources from any land in the region, whether occupied
by the English or not.[60] Foraging rights were a necessity to a people who
remained determined to retain their traditional way of life. However,
those rights were not always recognized by the native people's neighbors. In 1686, for example, the Indians of Askiminikansen on the Pocomoke River complained that "John Kirk and John Carter will not
suffer their [the reservation's] Indians to hunt upon their [Kirk's and
Carter's] land"; further, if they "catch any beaver," Colonel Colebourne
would "challenge the [ownership of the] skins."[61] The Eastern Shore
Indians continued to complain about the infringement of their hunting,
crabbing, fowling, and fishing rights well into the eighteenth century.[62]

The most critical treaty year for the Eastern Shore Indians was 1678,
when the Nanticokes, Pocomokes, and Assateagues all signed new
agreements with Maryland's Lord Proprietor. The texts of these treaties
contain almost nothing that was not previously stated in 1668, but the
Maryland government took this occasion to extend formal recognition
of land rights to the three tribes. In a proclamation separate from the
treaties, the Lord Proprietor recognized the existence of seven "Indian
towns" in the Pocomoke, Wicomico, and Nanticoke river drainages.
These "towns" were not established as reservations in the same fashion
as the Choptank reservation was earlier, since the Nanticokes, Poco-

mokes, and Assateagues were not given legal title to the town lands. The purpose of the proclamation appears to have been to warn English settlers not to take up lands on or near the Indian towns, which ranged in size from about 10,000 acres down to about 1,000 acres. The territories described in the 1678 act certainly did not cover all of the lands the three tribes inhabited or made use of at this time, but they did encompass the core areas occupied by Indian people. For the first time the Lord Proprietor was acknowledging that the Nanticokes, the Pocomokes, and the Assateagues had a legal right to remain on the land, and that they were not simply impediments to the further expansion of English settlement.

The 1678 recognition of the Eastern Shore Indian towns probably was spurred by the Maryland government's desire to end the state of constant warfare that existed with Indian groups on the colony's northern frontier. A complex series of events during the 1670s had left Maryland at war not only with the Iroquois but also with the colony's former allies, the Susquehannocks.[63] By 1678 Maryland was seeking a comprehensive peace with all its Indian enemies, and the colony may have decided that it was now time to stabilize the situation on the Eastern Shore as well.[64] Events in southern Somerset County during the 1660s probably had convinced the colony's leaders that Indian lands had to be protected in some fashion if there was to be peaceful coexistence on the Eastern Shore. As more and more settlers arrived in Somerset County, the northern part of the county became the main focus for further expansion. This circumstance increased the likelihood of conflict between the English and the Nanticokes, something that the Maryland authorities wished to avoid.

Since the wording of the treaties between the Maryland colony and the Eastern Shore Indians scarcely changed after the first treaty, the terms of the subsequent treaties obviously were not developed through negotiation with the Indians but were dictated by Maryland officials. Consequently, the treaties addressed English concerns much more than Indian concerns. Under these treaties the Indians received very little in the way of guarantees that their rights and interests would be protected. All that they were offered, in essence, was peace with Maryland's proprietary government, a certain amount of protection against personal violence from English neighbors, and the right to continue their traditional hunting and foraging activities. The treaties by themselves did not guarantee Indian land rights. Any protection of these rights had to come through separate legislation or through some specific action by the Lord Proprietor. Since Maryland was a proprietary colony rather than a royal one, the proprietor in theory could set aside unpatented land for the Indians without seeking the approval of the Maryland assembly.

When the Lord Proprietor formally acknowledged the existence of the Eastern Shore Indian towns in 1678, he must have had some understanding of the fact that these towns had to include considerably more than just the village sites themselves if the tribesmen were to survive. Thus the 1678 proclamation not only recognized the towns but also defined a three-mile-wide buffer zone around the towns where the English were not to settle. Unfortunately for the Indians, the Lord Proprietor did not follow up his proclamation with an order that the boundaries of these towns were to be fixed by survey. Without precisely defined boundaries, the towns remained vulnerable to English encroachment.

The two largest of the Indian towns recognized in 1678, Askiminikansen on the Pocomoke River and Chicone on the Nanticoke River, already contained some land patented by the English. In each case, however, the patents were held by men who had no interest in displacing the native people who lived there. The land at Askiminikansen was patented by William Stevens, one of the most powerful figures in Somerset County and a man whom the Lord Proprietor sometimes used as his agent in negotiations with the Eastern Shore Indians. At Chicone there was Thomas Taylor, formerly a licensed Indian trader and then a high-ranking militia officer who was usually the person sent by the proprietor to deal with the Nanticoke "emperor" during this era.[65] Taylor had acquired the rights to a tract of land in the heart of the Chicone Indian town called Handsel from its original English patentee. In both cases the patents encompassed the main Indian residential sites within the town lands, and it is likely that these were friendly patents held by Stevens and Taylor to protect the Indian towns from other Englishmen.

The Indian towns that were established by the proclamation of 1678 included sites on the Pocomoke, Wicomico, and Nanticoke Rivers. Apart from Askiminikansen, which was a large neck of land between Nassawango Creek and the Pocomoke River, two other tracts in the Pocomoke River drainage were set aside for the Indians. One called Queponqua was located east of the river across from the upper portion of Askiminikansen (see fig. 3.2). The other town was situated at the head of Dividing Creek. This town, whose Indian name was Parahocon,

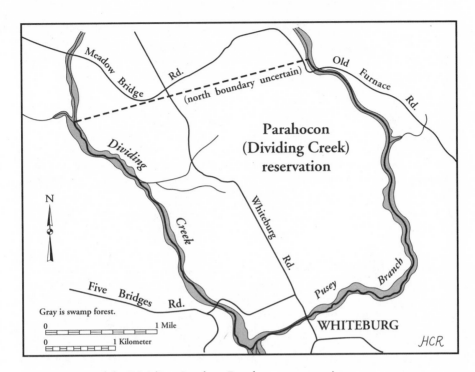

Fig. 3.4 Map of the Dividing Creek or Parahocon reservation

stood some distance up the creek from the Pocomoke River proper, on the present-day border between Somerset and Worcester Counties (fig. 3.4). The two Wicomico drainage towns were Tundotank (Tundotenake), the principal town of the Wicomico Indians, and another town whose Indian name is not recorded but which lay on Rockawakin (formerly Cottingham's) Creek (fig. 3.5). The two Nanticoke drainage towns mentioned in the proclamation were Puckamee, on the east bank of the Nanticoke River upstream from Barren Creek (fig. 3.6), and, nearly across from it, the Nanticoke town that was normally called Chicone by the English. The latter town, which was the seat of the Nanticoke "emperor," was located along the west side of the Nanticoke between present-day Chicone Creek and Marshyhope Creek in Dorchester County (fig. 3.7).

The actual boundaries of these towns were not defined in the 1678 proclamation, and none of the towns except Askiminikansen and Chicone were ever surveyed. However, the locations of the other towns can

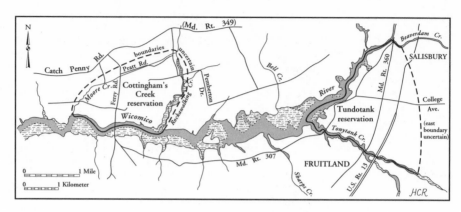

Fig. 3.5 Map of the Tundotank and Cottingham's Creek reservations

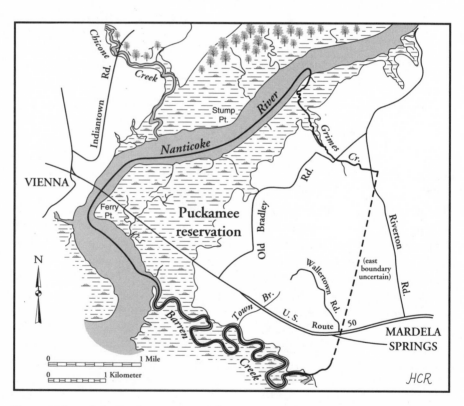

Fig. 3.6 Map of the Puckamee reservation

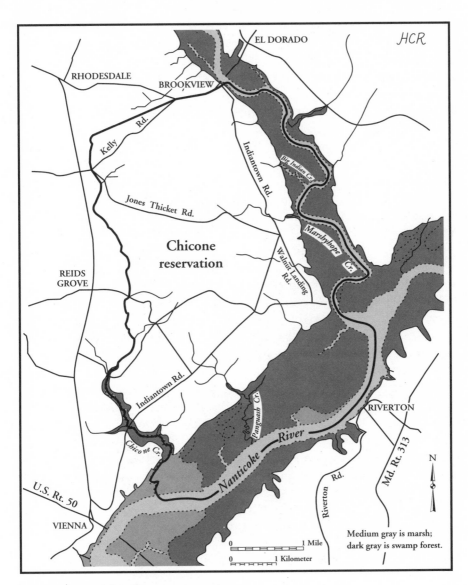

Fig. 3.7 Map of the Chicone reservation

be established through the use of the proprietary rent rolls for Somerset County. The Lords Baltimore were owed an annual rent by everyone who patented land in Maryland, and in order to ensure that this rent was paid, the Calvert family kept their own records of the landholdings in the colony. Using these records, it is possible to discover not only the locations of the towns but also approximately how long the Indians remained in them.[66]

The earliest surviving rent roll for Somerset County dates to 1707. By that year, the only Indian towns in the county that apparently still had Indian populations living on them were Askiminikansen and Tundotank.[67] Queponqua (Quapanquah) was still probably in Indian hands, but according to the rent roll the tract of land had no Indian residents. It was probably being used only as a hunting territory by people based on the adjacent Askiminikansen reservation.[68] The survival of Askiminikansen is not surprising, since even by itself it was the largest of the Somerset County reservations and the main residential area for both the Assateagues and the Pocomokes. Indian complaints about encroachment resulted in a formal boundary survey of the reservation in 1686, and that action seems to have provided the Indians there with the protection they needed to survive into the next century.

The survival of Tundotank is less easy to explain. The town area was small to begin with, and neither the proprietary government nor the Somerset County government ever properly defined its boundaries. The Wicomico Indians were still living at Tundotank in some considerable numbers in the 1680s, even though this part of the Wicomico River drainage had become a major focus for English settlement. In 1682 the Somerset government sent a force of twenty men to Tundotank to arrest two Indians accused of hog stealing.[69] The fact that such a strong force was deemed necessary suggests that the "king of Wicomico" and his subjects were still powerful enough to represent a threat to English security. After this incident there are no more references to the Tundotank Indians in the Somerset County records. Presumably the chief and most of his people left the town sometime after the 1682 incident and joined either the Pocomokes and Assateagues at Askiminikansen or, more likely, the Nanticokes at Chicone. However, some Indians must have stayed behind, since 1707 rent roll entries refer to the town as if it were still in existence, i.e., Indian-occupied. The town survived in some form until the mid-eighteenth century, since most of the town's land was not patented by any English planter until 1721, and the probable site of the village proper was not patented until 1764.[70] Tundotank is undoubtedly the Indian town referred to by the Nanticokes in 1767 when they complained about the loss of land "at the head of Wicomico 4 miles below Venables Mill."[71]

By contrast, the other Wicomico River Indian town recognized by the 1678 proclamation probably passed out of Indian hands in less than a generation. This town was on Cottingham's Creek, which is now called Rockawakin Creek. The name Rockawakin derives from the Indian place-name "Rotkawawkin" or "Rocahowan," a name which was used by English settlers for the upper portion of the Wicomico River in the seventeenth century. The Cottingham's Creek town was probably called Rotkawawkin by its inhabitants, and like Tundotank, it may have been occupied by a non-Nanticoke group, perhaps the Wicomicos, who were nevertheless part of the Nanticoke paramount chiefdom.[72]

The two Nanticoke River towns definitely were inhabited by Nanticoke Indians, and the larger one on the west bank was Chicone, the "emperor's" own town. The boundaries of this town were surveyed in 1698, when the Nanticoke reservation was formally created by an act of the Maryland Assembly. The town of Puckamee, across the river, probably had passed out of Indian hands by this date, since it did not receive similar legal recognition. Puckamee was certainly gone by 1707, for according to the Somerset rent roll, the lands north of Barren Creek were occupied by English planters, and no Indian occupants were mentioned.

The town called Parahocon, located on Dividing Creek, is another Indian town that went out of occupation relatively quickly. In fact, in the four years following the proclamation, virtually all of the land contained within the town was patented by English colonists. There are no references to the Parahocon reservation after its creation in 1678, although there is a mention of a Somerset colonist stealing "beans and pease" from the "Parrahawkin" Indians in 1676.[73] Since this town is only a few miles from Askiminikansen, it is likely that the people of Parahocon joined the other Pocomoke Indian groups at the larger up-river Indian town well before 1700.

The Indian towns recognized in 1678 show an obvious twinning pattern (see fig. 4.1), with three pairs of towns occurring on the east and west banks of the main rivers of the region in close proximity. The three pairs, Askiminikansen and Queponqua, Tundotank and Cottingham's Creek, and Chicone and Puckamee, may in reality have been only three towns, each of which had a main village on one side of the river and a hinterland beyond. Having a "town" that took in both sides of a river was a traditional Algonquian Indian pattern,[74] and the legal establishment of such a "town" would have protected Indian access to the rivers with their fish and emergent plant resources. If this is the case, then the almost total absence of references to Queponqua, Puckamee, and Cottingham's Creek in the county and provincial records after 1678 would be explained. Indian towns that had few or no full-time Indian residents would generate little official business and probably would be the first towns to pass out of Indian control as a result of encroachment by English settlers.

In reality, the 1678 Indian towns proclamation provided little protection for any Indian lands except in the two cases where the town boundaries were formally surveyed. The proprietary government's more loosely delimited Indian towns could not be defended against encroachment by Somerset County's English population, most of whom were probably hostile to the whole idea of a permanent Indian presence in their vicinity. The Pocomokes and Assateagues complained of constant harassment by the English until 1686, when the boundaries of Askiminikansen Town were finally surveyed. The Nanticokes were probably still strong enough in the late seventeenth century to discourage large-scale encroachment on Chicone until the town boundaries received formal recognition in 1698. Elsewhere, encroachment does not even seem to have slowed down significantly as a result of the 1678 proclamation. Of the other 1678 Indian towns, Parahocon, Puckamee and Cottingham's Creek disappeared relatively quickly, and Queponqua continued only as a hunting territory for Askiminikansen across the river. Tundotank managed to survive as an inhabited Indian town into the eighteenth century, but it is doubtful that more than a handful of Indians continued to live there after the 1680s.

The proclamation of 1678 was the first attempt by the Maryland government to give the Indians of the Eastern Shore south of the Choptank River some defensible rights to the lands they inhabited. It is worth noting that this was done by the Lord Proprietor's proclamation rather than by an act of the Maryland assembly. This fact hints at a difference in viewpoint between the Lord Proprietor and the assembly, a body made up of the elected representatives of the colony's English population. The tobacco planters who dominated the assembly were probably less concerned about Indian land rights than the proprietor, and they were inclined to see Indian reservations as a "waste" of land that would otherwise be available for patenting by English colonists. The proprietor and his representatives, on the other hand, were more concerned with "foreign" policy issues, like the conflicts with the northern Indians, and with the preservation of the fur trade. Since the duty paid on furs exported from Maryland directly profited the Lord Proprietor, he had a clear financial interest in the protection of the Indians who made that trade possible.

The difference in viewpoint between the proprietor and the planters' interests represented in the Maryland assembly may also have been behind the long delay in the formal creation of the Chicone reservation. It was not until twenty years after the Indian towns proclamation of 1678 that the assembly finally passed an act to create the Nanticoke reservation at Chicone. It is clear that the Nanticoke Indians had wanted the reservation to be formally recognized and to have its boundaries defined long before this actually came to pass. There is evidence of rising tensions between the Nanticokes and the English just before the passage of the 1698 act. The assembly may have acted because it feared that alienating the tribe further might push it into an alliance with the Iroquois, who were now the dominant Indian power to the north of Maryland. Certainly the creation of the Nanticoke reservation on Broad Creek several years later was prompted by a desire to quiet the Nanticoke Indians at a time when Maryland feared trouble from "foreign" Indians, in the latter case the Tuscaroras.[75]

During the last quarter of the seventeenth century, the Maryland government's Eastern Shore Indian policy centered on the Nanticokes, who were the last tribe in the region that had any real economic or military significance. The Choptanks were firmly allied with the English and in any case were not numerous or well organized enough to pose a credible military threat; they were no longer an important factor in the fur trade, either. The Assateagues and Pocomokes, for their part, were still in the process of consolidating at the Askiminikansen reservation. Both tribes appear at that time to have been aggregations of several smaller tribes or bands, most of whom were refugee groups from the lower Pocomoke River drainage or from the seaboard side. These groups had been pushed north out of Virginia or out of southern Somerset County by the tide of English settlement. The Pocomokes and Assateagues were preoccupied with protecting their reservation, which was their last refuge in Maryland, from further encroachment, and they took no part in events farther afield. They, like the Choptanks, were only involved in the fur trade on a local scale; they were not viewed as a military threat by the Maryland government.

The Nanticokes, however, were still moderately important players in Maryland's interminable struggle with the Five Nations of the Iroquois, and because of their geographical location they were also a significant factor in Maryland's ongoing boundary dispute with the Delaware colony. The Dutch were now gone from Delaware Bay. But they had been replaced there by Englishmen whom Maryland's Lord Proprietor did not like any better. Delaware was legally part of the New York colony, and New York refused to recognize Maryland's territorial claims to a large part of what is now Sussex County, Delaware. This disputed area included the northern part of the Nanticoke tribal lands. Ultimately the Maryland-Delaware boundary problem was solved by the surveying of the Mason-Dixon Line, but that was not to happen for another seventy-five years. Since the Nanticokes still had the power to influence events in this critical border area, keeping the Nanticoke "emperors" on Maryland's side in any dispute with Indians or other Englishmen became a goal of the proprietary government. In particular, Maryland feared what might happen if a pro-Iroquois paramount chief took power within the Nanticoke tribe. For that reason, each new Nanticoke "emperor" was expected to reaffirm the 1678 treaty with Maryland. No other Eastern Shore Indian group was required to do this when a new leader took office.

The Nanticokes were governed by hereditary paramount chiefs who were called in the Nanticoke language *talleck*, but whom the English referred to as "emperors." The first leader mentioned by the Maryland authorities is Unnarocassimmon; he was already talleck in 1669, when the first Maryland-Nanticoke treaty was signed. He was probably the same person as Cockasimmon, "king of the Nanticokes," who was mentioned in a Virginia court document dating to 1655. Unnarocassimmon appears to have died in 1686, for he was succeeded first by his brother Ohoperoon and then in 1693 by his (Unnarocassimmon's) son Ashquash. Ashquash's accession as talleck (recorded as "emperor" by the English) sparked a major crisis in Nanticoke-English relations, for he refused to renew the peace treaty that his father and uncle had signed when they reigned as Nanticoke chiefs.[76] The reasons for the refusal are unknown, but the Nanticokes certainly had a long list of grievances against the English by this time. Ashquash obviously had considerable popular support within the tribe, which indicates that discontent with the Maryland authorities was not confined to the ruling lineage alone.

Since Ashquash declined to sign the treaty, the governor and council of Maryland refused to recognize him as talleck of the Nanticokes. For a time the Marylanders considered giving two of the chiefs of the reliably friendly Choptank Indians authority over the Nanticokes in Ashquash's place.[77] However, the Choptank chiefs undoubtedly understood that their rule would be unacceptable to the Nanticoke tribe, which must have felt that the paramount chief of the Nanticokes had to be a Nanticoke person, preferably someone from the tribe's ruling lineage. In the end, the Choptank chiefs Nectanoughtough and Tequassino refused to be made rulers of the Nanticokes, stating that Ashquash was the only proper person for the job.[78]

After that, the Maryland authorities abandoned the idea of making a new talleck. Instead they selected two Nanticokes who were not of the Unnarocassimmon-Ohoperoon-Ashquash lineage to rule jointly. Panquash, the principal "great man," was appointed to be "commander in chief" of the Nanticokes, and Annatoughquan (or Annatocqin) was chosen as his lieutenant. Nothing more is known of these two individuals before their selection as leaders of the tribe, and neither man was ever given the title of talleck. We can presume that Panquash and Annatoughquan were chosen by the English because they were judged to be more pro-English than Ashquash. Certainly they did not delay in signing the same treaty with Maryland that Ashquash had been offered earlier.[79]

There is good evidence that the Nanticokes were not happy with this English intervention in their internal politics. In 1697 they attempted to appoint a talleck again, but the Maryland authorities intervened to prevent it.[80] The name of the proposed new "emperor" is not recorded. However, since Maryland's governor in 1698 instructed the Nanticoke leaders to "take no notice of the felton [felon?] who calls himself emperor of the Nanticoke," it is more than likely that the chief proposed by the tribe in 1697 was Ashquash again.[81] Ashquash had been declared an enemy of the Crown in 1693, so from the English point of view he could properly be labeled a felon.[82] Nanticoke discontent with the arbitrary interference of the Maryland government remained strong. Finally in 1705, after making peace with the English, Ashquash became the acknowledged "emperor" of the Nanticokes, and Panquash and Annatoughquan lost their authority over the tribe.

The Maryland government probably felt that it could intervene directly in the selection of the Nanticoke paramount chief because by 1693 the Nanticokes were weaker militarily and less important politically than they had been only a decade earlier. The intermittent war that Maryland had been conducting with the Five Nations had quieted down. Even though sporadic violence along the colony's northern border would continue into the eighteenth century, technically Maryland was at peace with all its northern neighbors, both Indian and English. The English population of the Eastern Shore was also much larger. In 1701 over 1,600 taxable persons lived in Somerset County alone, as compared with only 386 in 1671.[83] This meant that a military force that was more than adequate to deal with the Nanticokes could be raised quickly and easily if serious trouble ever broke out. Finally, by the 1690s the Chesapeake fur trade was no longer of any great economic importance and had become a local rather than a colonywide concern. All of these factors made the maintenance of friendly relations with the Nanticokes less important to Maryland's provincial government.

After 1693 Maryland abandoned the polite fiction that the Nanticokes were their own masters. From this point onward, the colony's only real anxiety about them concerned their relationship with the Five Nations. The fear remained that the Nanticokes, who were no longer regarded as a military power themselves, if sufficiently provoked might still threaten the safety of the province by allowing the Iroquois access to the Eastern Shore. Consequently, the Maryland government's interest in the tribe waxed and waned as the perceived Iroquois threat grew or diminished.

Maryland's troubles with the Iroquois also had an impact on the other major Eastern Shore Indian groups in the 1680s. The Choptanks felt so threatened by the Five Nations that many of them abandoned their reservation in 1683 and sought refuge with the Pocomokes and Assateagues at Askiminikansen. This was not intended to be a permanent move, since the Choptank chief Ababco was careful to get a guarantee from the provincial government that the tribe's rights to its reservation would be protected during their absence.[84] Choptank fears about the Iroquois were certainly justified, because in 1685 the Oneidas took fifty of Ababco's subjects prisoner and transported them out of the region.[85]

The movement of some Choptanks to Askiminikansen probably helps to explain why the Maryland government ordered a boundary survey for that Indian town in 1686. Ababco was the Indian leader most trusted by the Maryland English, and his relocation to Askiminikansen may well have focused the colony's attention on the encroachment problem there. It is clear that at least two of the three main Choptank bands were living at Askiminikansen in 1686. Listed among the various tribal groups in residence under the Assateague "emperor" are the "Transquakings" and the "Hatsawaps." Both of these names appear elsewhere as Choptank band or tribe names.[86] It is not clear when Ababco's people moved back to the Choptank reservation, but it must have been before 1694. By 1693 Ababco was dead and his son Nectanoughtough had taken his place as chief of what came to be called the Ababco Choptanks.[87]

It is interesting to note that Ababco did not move into Nanticoke territory when seeking protection from the Iroquois, even though the principal Nanticoke town of Chicone was much closer to the Choptank reservation than the Pocomoke-Assateague reservation at Askiminikansen. The Choptanks probably were worried that the Nanticokes were too friendly with the Delaware Indians, whom they in turn suspected of being in alliance with the Iroquois who were raiding Choptank lands.[88] Even the Choptank chief Tequassino, who in contrast to Ababco generally seems to have been friendly toward the Nanticokes, implied in 1681 that the Nanticokes might be contemplating war as allies of the Iroquois. This tension between the Choptanks and Nanticokes never entirely faded, although it did not stop frequent interaction between the peoples of the two neighboring reservations. Some Choptank Indians, perhaps those who did not go to Askiminikansen with Ababco, were living with the Nanticokes as late as 1693 and had to be ordered by the Maryland government to "withdraw to their several and respective towns" in that year.[89]

The late 1670s and early 1680s form a poorly documented period for the Assateagues and Pocomokes. Both tribes probably continued to absorb refugee Indian groups over these years, since the two surviving seventeenth-century lists of tribes or bands resident at the Askiminikansen reservation, dating to 1678 and 1686, are significantly different from each other. In addition to the Choptank bands that appear in the 1686 list but not the 1678 list, several other tribal names mentioned in the later list are otherwise unknown.[90]

It is likely that the introduction of these other Indian groups caused considerable friction, not only with the Pocomokes and Assateagues who were already resident there but also with the English inhabitants of the surrounding region. Early in 1686 James Rounds, an important Somerset planter with lands near Askiminikansen, apparently requested that the provincial government take some action to quiet the Indians. As a result of this request, the Maryland council ordered William Stevens, a Somerset County resident who was a member of the council, to present thirty matchcoats to "several Indian Kings on the Eastern Shore," who were probably the chiefs of those tribes assembled at Askiminikansen.[91] In the same year both the Pocomokes and the Assateagues made several complaints about their English neighbors. The most serious incident was the robbery of an Indian "quiankason" (*quiocosin*), or temple–mortuary house, by a prominent local planter named Edmund Hammond.[92] The lower Eastern Shore tribes all seem to have buried their kings aboveground in their temples along with offerings of roanoke and other precious goods. The Indians complained that Hammond "upon the like occasion of one of their kings dyeing" had stolen "skinns and roanoke from the place where he was layd."[93] In addition to the Hammond theft, there were also the now familiar complaints about encroachment and interference with Indian hunting rights.

The Indians of Askiminikansen were not completely happy with the response of the Maryland government to their complaints, and in particular they protested about the poor quality of much of the land laid out for their use as a result of the reservation boundary survey of 1686.[94] However, the decade after 1686 was relatively quiet as far as the Pocomokes and Assateagues were concerned. The only evidence of friction with their English neighbors was a 1689 complaint that the Indians sometimes killed colonists' livestock.[95] The boundary survey apparently did stop encroachment for a time, and by the early 1690s the Choptanks had returned to their own lands on the Choptank River. The other nonlocal Indians resident at Askiminikansen either left the reservation or assimilated with the Pocomokes and Assateagues. The Askiminikansen reservation was a large one, approximately ten thousand acres, and Indian protests notwithstanding, the land was quite productive. There were good corn lands in the southern part, and the swamps of the Pocomoke River and Nassawango Creek provided good hunting, fowling, and fishing areas. For about a decade after 1686, the Assateagues and

Pocomokes benefited from more stable conditions than they had ever had before at that site, or would ever have again during their period of residence there.

The Reservation Period

By 1698 what can be called the reservation period of Maryland Eastern Shore Indian history had begun. All of the major tribes now had a clearly dependent status with respect to Maryland's provincial government and were settled on government-created reservations with well-defined boundaries. The Eastern Shore Indians were by no means strictly confined to the reservations, however. They had previously been able to move through and exploit a huge stretch of territory on the Eastern Shore that extended into both Virginia and Delaware. They gradually lost this option as English settlement essentially privatized the resources of larger and larger blocks of land, but near some tribal tracts, large foraging areas remained. The reservations on the Choptank River, at Chicone, and at Askiminikansen increasingly became the foci of the Indians' political, social, and economic lives.

The decline in the fur trade was also a factor in limiting the Eastern Shore Indians' economic choices. By the late 1690s the Chesapeake Bay fur trade had dwindled to a point where it was no longer worth fighting over by the major regional powers, although a handful of Eastern Shore merchants still did very well exporting locally obtained furs. In 1695, 80 percent of all the furs being shipped from Maryland ports originated on the Eastern Shore, and most of these came from the two lower counties, Somerset and Dorchester, which contained the Choptank, Nanticoke, and Pocomoke-Assateague reservations.[96] The Eastern Shore Indians produced very little beaver anymore, but there was a good market for mink and raccoon skins, which for a time the Indians were able to harvest in large numbers. The days when the Chesapeake fur trade was a major factor in the economic and political life of the Maryland colony were gone, however, and within a generation the remaining trade was to decline and then disappear as well.

The Indian wars that had once so preoccupied Maryland's provincial government also had receded into the background, although the Iroquois of the Five Nations were still feared by Maryland authorities. The Wicomiss, the Susquehannocks, and the Delawares were, however, no longer even potential threats to the colony. These groups had been destroyed, had joined with the Iroquois, or had left the region for other destinations. The remaining Eastern Shore tribes were too small to represent a credible military threat anymore. The Nanticokes remained somewhat suspect in the proprietary government's eyes, but only because their territory was viewed as a likely invasion route for the Iroquois. The Maryland government's preoccupation with the Iroquois threat to the Eastern Shore continued well into the eighteenth century. In the minds of Maryland officials this danger was real enough to influence policy right up until the Seven Years' War and even beyond.

The Nanticokes and their Indian neighbors suffered many reverses during the seventeenth century, but most of the tribes in the region escaped the almost total devastation that was so often the fate of both the Maryland and Virginia coastal plain tribes on the western shore. The Maryland Eastern Shore Indians were saved from the worst effects of European contact by the long delay in the actual settlement of the region by English colonists. The Calvert family's deliberate policy of restricting the availability of Eastern Shore lands meant that Indian people who lived between the Choptank and Pocomoke Rivers did not have to confront the problem of English settlement until after about 1660, a circumstance that especially benefited the Choptanks and the Nanticokes. The tribes of the upper Eastern Shore were destroyed or lost their lands during the mid-seventeenth century, but these Indian groups were as much the victims of the Susquehannock-Iroquois rivalry as they were of the English. Maryland's fur-trade-driven Indian policy certainly contributed to the destruction of the upper Eastern Shore tribes, but actual English settlement in the region was not a serious factor in this process.

The Indians who lived south of the Choptank River on the Maryland Eastern Shore were in more or less continuous contact with the English from 1620 onward. This meant that unlike other Chesapeake Bay Indian groups, they had forty years in which to adapt themselves to the English presence before becoming direct competitors with the English for the land itself. During these four decades the lower Eastern Shore tribes successfully modified their traditional economy to take advantage of the availability of European goods and to accommodate themselves to the demands of the fur trade, while maintaining a traditional way of life in virtually all other respects. The Eastern Shore Indians' response to the seventeenth-century English intrusion into the Chesapeake world was a flexible and opportunistic one. Indian groups formed mutually profitable economic alliances with individual English traders and gradually learned how to take maximum advantage of the economic and political leverage that the fur trade gave them. In the latter part of the century, however, the tribes confronted an increasingly threatening outside world that left fewer and fewer behavioral options open. By the end of the seventeenth century, the reservations held out to them their only chance for survival as separate peoples on the Eastern Shore.

Four

The Maryland Reservations
after 1700

THE EIGHTEENTH CENTURY saw the continued growth of the
English population of Maryland's lower Eastern Shore and also
brought some quite fundamental changes in the region's agricultural
economy. In the seventeenth century Somerset and Dorchester Counties
had been settled by planters who produced tobacco as their principal
cash crop and raised livestock and grew corn mainly for their own use.
However, tobacco never proved to be as profitable for lower Eastern
Shore planters as it was for planters on the western shore, and by the
eighteenth century many farmers began producing cereal grains as a
cash crop instead.[1] In Maryland this was particularly true in the northern part of Somerset County, which had the fastest-growing population
in the region in the early eighteenth century.

These economic and demographic changes directly affected the Maryland Eastern Shore Indian tribes, since they brought even larger numbers of English settlers for the first time into the near vicinity of the
Askiminikansen, Chicone, and Choptank reservations. That vicinity
was the land from which the native people drew many necessary resources through hunting and gathering, and now it gradually filled up
with English farms. The change from tobacco to grain as the area's principal cash crop was detrimental to the Eastern Shore Indians' traditional way of life in another way. Successful grain farming demanded
that much more of a planter's total landholdings be under cultivation at
any one time than was the case with tobacco, so the large blocks of
fallow land characteristic of seventeenth-century tobacco plantations
gradually disappeared from the landscape. That reduced the amount of
land available to deer and other game animals and the people who had

hunted them. Thus over time, the native people were cut off from re-sources that lay beyond their reservation boundaries, and they had to make do with what the reservation lands themselves could produce. As the surrounding English population increased, however, the problem of settler encroachment on these now vitally important reservation lands also grew. Ultimately, economic and demographic forces combined to make the Indians' way of life in the Indian towns untenable. The Mary-land tribes responded by giving up their reservations and either becom-ing detribalized or moving north to join with other Indian groups in Pennsylvania. The Gingaskins, on the other hand, were hemmed in at close quarters and had nowhere to go, but they did retain easy access to their old foraging territory in the marshes and barrier islands that bor-dered the Atlantic. Thus in spite of having a tiny reservation, they held on longer than anyone else. Their eighteenth-century history is different enough, and extends later enough, that it is examined in the chapter after this one.

The Reservations and Their Populations

As the eighteenth century began, the four major tribes of the Mary-land Eastern Shore still inhabited the three principal reservations that had been carved out their traditional homelands in the seventeenth cen-tury: the Choptanks had their lands on the Choptank River, the Nan-ticokes had theirs on their own river, and the Pocomokes and Assa-teagues lived on the Askiminikansen reservation on the Pocomoke River (fig. 4.1). These four groups also still functioned as semiautonomous social and political units whose separate status within the Maryland colony was recognized by law. All four tribes apparently lived outside of English colonial society as a matter of choice, maintaining their own languages, religious beliefs, and patterns of social organization. Inter-action with the English majority during the early eighteenth century was basically limited to the economic sphere, just as it had been throughout the seventeenth century. At this time the reservations were still suffi-ciently large and productive to support the tribes. The native people re-lied heavily on English-manufactured goods, especially cloth and metal tools, but they seem to have managed to generate enough of a surplus through their traditional economy to trade for the goods they needed. Indian men sold part of what they produced through hunting and trap-ping; men and women occasionally worked for English colonists as

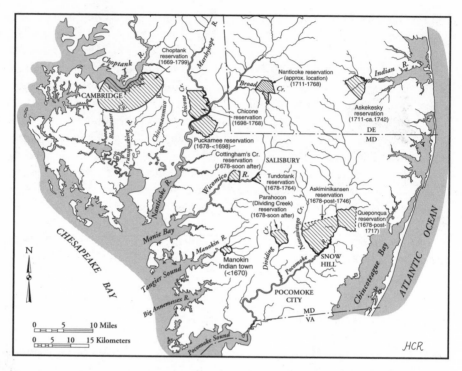

Fig. 4.1 The Maryland Eastern Shore reservations in the eighteenth century

hunters or farm laborers; and people produced some handicraft items for sale, principally "Indian bowls." Together, these activities brought in enough English manufactured goods to meet basic needs.

By the beginning of the eighteenth century, the four tribes had had several decades of experience trading with the English, but even so, trade still usually took the form of barter. The Choptanks, Nanticokes, and Pocomokes and Assateagues do not appear to have used either money or tobacco at this time as mediums of exchange. Roanoke and peak retained their earlier importance as standards of value within the exchange system. This conservatism in trading practices typifies the Maryland Eastern Shore tribes' reaction to contact with Anglo-American society. The native people were willing to trade for certain categories of English-manufactured goods, mainly guns, woven cloth, and iron tools, because these items were technologically superior to the deerskins and stone tools that were their functional equivalents in pre-Contact Indian times. However, the people showed no discernible enthusiasm for adopting other elements of English culture or abandoning traditional Indian standards of value or patterns of behavior. The Indians traded with the English for compelling practical reasons, but they modified their own way of life only just enough to accommodate the new economic reality that the English presence created.

It is difficult to determine just how many Indians there were on the three major reservations at the beginning of the eighteenth century. For one thing, the tribesmen tended to be highly mobile. Not only did they continue to follow their age-old annual cycle of farming and foraging, but also individuals and groups of Indians ranged quite widely through nonreservation lands, sometimes even traveling to the western shore or temporarily leaving the boundaries of the Maryland colony entirely.[2] Another problem is that the Indians living in these legally recognized Indian towns were not required to pay poll taxes, tithes, or quitrents to the county or provincial governments, and they did not vote in elections. Consequently the county governments of the Eastern Shore had no reason to keep records on the individual members of the tribes. The native people are only mentioned in the county or provincial records when they committed a crime or were the victims of one, or when they sold or leased land. For the most part, these few and scattered references to Indians do not provide enough information to support reliable population estimates.

Before the eighteenth century there is no evidence of any significant migration out of the Eastern Shore region by the Choptanks, Nanticokes, or Pocomokes and Assateagues. The populations of the major reservations actually may have been larger in 1700 than they had been in the 1660s when English settlement began in earnest in the region. As the smaller Indian towns were abandoned in the late seventeenth century, the population of the remaining larger Indian towns (i.e., reservations) probably grew.

At the beginning of the eighteenth century, the Choptanks still occupied a single large and unified reservation on the Choptank River above the English town of Cambridge. There had been a significant amount of encroachment on the western third of the reservation in the 1690s, but most of the 16,000-acre tract was still in Indian hands. In contrast to Askiminikansen, there does not appear to have been any significant movement of outlying Indian groups to the Choptank reservation until after 1720. The inhabitants in the early eighteenth century probably consisted only of the members of the three original Choptank bands that were recognized by treaty in 1669: the Ababco, the Hatsawap, and the Tequassino, called by the English after the tribes' rulers named in the treaty. At the beginning of the century, each band still had a separate ruler or rulers, and each band probably lived at a different location on the reservation.

A population estimate is easier to make for the Choptanks than for the other three tribes. Deeds for Choptank land recorded during the first quarter of the eighteenth century sometimes included the names of ordinary Indians, and not just the names of the "kings," "queens," and great men who usually signed such deeds. In particular, three deeds recorded in 1722 contain the names of many Choptanks who had no positions of authority and apparently were just members of the tribe.[3] There are a total of fifty-six different signatures on these three deeds, including those of the "queens" of the Ababco and Hatsawap Indians, two of the three Choptank bands. One of the deeds even states that the purchase was being made with the "full, free and unanimous consent of all the Indians" who were under the authority of the two Indian chiefs. At least thirty-nine of the fifty-six individuals signing the deeds were men, and if we assume that the ratio of adult males to total population is roughly three to ten, then the minimum Choptank population would have been about 130 persons. The total Choptank population might have been larger than this, since we do not know whether all adult male Choptanks signed the deeds. It is certainly unlikely that the 130-person figure is too large, and it may well represent a significant underestimate of the true total.

The Nanticokes formed the largest tribal group on the entire Eastern Shore at the beginning of the eighteenth century. However, determining Nanticoke numbers is made particularly difficult by the fact that even though some of the towns the Nanticokes had occupied in the seventeenth century probably had been lost already, the people were still living at several different locations in both Maryland and southern Delaware. In 1697 the Maryland authorities acknowledged that the tribe inhabited ten different towns. Some of these towns had "fewer than twenty families," but even so, the Nanticokes must have had a total population of several hundred.[4] A late eighteenth-century writer who lived in Dorchester County estimated the tribe's population early in the century at 500.[5] Additional evidence to support a total of several hundred at that time is given by a southern Delaware clergyman who wrote in 1722 that his parish contained less than 120 Indians, all of whom lived in a single town on the Maryland border.[6] The Indian town referred to was probably Broad Creek, and if a hundred or more Nanticokes were living there at that time, then the total Nanticoke population for the Maryland and Delaware towns together cannot have been much smaller than the 500-person figure.

There is no evidence at all for the size of the Pocomoke or Assateague populations living at Askiminikansen in the early eighteenth century. The Pocomokes by then were probably an amalgam of several Pocomoke River drainage tribes. The Assateagues resident at Askiminikansen had their own independent chief and probably lived separately from the Pocomokes. The historical records contain references to an upper Indian town distinct from the Indian town located in the Snow Hill vicinity on the southern part of the reservation.[7] It is probable that the upper town, which was near the smaller Assateague-dominated reservation of Queponqua, was the Assateague town and that the lower town was occupied by Pocomokes. However, the Pocomoke "king" usually took the lead in dealing with the English, and it is likely that the Pocomokes were numerically the stronger group living on the reservation. Even so, it is doubtful that the Pocomokes were as numerous as the Choptanks, and they certainly were a smaller tribe than the Nanticokes.

In addition to these major tribes, who had managed to hold onto some of their original lands and had preserved a considerable degree of political autonomy since initial contact with Europeans, a significant number of other Indians were still living on the Eastern Shore in the early eighteenth century. Some of these people were members of the major tribes who had chosen to live off the reservations and had found places for themselves in English society. Others were the remnants of displaced tribes who had been forced off their traditional lands as a result of English expansion. Among these were the poorly known tribes of the seaboard side. During the seventeenth century these tribes had moved up the Atlantic coast of what is now Worcester County, being driven from one location after another by the steady northward expansion of English settlement, until sometime before 1705 they established a new Indian town called Askekesky on the Indian River. That site is now in Delaware, but it was then considered, at least by the Maryland authorities, as Maryland territory. In 1705 Robin, leader of the Askekeskys, petitioned the Maryland government to grant his people a thousand acres of land at the head of Indian River. Robin stated that the tribe had already been expelled from Buckingham and Assawoman, two locations in northern Worcester County, and that it had been forced to retreat from a previous settlement at the mouth of Indian River up to its head. He also reported that the Indians had "already what rights the Proprietary and Governor of Pennsylvania can give," indicating that he understood that the Indian River region was disputed territory between the colonies of Pennsylvania and Maryland.[8]

In 1711 these Indians, "called by themselves the Askocksy Indians," received a Maryland patent for one thousand acres on the south side of Indian River.[9] The tribe was then led by "Weacomoconus their Queen" and Robin "the Interpreter and Ambassador." For the next thirty years the Indian River Town, also called Askekesky or Ashquesonne Town, was treated by the Maryland authorities as another of the officially recognized Eastern Shore Indian reservations. The Indian River Indians always seemed to be led by a member of the Robin dynasty, which consisted of Robin the Interpreter, "Young Robin," and "Robin the Indian son of Young Robin, grandson and second heir to King Robin the Interpreter."[10] There is, however, a 1742 reference to an unnamed "Queen" of the Indian River Indians as well.[11]

The legally recognized Indian towns on the Maryland Eastern Shore were partially successful in protecting their traditional way of life into the eighteenth century. The major towns or reservations were large and productive enough to support sizable resident populations. However, these particular reservations were vitally important to the survival of Indian cultures for reasons other than economics. Large towns like the Askiminikansen, Chicone, and Choptank reservations served as buffers or filters that softened the impact of English culture on the Indian way of life. Indians resident in these towns did not have to interact on a frequent basis with the English colonists, and therefore they could continue their age-old ways and beliefs, even if these ran counter to English cultural norms.

During the colonial period in eastern North America, close contact between Englishmen and Indian people almost invariably meant conflict, retreat, or assimilation for the native people. The English colonists believed that Indians were savages who were culturally inferior, not just to themselves but to all Christian Europeans. Indian ways that did not conform to Christian European standards were automatically judged to be wrong, and Indians who either could not or would not adopt at least a veneer of European behavior were at a great disadvantage if they had to interact on a regular basis with the English. Indian cultures seem to have survived best when contact with the English was infrequent, limited in scope, and formally structured, as it was on the Maryland Eastern Shore in the seventeenth century. The reservation system allowed the successful but increasingly fragile modus vivendi that had developed between Indians and Englishmen on the Eastern Shore to continue for a few more decades into the eighteenth century. Soon, though, the decline in the importance of the fur trade and the colonists' desire for the last remaining Indian lands would result in the destruction of the reservations, the withdrawal of most remaining Indians from the region, and cultural submergence for the rest.

Apart from size, another important advantage that the three major Eastern Shore reservations had was that they were not cut off from one another by areas of heavy English settlement. The Choptank, Nanticoke, and Pocomoke Rivers all rise in the poorly drained mid-peninsular area of the Delmarva, which was the last part of the Eastern Shore to be settled by Europeans. This meant that the lands upstream from the three reservations remained relatively open to Indian people well into the eighteenth century. When the Maryland provincial government created the Broad Creek reservation on the upper Nanticoke River in the 1711, they were not giving the Nanticokes any lands the tribe did not already occupy. The Broad Creek reservation was created near the site of an existing Nanticoke town that had been in that approximate location for at least the previous century.[12]

The availability of this extensive hinterland upstream from the Askiminikansen, Chicone, and Choptank reservations had important social as well as economic consequences for the Indians of the Maryland Eastern Shore. In practical terms the three major reservations shared common boundaries, and travel and communication between the reservations could take place without the need to pass through territories controlled by the English. Such travel between reservations is well documented during the late seventeenth and early eighteenth centuries, and contacts between the populations of the three reservations became, if anything, even more frequent as the eighteenth century progressed.[13] The ability of the native people to interact with relative freedom among themselves undoubtedly helped to preserve Indian culture on the reservations. Members of the four tribes might come together for religious ceremonies, political decision making, or cooperative economic endeavors. Contacts with other groups who shared similar customs and values undoubtedly helped prevent the loss of cultural identity by the tribes.

In the early eighteenth century the size of the reservations allowed most Maryland Eastern Shore Indians to live lives that were surprisingly like those of their ancestors. Only a small minority of tribesmen could speak or understand English, and certainly people spoke only their native languages to each other. Retention of the aboriginal languages shows up in the people's personal names, as well (see Appendix B). Even as late as 1792, a visitor to the Choptank reservation commented that the Indians "speak their language exclusively among themselves."[14] Communication between the tribes and the English was in the hands of a small number of interpreters, who presumably had acquired a knowledge of the other group's language to facilitate trade. The county governments of Somerset and Dorchester continued to appoint official Indian interpreters and to pay them out of the county poll tax until the 1720s.[15] Maryland's provincial government also appointed official Indian interpreters for the Eastern Shore; it was members of fur-trading families like the Nutters and Covingtons who most often held these posts.[16]

On the Indian side, the status of the interpreters is not so clear-cut. Indian chiefs and paramount chiefs did not normally speak to the English authorities except through interpreters, and there is no evidence that these hereditary tribal leaders felt any more obliged to learn English than did the majority of their subjects. Indian leaders normally were accompanied by tribal councilors or great men when they met with English officials, and on the Eastern Shore interpreters seem to have belonged to this class. Among the Choptanks these great men often had English as well as Indian personal names, a trait that links them to the other Indian interpreters who are identified as such in the late seventeenth- and eighteenth-century English records.[17] The question remains open whether some great men earned that designation because they were interpreters, or whether some individuals who were already great men became interpreters because of their greater need and opportunity to interact with the English.

In the case of the Indian River Indians, it seems clear that status as an interpreter could bring with it political authority. Robin, the first recorded leader of these Indians, was not usually called the "king" of Askekesky, even though he took the lead in all of their dealings with the English, as did his son and grandson of the same name. The English typically referred to Robin simply as Robin the Interpreter. For a group like the Askekeskys, who wandered for years without lands of their own, the ability to negotiate with the English must have become a vitally important survival skill. Robin may have emerged as a tribal leader precisely because he was the one person in the tribe who could deal most effectively with the English.

The English religion, like the English language, spread only very slowly through the Maryland Eastern Shore tribes. Most of the native people do not appear to have accepted the Christian religion even by the latter part of the eighteenth century. This slowness is due in large measure to the fact that the Anglican clergy in the region was not particularly active in proselytizing Indians. When the Maryland clergy was questioned by the bishop of London in 1724 about the spiritual welfare of the "Infidels" in the colony, none of the Maryland rectors showed much enthusiasm for missionary work among the Indians. The Reverend Alexander Adams of Somerset County, whose parish included Askiminikansen Town, briefly remarked, "No means used to convert the Indians; their language unknown to us."[18] The rectors of the two Dorchester County parishes that contained the Choptank and Nanticoke reservations both noted that they had Indians in their parishes who lived "under the free Government of their own petty princes," but both admitted that they had made no effort to convert them.[19] At about the same time the Reverend William Becket of Delaware, whose parish included some of the Nanticoke-occupied lands in western Sussex County, described the Eastern Shore Indians as "extremely barbarous and obstinately ignorant of the Christian religion." Becket also added the observation that the Indians had "an idolatrous catica of their own."[20] Presumably this comment refers to the survival of pre-Contact religious practices among the Indians.

Indian personal names are essentially absent from the surviving Maryland Eastern Shore parish registers,[21] although some native births, deaths, and marriages probably are recorded under English names. Indian people who lived off the reservations were obliged to pay tithes to the established church, and the off-reservation people who found places for themselves in English colonial society undoubtedly had to become at least nominal Christians. This process can be seen to have been under way as early as the 1680s, when a Somerset County Indian named John Puckham converted to Christianity and married his wife in an Anglican ceremony.[22] Indians like Puckham who converted and lived among the English invariably seemed to adopt both given names and surnames in English, a fact that makes them extremely difficult to identify as Indians in parish records.

The persistence of traditional religious beliefs among the Maryland

Eastern Shore Indians is best exemplified by their burial practices. The custom of preserving the bodies of their chiefs aboveground in mortuary temples, or *quiocosin* houses, survived well into the eighteenth century. William Vans Murray, who visited the Choptank town of Locust Neck after the American Revolution, noted that the body of the Choptank king Winacaco, who died ca. 1710, was still being preserved in a "Quacasun" house seventy years later.[23] There are also accounts of the Nanticokes who left the Eastern Shore in the mid-eighteenth century carrying the bones of their ancestors, and even their recent dead, with them. The Reverend John Heckewelder observed this phenomenon in the 1750s when a party of Nanticokes, "loaded with such bones, which, being fresh, caused a disagreeable stench," passed through the town of Bethlehem, Pennsylvania.[24]

The specific form of political authority that was exhibited by all four of the major Maryland Eastern Shore tribes in the early eighteenth century is another trait that appears to have survived from pre-Contact times. Before the coming of the English, the Algonquian-speaking Indian groups of the Maryland coastal plain typically lived in ranked societies that were headed by hereditary chiefs. Immediately below the chief was a relatively small upper class consisting of the chief's councillors, war leaders, and priests, and below them were the ordinary members of the tribe. This three-tier system remained in place among the Maryland tribes throughout the first part of the eighteenth century.

Beginning in the late seventeenth century, English interference in the succession of the Nanticoke "emperors" was the rule rather than the exception, but it is clear that whatever the English may have wanted, the Nanticokes themselves preferred the rule of their traditional hereditary monarchs. After the paramount chief Ohoperoon died, the tribe continued to push for the selection of Ashquash, his nephew and the son of the "emperor" Unnarocassimmon, as the next "emperor," even though the English distrusted him and wished to appoint someone else. It was not until the English passed over William Ashquash, the son of the paramount chief Ashquash, and appointed Panquash and Annatoughquan as corulers of the tribe in 1713 that the hereditary principle finally ceased to determine who was to be the Nanticoke "emperor."[25] Among the Choptanks the descendants of Ababco, Hatsawap and Tequassino continued to rule their separate bands until the consolidation of those bands at the Locust Neck village in the 1720s. The last generation of their descendants to rule the separate bands were all women who were apparently the daughters or granddaughters of the three earlier Choptank chiefs.[26]

The last recorded ruler of the Choptanks of Locust Neck, met by William Vans Murray in 1792, was also a woman.[27] The apparent willingness of the Choptank people to accept women as their monarchs underlines another enduring cultural difference between the English and the Indians: women had considerably more authority in traditional Choptank society than they did in eighteenth-century English society. This is apparent not just in the area of political power but also in the ownership of land. Choptank Indian "queens" are signatories to most of the property transfers made by the tribe. The English purchasers of Indian lands tended to treat the female chiefs as co-owners of tribal lands along with their husbands, who may or may not actually have had a hereditary claim to add to their wives' rights; thus the purchasers were careful to get the "queens'" signatures and consent to land sales.[28] This acknowledgment of the Choptank woman's right to have a say in decisions about land was not just confined to the chiefs. Several Choptank women who had no special status in the tribe also signed deeds as parties consenting to the transfer of lands.

We know less about the place of women in the other major Maryland Eastern Shore tribes during the eighteenth century. Henry Norwood's mid-seventeenth-century account of the Kegotanks just south of the Virginia border includes several references to Indian "queens," one of whom seems to have exercised independent political authority in her town.[29] However, the eighteenth-century records that mention the Pocomoke and Assateague Indians refer only to "emperors," "kings," and great men. This may simply be a consequence of the fact that it is the county court records that contain most of the surviving eighteenth-century references to the Assateagues and Pocomokes. Even among the Choptanks, men seem to have taken a more prominent role than women in dealings with the local English authorities. Choptank "queens" as well as "kings" typically had great men as their councillors when meeting with the English. The Indian River people had "queens" who exercised authority on some level in the eighteenth century; however, it was the men of the Robin dynasty who dealt directly with the English. This general pattern of male predominance in legal matters may simply have been an accommodation on the Indians' part to the prejudices of the English, who certainly saw law courts as the domain of men.

In the early eighteenth century, the Indians of the Maryland Eastern

Shore were more willing to accept English goods than English ideas, but even in the realm of material culture, change proceeded at a slow pace. The things that the reservation Indians needed and wanted from the English were principally cloth, metal tools, and guns, all items that had been staples of the Chesapeake Bay Indian trade since the early seventeenth century. These goods caused little disruption of traditional lifeways at the same time that they made the age-old subsistence activities of farming, hunting, and fishing more efficient. For example, by 1754 the Choptank Indians had adopted the use of oyster tongs from the English,[30] making it possible to harvest more oysters in deeper waters, rather than having to dive for them.

By the late seventeenth century, two items of European manufacture—the matchcoat and the gun—had become so important to the Eastern Shore Indians they became standards of value within Indian society. Indian men considered guns for hunting a necessity, so that the Maryland government's early attempts to keep guns out of their hands met with complete failure.[31] Although the Lord Proprietor kept in place an official policy that forbade the transfer of "any manner of Gunns . . . powder, Shot, Bullets or other Ammunition whatsoever" to the Maryland Indians, by 1676 this ban was ignored even by the proprietor's own officials.[32]

The matchcoat, a cloaklike garment by now made of European cloth, is not mentioned in the early seventeenth-century records as an important item in the Chesapeake Bay Indian trade. Most cloth vended to the Indians in the 1630s and 1640s was sold by the yard from long, uncut bolts. However, later in the century cloth usually was sold or traded to the Indians in the form of precut "matchcoats," although some late seventeenth-century references simply mention "trade" or "trading" cloth.

By the 1690s Eastern Shore Indian men in particular always seem to have owned a matchcoat and a gun, even if they possessed nothing else of European manufacture. When an English planter seized the property of Harry Will Tom, an Ababco Choptank man, in 1690 to pay a debt, the three items taken were his gun, his matchcoat, and his stock of traditional shell money called peak.[33] That same year the Dorchester County court charged another Choptank named Cutiwilson Jack with selling a gun thought to have been stolen.[34] By the reservation period, the Maryland government had recognized the importance of guns and matchcoats to the native people. In 1694 the colony passed a law forbidding traders to buy guns or matchcoats from the Indians for "Liquor," and guns and matchcoats were considered suitable presents to give to tribal leaders when they visited the governor in Annapolis.[35]

The most serious consequence of such dependence on English-manufactured goods was that Indian men and women now had to produce enough salable goods to pay for things that they needed but could not make themselves. Apparently they were still able to afford essential items at the beginning of the eighteenth century, but it became harder and harder for them to pay for such goods as the fur trade disappeared and English settlers further encroached upon the reservation lands.

The Eastern Shore Indians of Maryland never became cash-crop farmers, even though agriculture was even more important to them as a subsistence activity during the reservation period than it had been before. During the eighteenth century complaints about encroachment referred increasingly to the loss of corn-growing lands as being a direct threat to the Indians' ability to feed themselves. Indians also began to fence in their cornfields "in the English manner" early in the eighteenth century, a practice that is completely undocumented for the seventeenth century.[36] Yet there are no records of Indians selling agricultural produce. Beginning in the late seventeenth century, the Choptanks, Nanticokes, and Pocomokes all seem to have adopted animal husbandry from the English, raising both horses and pigs. However, there is only one recorded sale of Indian livestock to an English purchaser, so it is likely that they kept the horses and pigs for their own use.[37]

The making of handicraft items for sale to the English was one way that Indian people brought in extra income during the early reservation period. Beginning in 1695 and continuing until 1726, there are several references in the Somerset county probate inventories to "Indian bowls." These were probably ceramic bowls made by the Indians but used on English plantations or farms; the bowls were very likely the Eastern Shore equivalent of colonoware, a variety of pottery found at many colonial-era plantation sites on Virginia's western shore. The bowls were most numerous in inventories dating to the period 1695–1715, fading in popularity rapidly after that.[38] The fact that several English households owned a dozen or more of these bowls suggests that the Indians were making them in quantity for sale during the early reservation period.

The Indians continued to use traditional forms and materials when making items for their own use. One of the clearest examples of this conservatism in material culture can be seen in Indian housing. During the eighteenth century the populace of the major tribal groups continued to live in a type of house that the English called a "cabin." Robert Beverley noted in 1705 that the term was commonly used in Virginia for an Indian house, and it was also the term used to describe the Nanticoke dwellings at Chicone in the 1660s.[39] The English inhabitants of the Eastern Shore invariably lived in "houses" during the early eighteenth century, as did African slaves,[40] so *cabin* appears to have been a term entirely restricted to Indian dwellings. A cabin would therefore have been a traditional bark- or mat-covered Indian house of the type that was also called a "wigwam" by the English, *yihakan* (yee-hah-kahn) by the Powhatan Indians. An English traveler reported that the Indians of the lower town at Askiminikansen inhabited "wigwams" as late as the 1740s, and all but one of the Indian dwellings observed on the Choptank reservation in 1792 were "wigwams."[41]

In the absence of any full-scale archaeological excavation of a reservation Indian town on the Eastern Shore, we do not know precisely what an early eighteenth-century Indian cabin or wigwam looked like, but we do have one surviving inventory of the contents of a Pocomoke cabin. In 1706 the dwelling of Machicopah, a Pocomoke man, was burned by an English colonist; Machicopah's wife was injured in the fire. The tribe complained to the Somerset County court and sought compensation for the possessions that had been destroyed.[42] Machicopah's losses included several English goods: a gun, three brass kettles, a shirt, and one new "streak of white" blanket. Everything else in the cabin was probably of Indian manufacture: twenty-seven arm's lengths of roanoke, two Indian belts, four "Indian baskets," six round mats, twenty bowls, two chests, one raw doeskin, ten bushels of corn, and two bushels of "dry roasted ears or soft corn roasted or dryed."

This brief inventory is a very revealing document. From it we can see that Machicopah owned precisely the same categories of English goods that his ancestors had been seeking through trade with the English and Dutch for several generations. Otherwise his possessions, with the possible exception of the two chests, were the products of traditional Eastern Shore Indian culture. The roanoke and the Indian belts, which were presumably wampum belts, demonstrate the continuing importance of shell beads among the Pocomokes. The baskets, mats, and bowls were all common Indian-made utilitarian items. Some of Machicopah's twenty bowls were probably craft items that he or his wife had made for sale to the English. The couple's other economic activities included hunting, attested to by the raw doeskin, and growing corn. It is interesting to note that part of the corn had been dried or roasted on the ear, a traditional Indian method of processing corn.

Machicopah was not a chief, and he was probably not even a great man, since his name was not mentioned in any previous or subsequent encounter between the Pocomoke tribal leaders and the Somerset authorities. Instead he appears to have been an ordinary man whose cabin was probably one of those forming the lower town on the Askiminikansen reservation. Machicopah's family subsisted through a combination of farming and hunting, and they generated enough of an economic surplus, perhaps through the sale of hides and pelts and the making of "Indian bowls," to trade for the English-manufactured goods they needed. Most of the items used in everyday life, however, he or his wife probably made themselves using traditional materials and techniques.

Machicopah's inventory provides a window into the material world of one Indian family; a second inventory made in the same year gives us a somewhat different view. In 1706 three Englishmen who lived near the Chicone reservation in Dorchester County broke into the "Quiacason or Sepalchre House" of Ashquash, "King of the Nanticoke," and stole goods valued at £100. The Nanticokes complained to the Maryland provincial government about this crime and submitted an inventory of the items that had been taken.[43]

Since the "emperor" Ashquash was still alive in 1706, we can assume that the stolen items were either mortuary goods placed in the quiocosin house for his ancestors or, more likely, his own wealth being stored there. Among the Powhatan Indians of Virginia, temples, or quiocosin houses, were used as sacred and therefore off-limits repositories for the valuable property of living chiefs.[44] In either case, the Ashquash quiocosin house inventory is not strictly comparable with the Machicopah one, since it was not a residence and thus did not contain ordinary household items. Even so, both the Ashquash and Machicopah inventories reflect Indian views on the value and significance of material things at the beginning of the eighteenth century. The Ashquash quiocosin house contained goods appropriate to the high status of the Nanticoke paramount chief, just as Machicopah's house contained the kinds of goods that were in more general use by ordinary Indians. The Ashquash inventory makes it immediately apparent that a Nanticoke "emperor" owned European-manufactured goods of much greater value and variety than did an ordinary Pocomoke man.

The "emperor" Ashquash owned fourteen red and blue matchcoats and twelve new white shirts, in contrast to Machicopah's single blanket and shirt. Additionally Ashquash had twelve pairs of stockings, eight "striped snuff gowns," two petticoats, and twelve yards of printed calico. There were no guns or brass kettles in the inventory, probably because these were items in everyday use that would not be put aside into storage. The only Indian-made goods in the quiocosin house inventory consisted of wampum in several forms: over a hundred arm's lengths of "long wampum" and "short wampum" are mentioned, plus four wampum wristbands and six wampum collars. In comparison, Machicopah owned twenty-seven arm's lengths of roanoke and two belts that may have been made of either wampum or roanoke. Mussel-shell roanoke was a less valuable variety of beads than wampum, which were the harder clamshell beads that were usually called wampumpeak or just peak in the seventeenth century.[45] Clearly roanoke and wampum were still prized by the Eastern Shore Indians in the eighteenth century, and these beads continued to play a role in Indian society as a standard of value in trade, as an indicator of status, and probably as an essential category of mortuary goods.

A comparison of the Ashquash and Machicopah inventories indicates that even at this relatively late date, English and European trade goods were still concentrated in the hands of tribal rulers, and these rulers were considerably richer than their subjects. One other commodity mentioned in the Ashquash inventory hints at the basis for the difference in wealth: the quiocosin house contained 190 mink skins, whose collective worth probably equaled half the value of all the stolen European trade goods. The paramount chief Ashquash, like his seventeenth-century predecessors, was obviously still trading furs in considerable numbers and probably for that reason could afford to buy large amounts of European goods.

Except for the furs, virtually everything in the quiocosin house inventory is an item of apparel or personal adornment, whether European-made or Indian-made. However, even though Ashquash owned much more European-style clothing than did the typical English resident of the Eastern Shore, he probably still did not dress exactly like an Englishman. There are no representations or descriptions of early eighteenth-century Indian costumes anywhere on the Eastern Shore, but the kinds of clothing that Ashquash owned suggest how he may have dressed. The items of men's clothing listed in the inventory were matchcoats, shirts, and stockings—but there is no mention of other English-style clothing such as shoes, coats, or trousers. The "emperor" of the Nanticokes probably wore a matchcoat over a long linen or woolen shirt belted at the waist, with leggings or stockings below.[46] A similar style of clothing is recorded for various Algonquian groups living in Pennsylvania, New York, and New England during the eighteenth century.[47] Machicopah's inventory mentions only a blanket and a shirt, which suggests that he wore a simpler variant of the same outfit. A seventeenth-century engraving of Delaware Indians shows them wearing wampum wristbands and collars that were probably similar to the Nanticoke examples.[48]

Ashquash and Machicopah were from two different tribes and belonged to two different social levels within their respective tribal societies, yet from a material-culture perspective, the parallels between their lives are strong. The two men were part of communities where traditional building forms, such as the Indian cabin and the quiocosin house, were the norm. Both men were involved at some level in the fur or hide trade, although beaver pelts had ceased to be the main commodity in that trade. Ashquash and Machicopah accumulated wealth in the form of roanoke and wampum rather than in the English forms of money and tobacco. They owned and probably wore English-made clothes in preference to traditional Indian deerskin garments, but the kinds of English clothing they wore and the way they wore it would immediately have identified them as Indians rather than Englishmen.

Neither man was poor by the standards of the day, and Ashquash was in fact quite well-to-do, but the things that these two Indians owned were not the same things that Englishmen of similar wealth levels would have owned. It is particularly notable that the valuable goods Ashquash placed in the quiocosin house did not include any silver items. An English colonist who owned a dozen shirts would also have owned some silver plate. Silver functioned as both a status indicator and a form of stored wealth in colonial English society, but it does not appear to have had a similar role in eighteenth-century Nanticoke society. The Ashquash and Machicopah inventories bolster the view that reservation Indian society was essentially conservative. By the beginning of the eighteenth century, certain categories of English goods had replaced certain categories of functionally equivalent Indian goods, but English material culture showed no sign of overwhelming the Maryland Eastern Shore Indians.

Continuing Conflicts

We only know about the things that Ashquash and Machicopah owned in 1706 because those possessions were either stolen or destroyed by Englishmen. On one level these instances of theft and arson can be viewed as isolated criminal acts committed by individuals, but they were also symptomatic of the increasing tension between the reservation Indians and their Anglo-American neighbors in the early eighteenth century.

Two main factors were fueling conflict between the two sides on the Maryland Eastern Shore. The first was the decline of the fur trade; by the 1720s it had essentially ended, and the era of the Chesapeake Bay fur trader was over. The second factor was the shortage of vacant land for the continually growing English population of Maryland. English settlers had been drawn to the Eastern Shore in the 1660s by the promise of cheap and readily available unpatented land, but by 1700 there was little such land left in Somerset or Dorchester County except in the upper drainages of the Pocomoke, Nanticoke and Choptank Rivers and in coastal areas where unproductive salt marsh predominated. Eighteenth-century Eastern Shore planters and would-be planters could no longer expand their landholdings cheaply and easily. The Choptank, Nanticoke, Pocomoke, and Assateague Indians owned the best and most productive of the remaining unpatented land on the central Eastern Shore, yet as long as the native people continued to live on that land, English planters could not get their hands on it.

Land disputes were the most common kind of conflict that arose between the Eastern Shore Indians and the Maryland colonists in the eighteenth century. However, there were some other problems as well. In 1702 there were two housebreakings by Indians in Somerset County. Nat and Ned, both simply described as "Indians," stole goods from the house of John Rounds, an English colonist who lived near Askiminikansen. The same year Nat broke into the house of John Dryden; in this case his accomplice was a black slave named Ceasor.[49] Overall, though, very few Indians were charged with serious crimes against the English. Eastern Shore Indians had been accused of several crimes of violence against colonists in the seventeenth century, but not a single example of such a crime was recorded for the whole of the eighteenth century.[50]

There were also relatively few recorded instances of the theft of Indian goods by English colonists, although this category of crime was probably underreported. The most serious crime against property of the early years of the eighteenth century was the already mentioned incident at Ashquash's quiocosin house. Another important Nanticoke man, Panquash, had his cabin broken into in 1703.[51] The most common serious offense perpetrated by English colonists on the Indians was arson. The burning of Indian houses or fences typically arose out of land disputes, as did one of the two recorded assaults by Englishmen on Indian people during the early eighteenth century.[52]

Both violent and nonviolent crimes by Englishmen against Indians were probably more common than the official record indicates. Even the Maryland provincial authorities acknowledged that it was practically impossible to get local juries to convict English defendants in these cases, so there would have been little reason for Indians to report most such crimes to the county courts.[53] The three individuals who broke into Ashquash's quiocosin house, for instance, were identified; but there is no evidence that they were ever punished. Indians were sometimes compensated for their material losses, and that seems to be the main reason why any of these crimes were reported. Panquash got sixty doeskins to pay for the break-in at his cabin.

Apart from criminal matters and land disputes, the only other significant area of legal conflict between the English and the Indians of the Maryland Eastern Shore concerned the status and treatment of Indian servants. During the early eighteenth century, a small number of Indians became indentured servants in English households. Suits brought by servants against masters were extremely common in colonial Maryland, and it is difficult to say whether Indians received worse treatment than other servants. The 1728 complaint of a Pocomoke boy named Quinackin that he was being illegally held as a servant had the form of a typical servant-master dispute; he was freed by the Somerset court.[54] Another incident that occurred in Somerset County in 1722 suggests that Indian indentured servants, like free black indentured servants, risked being illegally sold as slaves to masters outside the province. However, the Somerset court took quick action to punish county resident Marcus Andrews when he sold his Indian boy outside of Maryland, so we can assume that this practice was not tolerated.[55]

The latter case illustrates the fact that in early eighteenth-century Maryland, Indians had a status in law and custom which was more closely equivalent to that of whites than blacks, though it was not by any means equal. The native people of Maryland differed from the Virginia reservation inhabitants in that they never had a treaty that said they were to be defended in their persons and property "as if they had been Englishmen." Yet by the same token, Maryland did not pass a "black code," as Virginia did in 1705, trying to eliminate most civil rights for all nonwhites. The statutory restrictions that constrained the lives of blacks, whether slave or free, did not apply to Indians in Maryland. In 1717 Indians lost the right to testify against whites in courts of law,[56] but in view of the limited access the Indians had to the Maryland court system anyway, this restriction probably meant little in practical terms. It was not until 1717 that Indians had the right to petition county courts for redress against anyone at all.[57] During the preceding two decades, Indian disputes were handled by special magistrates appointed to deal with Indian affairs, as set forth in a law of 1697.[58] Before that time, Indians with complaints against Englishmen had to petition the governor and council directly.

Indian plaintiffs were not treated with absolute fairness even when they did gain access to Eastern Shore courts, since both judges and juries often failed to punish English colonists who committed offenses against Indians. However, while the majority of Eastern Shore whites may have viewed Indians as their inferiors, they still did not place Indians in the same category as blacks. Indians faced considerable de facto discrimination in Eastern Shore courts, but Maryland's laws never provided a legal pretext for that discrimination, and there seems to have been a general attitude on the part of the justices that Indians should not be treated as badly as blacks routinely were. The Somerset County court, for example, did not show the same zeal to punish those who sold free black indentured servants outside of Maryland that they did to punish Marcus Andrews, even though the selling of a free black servant was just as illegal.[59] Unlike free blacks, eighteenth-century Indians who lived off the reservations had the same tax status as white persons and could marry whites.[60] In fact, there was no legal bar to stop Indians as individuals from completely assimilating into the white community, and during the late seventeenth and early eighteenth centuries, this certainly happened from time to time.

Conflicts inevitably escalated as more and more English people settled near or even on Indian lands. Legal protection of those lands became a necessity to Indian people. One would expect the Choptanks, as quitrent-paying landowners, to have been in a more secure position than the other Maryland Eastern Shore tribes in retaining their lands. Yet it was precisely because they did own their reservation outright that they nearly became the first of the tribes to be entirely dispossessed. Since the Choptanks could legally transfer land to the English, they came under intense pressure by the 1690s to sell some particularly desirable parts of their reservation. At that time the western end of the reservation extended into what had become a very heavily settled part of Dorchester County; the tribe's lands even included the site of the English town of Cambridge, which was emerging as the principal economic center of the county.

The Choptanks began complaining about encroachment shortly after they returned to their lands from Askiminikansen in the early 1690s,[61] and by late in that decade the problem became acute. In 1698 Nectanoughtough, chief Ababco's son and successor as leader of the Ababco segment of the Choptanks, asked the proprietary government to intervene to protect his tribe's lands.[62] The Ababcos lived on the western part of the Choptank reservation at this time, so their territory was most vulnerable to trespass by English people. Nectanoughtough's protest accomplished little or nothing.

The Ababcos apparently tried to deal with the encroachment problem by selling or leasing the western end of the reservation to English planters. In 1702 Winacaco, the successor to chief Nectanoughtough of the Ababcos, sold the "lowermost part" of the Choptank reservation to John Kirke. A few months previously Winacaco had leased two other, smaller parcels of land within the western half of the reservation to two other planters for twenty and thirty years, respectively. In each instance his tribe was paid in matchcoats.[63] The price of the parcels varied enormously. John Kirke paid only forty-two matchcoats for a parcel of at least 3,000 acres, while John Brannock paid forty matchcoats to lease 500 acres. The difference is probably a reflection of the fact that by 1702 the Ababcos did not really control that end of the reservation where Kirke's tract lay. The forty-two matchcoats were probably a token payment to formalize a transfer of control that had already taken place. Winacaco reserved the right to "hunt and fowle" on those lands and to "build Hunting Cabbins on any part not cultivated to dwell the winter seasons in," but this provision in the deed rapidly became meaningless as English settlement in the Cambridge area increased.[64]

The eastern end of the Choptank reservation, the portion occupied by the Hatsawap segment of the Choptanks, had a somewhat different history. It seems that by the 1690s chief Hatsawap (or Hachwop), who was one of the three Choptank "kings" mentioned in the 1669 treaty with the English, had also become fearful of English land hunger. Hatsawap's strategy for protecting his segment's core territory apparently was to transfer nominal ownership of the land to a prominent and sympathetic English inhabitant of Dorchester County. In 1692 he gave Francis Taylor, wife of Thomas Taylor, the title to a part of the Choptank reservation that included the Locust Neck Indian Town.[65] Thomas Taylor was an influential county justice who often served Maryland's provincial government as an envoy to the Nanticokes. Taylor was also the nominal landlord of the Nanticoke paramount chief, since he was the owner of record for a land grant that included the site of the Nanticoke Fort at Chicone.[66] The Taylors paid chief Hatsawap nothing for Locust Neck, and they never attempted to occupy the property. Indeed, the tract of land given to Francis Taylor remained in Indian hands until the Choptank reservation was abolished in 1799. This transaction was clearly a legal fiction designed to protect Locust Neck from English encroachment.

Hatsawap's strategy clearly worked, since by 1721 Locust Neck became the home of all the remaining Choptanks who were descended from the Ababcos, Tequassinos, and Hatsawaps. By that time the Choptank lands west of Indian Creek, which was the western boundary of Locust Neck, had virtually all been sold to English colonists. The largest single sale was in 1704, when Thomas Ennalls bought the central portion of the Choptank reservation, 4,660 acres in all, from Winacaco, Noockyousk, and Patchyouske and Patasuske, rulers of the Ababco, Hatsawap, and Tequassino Indians, respectively.[67] Ennalls paid a substantial price for the land, 6,000 pounds of tobacco, £40 "sterling money," and 320 matchcoats. This was the first recorded transaction in which the Choptanks accepted either tobacco or money, rather than goods, for land; by the 1720s money payments became the rule rather than the exception.

Land sales to the English were voluntary in theory, but circumstantial evidence indicates that English encroachment preceded any actual transfer of ownership. Under such circumstances the Indians may have believed that outright sale of the land was the only way to get any benefit from it. The Choptanks became alarmed by the rapid pace at which they were having to give up their land, and in 1719 and again in 1721 they complained to Maryland's provincial government about the actions of the English settlers in Dorchester County.[68] In 1719 they said specifically that they had been "driven back" to Locust Neck, and the lands they sold were probably those already being used by the colonists without permission. Locust Neck became the refuge area for the Choptanks because it was relatively isolated, and also because it was the nominal property of the Taylor family, so that it could not be sold.

By 1721 the people's continued possession even of Locust Neck was being threatened. In that year William Trippe, a local planter, bought the rights to an old land grant called Guinea (or Genney) plantation.[69] That tract was located on Locust Neck and had been laid out "at the upper Indian Town" by Indian trader John Edmundson in 1665.[70] The Edmundson grant should have been invalidated by the creation of the Choptank reservation in 1669, but it is hard to see why Trippe would have bought the grant at all unless he intended to make some sort of claim on the land.

The Maryland government acted relatively quickly in response to the Choptanks' 1721 complaint, decreeing that a new survey be made of their lands that year. Two years later the assembly finally resolved the problem of Choptank land sales by forbidding the Indians to sell any more land within the newly defined reservation boundaries and by invalidating any land sales made since the 1721 resurvey.[71] The Choptanks also were forbidden to lease any lands to the English, and the leases already in force were to terminate within seven years. In effect, the Choptanks now held what was left of their reservation under the same terms as the other Eastern Shore tribes; they could occupy and use the land, but they did not really own it. The lands sold before 1721 were gone for good, but Locust Neck remained in Indian hands until termination occurred in 1799.

The Nanticokes made their first postsurvey complaint about English encroachment in 1698, the same year that their reservation was established.[72] The complaint undoubtedly referred to individuals who had claimed land inside the reservation before its boundaries had been formally defined. Two of the four Englishmen mentioned in the complaint were Christopher Nutter and Nehemiah Covington Jr., both long-established Eastern Shore Indian traders who were also both officially designated Indian interpreters for the region. Nutter had been involved with the Nanticokes since the early 1670s and had bought the Handsel land grant from Thomas Taylor in 1693,[73] a grant that included the Nanticoke Fort at Chicone. Covington relocated to the Nanticoke region from southern Somerset County, where he had owned the site of the Great Monie Indian town originally patented by his father, Nehemiah Covington Sr.

Neither Covington nor Nutter seems to have been trying to remove the Nanticokes from Chicone, but the Indians may have felt that the two Englishmen were getting too close to their core territory and were attempting to exert too much influence on the tribe. Christopher Nutter's purchase of Handsel seems to have represented an attempt on his part to take Thomas Taylor's place as the Nanticokes' principal English contact. The confusing political events of the 1690s involving the Nanticokes and the English probably had something to do with Nutter's more active role in Nanticoke affairs. Nutter took part in almost every important negotiation between the Nanticokes and Maryland's provincial government during the last quarter of the seventeenth century.[74] The 1702–3 probate inventory of Nutter's estate indicates that he was actively involved in the Indian trade up to the time of his death. It lists large quantities of commodities like guns and cloth that were typical trade goods, as well as furs and twenty-nine "Indian bowls," the second largest number of such bowls in any recorded Eastern Shore estate.[75] There can be no real doubt that Nutter's main trading partners were the Indians at Chicone. His death seems to have destabilized Nanticoke-English relations for a time, and it probably also contributed to an internal Nanticoke political crisis. Nutter's emergence as the tribe's principal English contact had coincided with the 1693 appointment of Panquash and Annatoughquan as the joint leaders—temporarily—of the Nanticokes. His death coincided with the reemergence of Ashquash, the son of the seventeenth-century "emperor" Unnarocassimmon.[76]

Nutter's death probably made Chicone more vulnerable to encroachment, since no Englishman of comparable stature took over his role as a patron of the Chicone Nanticokes. The robbery of Panquash's cabin in 1703 and of Ashquash's quiocosin house in 1706 suggest that the Nanticokes were increasingly being viewed as fair game by their non-Indian neighbors. Powerful merchant-planters like Christopher Nutter may have taken economic advantage of the Indians, but at least they could ensure that other, lesser men in the neighborhood did not harass their trading partners. Without the protection of such a patron, the Chicone Nanticokes were increasingly vulnerable to all sorts of predatory acts.

Since the Nanticokes did not "own" (in English terms) either Chicone or the reservation that Maryland created for them at Broad Creek in 1711, there are no recorded sales of tribal land to the English. However, there is evidence of continuing trespasses by neighbors. The paramount chief Ashquash and his son William Ashquash fenced their fields "after the English manner," probably to discourage encroachment on the tribe's key agricultural lands.[77] Nevertheless, by 1721 the Nanticokes reported that because of illegal English use of reservation land, they now had "not enough land to make cornfields."[78] In 1713 Ashquash himself gave up and left Maryland entirely; he went to live among the Susquehannocks, probably because of English harassment and the failure of the Maryland authorities to do anything about the robbery of his quiocosin house. The Nanticokes continued to complain about that incident and seek compensation for it even after their "emperor" left the Eastern Shore.[79] With Ashquash's departure, political authority at Chicone shifted back to Panquash and Annatoughquan, although neither man was ever given the title "emperor." Based upon their past performance, it can be assumed that they were more accommodating to the English authorities than Ashquash had been.

Ashquash's departure seems to have been a personal decision, since most of the Chicone Nanticokes, including his son William Ashquash, remained at the Chicone site. However, significant numbers of Nanticokes were moving north into Pennsylvania in the early years of the eighteenth century. The first reference to Nanticokes in Pennsylvania dates to 1707, when people from seven different towns, presumably on the Eastern Shore, appear in that colony's records.[80] None of the towns named in the Pennsylvania documents can be identified with Chicone—although there was never any evidence that "Chicone" was what the Nanticokes themselves called their town in the first place. At this point the Nanticokes who left Maryland and accepted the protection of the Five Nations (soon to be Six Nations) in Pennsylvania probably were going as individuals or family groups, rather than as part of an overall planned tribal migration.

The next really serious conflict between the English and the Nanticokes came in 1721, after the heirs of Christopher Nutter sold their grant for the Handsel tract to a Dorchester planter named John Ryder.[81] Ryder almost immediately tried to seize the 700 acres of Handsel, including the site of the former Nanticoke Fort among whose inhabitants was William Ashquash. Ryder burned down William Ashquash's cabin and destroyed his fences, claiming that the Indians had abandoned the land. In their complaint to the English authorities, the Nanticokes stated that they had temporarily left that part of the reservation to go hunting. The Maryland government sided with the Nanticokes. Ryder was ordered off the reservation, the Chicone reservation was resurveyed, and the Nanticokes' hereditary right to use the reservation land in perpetuity was reaffirmed.[82]

After the Ryder incident there were no more overt attempts to seize the Chicone reservation lands, but the Nanticokes continued to have problems with their English neighbors. As early as 1717 the tribe had begun leasing portions of the Chicone reservation to Englishmen for annual payments of corn, trade goods, or money.[83] Some English colonists preferred leasing Indian land to purchasing it, since the annual sums paid to the Indians could be less than the quitrents that would be owing on the land if the colonists owned it outright. Samuel Cratcher, who leased land on the northern part of the reservation, even stated that "he had rather pay rent to the Indians than the Proprietary," an attitude that did not please the Maryland provincial authorities.[84]

The English tenants on Nanticoke lands often did not pay their annual rents, however, or if they did, they paid them in greatly overpriced trade goods. Neighboring Englishmen also probably cut timber on Chicone without the Indians' permission, a practice that steadily reduced the tract's capacity to support its native population.[85] Eventually the abuses at Chicone became so severe that the proprietary government took direct control of the reservation. In 1753 Chicone was made a proprietary manor, which meant that legally the reservation became the property of the Lords Baltimore again.[86] This change in legal status did not infringe on the Nanticoke Indians' right to occupy the land, but it did halt the leasing of that land to English tenants. The Broad Creek Nanticoke reservation also became a proprietary manor at the same time.[87] Both tracts remained in that status until after their Indian residents had moved away.

From the mid-1690s onward, the Indians of Askiminikansen also had to contend with increasing threats to their lands. In particular, the year 1696 marked the beginning of a more than thirty-year struggle by King Daniel of the Pocomokes to prevent a father-and-son team of Somerset County planters, John Parker and John Parker Jr., from taking over key portions of Askiminikansen Indian Town.[88] The Parkers were not the only Englishmen who attempted to seize Pocomoke and Assateague lands in the eighteenth century, but they were certainly the most persistent and ultimately the most successful. The story of the Parkers and chief Daniel is an excellent case study of how the Maryland Eastern Shore Indian reservations were dismembered and finally destroyed by land-hungry English planters. The dismemberment went on despite the laws and policies of Maryland's colonial government, which seems to have made repeated efforts to stop the encroachment process during the early and middle years of the eighteenth century.

Only two Englishmen had obtained land grants within the boundaries of Askiminikansen before 1695. The first was William Stevens, who had patented most of the southern half of the Indian town in 1665.[89] Stevens was a rich and powerful Somerset County planter who was a member of the Maryland council and who repeatedly served as the provincial government's representative in dealings with the Eastern Shore Indians. As was the usual pattern for the first generation of Indian town grantees, Stevens made no attempt to displace the Indians from his grants, even though he had the legal right to do so up until 1678, when Askiminikansen received formal recognition as an Indian reservation.

The second Englishman to patent land in Askiminikansen was Francis Jenkins, who was probably the wealthiest merchant in Somerset County during the last quarter of the seventeenth century, and who also served as a member of the Maryland council. His motives for patenting 300 acres in 1683 are readily explainable.[90] His grant, called Castle Green, was in the northeastern part of the reservation. It was described in the original patent as being located "whereon an Indian fort now stands," and a later document notes that the grant was "situate at the upper Indian town on Pocomoke."[91] Obviously Jenkins was following the typical strategy of seventeenth-century Indian traders and was securing his prior claim to the upper Indian town, the second of the two main Indian settlements on the Askiminikansen reservation. Jenkins, like Stevens, left the Indians in undisturbed occupation of their lands.

In 1695, however, a very different sort of man patented 400 acres of land within the boundaries of Askiminikansen. This was John Parker, and he was not a merchant or a government official or a wealthy landowner. Parker was a landless former indentured servant who was attempting to establish himself as a planter in Somerset County.[92] He wanted nothing from the Indians except the land they lived on. Over the next thirty years, he and his son John Jr. used a variety of tactics, mostly illegal, to compel the Indians to leave. The Parkers kept up the pressure on the Indians until they finally did leave the region, and at that point John Parker Jr. emerged as the largest landowner in the former Askiminikansen Indian Town.[93]

During the earlier part of John Parker Sr.'s life, his predatory acts were directed only against the Pocomokes of the lower Indian town at Askiminikansen. In 1712, however, he was able to buy the Castle Green grant from the heirs of Francis Jenkins.[94] Thereafter, he and his son began encroaching as well on the upper Indian town, which was located on the part of the reservation that was probably controlled by the Assateagues. In 1722 and again in 1726, the chiefs of the Assateagues and

Pocomokes jointly petitioned Maryland's proprietary government about the Parkers' moving in on Indian lands. In the latter petition they complained that Parker and his son had established plantations so close to the Indians that they, the Pocomokes and Assateagues, "shall quit their towns" unless the Parkers and another encroaching English planter were removed from the Indian lands.[95] No effective action resulted. The Parkers risked very little by moving in on Indian lands, since no matter how blatant their actions were, local magistrates and juries would not apply any real sanctions against them. On the other hand, when Indians like King Daniel tried to use English law and English institutions to defend their lands, they found that the deck was always stacked against them. Indian leaders eventually realized that without the support of local government officials, the Maryland provincial government could not protect reservation lands even if it wished to do so. When disillusionment finally came, the Indians began leaving the Eastern Shore in large numbers.

It would appear that most of the Pocomokes and Assateagues did indeed leave the Askiminikansen reservation in the late 1720s or early 1730s. There is only one more recorded petition by King Daniel, made about 1728 to the Somerset County court, about the actions of John Parker Jr. on the Indian lands.[96] After 1729, there are no further references to King Daniel in either the Somerset County or Maryland provincial records, and there are very few mentions of Indians living within the bounds of the reservation at all. The most likely explanation is that King Daniel and the Assateague chief and most of their subjects left Maryland to join other refugee Eastern Shore Indians in Pennsylvania. Only a small remnant was left behind.

The main reason why the Maryland provincial authorities tried as hard as they did to maintain good relations with the Eastern Shore Indians, even after the decline of the fur trade, was their continuing fear that if the Indians were pushed too far, they would make a common cause with hostile Indians from outside Maryland and join with them in an attack on the colony. The apparent conflict between the Eastern Shore Indians and the Iroquois tribes and their tributaries living in neighboring Pennsylvania ceased during the last decade of the seventeenth century; the Senecas and Susquehannocks made peace with Maryland in 1696.[97] Thereafter, the Five (later Six) Nations seem to have always been willing to offer refuge to Eastern Shore Indians who chose to leave Maryland, allowing them to resettle on lands in Pennsylvania that had been conquered from the Susquehannocks earlier in the seventeenth century. In fact, the Iroquois actively sought to populate the former territory of the Susquehannocks with other Indian groups who were willing to accept Iroquois authority. Not only the Eastern Shore Algonquians but also the Piscataway/Conoy Algonquian-speakers of Maryland's western shore moved to Pennsylvania in large numbers during the early part of the eighteenth century.[98]

The Maryland authorities certainly wanted a peace with the Iroquois, but they were suspicious of the increasingly close ties between the Eastern Shore tribes and these "foreign" Indians that the peace had brought. Apparently the fear that the Maryland Eastern Shore Indians might invite the Five Nations to attack the colony was widely held both by officials of the Maryland government and by ordinary colonists. In 1706, for example, a colonist named James Smith was prosecuted by the Somerset County court for spreading a "false rumor" that the Seneca Indians were at Broad Creek, the more northerly of the two main Nanticoke Indian towns. The rumor caused a number of the English inhabitants of Somerset County to abandon their plantations temporarily and draw together for defensive purposes at more secure locations in the county.[99]

The concern that the Nanticokes in particular might conspire with various northern Indians to work harm on the Maryland colony strongly influenced the proprietary's Indian policy in the early eighteenth century. In 1713, when the paramount chief Ashquash abandoned his tribe to go and live among the Susquehannocks (then tributary to the Five Nations), the governor and council of Maryland sent three high-ranking envoys north to the Susquehanna region to meet and talk with Indian leaders there. The task of the envoys was to find out what Ashquash was doing in Pennsylvania and to refute any charges against the Maryland government that he might make. One particular worry was that Ashquash might recruit northern Indians to "reduce his own people" or "otherwise molest this Government."[100] The Maryland authorities obviously feared that Ashquash would invite the Susquehannocks or the Iroquois to intervene in his ongoing leadership struggle with Panquash and Annatoughquan, the two Nanticoke leaders whom the English favored.

No conflict with the northern Indians resulted from the Ashquash incident, but a generation later the Maryland government's suspicions about Indian conspiracies on the Eastern Shore seem finally to have been vindicated. In the spring of 1742 some leading Nanticoke Indians met secretly with envoys from the Shawan (Shawnee) Indians, supposedly to plan a general Indian uprising on the Eastern Shore that would be supported by a large number of warriors from Pennsylvania.[101] Even though the planned uprising failed before it had properly begun, the 1742 conspiracy still remains the most important collective act of resistance against the English that the Eastern Shore tribes ever made, either in Maryland or in Virginia. The conspiracy also marked the beginning of the end for the Maryland tribes as organized political entities within the colony. After 1742 they no longer controlled their own affairs to any meaningful degree, and most of the Indians still remaining chose to leave Maryland entirely.

The Maryland colonial authorities' first evidence of the conspiracy came in June 1742, when a Dorchester County official reported that all of the Indians in his county, which contained both the Chicone and Choptank reservations, had abandoned their towns. He further reported that the entire population of the reservation at Broad Creek in neighboring Somerset County (now Sussex County, Delaware) was also gone. All of these Indians had gathered together at a place called Winnasoccum, in the swamps at the head of the Pocomoke River, "under a Pretence of Hunting," but contrary to their usual practice, they had taken with them all of their old men, women, and children and all of their goods.[102]

In response to this report, the Maryland provincial government immediately sent a militia unit to Winnasoccum to seize the Indians' guns, capture the tribal leaders, and take them to Annapolis for questioning. All of these aims were accomplished without violence. A number of Indians were interrogated both in Annapolis and in Dorchester County. The testimony of the various Indians is quite consistent. In the middle of May 1742, twenty-three Shawnee Indians had come to the Nanticoke town of Chicone and met with the leaders of the Chicone and Broad Creek Nanticokes and also with the "Indian River Queen."[103] The Nanticokes then sent two envoys of their own to Conoy Town on the Susquehanna River. These men returned in a few days with a small party of Shawnees that included a war captain. The Nanticoke leaders and the Shawnee war captain then moved to Winnasoccum and invited the other Maryland Eastern Shore tribes to join them there. All of the legally recognized tribes, the Choptanks, the Pocomokes, the Assateagues, and the Indian River Indians, did so. They built a fort, and an "Indian River Doctor" prepared a potion of some sort.[104] The Indians remained at Winnasoccum for a few days and then dispersed again.

While the twenty Eastern Shore Indians questioned by the Maryland authorities were in general agreement about the chronology of events, their interpretations of the events varied quite markedly.[105] The Choptank witnesses testified that the purpose of the meeting at Chicone with the Shawnee Indians was to organize an uprising to destroy the English of Somerset and Dorchester Counties, and that this uprising was to be coordinated with a general Indian attack on the English inhabitants of Maryland and Pennsylvania that would be supported by the French.

The Pocomoke and Assateague Indians who were questioned told a quite different story. They stated that they had been called to Winnasoccum to meet with the Chicone Indians for the purpose of hunting and "to make a new emperor."[106] These Indians denied any knowledge of a conspiracy with the Shawnees. The third version of the story came from Panquash, Dixon Coursey, and Captain John, the Nanticoke Indian leaders who were most closely implicated in dealings with the Shawnees. These men also said that they had gone to Winnasoccum in order to make a new "emperor" and to hunt. They took the old men, women, and children of the tribe along only because they had no food for them at Chicone. (This excuse was plausible, since June was a season for foraging before a new corn crop came in.) In this version of the story, the potion prepared at Winnasoccum by the Indian River doctor was a medicine to cure Panquash "of a Cough."[107]

The English authorities were understandably skeptical when presented with the Nanticoke leaders' account of events and chose to believe the Choptank version instead. Maryland governor Samuel Ogle gave the Indians a stern warning and required the leaders of each of the separate Indian towns to sign a new treaty with the proprietary government. The texts of all the 1742 treaties are practically identical.[108] The treaties firmly established the principle that the Eastern Shore tribes were subject peoples under the direct control of Maryland's Lord Proprietor. The traditional Indian privileges (necessities) of "Crabbing, Fowling, Hunting and Fishing" were confirmed, but no Indian was to be allowed to carry a gun unless it was licensed by the governor of the province. The Eastern Shore tribes were forbidden in the future to meet with the Chicone Nanticokes to select an "emperor," and this restriction applied even to the Broad Creek Indians, who were themselves Nanticokes.

The Fading Out of Tribal Communities

The 1742 treaties ended the pretense that the Eastern Shore tribes had any political independence from the English and further undermined the tribes' internal political structure by curtailing the influence of the tribal chiefs. The hereditary "kings," "queens," and "emperors" who used to have authority over the tribes were already gone from the scene. In 1742 the Choptanks, Nanticokes, Pocomokes, and Assateagues were led by men without royal titles who appeared to have had no connection with the previous generation of Indian rulers. The Nanticokes had not had a paramount chief for some time before the abortive 1742 attempt to make one at Winnasoccum. The last reference to an "emperor" of the Nanticokes in the Maryland provincial records dates to 1725, when Henry Coursey is called by the title.[109] The Chicone Nanticokes were ruled in 1742 by Sam Panquash, who may have been the same Panquash who took over from "emperor" Ashquash in 1713, and by Dixon Coursey. The Courseys were a Chicone Nanticoke family that rose to prominence at about the time of Ashquash's departure from the province.[110]

The only royal title in evidence among the 1742 conspirators belonged to the Indian River "Queen"; however, she is not mentioned in the subsequent treaty, which was signed on her people's behalf by an otherwise unknown Indian River man named Tom Hill and also by Robin, the hereditary interpreter for that group. There is no mention of the Indian River "Queen" or, for that matter, of the Indian River Indians in the Maryland records after that time. In 1741 these people had sold off the last of their reservation at Askekesky. After the failure of the 1742 conspiracy, the people at Indian River seem either to have left the Eastern Shore entirely or perhaps to have merged with some other Eastern Shore group.[111]

Some Pocomokes and Assateagues remained in Maryland for a time, and a few hundred acres of reservation land in the vicinity of the lower Indian town may have stayed in Indian hands as late as 1746. A deed recorded in that year mentions "the natives, to wit the Indians of Askiminiconson Town," who it would appear were still living on part of the original grant called Partner's Choice that was patented by William Stevens in 1665.[112] An English traveler who visited the Eastern Shore in the 1740s also describes an Indian village near the town of Snow Hill, which was probably the same small remnant of the lower Askiminikansen town.[113] The Pocomokes and Assateagues who met with the Nanticokes at Winnasoccum numbered only sixteen people altogether.[114] Even if only the adult male Pocomokes and Assateagues went to the meeting, this figure would still suggest that the total Pocomoke and Assateague population resident on the Eastern Shore at that time amounted to around fifty persons. The last mention of Askiminikansen

Indian Town in the county or provincial records dates to 1750, but it is not clear whether any Indians were still living there at the time.[115] Unlike the Choptank and Nanticoke reservations, the Askiminikansen reservation was never formally abolished. It simply eroded away, becoming progressively smaller until it ceased to exist.

As the second half of the eighteenth century began, it seems that only the reservations at Locust Neck (formerly Choptank) and Chicone in Dorchester County still supported viable Indian communities. The last reference to Indian residents at Broad Creek dates to 1755, and in that record only two persons are mentioned.[116] Most Nanticokes apparently decided to abandon Maryland in the aftermath of the 1742 conspiracy. In 1744 the tribe requested permission from the governor of Maryland to "remove to the Six Nations" and agreed to live wherever the Six Nations should decide, a clear indication that they were accepting tributary status under the Iroquois.[117] Maryland's governor granted permission for the Nanticokes to depart, although some members of the tribe chose to remain behind at Chicone. Two such people were James Cohonk and Peter Monk, both of whom had testified against Panquash during the government inquiry of 1742.

After 1750 the Indian towns at Chicone on the Nanticoke River and Locust Neck on the Choptank River continued to lose population at a rapid rate. Maryland's governor estimated in 1761 that the total number of Indians living on all the reservations in the colony was only 120 persons, and since the western shore reservations had effectively ceased to exist by that time, we can assume that all or nearly all of these Indians were Choptanks and Nanticokes.[118] As the two Dorchester County reservation communities got smaller, there seems to have been a considerable mixing of population between the two. Even in the early eighteenth century there had been some movement by individuals between Chicone and Locust Neck. William Ashquash, the Nanticoke paramount chief's son, apparently left Chicone and moved to the Choptank reservation after his conflict with John Ryder in 1721. By 1727 Ashquash was listed in a deed as a Choptank Indian, and as late as 1754 he was still living at Locust Neck.[119] In the late 1750s the mingling of the two reservation populations reached the point where the distinction between the Choptank and Nanticoke tribes seems to have been fading away. Additionally, it appears that some members of other Eastern Shore tribes had moved to the two reservations in the 1740s or 1750s, after their own Indian towns ceased to exist.

The conflicts caused among the native peoples by this mixing of tribes and the concomitant erosion of tribal identity came to the surface in 1757, when a controversy developed over who was to be recognized as chief of the Nanticokes.[120] The two candidates were Peter Monk and George Pocatyhouse, both of whom apparently lived at Chicone. The chief supporters of Monk, however, were members of the Bishop family, who were Choptanks, not Nanticokes. The supporters of Pocatyhouse consisted mainly of members of the Ashquash and Cohonk families, who do appear to have been Nanticoke by descent. The Pocatyhouse party complained that Peter Monk was not himself a Nanticoke but was in fact "a Descendant of the Indian River Indians." Pocatyhouse, on the other hand, was a descendant of the former Nanticoke leader Panquash. Governor Sharp of Maryland ended the controversy in 1758 by appointing George Pocatyhouse as "Chief Man" of the Nanticokes.

During this period the Indians of Locust Neck and Chicone suffered "continual frauds Trespasses and Incroachments" from their English neighbors, and they petitioned the Maryland authorities for redress in 1754, 1755, and 1759.[121] The latter petition complained that "the White people" burned down the Indians' cabins when they left them to go hunting and further stated that the Indians would soon be "quite Destroyed and Totally Pushed out of this Nation." In each case an inquiry was ordered and the Indians' rights were to be upheld, but the hostility exhibited by the neighborhood in general toward Indians was insuperable. The Indian picture for the 1750s is one of rapid disintegration, with both the economic base and the social structure of the reservations crumbling under pressures from outside. By the 1760s many of the remaining Eastern Shore Indians, especially the Nanticokes, apparently decided that the only option left to them was to leave Maryland for good.

In 1767 three Nanticoke men who had formerly lived in Maryland but had since "been incorporated with the Six Nations" at Otsiningo in New York returned to the Maryland colony along with several other Six Nations people. The purpose of their visit was to invite the "Indians at Locust Neck and on Nanticoke" to give up their lands in Maryland and return with them to Otsiningo.[122] This invitation seems to have been extended at the request of certain residents at Chicone and Locust Neck who wished to move north and "be one People" with their "Brethren of the Six Nations." The Maryland authorities granted permission for the three Nanticoke emissaries to meet and talk with the Indians at the Choptank and Nanticoke reservations and to take away with them any persons who were willing to leave those communities.

There is no record of how many Eastern Shore Indians left Maryland that year, but since Chicone appears to have been abandoned by the Nanticokes at about this date, we can assume that most of what remained of the tribe went away with the emissaries of the northern Nanticokes. In 1768 the Maryland legislature passed a bill authorizing the purchase of all remaining rights to Chicone from the Nanticoke Indians. The bill states that the remaining Nanticokes, "who have incorporated themselves with the Six Nations," petitioned the assembly for the right to sell their claims to the land. The same bill also authorized the sale of the 3,000 acres of the Nanticoke reservation at Broad Creek.[123] There are no references to Indians at Chicone after 1770; by 1785 the reservation lands were entirely in the hands of Anglo-American farmers (fig. 4.2). The few Nanticokes who remained in Maryland probably moved to the Choptank reservation. After that, the Indians at Locust Neck are sometimes called Nanticokes rather than Choptanks, a usage which probably reflects the fact that from about 1770 there was only one Indian town left on the Maryland Eastern Shore, a small mixed Choptank and Nanticoke one at Locust Neck.

There are, in turn, very few references to the Indians of Locust Neck during the remainder of the eighteenth century. Just before the American Revolution, William Eddis wrote a short account of the Maryland Indians in which he mentioned "the remnants of a nation" living in "Dorset county on the eastern shore." He remarked that these Indians "retain considerable tracts of valuable land," but that "spiritous liquors . . . and smallpox" had reduced their numbers to less than twenty persons.[124] There can be no real doubt that Eddis was referring to the Locust Neck Indians. Soon after the Revolution the new state of Maryland attempted to buy the remaining Indians' lands in Dorchester County, but the Indians declined to sell.[125] In 1792 William Vans Murray visited the Locust Neck Indian Town and compiled a short vocabulary of the language still spoken by the people, which he considered to be the Nanticoke language. At that time only nine persons were living at Locust Neck, in "Five wigwams and a board house" (fig. 4.3). He recorded that "many of them migrated to the Six Nations about twenty-five years since," a clear reference to the events of 1767–68.[126]

Finally in 1798, the Maryland assembly voted to purchase the remaining Choptank reservation lands from the five Indians still living

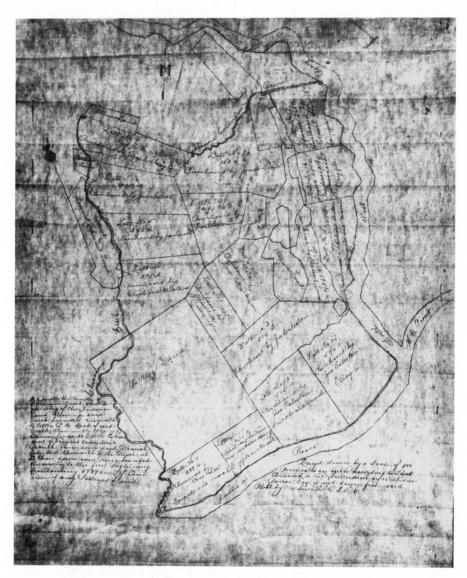

Fig. 4.2 Plat of the Chicone reservation in 1785. (Courtesy of the Maryland State Archives, Maryland Survey Papers [Division Plats] MSA A 65–135)

Fig. 4.3 Aerial view of the last part of the Locust Neck Indian Town to be inhabited by Indians

there and to abolish the reservation. The sale of Locust Neck was completed on April 10, 1799, and at that time the reservation still encompassed an estimated four thousand acres.[127] The Indians, who were listed as Mary Mulberry, Henry Mulberry, Henry Sixpence, Thomas Joshua, and Esther Henry, were given annuities ranging from $30 to $160 a year, and each family was allowed to retain possession of twenty acres of land for life. The last of these twenty-acre parcels of land reverted to the state of Maryland in the late 1830s when Thomas Joshua died.[128]

Detribalized Indian Citizens

We do not know how many Indians were already living off the reservations when Locust Neck was abolished in 1799. Several hundred Indians certainly must have left the various Maryland Eastern Shore reservations over the course of the eighteenth century, but it is impossible to determine the number of ex-reservation Indians who remained in the region, in contrast to the number who left the Eastern Shore entirely and joined with the Six Nations. The decision to stay or to go appears to have been made on an individual basis. Since the Indians who did choose to stay lost any claim to special legal status, they are very difficult to locate in official records.

The loss of a legally recognized Indian identity can be seen fairly clearly in the case of one Choptank Indian named Abraham Bishop. The Bishops were one of the most important Choptank families living on the Locust Neck reservation during the second and third quarters of the eighteenth century; the first Bishop from the tribe appeared in the Dorchester County records in 1722, in the person of "Atuckqueawatow alias Tom Bishop."[129] Tom Bishop surfaced repeatedly in the records as a Choptank leader; toward the middle of the eighteenth century, Abraham Bishop showed up as well and may have been Tom's son or grandson. Both men were called "Indian Chiefs of Locust Neck" in 1755.[130]

The last time the name Abraham Bishop appeared in association with the Choptank tribe or the Locust Neck reservation was in 1790, when he gave a deposition about the boundaries of the Indian town.[131] That same year a prominent white landowner in the region, Henry Hooper, conveyed a slave girl named Pleasant to Abraham Bishop.[132] A 1797 notation refers to a "free Negro" named Abraham Bishop who was living in Dorchester County. This Abraham Bishop had two sons named

Thomas and Abraham, who like Pleasant were formerly slaves of Henry Hooper.[133] There was no mention of an Abraham Bishop in the first federal census of Dorchester County, made in 1791, but the 1800 census listed him among the "Other Free Persons" residing in that county.[134] In the nineteenth century the descendants of Abraham Bishop were classed as "free Negroes" or "free colored."[135]

Clearly Abraham Bishop the Choptank Indian and Abraham Bishop the free black man were the same person. Sometime after 1790 Bishop apparently moved off the Locust Neck reservation and established himself on a small farm along with his ex-slave wife and ex-slave children, Pleasant, Thomas, and Abraham. At the time of the first federal census, Abraham Bishop was still reckoned to be an Indian living on the reservation, so he was not counted in 1791. Indians on reservations were not citizens, so their names were not recorded in that census. By the time of the 1800 census, though, the Locust Neck reservation had been abolished and Bishop was a legal resident of Dorchester County who was regarded as a free black man.

As far as Dorchester County officials were concerned, Abraham Bishop ceased being an Indian when he stopped living in a legally recognized Indian community. Since he was a free nonwhite person married to a black person, his new legal status logically became that of a free black. No white person at that time could marry a slave or a black. Bishop's children had once been the slaves of Henry Hooper, and the law in Maryland mandated that the children of a slave woman should be slaves even if their father was a free person.[136] Thus it is clear that Bishop married his wife while she was still a slave. County officials probably believed that by moving off the reservation and residing with his ex-slave wife and children, Abraham Bishop was tacitly accepting a new official identity as a free black. Northampton County officials would make the same assumption about detribalized Gingaskin Indians later in the nineteenth century.

This process of Indians marrying non-Indians, moving off the reservations, and merging into the general population of the Eastern Shore had been going on since the seventeenth century. The first two Indians whose baptisms were recorded in Somerset County, John Puckham and Richard James, were both Indians who married women of other races. Their children were not reckoned to be Indians by the county or provincial authorities; instead they received their official racial identities from their mothers. Puckham's children were considered free mulattoes because Puckham had married "Jone Johnson, negroe," while James's daughter was seemingly considered white because her mother was of English descent.[137]

The loss of a recognized Indian identity could also occur even without marriage to a non-Indian. During the second quarter of the eighteenth century, a few individuals were listed in the Somerset County tax records both as Indians and as the taxpaying heads of free households.[138] Since Indians living on the reservations paid no taxes, these persons must have been Indians who had moved off the reservation and set up English-style households on nonreservation lands. At least as far as their tax status is concerned, these off-reservation Indians appear to have been treated in the same fashion as whites, since only the adult males of the households are listed as taxable persons (the women would have been taxed as well, had their status been nonwhite). Even so, the men's identity as Indians had not been forgotten by the authorities, since they were called "Indians" in the records. After about 1750, however, the Somerset tax records no longer identify anyone as an Indian, and the off-reservation Indians seemingly merged into the general population of the county. It was probably not a coincidence that this happened at about the time that the Askiminikansen reservation ceased to exist and the Broad Creek Nanticoke reservation lost all or nearly all of its resident Indian population. No administrative purpose was served in keeping track of who was an Indian and who was not once the reservation communities were gone.

Most of the Maryland Indians who merged into the general population of Somerset County before 1750 appear to have achieved eventual acceptance as white persons. After 1750, though, the Indians who had not already made this social and legal transition were more likely to be classified as blacks by county officials. For example, in the year 1757 a man named James Scokem is listed for the first time as a head of household in the Nanticoke Hundred of Somerset County, a sparsely inhabited part of the county which contained the Broad Creek reservation. James Scokem was classified as a free black, although before 1757 there was no free black Scokem family living in the county, nor is there any recorded manumission of a slave who could have been James Scokem.[139] In fact, the name Scokem is unknown in the whole region except among the Nanticokes of southern Delaware, where in the nineteenth century the name appears in the form of "Sockum."[140] James Scokem almost certainly was a Nanticoke man who left the Broad Creek reservation, and who like the Choptank Indian Abraham Bishop was reclassified as a free black when he did so. Although James Scokem's wife Rachel was also classed as a free black, there is nothing in the records to suggest that she had this racial identity before 1757, so this probably was not another case of an Indian taking on his spouse's racial identity. Scokem's classification as a free black by Somerset County officials seems to have been an arbitrary decision, based perhaps on his nonwhite appearance or on the prevailing community attitudes about the proper status of non-Europeans.

Once the reservations were gone, "Indian" ceased to be a valid legal identity in both Virginia and Maryland, and the only remaining categories for free persons were either white or free black. For Eastern Shore Indians in the late eighteenth century, that usually, if not invariably, meant reclassification as free blacks. By the early nineteenth century on the Maryland Eastern Shore, even the awareness that there were still Indians present, and that not all people classified as free blacks were of African descent, seems to have faded from the minds of the white inhabitants of the region. This does not mean that the Scokems and the other Indian-descended families had forgotten who they were, but certainly the white officials who kept the county records no longer knew or cared about such distinctions in racial identity.

Five

Virginia's Gingaskin Reservation after 1700

T HE EIGHTEENTH CENTURY saw patriarchy grow among the English of Virginia and Maryland, along with social dominance by a few merchant-planters, a heavy reliance on slave labor in farming, and a continuously low legal status of all nonwhites. The last-named is crucial in understanding the eventual disappearance of the Eastern Shore reservations, especially the Gingaskin one. Even though the Virginia Eastern Shore had very few truly rich planters, there were plenty of prosperous, slave-owning farmers whose interests lay in controlling the native people who remained. Controlling eventually came to mean forcible expulsion, an extreme attitude triggered by the fact that the Gingaskins, unlike the native people north of them, seem never to have considered moving from their homeland.

The higher echelons of English society, including politically powerful neighbors of the Gingaskins, now lived increasingly in multiroomed houses with glass in the windows and well-made furniture inside. They wore imported clothing of fine-textured cloth. They were people who had never experienced servitude of any kind themselves, and whose longevity enabled them to establish and dominate more stable, more closely related family households (with a corresponding decrease in regard for inferior nonrelatives). They had slaves to keep the house in order, practice the basic plantation crafts, and till the fields. And they had the leisure to devote themselves to politics, socializing, and living in an increasingly refined, well-regulated manner that included scheduling their lives by clock time and using the day's hours wisely.[1]

Most people on eighteenth-century plantations were far from privileged, however. Any Indians who became servants found themselves working with slaves. Most slaves and hired or indentured workers spent much of the year in small, one-race, predominantly male groups at "quarters" (outlying farms), living in extremely spartan conditions. These included a shack for shelter, a few portable cooking utensils, and shabby pieces of bedding; white servants' quarters had more substantial household belongings, including an occasional bedstead.

Workers' living conditions actually resembled the back-to-basics lifestyle of traditional Indians, and the small, scattered quarters resembled traditional Indian hamlets.[2] For that matter, they resembled the living conditions of most English people in the previous century. The major differences between the surviving Indian communities and lower-echelon non-Indians were in the food, which was sparser and starchier for servant men with less time to fish; the greater variety of ages and genders of people in the Indian towns, whose women still did the farming; and servants having to take orders day in and day out. The Gingaskin Indians had a better diet and more personal autonomy.

In the eighteenth century the Eastern Shore (and later the western shore) shifted to more diversified crops, especially in Maryland, where grains, fruits, and vegetables were raised for the Philadelphia market. Tobacco production on the Virginia Eastern Shore reached a peak in 1703, but raising tobacco as a cash crop had essentially come to an end by 1727, after which planters produced mainly corn but also wheat, oats, hogs and cattle, lumber, and other things. The Virginia Shore, like the Maryland sector, became a major exporter of foodstuffs to more northerly colonies. Farming households also did more domestic manufacturing, evidenced by things like spinning wheels and looms in estate inventories and by the numbers of shopkeepers and craftsmen, especially weavers and shoemakers. Raising wheat, oats, and barley required plow agriculture, which in turn required fields cleared of stumps (fig. 5.1), an effort which was worthwhile because those crops did not exhaust the land as fast as tobacco and corn did. Wheat in bread meant somewhat better nutrition for people, and oats meant better-nourished horses.[3] It is unlikely that the surviving Indians of the Virginia Eastern Shore shared these things to any great extent, unless they became domestic servants.

The Gingaskins continued to practice their traditional economy throughout the eighteenth century, as far as the records show, in spite of their tiny land base. Women farmed, and men continued to forage successfully thanks to the reservation's access to the eastern marshes

Fig. 5.1 Flat farmland in Northampton County showing modern clear farming and fairly large fields

and waterways via Indiantown Creek (fig. 5.2). However, keeping the traditional economy meant that the Indians' land continued to consist mainly in forest punctuated with overgrown, fallow fields, which now looked messier and less productive than those off the reservation. Not joining the prevailing market economy also meant that the Indians fell behind in material prosperity. Thus the more powerful of their neighbors became increasingly unimpressed with the way the Indians ran their lives. How much the Gingaskins themselves minded their "poverty," given their traditionally spartan but more relaxed way of life, is impossible to say. However, their upper-class neighbors perceived them as poor and indolent, which did not bode well for their future in an increasingly stratified, patriarchal society.

The Gingaskin Indians became somewhat more anglicized in the course of the eighteenth century. (They probably also borrowed from their African-descended neighbors, though documentary evidence for it is all but nil.) Gingaskins acquired English surnames, which probably accompanied the (undocumented) demise of the Accomac Indian language. Indians with both first and surnames appear in the seventeenth-century records (see Appendix A), but in those early times they may have been detribalized. Indians with only English first names appear as late as 1721, like "Quinney the Indian" who bought a boat at an estate sale, but surnames were becoming the rule. Some of them may have been derived from English first names; Jeffery was the sole name of a Gingaskin man in 1704, and by 1800 it was a Gingaskin surname.[4] Other last names entered the community by unrecorded routes, sometimes appearing only briefly (Cross, Daniel, Drummond, Rozario, Shepherd, Sunket)[5] and in other cases remaining for the duration (Bingham, Baker). The surname West emerged among the Gingaskins with "John West Indian" in 1707 and lasted until after the reservation was terminated. The name Press first appears in the Northampton County records as a mulatto one in 1732, but it was a purely Gingaskin name from the mid-eighteenth century until the end of the reservation era and beyond. Not only that, but in every generation from the late eighteenth century onward, there was a son named Edmund Press.[6]

Fig. 5.2 Indiantown Creek, Northampton County, looking across to the northern waterfront of the old Gingaskin reservation

Still other names came into the Gingaskin community through marriage around 1800 with identifiable free blacks. Driggus, or Rodriggus, had been a free black name since the mid-seventeenth century; it appeared among the Gingaskins in the early nineteenth century. Bevins or Beavans, originally an English name, became established in the free African-American community by the mid-eighteenth century, and it appeared among the Gingaskins after a marriage of 1797. The name House was acquired through a marriage of 1788; the wives in the Beavans and House marriages were named Press. Men named Francis married Gingaskin wives in 1792 and 1796; both husbands plus the current Edmund Press would get the Indians into serious trouble in 1812. Still other free black names such as Collins, Carter, Stephens, Weeks, and Trower (rhymes with "flower") entered the Gingaskin community near the end of the reservation era.[7]

Most other aspects of the eighteenth-century Gingaskins' lives were never written down; we know only about their business dealings with whites and about the squabbles they got into with non-Indians and with each other. Gingaskin women continued selling mats and baskets at least through the 1720s, for these appear in estate inventories.[8] The men usually appear in other guises, as did the Indian Philip Rozario, who was probably (but not certainly) a Gingaskin. He bound himself as a servant to a white man in 1714, when he was twenty-one. His master subsequently hired him out to a mariner, and when neither man listed Rozario as a tithable the next year, both got into trouble. In 1719 his master died, and he was listed as part of the estate. By 1724 Rozario was free, and he was taken to court on unspecified charges and ordered to pay four barrels of corn. The following year he sued a white man for debt, but the case was settled out of court. In 1730 a white man sued Rozario, and the case was dismissed when neither man appeared in court. The next year Rozario and a different white man were involved in a suit for debt, with the same result. By 1752 Rozario had died, and his estate was so small that the sheriff had to settle it. In 1762 another Philip Rozario, possibly a son, was bound out as an indigent child.[9]

Other Gingaskins were poor enough that local officials took action about it. From the 1750s onward the county's Overseers of the Poor took their children and bound them out as indentured servants to be sure they had adequate support; the alternative was the parish having to pay for them. This was the fate of the Indians named Major Drummond and Brit Sunket, as well as several Bingham children, some labeled Indians and some not. An Indian named Scarburgh Bingham was bound out in 1760 and 1762, and his son Southy Bingham was bound out in 1780 (without an ethnic label), poverty being hereditary. Another, possibly Indian, Press named John was imprisoned for twenty days in 1771 for debt. And in 1775 the churchwardens of Hungars Parish paid a white man for boarding an unnamed Gingaskin Indian, for reasons not given.[10]

Some Gingaskins landed in court at fairly regular—though well-spaced-out—intervals, usually because of internal squabbles. For instance, in 1732 "Ibbey Indian Woman" complained "that she has been abused by will [William Custis] Priss Molatto in such manner that she's afraid to go to her place of Abode." Press was taken into custody until he posted a bond for good behavior. In 1749–57 John Daniel sued several other probable Gingaskins (their ethnic identity was not recorded, but the names are right), including two successful prosecutions of William West, first for trespass and assault and battery and then for debt. Interestingly, the jury in the debt case ruled that West "hath [improperly] occupied and tended six Acres of the Lands of the Tributary Indians residing in this County . . . by the space of one year"; West was fined £3 (a steep price). Six acres was a lot of ground for one person using digging-stick agriculture; West may have been using a plow, English-style. If West was Indian, then he was the only Gingaskin male recorded as farming land before the early nineteenth century. Several other intra-Gingaskin disputes arose in subsequent decades, often without details being recorded in the county order books. There were also Gingaskins involved in court cases with outsiders; usually it was the Indian who was prosecuted. The charges were not always specified, but they included debt and theft of a gimlet from a white man (the result in this case was acquittal).[11] As usual, these records show a negative side of the Indians; in fact, their rate of getting into trouble was about equal to that of non-Indians in those days.

The Gingaskins' hold upon their reservation land was reasonably secure in the first two-thirds of the eighteenth century. They had their 1680 patent recorded in the county deed books in 1712. In 1757 a new road was run to their reservation. The location of it is vaguely worded, but it may have been part of modern County Route 631, which runs eastward from the county seat to and now through what used to be the reservation (fig. 5.3).[12]

In 1769, though, the Gingaskins' poverty, in white eyes and possibly

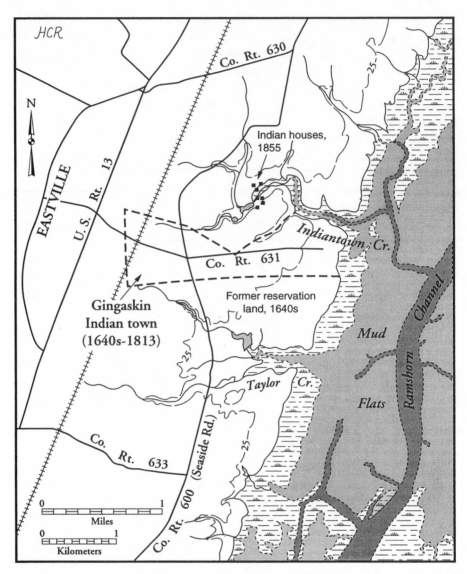

Fig. 5.3 Map of the Gingaskin reservation and vicinity

their own, resulted in the first of a series of land transactions that would ultimately lead to losing their land. The vestry and parish of Hungars petitioned the General Assembly that a law be passed enabling the leasing out of part of the reservation. The reason was that "the said Indians [male ones] neglect to cultivate [the land by plowing] and by pursuing their ancient custom of hunting, fishing, and fowling, leave their aged, sick, and disabled, to languish in distress, and to become a charge and burthen to the said parish, which is unreasonable." The poverty was real, but it was not the men's tasks, which had always brought in food and which now included farming, that were the sole cause of it. A more likely cause is social disorganization, as shown in the intratribal court cases, combined with increased out-marriage; the result was a dilution of tribal ties that left marginal people unsupported. The General Assembly agreed with the parish, and 200 acres were vested in the churchwardens to lease out, 50 acres of that being kept in timber for building and repairing leased houses. Fewer acres were actually disposed of, since the churchwardens found that 100 acres would support the Indians.[13]

The churchwardens set about paying the people's living expenses, but they did not (or could not) prevent "divers encroachments" being made on Indian land. In 1773 the Gingaskins themselves petitioned for and got tribal trustees appointed to do that job.[14] The tribe apparently had all its adults sign the petition; their hereditary leaders were long gone.

Background to Gingaskin Allotment and Termination

The legal termination of the Gingaskins, done essentially against the Indians' will, was a drawn-out process that began in 1784 and ended in 1813. Social termination, meaning the "disappearance" of anything Indian about them or their descendants, did not occur then or later: it has not yet entirely happened.[15] The breaking up of the reservation, which meant the end of the tribe as a legal entity, was due largely to white people's anxieties about the Gingaskins' associations with local free blacks. These connections had gradually intensified at the same time that the downhill slide of free blacks' status in Virginia had made the Gingaskins' "treaty rights" look substantial by comparison. The Indians' white neighbors assumed—probably correctly—that residence on the reservation would look attractive to free African Americans; they also assumed—incorrectly—that the reservation was therefore becoming a serious nuisance to law-abiding citizens.

For three decades before they yielded, the Gingaskins were steadily pressured by white neighbors who had grave fears about nonwhites in general, amounting almost to paranoia. The Gingaskins' partially traditional lifestyle, so little comprehended by Anglo-Virginians, must have exacerbated the situation. Other white fears resulted from the Eastern Shore's very extensive shoreline and its concomitant vulnerability to raids from outside, as well as insurrection from inside. The Eastern Shore was badly harried by the British during the American Revolution, especially during 1779 and 1781, which left bad memories; the same thing happened again in the War of 1812, during which the Gingaskins were finally terminated. Attack from outside and a local population with divided loyalties could—and did, during the Revolution—make for chaotic times that left horrid memories for generations to come. Fueling all of these anxieties was the knowledge that the southern peninsula was geographically isolated from the mainland, so that help from other white Virginians was distant at best and impossible to send for or receive during really bad weather.[16]

The fears of the Gingaskins' neighbors about the supposedly subversive influence of free nonwhites upon the slaves ran high during the eighteenth century, slowing only temporarily during the liberal time of the American Revolution and early Federal period; the fears escalated greatly thereafter. Northampton County was a community heavily committed to slavery before the Civil War. Between 1790, the date of the first national census, and 1850, the portion of the county's population made up of slaves was between 43 and 50 percent. That proportion guaranteed considerable interracial contact and communication between whites and nonwhites, unlike the more heavily slave-populated regions in the Deep South.[17] But Northampton County whites were nevertheless decidedly pro-slavery, with all the attitudes the term implies. Those attitudes have been thoroughly documented in Winthrop Jordan's *White over Black*; the one that most concerns us here is the then-common belief that the presence of free nonwhites would automatically incite the slaves to resist, by insurrection or in other, more subtle ways. Free blacks were seen by many whites as an inherent threat to their control over their slaves, the major source of labor on the farms and in the shops, and thus as a threat to the whole structure of the community itself. Even a few free local blacks could be a source of anxiety; when the free African-American population was proportionally large, and especially when it was growing, white anxiety became acute.

Northampton County's free African-American population had roots far back in the seventeenth century, but until the American Revolution it seems to have been fairly small. Douglas Deal, who has specialized in the subject, estimates that it made up about 4 percent of the county's people in the 1720s.[18] Even that was a fairly high percentage for Virginia in 1790. Northampton's community would continue

Table 5.1. Virginia counties with the four highest free black populations
(% of total county population)

County	1790	1800	1810	1820	1830	1840
Northampton	6.6	10.4	12.1	13.0	15.4	
Charles City	6.5					14.0
York	6.8			14.4		13.8
Accomack		9.8	11.8	13.2	15.3	16.7
Nansemond		8.2	12.3		14.4	
James City			10.3	14.8	14.9	
Surry	5.9					16.5
Southampton		8.2				

Note: Cities such as Richmond, Petersburg, and Fredericksburg are omitted here;
after 1800 they had a higher proportion of free blacks in their population than
any county. Northampton dropped to 9.8 percent in 1840, far out of the top four.
(Figures calculated from county totals on U.S. Census Population Schedules.)

to be both large and rapidly expanding, compared to other counties
(table 5.1).

Note that Northampton's proportion of free blacks in the population
decreased seriously after 1830 (more precisely, 1831); the percentage
did not reach even 10 percent again until the Emancipation Proclamation had freed all blacks. Many other Virginia counties saw a decrease
in free blacks in the very racist 1830s, but Northampton had the second
largest percentage decrease in the state, and the largest among counties
that had big free black populations to begin with. It would seem, then,
that Northampton's situation with regard to free nonwhites was more
polarized than elsewhere.

There is some concrete evidence that the white population of Northampton was indeed more anxious about the free black "threat" than
the rest of the state. There were no social scientists to circulate question-
naires back then, but some kinds of historical documents can be used to
gauge attitudes among aggregates of people. A major genre in Virginia
in the eighteenth century through the Civil War is the legislative petitions, which both individuals and groups of citizens sent to Richmond
requesting that laws be passed. Northampton County filed more anti–
free black petitions in the state legislature than any other Virginia
county, and they began at an earlier date. In 1722–23 the county's

white citizens complained that they suffered damage because of "the great Number of ffree Negros Inhabiting within this County [then 4 percent of the population] are a great Grievance, more particularly because the Negro women pay no Taxes." In 1758 the citizens specifically asked the colonial government to have all free blacks deported. Northampton was also the source of anti-Gingaskin petitions that included strongly anti–free black sentiments. A few other Virginia counties produced petitions before 1831, but none of them were as early or as virulent as that Northampton one of 1758.[19]

Finally, in the terror-ridden aftermath of the Nat Turner Insurrection of August 1831, many (but by no means all) Virginia counties sent petitions to Richmond asking the state government to do something. Usually these petitions were prefabricated printed compositions; three versions circulated in the year following the insurrection, none of them suggesting any particular course of action. Only Northampton County's petition specified a solution to the free black "threat," namely, raising county funds to deport all free blacks who could be persuaded to leave. Only Nansemond County even came close to that definite a plan, sending one of the printed petitions in 1831 but going on in 1833 to ask for state funds for a deportation; the assembly failed to approve that less self-sufficient proposal.[20] Permission for Northampton County's plan came in 1832, and also permission for a change in the system of fund-raising in 1839. The county's legally funded program resulted in many free African Americans leaving in the decade of the 1830s. Local tradition, however, speaks of sometimes violent pressure being put on free nonwhites to be "willing" to leave. The then-reservationless Gingaskins would fall prey to that pressure. The evidence is good, then, that white anxiety about free blacks was higher in Northampton County than elsewhere, and that it led to more action being taken.

White slave owners wanted to control nonwhites, but they were foiled by the Gingaskins and, to a lesser extent, the free blacks. The Gingaskins especially could resist white control because they had treaty rights, albeit by tradition since they were not actually signers of the Treaty of Middle Plantation. Their treaty status enabled them to carry guns and, if prosecuted, to have jury trials just as whites did. They also could not be taxed out of any land they owned and then pressured into leaving, since the reservation was tax-exempt. Those few rights seem limited by modern standards, but compared to the legal position of free African Americans, especially as the nineteenth century dawned, the Indians were privileged people. There may well have been something to the white citizens' complaint that the Gingaskin reservation had become a "resort" for free blacks. The Indians' better legal status may have been a drawing card, making marital connections with Indian people desirable.

As time went on, the legal disabilities increased for nonwhites living outside a reservation. The seventeenth century was harsh enough: in 1668 the Virginia Grand Assembly stated flatly that blacks, even free ones, should not be "admitted to a full fruition of the exemptions and impunities of the English." After that the rising tide of antiblack legislation was halted only briefly by the American Revolution. In 1691 it became unlawful in Virginia for whites to marry any nonwhites whatever. In 1705, as an influx of black slaves continued to reach Virginia and more mulattoes—and quadroons and even octoroons—appeared in the colony, a "black code" was passed barring all nonwhites (including Indians away from their reservations) from holding office, serving in the militia, testifying in court against anyone (later modified to forbid testifying against whites), and even raising a hand against any white person for any reason. It was also made legally difficult to qualify as white: one had to be more than seven-eighths European in ancestry (modified to more than three-quarters in the slightly more liberal Federal period). In 1723 nonwhites were forbidden to vote.[21]

Manumissions were legalized in Virginia during the American Revolution, to encourage blacks to fight for Virginia instead of the English.[22] The result was mixed, as were the loyalties among white Eastern Shore residents. One historian has written that there was actually a mini–civil war on the southern Eastern Shore and in the Norfolk area. The result of the manumissions was a great increase in Virginia's free black population and, by the 1790s, a great increase in white fears about its attitudes and activities. The relative liberality of the early Federal period, due to both abolitionist movements and the influence of egalitarian-minded Baptist and, especially on the Eastern Shore, Methodist congregations, was short-lived. It was damaged in 1792 and the years following by the French and slave refugees from the Haitian revolution, who settled heavily in Virginia and caused Virginia more than any other state to seethe with rumors of plots. A 1792 plot for insurrection in Northampton County may have been a response to this event, though documentary evidence is lacking.

Liberality petered out altogether by 1806, when Virginia passed a law requiring all manumitted slaves to leave the state; the states to the north and west of Virginia did not want the migrants, so they soon passed legislation forbidding them to enter. Other discriminatory laws followed. Free blacks needed permission from the county to own firearms as of 1806; Samuel Beavans, the husband of a Gingaskin wife, got such a permission in 1811. The Overseers of the Poor, who could bind out indigent children without their parents' permission, were now forbidden to allow masters to teach nonwhite children to read. Free blacks in debt could be declared vagrants and sold as servants for a period of time. They were barred from being river pilots, the highest-paid job on a boat. They had to get a permit to sell agricultural produce, the assumption otherwise being that it was stolen. They had to carry certificates stating that they were of free birth, without which they could be arrested and sold as slaves. They had to get official permission to leave their home county, even on legitimate business. All of these laws were ultimately aimed at making living conditions for free blacks so miserable that they would leave. There were major colonization movements, hoping to send them to Africa, in the 1790s and 1820s. Some newly freed people did leave; others stayed, either by lying low and letting local whites neglect to enforce the law or by getting white friends to petition that they be allowed to stay. Many free blacks had such friends; white citizens may have feared free blacks in the aggregate, but they all knew individual free people whom they liked and respected. These legal disabilities meant that to an increasing extent in the eighteenth and early nineteenth centuries, free black citizens had some freedom but little real security.[23]

Ira Berlin has written that even with increasingly repressive laws, white slave owners failed to control free blacks fully because they did not have the time and manpower to force that segment of the population to conform in its every action with their wishes and values. Nonwhites' social resistance to white control could and did take many forms, many of them subtle and perfectly legal, such as avoiding working for white landowners, even when extreme poverty was the alternative. The illegal activities in which some nonwhites engaged were widely believed by whites to be both frequent and an overt flouting of white control. There may have been some deliberate display of disdain, but the frequency of the crimes was in fact quite low.

A survey of the Northampton County order books between 1750 and 1810 shows a limited number of free black appearances, and very few of the people involved could be called criminals. The vast majority of these court records involve indigent children being bound out, distantly followed by some women being prosecuted for bearing bastards, the father's race never being specified. Many more white children were bound out, in proportion to the larger white population in the county, and some white women were presented for bearing bastards, sometimes by black men.

In six decades there were only six prosecutions of free blacks for theft: three women were convicted, and two women and one man were acquitted. Several other free blacks, two of them women, were involved in two debt cases and half a dozen trespass and assault cases, sometimes as plaintiffs and sometimes as defendants, sometimes opposing fellow free blacks, other times whites. The outcomes varied, apparently according to the merits of the cases rather than for racial reasons. Only three nonwhite crimes that were committed against persons (rather than property) reached trial stage during those sixty years. A robbery and a rape were committed by slaves in the late 1790s, and the men who committed them were convicted. The third case was a stabbing done by one of the three free black women who got into trouble for fighting with other free black women. Esther Collins, who was tried for seriously wounding her opponent with a knife in 1803, was convicted of theft in 1808. She lived within the area of the Gingaskin reservation, after it was divided up and possibly before.

As for subversive activities, there were three cases in the county between 1750 and the termination of the Gingaskin reservation. One was minor: a free black man was acquitted in 1806 of "dealing with a slave." The other two cases were full-fledged plots for insurrection against the white people and were both nipped in the bud. In 1792 a free black man was convicted of plotting an insurrection against the whites, while the slaves accused with him were acquitted. The second case, in 1812, involved a Gingaskin Indian and will be discussed below.[24]

For a population that numbered less than 700 people in 1750–1800 and about 900 people in 1810, especially for a poverty-stricken social group living under a discriminatory legal system, the Northampton County free blacks' record is not one that suggests even a *moderate* amount of criminality. Yet the white landowners of Northampton County persisted in believing that the county's free African Americans were a major source of civil strife. Much of that belief must have been based upon prejudice against the people's lower-class origins and continuing lower-class way of life. It was the latter that put the free blacks into contact with the Gingaskins. It therefore behooves us to examine that population's origins and to compare its lifestyle with that of the reservation Indians.

Before the American Revolution the free black population in all the American colonies was small; in Virginia it has been estimated at about 350 in 1691 and about 2,800 in 1782. The five sources from which it sprang practically guaranteed its lower-class position. Some of its members were descended from Africans who were indentured servants rather than slaves or from African slaves who had managed to save the money to purchase their freedom. According to law, free black mothers passed their status on to their children, regardless of the race or status of the father. Both routes to freedom were possible in the mid-seventeenth century, and Douglas Deal has traced family histories that show them on the Virginia Eastern Shore.[25] The population's third source, a minor one before the Revolution, was emancipation of African slaves by their masters for reasons other than purchase. In 1691 Virginia passed a law requiring the removal of such people after emancipation (repealed in 1705), and in 1723 another law forbade any emancipations except for "meritorious service."[26] The population's fourth source was white mothers who had mulatto children by black fathers, free or slave; again, the mother's free status was passed on to her children. There were four such cases in Northampton County in 1750–1810. The fifth source was white fathers who had mulatto children by black slave women and emancipated them. Many slave mothers had mulatto children, judging by the great increase of mulattoes mentioned by writers of the early eighteenth century.[27] Such births do not appear in court records: slave mothers were not allowed to have husbands whose legal rights a lustful master could defy; they also did no damage to their masters by producing more slaves for them. Most white men, however, were content to leave their mulatto children in slavery; emancipations, which required legal action, were few in Virginia even before 1723. (And any enslaved Indian had a hard time making an emancipation stick: in 1728 such a boy, freed by his master's will, was taken into custody and sold by the parish churchwardens "as the Law directs.")[28]

Even in the more fluid seventeenth century, the socioeconomic status into which free black children were born was generally low. Deal has shown that such families on the seventeenth-century Eastern Shore were usually economically marginal, due in part to the sheer difficulty of functioning in a heavily prejudiced white system. Additionally, the founders of free black families always got a late start in life as citizens. Indentures and former slavery ate up people's productive years. Not only that, but in a family that was still purchasing the freedom of some of its members, any money that could be hoarded beyond bare subsistence needs had to be used to buy a spouse's or children's freedom rather than land. The mulatto children of white women or white men usually fared no better. Virginia's governor wrote in 1723 that "most of them are the Bastards of some of the worst of our imported servants and Convicts." [29] These parents were not likely to be well off economically at any time in their lives, and the children's illegitimacy carried a disabling stigma of its own. The relatively few prosperous white fathers who freed their mulatto children did so without formally recognizing them—the children are recorded as belonging to the mother, without a father being mentioned—and without feeling impelled to help them to any great extent afterward. Herbert Klein vividly contrasts this Virginia practice with the recognition and help that white Cuban fathers often dispensed, some going to the length of sending mulatto sons to college.[30] Free black children in Virginia were apt to be mulattoes rather than purely of African descent before the Revolution.[31] But paler skin did not help much: though many of them came from honest, hardworking families, such children nearly always "grew up poor."

The day-to-day lives of free blacks paralleled Indian ones in many respects, making the two communities congenial at the same time that they both contrasted increasingly with the lives of the better-off whites who ran the county. Most free blacks in Virginia worked as farmers, laborers, laundresses, seamstresses, and boatmen, the latter being a much-favored occupation because an all-black boat crew (possible before the legislation about pilots) could operate independently of whites. People in these occupations, whether black or white, often resembled the Indians in not operating on clock time. Boatmen were at the mercy of the weather; farmers and farm laborers had to pace themselves while working in the hot sun; and laundresses, seamstresses, and laborers may well have worked less enthusiastically because they were doing others' work.[32] As the eighteenth century went on and the white elite became more time-conscious, these people who worked on a traditional daily, monthly, or seasonal basis were increasingly perceived by that elite as being lazy.

Many free black farmers were tenants, and as such they were just as likely to get into debt as were poor whites. However, from the late 1790s onward they could be sold into servitude for those debts (or taxes, or fines), and servants' wages were extremely low. Getting into any trouble that resulted in a fine or debt therefore meant having to work for someone else for a long time to pay it off. Free black children, like those of poor Indians and whites, were apprenticed to more prosperous people so as to earn their keep. But the free black children were usually apprenticed to farmers, not to craftsmen who could teach them a trade. And after 1804 no master was to teach a free black child to read.[33]

A few free blacks refused to do wage work at all—fewer than some whites liked to claim—as an assertion of independence and to show the whites how much they relied on black labor. That, of course, aroused even more white dislike. Those who worked, even when they worked hard, did not make much, so practically all free black women were working wives (like Indian and many poor white wives). That fact inhibited the rise of patriarchy among the "lower orders," in another contrast with the elite.[34] Finally, many free black families, like other poor families, had to supplement their limited diet by foraging: hunting, fishing, berry picking, and the like. The working wives, the greater gender equality, and the foraging to supplement farming were all traditional Gingaskin customs. Most non-Indian people in Virginia continued living in "one- or two-room wooden houses with rude lofts, wooden chimneys, and earthen or wooden floors" until at least the last third of the eighteenth century, after which the middling classes began building somewhat larger frame houses. Though the middle stratum of Anglo-Virginian society began to acquire more furniture and changes of clothing after 1700, poor people's houses continued to be sparsely furnished, often without beds, and family members went on sleeping in their clothes.[35] The Gingaskins adopted the smaller Anglo-style houses sometime in the eighteenth century; they are spoken of as living in "houses" rather than "cabins" by 1812. Thus the "poor folks" among free blacks and whites were more congenial culturally with the Indians than had been the case in the mid-seventeenth century.

There were also ample opportunities for Indians and less prosperous non-Indians to meet. The communities in which free blacks lived and the social ties they maintained were complex and perfectly capable of including Indians. Many people, especially if indentured themselves, had close ties with slaves and servants locally. They were often fellow workers on farms, and the discrimination to which all of them were subjected could create real fellow feeling. (Other free African Americans, especially some mulattoes, distanced themselves from slaves in order to cultivate a better image with the whites.) Free black settlements, where they existed, often had a fluid membership and a rainbow-hued procession of visitors. The residents "squatted in shanties on scraps of land that no one else seemed to want. Tucked away well off the main road, these isolated cottages and shacks occasionally grew in number until they formed a small village whose general location was familiar to whites but whose fluctuating membership remained shrouded in mystery." Family composition fluctuated, too, not only from the usual family life history of children growing up and older members dying but also through members' employment (men on cargo boats were away for days or weeks; some jobs with white employers required living-in) and because of getting in trouble with the law, usually for debt. The free black settlements at any one time might not have many nuclear families, with a father, a mother, and their children. Instead families were likely to have three or more generations of people who were tied together in a variety of ways by blood, marriage, and adoption.[36] Visitors to the settlements could include whites, other free blacks, Indians, and even slaves, for slaves were sometimes allowed time off by their masters. The visitors could be of either sex, though they were probably more often male, and they might come to socialize, to court future spouses, or (especially in the case of higher-class white males) simply to engage in sexual liaisons.

Socializing with people from other communities (and races) was primarily a male phenomenon among the free people of eighteenth-century Virginia. Ever since humans began to practice plow farming, where men do the farming as well as the herding, women have been expected to remain close to home in the "domestic sphere." Thus for the last few millennia among many Old World peoples (though not among Native Americans and not in some African cultures), it has been men who had more freedom of movement and more opportunity to fraternize with people outside their own homes. Eastern Shore free black men (and later Gingaskin men) joined their white counterparts in this freedom, though the hard labor they performed often limited their time for it. Eighteenth-century Virginia saw the establishment of neighborhood stores, which often doubled as taverns. The multiracial customers at these centers were nearly all male; women usually sent male relatives, friends, or servants to buy things from them. Indeed, they were not congenial places for women. The leisure-time activities for gatherings of men—drinking, gaming, horse racing, arguing, and fighting among social equals—made for a competitive, violent world.[37] There was also a more gentle camaraderie as well. "After a long day in the woods, they might share a jug of sour mash and laugh at the aristocratic pretensions of local nabobs. . . . Common interests and the tedium of daily life drew [a free black man] and his neighbors together." Women, on the other hand, tended to form social circles, visiting each other's homes within a narrower geographical area, and emphasizing cooperation and charity. The Gingaskins would have fitted into these patterns nicely. The sexual segregation in non-Indians' work and leisure pursuits paralleled that in traditional Indian society; so did the allocation of competition to males and cooperation to females. The major place for both sexes to meet in Eastern Shore neighborhoods, especially in late eighteenth century with the Second Great Awakening, was the churches. The lower orders were drawn to the more evangelical forms of Christianity, for unlike the established Anglican (later Episcopal) Church, these forms placed very strong emphasis on equality of all believers before God, as well as a release of emotions that was not possible when working under upper-level white supervision.[38]

It may not be overstating the case to say that "under the pressure of common conditions, poor blacks and whites [and the Gingaskin Indians] became one. They lived together, worked together, and inevitably slept together, hopelessly blurring the color line."[39] Matters were made more complicated by the common practice of higher-class white males—and, more rarely, females—forming temporary or long-term liaisons within these communities. The economic and legal status of subsequent free black generations remained low. But any "whitening" of the population was seen as an advantage in color-conscious Virginia, for quasi-recognized kinship ties with the white fathers might confer advantages in time of trouble.[40]

The Gingaskins participated in some eighteenth-century liaisons with whites (one of the children produced was Brit Sunket, son of Elishe Sunket), and they also formed social and kinship ties with free blacks in the late eighteenth century. The small size of their population necessitated out-marriage, and the people in the poor white and free black communities had a lifestyle that in many ways resembled the Gingaskins' own. Once the Indians' native language was lost, the only major social difference between Indians and the poorer, free non-Indians was the reservation on which they lived. There they had somewhat better civil rights than other nonwhites, and they were exempt from the taxes that everybody else had to pay. Free blacks and some poor whites would have been congenial, as well as willing, partners. The Gingaskins probably sought such spouses, given their small population, as well as the other way around. But however the connections occurred, they brought the Gingaskins under more intense scrutiny by whites, resulting in more pressure to terminate the reservation and detribalize. That was especially true in wartime.

The American Revolution was a time of serious strife on the southern Eastern Shore. The white citizenry was badly divided about whom to fight for, with consequent bitter feelings that disrupted communities and even families. Both the Americans and the British offered slaves their freedom in exchange for going soldiering in their cause. The British made the offer first, and desertion of farms by slaves—who then guided British and loyalist boats into the creeks on raids—became common.[41] That did not sit at all well with pro-American white Virginians; they expected loyalty to a cause, their cause. In Northampton County that simply added to the disaffection driving people apart. The county's eventual winners, the pro-American whites, had ample reason to distrust nonwhites who either had fought for the British or seemed to have opposed them only after being promised freedom.

The southern Eastern Shore was exposed to repeated raids. In the summer of 1781 raids by British forces or American loyalists from the western shore became an "almost daily" occurrence.[42] The raiders plundered and burned whatever they could find. Northampton was not the only county to suffer in this way (Nansemond County suffered severely), but its white freeholders felt strongly that their county's isolation had attracted British plunderers. The raids and the perceived exhaustion of the soil on their farms led them to ask permission in 1782 to pay their taxes in salt, rather than the more usual tobacco, hemp, or flour. By 1783 none of the county's four warehouses for the inspection of tobacco was still in operation, seriously hindering economic recovery. Everyone was hurting, but Northampton County's whites were unusual in petitioning Richmond in 1784 for an amelioration of the debt collection laws.[43] The same year saw the first petition against the continued survival of the Gingaskins' reservation. The "liberal" period in white attitudes toward nonwhites evident in other parts of the fledgling United States did not extend to Indians in Northampton County.

The Allotment and Termination of the Gingaskins

In November 1784 white landowners in the county asked the Virginia legislature to allow part of the reservation to be leased out.[44] That in itself was nothing new, but the complaints about the reservation's inhabitants had a new vehemence. The Indians, they claimed, were now very few: "five or six; whom fondness for fishing, fowling & hunting, the natural insolence of their disposition, & their disinclination to Agriculture" made into potentially dangerous neighbors. Worse than that, non-Indians were moving in: "the said Land is at present an Asylum for free Negroes & other disorderly persons, Who build Hutts thereon & pillage & destroy the Timber without controul to the great Inconvenience of the honest Inhabitants of the Vicinity, who have ever considered it a Den of Thieves & Nuisance to the Neighborhood." That statement about disorderliness and thievery was not, of course, historically accurate. The Indians' tax-free status also irritated the petitioners: leases would be a "saving to the Public (the Lands being at present exempt from taxation)." The signers of the petition included three neighbors of the Gingaskins, one of them Littleton Savage.

The General Assembly apparently allowed the leasing. Commissioners were appointed by the county to inquire into "all such persons as may be residing on the Lands appropriated to the use of the said Indians contrary to Law." Their report, filed in January 1785, stated that "the several families of free negroes and others [presumably whites], who have formed settlements within the bounds of the said lands," had done so with Indian permission but with no other claim to possession. They also found that a free black man, Abraham Lang, used Indian land because he had married one of the Indian women, even though for some years he had lived with another woman off-reservation. The county then appointed new commissioners and gave them broader power "to take into their Care & management the said Indians Lands." Four men were prosecuted in 1792 "for tending the Indians' Land," but the cases were dropped for reasons not given in the records.[45]

That was not enough for some white citizens in Northampton County. In October 1787 two more petitions went to Richmond, one written by Gingaskin neighbor Littleton Savage, the great-grandson of the Thomas Savage who knew Powhatan and Pocahontas.[46] The Gingaskin reservation had originally been taken out of his family's large plantation. Now that the extinction of the Gingaskins was at hand, he said, he expected the land to be returned.

The other petition, which Savage also signed and which demanded the sale of the whole reservation, specified why the Gingaskins were supposedly going extinct. There were now "not more than three or four of the genuine Indians at most," a judgment probably based upon the Gingaskins' physical appearance: most non-Indians then and now unrealistically expect "real Indians" to be nothing less than full bloods. The Indian men, most of whom followed their traditional occupations on the water without trying to make a profit, remained misunderstood. They allegedly let others till their lands because they themselves were "little disposed to industry and unacquainted with Husbandry, . . . while they abandon themselves almost solely to the employments of fishing and fowling, from which they chiefly derive a Maintenance." The women's horticulture seemingly did not count. Despite the leases recently approved, the petitioners went on to complain that "the greatest part of their lands have never been in [agri]culture, nor yielded them any support, but on the contrary have remained for many years waste and unemployed, while the Timber with which it was formerly abundantly supplied has been so wantonly pillaged by the adjacent Neighbourhood that it is mostly destroyed." Presumably non-Indian owners (not lessees) would be more effective in keeping the woodlot from being ravaged. The petitioners also complained about the reservation's tax-free status and its supposed harboring of miscreant free blacks. Therefore the petitioners wanted the reservation land sold out from under its residents and the money used "to the maintenance of such of the said Indians as appear to be genuine descendants of the Tribe to whom the said Land was granted."

The General Assembly rejected both petitions. However, it perceived that something was wrong, for without another petition's being submitted, in 1792 it passed a law allowing Northampton County to appoint trustees with the power of leasing land, distributing the money to Indians, and also settling disputes that arose among either themselves or the Indians. Trustees were duly appointed in 1793 "for protecting the rights of the Gingaskin Tribe of Indians."[47] One of these men, Griffin Stith, reported to the governor a few months later that the reservation lands had been surveyed. But he hinted strongly that he thought the denizens of the reservation were not worth taking much trouble over. "The known habits of Indolence and aversion from every kind of profitable labour in which these people live, were, I presume, the motives which had induced the late Governor to adopt in their favor so indulgent a means of vindicating their rights." Stith was not an ideal trustee, but it is unlikely that the county's justices could have found anyone less prejudiced.

Either the Gingaskins did not know about the petitions against them, or they knew but chose to ignore them. They continued not only to marry or adopt congenial outsiders (from necessity) but also occasionally to get into trouble of a mild sort. The Gingaskin who appears most frequently in the court records in the next two decades is Edmund Press. He was sued for debt in 1788 and sued again and complained against (with his wife) for disturbing the peace in 1793. Scarburgh Bingham, who had been bound out as a boy in 1762, died in 1793 while being sued for causes unspecified. Betty Drighouse lost her daughter Esther, and "Polly" (Molly Fisherman) Press, wife of Littleton Press, lost her son George when the children were bound out for indigence; in 1805 Molly Press went to court to have the executor of the white master's estate show cause why he "detains her child," and the boy was then freed.[48] The poverty of the Gingaskins seems well documented from these records. Some of the impoverishment was a lack of cash, a condition frowned upon according to prevailing white standards. Some of it may also have been due to prejudice because Indian men continued to downplay farming as an occupation, though that situation appears to have begun changing. By 1812 the Gingaskins claimed that their men had become farmers, an assertion difficult to corroborate since the Gingaskins of that decade, unlike the ones of the 1820s, left no mortgages or deeds of trust that might list tools and household goods as collateral. The male farmers in question may have been non-Indian husbands.

In 1794 several dozen nonwhite people in Northampton County registered the fact of their free birth. Virginia had passed a law the year before making it mandatory for urban free blacks to register or be arrested and sold; all free blacks had to register from 1803 onward.[49] Perhaps Northampton's rural people did it so early in reaction to the virulent local prejudice. Several people with Gingaskin connections registered. They included future Indian allottees Mary (Press?) Beavans, Betsy Collins, and William Weeks; also James Carter (with a Gingaskin wife and son), Samuel Beavans (with a Gingaskin wife), and Jacob Thompson (husband of the daughter of the only Gingaskin man and woman then married to each other).[50] Technically, Indians who lived on the reservation would not have needed certificates of freedom, but registering may have seemed a sensible precaution.

The tithe list for Northampton County in 1810 shows a few "Indians" and a considerable number of non-Indian men living at "Indian Town" as heads of household. The only Gingaskin men were Edmund Press and Thomas Baker; the lone Indian woman was Betty Drighouse (listed without a racial designation). Otherwise, all the household heads were non-Indians. None were slave owners, but most owned one or two horses.[51]

The event that triggered the reservation's dissolution occurred in June 1812.[52] On the eleventh of that month a court was called to examine several men charged with preparing for an insurrection among the slaves, which was to have taken place the previous week. "John Francis and Edmund Press, free negroes," and also Edmund Francis, Thomas Francis, Ben Wallace, and four slaves were tried; all were acquitted except John Francis, who was sent to be tried at the superior court. Edmund Press was a Gingaskin; John and Thomas Francis had been the husbands of Gingaskin women since the 1790s. The conspiracy was said to have been hatched at Thomas Francis's house, which was on the reservation. Edmund Francis, who turned state's evidence, testified that the conspirators molded bullets to use "to take the white people," among other things. There were several conspirators involved, so word of the plot must have leaked.

What was significant for the Gingaskin tribe was that one of its men and two of its married-in husbands were accused of a subversive undertaking, even though only one of them was actually convicted. The imminent outbreak of another war between the United States and the British cannot have helped soothe the white citizens' feelings. So now the trustees of the Gingaskin tribe went to work to try to persuade the Indians to take the first step toward dissolving the reservation and leaving the scene.

In December 1812, the very month the War of 1812 began, the Gingaskins and their trustees petitioned the Virginia General Assembly for division of the reservation and the allotment of individual shares in fee simple to qualified Indians. The petition does not admit any wrongdoing in the community on the part of the Indians, but it does echo the two petitions from the 1780s in its description of conditions then obtaining on the reservation. Part of the tribal land had been rented out since 1792, the money being distributed among the Indians. But in recent years the fences around the rental plots had decayed, and there was not sufficient timber left on the reservation to repair them; the plots were currently almost unrentable. Meanwhile, the "members of the tribe have greatly increased within these twenty years," so that rent money was entirely insufficient to support them. Future increase in population "will add to this difficulty; the Tribe having long since forsaken their original habits of Hunting fishing etc. for a living, and applied themselves to the cultivation of the Earth, & other civil employments." Now the Indians supposedly wanted their agricultural plots in individual ownership; the trustees certainly wanted to be relieved of their duties. Eleven Indians signed.[53]

Accompanying the petition was a letter from trustee George Parker giving more details, many of them negative. Parker felt that the reservation and the Indians had gone steadily downhill:

> in the early part of my acquaintance with this Land, a large proportion of it was in woods, and the only occupants of it were Indians, except of that part which was leased, which consisted of one Tenement only. Now there is no woodland of value on it, the Indian women have, many of them, married black-men, and a majority, probably, of the Inhabitants are Blacks, or have black-Blood in them; the houses & Housekeepers, are 13 or 14, and there are frequent applications to the Trustees to build more, which has been refused, on the ground of there being no woods to support them in firewood & Rails, and that every house built would so far increase the nuisance, as it would probably add one more harbour & receptacle for Rogues, & stolen goods; it is genuinely believed since the introduction of so many free negroes and mulattoes into the Town, that it has become a place of resort, for the most vicious part of the black population, for the most injurious and abandoned purposes; each one of the house-keepers has his little field of corn, oats &c and of course, it is difficult to prove, when they sell these articles, that they have been stolen, it is, however, genuinely believed, that much of what they do sell is obtained illegally, of this, however, the real Indians, of which there are but few now, are not accused or suspected, I believe.

Parker confirmed that the insurrection plot six months earlier had made the local whites eager for the reservation's demise.

The trustees had first suggested that the reservation be sold and the resulting money distributed, then that the leased land be sold and the remaining reservation land allotted to individuals. "They [the Gingaskins] would accede to neither of these proposals; it was then proposed to them to divide the whole of the Land among such as may be considered entitled, by Trustees & each to hold separately from the other; to this they have agreed." Parker and his fellow trustees wanted any law enabling allotment to specify that no "free-negro or mulatto," even one descended from "a female Indian," be allowed on the divided-up reservation, except for the men the Gingaskin women married. Thus the reservation land would "probably soon pass into the hands of white people, by contract," and the free black "nuisance" would be eliminated. "The families, now, I believe are 13 or 14, the whole number of the Tribe 50 or 60." [54]

In February 1813 the Virginia legislature passed a law allowing the division of the Gingaskin reservation and the allotment of parcels of the land to qualified Indians. [55] The plots would be held in fee simple; there was no restriction on who could live on them or how soon they could be sold. Since Indians legally remained "Indian" in Virginia only as long as they possessed a reservation, this law terminated the Gingaskins as a legally constituted tribal entity. Nothing protected the new landowners from being pressured into immediate sales or from taxation until they could gear up their economy for the new expense. As soon as they received their land, they were detribalized and legally on their own.

The dividing-up of the lands was done by local commissioners who did their work slowly and carefully. However, they made no provision for Indians who were then children; they allotted land to "those of the Tribe who are now of proper age to be housekeepers," which meant twenty-seven adults (fig. 5.4). The commissioners also laid off "the [new] public Roads through the said Lands." The Seaside Road (now County Route 600) was run through the reservation; presumably it had run around it before. And the road going eastward from the courthouse to the reservation boundary (now County Route 631, Willow Oak Road) was to be extended all the way to the waterfront, at Indian Town Landing. [56] Each Gingaskin adult received about twenty-five and a half acres of land.

If the white landowners of Northampton County expected the Gingaskins to sell and move out fast, they were disappointed. Most Gingaskins or their heirs held onto their land and relinquished it only during the fierce reactions to the August 1831 Nat Turner slave insurrection.

Only six Indians sold their land within three years of allotment, two of them retaining an interest in all or part of their allotments and some of the other sellers staying on in the area as landless people. Edmund Press, whose departure many whites may have hoped for, sold his land in April 1816, but he kept the right to live on it for the remainder of his

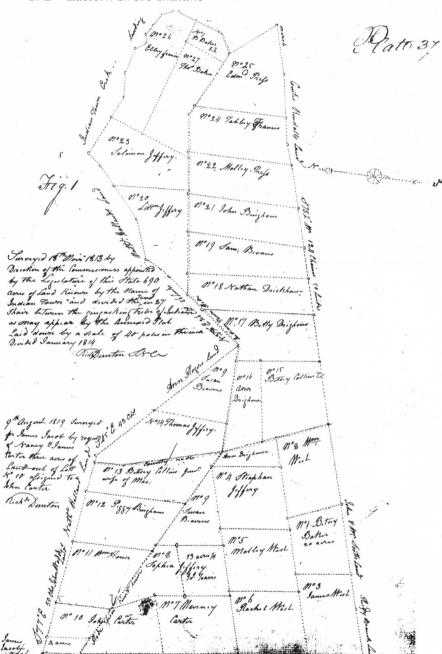

Fig. 5.4 Plat of the division of the Gingaskin reservation in 1813 (Northampton County Courthouse)

life. Solomon Jeffery kept a life interest in five acres in 1815, Rachel and Molly West sold their parcels altogether in 1814, William West or Weeks sold his plot in 1816, and James West sold his in 1814 but bought a nonreservation acre in 1816, retaining it until 1831. West also took the precaution of getting himself legally exempted from taxes because of his "Indian extraction" before he sold his allotment.[57]

Two more Gingaskins or their heirs held out considerably longer but sold their land apparently without direct compulsion being applied. William House sold twenty acres of his plot in 1814, but he did not sell the rest until a month before the Nat Turner Insurrection. Tabby Press Francis died in 1828 still in possession of her allotment. Two months later her widower, Thomas Francis, sold all except the house, one acre of land, and the timber growing on the whole allotment. Two daughters inherited what was left; "Susan Francis free negro" sold her reversionary rights in 1829 after her father's death, but her sister Louisa Francis did not sell her portion until 1857.[58]

That left nineteen other chunks of the reservation—more than two-thirds of the land—whose owners, or their heirs, still held onto all or part of their rights through the year 1830. Selling out quickly and leaving was not a Gingaskin pattern.

However, the Gingaskins' hold on their remaining land would prove to be precarious, as was their social position in the county. They were now officially free negroes, except perhaps for James West; former allottee William West registered as a free black person in 1827, and other allottees' children did so later. There continued to be occasional tensions with non-Indians; the Gingaskins involved were both landless ones (Rachel West, James West) and those who still had their allotments (Littleton Jeffery). George Press, son of Molly Fisherman and Littleton Press, registered as a free black man in September 1829, although he was the son of two Indians, one of whom had lived long enough to be an allottee. Two of George's siblings, Edmund and Betsy (or Eliza) Press, were prosecuted that same month for not "having a certified copy of the register of their freedom within the last twelve months." The two were taken to court again in December of that year, still not having their copies made. Meanwhile, the Overseers of the Poor bound out a Drighouse girl and an eight-year-old Edmund Press.[59]

No Gingaskins, with or without land, prospered in the 1820s. The county records show them mortgaging their property to stay afloat; there are also two estate inventories from that decade that show the relatively low value of the Indians' possessions. The property lists are interesting, though, because the livestock, farm gear, and household implements show that the Gingaskins' way of life by 1820 had become very anglicized. They owned horses, an occasional ox, cows, hogs, geese, turkeys, and chickens (no guinea fowl are mentioned). Some records indicate ownership of canoes, horse carts, and cart furnishings. Some Indians' farm gear indicated the practice of plow agriculture (e.g., William Weeks, Littleton Jeffery), while other families (e.g., William House) lacked it but sometimes had other income-producing tools (e.g., James West with a half interest in a canoe and black husband William Francis with shoemaker's equipment). Furniture in the people's houses consisted of several chairs and at least one bed with bedding; Charles and Ann Drighouse Pool had three feather beds in 1829. Mrs. William House and Mrs. Littleton Jeffery both had spinning wheels, while Peggy Bingham Francis (Mrs. William) had two of them; Mrs. Jeffery and Betsy Shepherd Collins each had a loom. Molly Press had a linen wheel and flax to spin on it when she died in 1826. Ceramic bowls (not "Indian" ones) and metal pots, pans, and spoons were common; Littleton Jeffery's more prosperous household had a considerable variety of these things, none of them very valuable.[60]

Just as the Gingaskins and their connections tended to hold onto their allotted lands, they also tended to rely on each other socially, in a network indicating that loosened tribal connections persisted nonetheless for some time. The best evidence comes from several marriages in 1826–31.[61] One of them occurred in 1828 when Mary Francis, daughter of the Gingaskin Ebby Baker Francis and her husband John (indicted in the insurrection plot of 1812), chose a free black man, George Stephens, as her guardian; five days later ward and guardian married. As Molly Stephens, she would appear later in the century as "the Ingin Queen."

The Nat Turner slave insurrection of August 1831 caused a wave of horror to sweep across Virginia and adjacent states. It caused more than that to surface in Northampton County: an active program of eliminating the free black population was undertaken there. It did not matter that no free blacks were involved in the insurrection, which occurred nearly a hundred miles away. "Whites directed their frenzied outrage not so much against slaves as against free negroes. . . . It made no sense to cripple valuable slave property or to limit the liberty of those who had none. The slaves' position, which sheltered them from white vigilantism, seemed to intensify the abuse heaped on the free negroes. Their presence reminded a people who professed, above all, to value liberty and despise tyranny that they themselves were tyrants. . . . The free Negro, in short, personified the dangers and guilt inherent in owning slaves."[62]

Where other Virginia counties only asked the state government to do something about the "menace" of free blacks, the Northampton County whites held a mass meeting at the courthouse around November 11 and decided upon a self-sufficient plan of action, which they got the state legislature to approve. The resulting law of 1832 allowed county money to be collected for the removal of "free people of colour"—a broader term that could include Indians—from the county. Even if some Gingaskins had applied and qualified for the new racial status set up the next year, "persons of mixed blood, not being negroes or mulattoes" (and none of them did, either through ignorance of the law or because of too much free black ancestry), it is unlikely that they would have escaped the pressure that their paranoiac white neighbors now put on them to leave.[63] Vigilantism cannot be documented in the surviving governmental records, but oral traditions about it in Northampton County were still strong nearly a century later. Many free nonwhites in the county chose to leave.

Most of the Gingaskins still owned and lived on allotments of reservation land; though sales had created some gaps, the people still essentially lived in a clump of contiguous holdings. Pressure was therefore brought to bear on Indian landowners to make them disperse if not leave. The pressure worked: November 1831 saw a spate of sales or court cases to get heirs to agree on selling. Most of the sales and court cases were dated within a six-day period, November 14–19, shortly after the mass meeting at the courthouse. Most of these sales lacked any retention by the sellers of life interests.[64] One such outright sale was of a plot with a boundary that is still visible as a farm lane through a field (fig. 5.5).

The mass nature of the 1831 sales is shown by the legally required separate acknowledgments of those sales: two allottees and several of the heirs came to the courthouse and did the acknowledging all at once, on November 14. And even a former Gingaskin allottee, who had long since parted with his share of the reservation, decided that he had better clear out: on November 8, 1831, James West and his wife sold the acre of land they had bought off-reservation in 1816. Ingress to the former reservation land was improved very shortly after so many Indians sold out; apparently the 1813 order about opening the road from the court-

Fig. 5.5 The lane marking the old boundary of the Betty and Nathan Drighouse allotments, Gingaskin reservation, in 1970

house in Eastville eastward to Indian Town Landing had not been fully carried out. Now a view was to be taken of "conveniences and inconveniences" for the new (white) landowners that would result if that road "shall be opened."[65]

In spite of all the pressure to leave and new white owners' immediate taking of possession, three Gingaskins and their heirs managed to retain entire plots of reservation land beyond 1831. Sophia Jeffery (married to free black Thomas Carter in 1803) had a plot of her own and one inherited from Stephen Jeffery, possibly a brother. In 1816 she sold half of her own allotment, but the buyer had to pay her in money and also build her a log house on the other half. In 1831 she sold her remaining half allotment, but she held onto the inherited parcel. She died sometime after 1831, and her heirs, Betsy Collins the elder (Mrs. Robert Powell) and then her daughter and granddaughter, resisted selling until 1846. Peggy Bingham (1788–1853, Mrs. William Francis from 1829) mortgaged her plot in 1822, resisted selling in 1831, and finally let the land go in 1835. She and her husband remained in Northampton County, for he bought two acres of nonreservation land in 1856.[66]

One of the very last Gingaskin descendants to sell her rights in an allotment from the old reservation was Molly Stephens, who in the 1860s styled herself "the Ingin Queen." Her mother, Ebby (Elizabeth) Baker, married the white man Hezekiah Shepherd in 1787 and became the mother of Betsy Shepherd Collins (allottee Betsy Collins the Younger); in 1792 Ebby married the free black man John Francis, who was tried for plotting an insurrection twenty years later. The Francis children were too young to be allottees in their own right in 1813; instead they inherited her plot together. Ebby never sold her land; two months after she died in 1835, her daughter Molly's husband bought out the interest of one of the two other Francis children. (Ebby is called "a free Indian woman" in that deed but a "free coloured woman" in a later one.) In 1838 Molly and George Stephens, "free negroes," sold Molly's and her sibling's shares in the allotment. However, Molly was still her remaining sibling's eventual heir, and she did not sell out until 1847. Only one other Gingaskin heir, Louisa Francis, held out longer.[67]

Many Gingaskin descendants who had lost their title to reservation lands stayed on in the county, as Molly Stephens did. In fact, some of them went on living in the immediate area. A map of 1855, made soon after the railroad was run down the Virginia Eastern Shore, shows a cluster of seven houses, called "Indian Town," on either side of the head of Indiantown Creek, north of the former reservation (see fig. 5.3).[68] It was primarily the mapmaker, however, who regarded the inhabitants as Indians. Legally the people were free blacks, and even some original Gingaskin allottees registered as such as the county courthouse. Mid-November 1831, at the same time as the spate of sales, saw registrations by allottees Molly Press Beavans, Betty Drighouse, Peggy Bingham Francis, and the children of several allottees (e.g., Peggy Francis and Molly Press). The next month allottee Sophia Jeffery and one of the two Betsy Collinses also registered. Allottees' children had been expected to register at least since 1829; they went on doing it.[69] It is in the records of the free black community, and the non-Indian community at large, that the later history of individual Gingaskin descendants lies.[70] That history is beyond the scope of this book.

Some Gingaskin descendants preserved a tradition of Indian ancestry, but public announcements of that ancestry were few. Part of their reticence in public may have stemmed from embarrassment at the behavior of Molly Stephens, who was all too publicly both Indian and a heavy drinker. She fit an all-too-common stereotype that non-Indians hold about Indians. Molly was a public nuisance by the early 1860s, according to the turn-of-the-century local historian Thomas Upshur.[71] Upshur's account is a bit florid by today's standards, but he relates an incident which probably really happened:

> Even as late as 1862, or later, one Mollie Stephens, when she got tipsy—as she frequently did—would shout, "I'm the Ingin Queen!" and persons much older than herself said that she was doubtless the daughter of the last Gingaskin King, a queen without maids of honor to minister unto her—a sovereign without vassals to command. Upon one occasion, when decidedly unsteady from too many potations of "fire-water," and she had, judging by the dusty and muddy appearance of her gown, been down in the gutter "feeling upward for the ground," she came dancing, as usual, through the piazza of the hotel . . . in Eastville, where some gentlemen were sitting, among them a certain attorney-at-law, who became one of our court judges, and who was attired, as usual, in the most tidy and careful manner, with immaculate white linen trousers and Marseilles vest. As Mollie passed him she shouted, "Ugh! Ugh! I'm the Ingin Queen! I'm the Ingin Queen!" and losing her balance at that moment, sat down suddenly in his lap. This raised a laugh at his expense, and he became so much incensed that he caused her arrest and incarceration, but recovered his temper a short time after, and had her released.

Molly had lived long enough to see drastic changes in the fortunes of the Gingaskins and their descendants. If the age she gave to the federal census taker in 1850 was correct, she was born in the year that the reservation was allotted. She grew up in a community of Indians and their non-Indian spouses that was still reasonably cohesive and grouped together geographically. Married in 1828 to George Stephens, a man some twenty years older, she saw as a young matron the breakup of most of the rest of the reservation; her mother was one of the few allottees who held out. She watched her people become "free negroes" regardless of the amount of their Indian ancestry, while the laws passed by the Virginia legislature became ever more stringent, aimed at making all "free negroes" leave. Many of Northampton County's free nonwhites and some of Molly's relations did leave. But Molly and her husband, who seems to have been a respectable, steady man, listed in the 1850 census as a wagoner, stayed on nevertheless. After her sister's daughter died, Molly turned loose the last rights to her mother's Indian land. She and her husband went on living on the twenty-five acres he owned elsewhere in the county; in 1850 he owned $900 worth of real estate. But after 1850 Molly's personal fortunes went downhill. Her husband died, as had most of her close relatives already, and by 1857 she was in financial trouble. She mortgaged the land she inherited from her husband in that year, and the next year she lost it when the mortgage was foreclosed.[72]

By 1862, when she had become a town character, Molly Stephens was landless, husbandless, and surrounded by white neighbors who openly thought her not only inferior as a nonwhite but also amusing when she claimed to be an Indian, like her mother's people. Their attribution of her "queenship" to being the "daughter of the last Gingaskin King" shows how little the local whites remembered about the real Gingaskins and how willing they were to romanticize—and make harmless—the early nineteenth-century Indians. For someone who remembered her relatives so differently, it must have been very hard.

Epilogue

The end of the Eastern Shore Indian reservations did not, of course, bring the story of the Eastern Shore Indians to a close. The Nanticokes seem to have taken in many people from other groups before 1750; those who subsequently went to live among the Six Nations maintained their tribal identity as members of the Wolf clan of the Senecas and traveled with the Six Nations in their migrations to Canada and to the American Midwest. Many descendants of the Nanticokes now live in Oklahoma, along with other tribes and clans of the Six Nations. That story has been told by C. A. Weslager in his book *The Nanticoke Indians Past and Present*.[73]

Other Eastern Shore Indians never left the region, even after the reservation system ended, and their descendants live there today. What these Indian people lost when their towns were abolished or allotted was legal recognition of their identity as a separate people and, later, of part of their ancestry. The loss in legal terms is well attested in the historical record; the retention or loss of an Indian identity in private is much harder to document.

Throughout the nineteenth century both the state governments and the federal government, by failing to acknowledge the existence of a nonreservation Indian population, tacitly adopted the viewpoint that there were no Indians on the Eastern Shore. Early federal census records for both Maryland and Virginia list any Indians who were not living on reservations as "Other Free Persons," a general catchall category for any free persons not classed as "White." [74] Most people in this category were free blacks, but it is clear that nonreservation Indians, lacking treaty rights, were included. In later federal census lists and in state and county records from the Eastern Shore, people of Indian descent were usually classed as "negroes," "mulattoes," or "free colored" persons. Census takers and other nineteenth-century government officials tended to lump anyone who was not perceived as white under one of these labels. The specific racial classification assigned to a nonwhite person seems to have depended on the subjective judgment of the census taker.

The administrative merging of the Indian and free black populations makes it very difficult to study or understand the real pattern of involvement between Native Americans and non-Indians on the Eastern Shore. Nineteenth-century scholars writing about contemporary Indian communities along the whole eastern seaboard often implied or stated outright that the people in these communities were not properly Indians at all. Many believed that even the surviving Indian reservations in the region had lost all their culture and even their racial identity through long interaction with the non-Indian populations that surrounded them.

In slave states like Maryland and Virginia, Indians who remained in their traditional homelands generally were considered so extensively intermixed with African Americans that they had forfeited the right to be treated as a separate racial group. This viewpoint became particularly common as the Civil War approached. The virulent racism in the American South at the time viewed everyone as being either black or white. After the Civil War this bipolar view of race continued in all of the former slave states, even those like Maryland and Delaware that had never seceded from the Union. There was no longer any room in southern society for persons who claimed to be neither white nor black. Racism of this sort certainly influenced the observations of the nineteenth-century Maryland historians John Leeds Bozman and James Thomas Scharf when they wrote about the Indians of the Eastern Shore. [75]

While some Virginia Eastern Shore Indians did take African-American spouses from at least the late eighteenth century onward, there is no historical basis for the common nineteenth-century assertion that the people on the Maryland reservations intermarried heavily with "negroes." There is not a single contemporary reference to a slave or a free black living in any of the Maryland Eastern Shore Indian towns any time before the dissolution of the reservations. The only Indians recorded as marrying African Americans were people who detribalized. There is also no evidence that the Maryland reservations became havens for runaway slaves or free black troublemakers, charges that were made about the Gingaskins in Virginia because intermarriages had occurred.

After the dissolution of the Eastern Shore reservations, it seems plausible that Indians remaining in the region would have drawn closer to the African-American community there; genealogies show that it did happen with the Gingaskins. Most nineteenth-century whites in both states were unwilling to accept Indians as equals, but there is no evidence of similar prejudice among either slave or free African Americans.

During the late eighteenth and early nineteenth centuries, free black settlements appeared to grow up on or near the sites where Indian reservations had been. One of the earliest on the Eastern Shore, a community now called Taylor's Gate, began to develop in the 1750s on the northern part of the former Askiminikansen reservation.[76] Two other free black communities, Rabbit Town and Santo Domingo, developed near the old Chicone reservation during the first quarter of the nineteenth century. Perhaps some early inhabitants of these free black settlements were Indians rather than African Americans. One of the surnames associated with early nineteenth-century Rabbit Town is Quash, which may equate with the common Chicone Nanticoke surname of Ashquash.[77]

However, even if Eastern Shore Indians lived in free black settlements during the early nineteenth century, and even if they were considered to be free blacks by white county officials, it cannot be assumed that these Indians had been completely assimilated into the free black population. Some of the Nanticokes of southern Delaware tried to reassert their identity as Indians as early as 1855.[78] Individuals and families alike maintained an awareness of their Indian heritage long after the Eastern Shore reservations ceased to exist and long after white officialdom ceased to believe that there were any more Indians in the region.

As the twentieth century began, the belief that there were no more real Indians on the Eastern Shore persisted even within the white academic community. When James Mooney of the Smithsonian Institution published his influential paper "The Aboriginal Population of America North of Mexico" in 1928, he stated flatly that "not a single full-blood survives" in the region, as though real Indianness required full-bloodedness. He was willing to concede only that about eighty Nanticokes and twenty Wicomicos of "mixt" ancestry still remained.[79] In

1907 he had written that "there are still individuals among the Maryland blacks who claim strains of Nanticoke, Piscataway, and Wicocomoco blood." Of the Virginia Eastern Shore he wrote: "The few [Indians] who remained at the beginning of the last century had become so mixed with negro blood that in the general alarm occasioned by the Nat Turner slave rising in 1831 they had been classed as full negroes and driven from their homes, so that their identity was lost. . . . there are said to be a very few mixed-bloods still living in the neighborhood of Accomac Courthouse (Drummondtown) in Accomack county; and also a few . . . near Fisher's Inlet, in southern Northampton County." [80] There were probably considerably more Indian descendants around in the counties than that.

It was not until pioneer ethnologist Frank G. Speck began researching the Nanticoke community at Indian River in southern Delaware that scholars began to pay serious attention to the question of surviving Native American groups on the Delmarva Peninsula. Speck's work inspired a few other researchers like Weslager to pursue the ethnohistory of the Nanticokes; these studies focused on groups living in Delaware, however. On the Virginia Eastern Shore, where Gingaskin descendants lived less cohesively and amid more prejudice, fewer scholars were interested until recently—and then racial identities got in the way. One of us (Rountree) made a tentative investigation in Northampton County in 1970 but found the Gingaskin descendants unwilling to talk to her because she is white.

Several formal organizations of people publicly claiming Indian descent appeared on the southern Maryland Eastern Shore in the 1980s; one began hosting a powwow in 1994.[81] There undoubtedly are individuals and families of Indian descent still living on the Maryland and Virginia Eastern Shore. However, the continued survival of reservationless Indian-descended groups remains a topic yet to be documented by scholars.

Six

Geography, Ecology, and the Eastern Shore Tribes

IN EXAMINING THE historical and social processes played out by the Eastern Shore Indian tribes and their English adversaries, we cannot simply describe what European writers saw and what people did in the Contact period. We need to go further, explaining why people acted the way they did, and that means including the heavy influences of both geography and ecology, themselves intertwined.[1] Geography often impacts human societies throughout their history, regardless of the kind of economy those societies practice. Geographical distances become even more important when a native population comes under pressure from outsiders and seeks first reinforcement and later refuge with other still-strong native populations. Ecology is a dominant factor in the lives of people who, like the natives of the Chesapeake region, make part of their living each year by foraging; ecology also becomes indirectly important to anyone who deals with such people—or tries to comprehend them, as we are doing. And we need to take into account the details of local ecology: not just where the fur-bearing animals were plentiful, but also where specific Indian foods could be found for the hungrier seasons.[2] Native people's continuing access to specific foods (and the lands producing them) had a great impact upon the survival of their traditional culture all across North America; on the Eastern Shore that access, coupled with geographical proximity to still-strong groups like the Iroquois, also determined whether they stayed or left the region.

The Eastern Shore Indians were not culturally uniform in late prehistoric times; there are hints in the records that the tribes of the Virginia Shore differed from both the Maryland Shore people and the western shore tribes across the Chesapeake. The historic Virginia and Maryland colonies did not act identically toward the aboriginal inhabitants, either, although both colonies stemmed from early seventeenth-century English efforts. They differed in the way they overran the peninsula and in their policies toward native people. The natives' reactions to being invaded and their decisions to leave or remain also varied from north to south. In all of these differences, geography and ecology played a major explanatory role. They are, after all, major limiting factors (though not absolute determining factors) in the two issues that most deeply affect the behavior of human populations: getting food and fending off enemies. So in this concluding chapter, we discuss how geography and ecology worked on the Eastern Shore's native tribes and the foreigners with whom they dealt later.

The principal variations in Eastern Shore geography and ecology that affected people were north-south ones. The Virginia Eastern Shore is narrower, lower in average altitude, and more southerly than the Maryland one. It is therefore poorer in the nut-bearing trees that prefer fairly high ground; the richest oak-hickory forests are to be found on the Maryland Shore. That means in turn that the populations of fur-bearing animals, most of which eat nuts, were smaller on the Virginia Shore— and not much worth exploiting in historic times. The altitude and the narrowness of the Virginia Shore prevent the streams from being long enough and rising high enough above encroaching salty waters to contain most of the emergent plants (*tuckahoe*) that could form a major part of the native people's diet. The streams also had fewer of the kinds of bark and twigs that attract beavers, and their waters were not visited in the barren, storm-prone early spring season by shoals of anadromous fish seeking freshwater spawning grounds. The more southerly latitude, on the other hand, made for a longer growing season for farming, and the narrowness of the peninsula also meant that people had fairly easy access to saltwater fisheries and to rich beds of clams and oysters to both the east and the west. Finally, the Virginia Eastern Shore is a harder place to reach from the western shore because of the ten- to fourteen-mile width of the Chesapeake Bay. The Maryland Shore, especially from Kent Island northward, was somewhat more accessible to Indians, whether friends or enemies, who came from either the western shore or down the Susquehanna River.

Thus the prehistoric stage was set for Late Woodland peoples who lived somewhat different lives, depending on what part of the Eastern Shore they inhabited. Those living in the Maryland part, whether the lower-lying southerly plain or the higher-standing, northerly hills, had ecological resources that would have enabled them to parallel closely the western shore Powhatans and Patuxents/Yoacomocos in their mixture of farming and foraging, with the threats of impinging Indian enemies from the north and west forcing the men to be hunters of people as well as of animals. Early eyewitness accounts of the Maryland Eastern Shore tribes' lifeways are extremely scanty, but what evidence there is does not contradict this assertion. The threat from Indian enemies is vividly demonstrated by the fact that several major Maryland Eastern Shore Indian towns were palisaded ones. John Smith described Tockwogh as such a town; archaeology has shown the same for the Nanticoke capital of Chicone; and later Contact period records mention palisades for Pocomoke and Choptank settlements as well.

The Virginia Eastern Shore people, especially the Accomacs, differed. John Pory observed at first hand that they raised more corn than any other native people he knew of, and at the same time they lacked the *huskanaw*, the rigorous initiation of boys into a warrior manhood. No palisaded towns are to be found in the historical records of that sector, nor have any been found by the very limited archaeological work done in the area so far. It would seem that the Accomacs and probably the Occohannocks as well were a more settled, less warlike people than those to the north. They had to be settled, of course, because they all but lacked tuckahoe in their territories and had to make up for it through farming. They also could afford to be more settled and forgo the huskanaw for their boys because in their relative isolation they had less to fear from other Indians.

As far as we know, all the aboriginal Eastern Shore tribes had chiefs who ruled their various towns. However, two tribes had paramount chiefs who ruled over the town chiefs when the English first began visiting the region: the Nanticokes and the Accomacs/Occohannocks. It is likely that the two groups developed these larger organizations for different reasons, rooted in the somewhat different ecological resources available to their people and the geographical closeness of other, potentially competitive tribes.

We proposed in chapter 1 that the Nanticoke population was the largest on the Eastern Shore because their river had the richest occurrence of edible tuber-producing wetland plants. Larger and denser human populations are apt to develop more complex polities to organize the people. As human populations grow in areas of rich resources and begin to compete for those resources, then chiefs and later paramount chiefs are likely to appear; that is especially true in places where it is also possible to monopolize the high-status goods whose possession validates a chief's position.[3] Scholars studying the Powhatans, Patawomecks, and Piscataways on the western shore agree that those factors were causes of the rise of those paramount chiefdoms, with their origins at or near the fall line.[4] The same can be said for the Nanticokes. The heart of their territory was rich, but expansion beyond their own valley and those of the Wicomico and Manokin Rivers was not feasible without going to war with the Choptanks and the Pocomokes. Also by 1608 they had become the major regional makers of white shell beads, one of the highly valued symbols of wealth in the Indian world.[5] John Smith, our source for that statement, calls the beads roanoke, but the value he assigns them indicates that they were peak, which was made from whelk and clam shells. Hard clams were plentiful in the salty-brackish shallows beyond the Nanticoke River's mouth, but whelks are decidedly saltwater mollusks, so the Nanticokes would have had to acquire them by trade from the east or south. An entrepreneurial chief based in a rich natural area was odds-on to become a paramount chief in time. Apparently the Nanticokes had had that much time: a Piscataway legend, recorded in 1660, told of the first Piscataway paramount chief coming over from the Eastern Shore thirteen "generations" (that is, chiefly reigns) back. There is linguistic evidence for that early political connection, too: the terms for "paramount chief" are nearly identical in Piscataway (*tayac* [/tayak/]) and Nanticoke (*telleck* [/tall!ak/]).[6]

It is less easy to explain the Accomacs' paramount chiefdom, which included the Occohannock paramount chief with his subsidiary town rulers. One of us (Davidson) has pointed out that there is no mention in the English records of the Accomac chief being paramount over the Occohannock one until John Pory's 1621 account.[7] But even by itself the Occohannock paramountcy is hard to account for. The edible natural resources are somewhat less rich on the Virginia Eastern Shore, though the people may have made up for it through their farming. Decent, flat farmland and small estuaries for fishing and shellfishing are so plentiful that the human population would have had to be very much denser before beginning to compete over them. The Accomac and Occohannock populations were among the smallest and least dense for the region as a whole. However, that deficit may have been due to an epidemic.[8] It is a pity that John Smith did not ask—or was not able to make people understand the question—about how things had been in the past. There is no evidence in his or anyone else's writings that the region formerly had more people, or that their paramount chief–headed political organization had existed for any length of time. It is therefore entirely possible that the western shore ruler Powhatan installed the brothers Esmy Shichans and Kiptopeke (or their predecessor[s]) as paramount chiefs nominally under himself at the time that he extended his sphere of influence to the Virginia Eastern Shore and began collecting tribute there.

In aboriginal times the Eastern Shore tribes tended to trade along an east-west axis, just as they forged their alliances in that direction.[9] The people in neighboring valleys to the north or south were apt to be political and economic rivals, against whom alliances elsewhere were sought.[10] In addition, most of the recorded trade was in nonlocal, high-status goods that the chiefs themselves wanted. No English records indicate that any utilitarian goods were traded, either east-west or north-south, among the native people. Instead there was a westward flow of shell beads from the Eastern Shore and an eastward flow of copper and puccoon (dye roots) away from it.[11] The ceramics that archaeologists find all up and down the peninsula are predominantly Townsend wares, once the basic Late Woodland pottery of tidewater Virginia and southern Maryland as a whole. With the rise of paramount chiefdoms on the western shore, other ceramics became important,[12] and some of these have been found on the Eastern Shore in indicative places. Potomac Creek pottery became common in the area occupied by the Patawomecks and Piscataways; small amounts of it have been in the Nanticoke area,[13] where we know from an oral tradition that the people were in contact with the Piscataways. Roanoke simple-stamped pottery became common in the lower James River and down into the Carolina Sounds; a small amount of it has been found in Northampton County.

Thus we postulate that whatever north-south contacts the Eastern Shore native peoples may have had were motivated not so much by trade as by political rivalry mixed with social reasons such as intermarriage. And there probably were many such contacts, for all of the Indian people were adept at canoe travel and spoke closely related languages.

The invasion of the Eastern Shore by English settlers began much earlier in the south than in the north. English farmers essentially took over the Accomac Indians' land in the 1620s through 1640s, the Occohannocks' lands in the 1640s through 1670s, the lower reaches of the Maryland rivers in the 1660s through 1690s, and the upper reaches of those rivers in the 1690s through 1750s. This northward-then-northeastward sweep was not entirely due to geography, that is, to a radiation outward from the colonial nuclei at Jamestown and St. Mary's City. It was a matter of simple radiation outward only in Virginia, where farmland was the main issue of contention between Indians and Englishmen.

The flood of settlers was a steady one in Virginia, and the Accomacs, now called Gingaskins, found themselves in a tiny 690-acre enclave by 1641. The Occohannocks in turn were confined in small and probably landlocked enclaves (locations impossible to determine) in a sea of foreigners by the late 1660s. The Gingaskins' land was at least located on the waterfront, and they retained their age-old access to the miles-wide seaside marshes and estuaries. But the native people, especially the Gingaskins, were now thrown into constant contact with English people, and some of their lifeways probably began to change early. The evidence for what their language and culture were like thereafter is extremely scanty. But small populations surrounded by much larger ones must of necessity learn the language and some basic elements of the other people's culture simply in order to defend their rights and survive. It was not long before they became adept at dealing with the English in court. There is no mention of an interpreter for them after the 1680s (and none was ever paid by the Virginia colony), and their appearances under English names soon increased, while Indian-language names all but ceased by 1700 (see Appendix A).

In Maryland, on the other hand, the English settlers were halted from the 1630s to the 1660s by a prosperous fur-trading enterprise that was endorsed by (and a source of profit for) some of the leading lights in the colony, from the Lord Proprietor on down. The native people got a reprieve precisely because the peninsula in their homeland was higher and much wider, supporting the oak-hickory and oak-gum forests and freshwater streams in which more fur-bearing animals, especially beaver, lived. The rivers there are also much longer; when English settlement did finally begin, the Indians could withdraw up those rivers. It was their good luck that English farmers, who would have preferred the richer soils upriver, were heavily dependent upon maritime shipping, which for a long time meant that settlers were reluctant to move very far from the easily navigable stretches of the rivers. The continuing fur trade also made further movement upriver difficult, even for those Englishmen who wanted to try it. The major English agents dealing with the Indians usually took care to patent the land on which the Indians had their villages; protecting their own investments in that way also protected the Indians from undue harassment by newcomers.

When the Pocomokes, Nanticokes, and Choptanks lost their down-river territories, they were left with the best, not the worst, of their old domain. After the early 1660s the native people concentrated in areas that were rich not only in fur-bearing animals but which were also rich in foods for human beings, especially nut-bearing trees and freshwater emergent plants. In the case of the Pocomokes and Nanticokes, the best soils in the whole river valleys were up there as well. And the upper river valleys are close enough together that the remaining tribal lands formed one huge, contiguous foraging range. Although the number of Indian towns dwindled, the people still had a large enough land base support-ing large enough towns that they could continue their traditional life-ways unabated. Among other things, they retained their languages far longer than the Gingaskins did (see Appendix B). When the fur trade wound down after 1690, the trader allies faded from the scene, the set-tlers moved in, and the Maryland tribes lost ground in the same way that the Accomacs and Occohannocks had: Englishmen patented their lands and then either waited until the Indians "left" (even on foraging trips) or moved in and pushed them out. When the crunch came, ironi-cally, it was the government officials of Maryland, the slower-moving colony in taking Indian land, who proved less sympathetic to Indian treaty rights.

The immediate reasons for the difference in levels of sympathy are not far to seek. Maryland and Virginia had quite different attitudes to-ward the native people about whom they made policy and with whom they made treaties. And once again, ultimately geography, ecology, and the resulting Indian lifestyles (this time in the late seventeenth and early eighteenth centuries) played a major part. Both colonies made treaties with Indians after serious episodes of unrest on the western shore. Both colonies had to fend off threats and/or attacks from strong Iroquoian-speaking peoples: the Susquehannocks and Iroquois for Maryland and the Tuscaroras, Susquehannocks, and Iroquois (especially Senecas) for Virginia. Yet the treaties that the two colonies made with their local Indians were different, so local factors must be adduced to explain the discrepancy.

The Virginia Algonquian-speaking Indians never did side with any of the "foreign" Indians that upset the Virginia colonists so. They were also reduced by 1680 to small, partially anglicized enclaves of people who could pose little military threat of their own (with the exception of the refuge areas of Pamunkey Neck and the Blackwater region).[14] The Virginia government aimed all its treaties at assimilating the natives, preferably into a lower stratum of society. Thus the 1677 Treaty of Middle Plantation contained a clause establishing civil rights for Indians in English-dominated Virginia: individual Indians were to be "well Secured & defended in theire persons goods and properties against all hurts and injuries of the English," and when they reported wrongs done against them to the governor, he was to proceed "as if such hurt or injury had bin done to any Englishman." The Indians signing the treaty are referred to in it as "Neighbour Indians," and the stated purpose of the treaty was to found a peace "upon the strong Pillars of Reciprocall Justice."[15] The Gingaskins and Occohannocks did not actually sign the 1677 treaty, but everyone seems to have assumed that it would cover them. In fact, Northampton and Accomack Counties had treated them all along as if they had English civil rights whenever they wanted to use them. Consequently most of the records about the Virginia Eastern Shore Indians are county records, for the Gingaskins and Occohannocks had learned how to put the county courts to full use. The Indians there seem to have felt at least partially like citizens of the Virginia colony.

It was different in Maryland. The Eastern Shore tribes in that colony were not only unanglicized but actively sympathetic at times with Indian enemies beyond the colony's borders, a situation that persisted into the mid-eighteenth century. So Maryland made its treaties with its local Indians as though they were foreigners, socially outside the colony, an evaluation with which the native people themselves must have agreed. Many of the treaties had a set formula, concerned mainly with prevention of crimes by Indians in English territory and the return of runaway servants; Indian rights were summed up in a provision designed to protect "the privilege of crabbing, fowling, hunting and fishing." Even more significantly, from the 1666 Piscataway treaty down through the 1742 treaties with the remaining Eastern Shore tribes, there was always a provision—aimed at Indian groups living anywhere inside the Maryland colony's boundaries—that read, "Forasmuch as the English cannot easily distinguish one Indian from another, that no Indian shall come into any English plantacon painted and that all the Indians shall be bound to call aloud before they come within three hundred paces of any English man's clear ground and lay downe their arms whether gun, bows or arrowes or other weapon for any English man that shall appear upon his call to take up." [16] The perception of foreignness and potential threat in English minds is inescapable. Thus it is not entirely surprising that the great majority of records about the Maryland Eastern Shore tribes are provincial council records, not county ones.

That may not be the whole story, however, for up until about 1700, the reservation Indians in Somerset and Dorchester Counties comprised about 15 percent of the population there. Apparently Indians could not petition the county justices for redress of grievances before 1717,[17] which eliminated them as plaintiffs in county court cases. Even so, interactions between Indians and Englishmen should have produced much more incidental court business than just the few native people accused of crimes. The dearth of recorded contacts may indicate that county officials were unwilling to regard Indians as a part of mainstream Eastern Shore society, even when the Indians in question, such as the Pocomokes, had lived peaceably next door to them for generations. It is likely that the native people returned the feeling.

The Indians eventually lost the contest for territory, not because of military victories by the English but because they were flooded out by hordes of English squatters. The English, including settlers in the New World and potential migrants still living at home, had a much larger population than any aboriginal Indian one, since they had practiced intensive agriculture and animal husbandry for millennia. That highly productive economy had allowed their population to grow more or less steadily and to be much less affected by the limitations of local ecology. Their political organization had also grown more all-encompassing (states have the right to meddle in many personal affairs that mere chiefdoms do not dream of invading)—and very acquisitive. The English who migrated to the Chesapeake region saw the land first as being owned by their monarch and second as being a place for themselves to practice intensive farming in the attempt to become wealthy. Thus in both Virginia and Maryland it was legal to patent the land on which Indian tribes still lived—as occupants, not owners. It was merely illegal to force them to move, which would create bad feeling and endanger the colony as a whole. The issue, to the settlers, was a practical one, not a moral one. Aboriginal inhabitants of the land were a stumbling block, to be tolerated only as long as they served some useful purpose. When the fur trade ended in Maryland, and when the Indians' potential military threat through alliance with "foreign" Indians faded, the toleration ceased.

Interestingly enough, the overrunning of the Eastern Shore Indians occurred during a period that was not nearly so racist as the nineteenth and early twentieth centuries would be. Compared to that later period, the eighteenth-century laws about Indians in Virginia were relatively moderate, and the ones about Indians in Maryland probably were based more upon cultural than biological issues. Both colonies limited the civil rights of Indians. From 1705 in Virginia and 1717 in Maryland, Indians were barred along with other nonwhites from testifying in court against whites,[18] a prohibition that must have had serious repercussions for the tribes whose land was being encroached upon by squatters and who now could only go to the governor in each colony's capital for redress. Virginia's law explained the ban on court testimony: an oath taken on the Bible would mean little to non-Christians. Virginia additionally passed other laws in 1705 that were aimed at keeping nonwhites socially separate from whites; the laws about keeping them illiterate and poor were a nineteenth-century phenomenon. Maryland was more liberal about the social separation for a while. But at the same time, neither colony in the eighteenth century forbade reservation Indians at peace with the English to own and use guns or individual Indians to own land if they became detribalized.

Nonetheless, the civil rights legally provided (or not) in the treaties and those informally accorded the Gingaskins, who always figured in court cases in Northampton County, had a serious impact upon the decision of Eastern Shore native people about staying or leaving as English settlers became a sea around islands of Indians. So too did the amount of ecologically based cultural conservatism the people had been able to maintain. Differences in civil rights and conservatism added up to different decisions in the north and the south.

The Maryland Eastern Shore tribes, culturally conservative and being essentially foreigners in an English colony, withdrew except for scattered individuals who chose to detribalize and a very few Choptanks who hung on at Locust Neck. In the 1740s through 1760s people migrated northwest to join the Iroquois, who were still strong and by then had a policy of adopting Algonquian-speakers. The people joining the Iroquois were sufficiently traditional in culture, language, and outlook that they would have found the Iroquois much more congenial than the English Marylanders (though by no means identical to themselves). In New York they could go on practicing a mixture of farming by women and foraging by both sexes, with extended families living and working together for subsistence rather than wealth, a political system that did not extract taxes from people, and a religion keyed to the annual economic cycle instead of one commemorating a sacred figure distant in both time and space. By keeping their large, contiguous reservations so long, the Nanticokes, Pocomokes, Assateagues, and Choptanks had remained conservative long enough to make accepting the Iroquois offer of refuge the obvious choice.

Most of the Occohannocks probably had joined the Maryland Eastern Shore tribes sometime before the migration. They had become tiny groups in Virginia when they sojourned in that colony in the decades of the 1690s through 1720s. But their movements to and from Maryland may have kept them fluent enough in their native language and adept enough at their traditional culture to make it feasible to join one of the Maryland tribes permanently at some point. As with the people they joined, some individuals probably detribalized under pressure from the English and were left behind.

It was the Gingaskins, far to the south, who did not leave. They had been left high and dry on a 690-acre reservation since the 1640s, but their land still had good access via Indiantown Creek to the marshes and estuaries to the east. Traditional farming by women and fishing and fowling by men remained possible, and the wording of the 1793 trustee's report hints that many Gingaskins practiced it still. But by the early 1700s their traditional political system had long been drastically changed, and they probably had lost their language as well. It is very likely that the Gingaskins continued visiting their Algonquian-speaking relatives to the north, at least as long as their linguistic fluency made communication feasible. They continued to be canoe-using people, and sociable ones as far as we know. Yet by the end of the seventeenth century they would have known that the Maryland tribes were going to lose their lands just as surely as they had themselves, so there would be little reason to move north. There may already have been enough acquired cultural differences between themselves and the Pocomokes and others, in addition to the ecologically based differences that existed from aboriginal times, that a union would not have been entirely comfortable. Meanwhile, the governor of Virginia still had the Gingaskins under his personal protection, both by an ancient proclamation and by an informal extension of the 1677 treaty to them. And the territory they clung to had all the ecological elements that their Accomac ancestors had had all along: farmland and saltwater marshes and streams. So why leave?

Unfortunately, staying on—as Indians—ultimately became an untenable goal. The Gingaskins were a classic example of marginal people by the mid-eighteenth century. They would not have been comfortable in the Iroquois-dominated world that the Nanticokes and others joined, and they did not fully fit into the Virginia English world either, even on a lower social level. Now with the removal of the tribes to the north, from whom they could have drawn marriage partners, the Gingaskins had to marry non-Indians, usually free blacks—themselves a marginal people in Virginia society. The Gingaskins' remaining Indianness coupled with their recent alliances with free black people irritated their white neighbors, who after the American Revolution could cease worrying about external threats from the French, the Iroquois, and (for a time) the British and begin concentrating on what seemed to be threats from within their own society. The whites' feeling of being threatened was heightened by geography: the southern tip of the Eastern Shore was isolated from help from the mainland. That meant in turn that the Gingaskins' position became endangered as well as marginal. The end of the tribe did not come because of losing so much land, as was the case with the native people to the north. It came because the Indians were forced, in a very racist era, to detribalize and change their identity to one that the white majority found more controllable. Even then, most of the Gingaskins' descendants stayed on.

Was colonial Chesapeake society, in either Virginia or Maryland, capable of including Indians who practiced traditional lifeways? No. The Indian and English ways of life were based upon differing methods of using their territories and the natural resources in them. The Indian way required very large tracts of land to support fewer people; the English way required less land per person, but when that flood of Englishmen poured across the Atlantic, there were many, many more people to feed.

Coexistence might have been possible—it was possible for the already heavily agricultural Gingaskins until racism disbanded them—if the English had been willing (or able) to stem the flow of migrants short of flooding out the Indians, or if the Indians had been more willing to adopt English farming practices to make room for newcomers. Neither accommodation happened, for either one would have required changing basic and long-held elements of the people's value systems. To change people's values is a long, hard, painful process; people will endure a great deal to avoid that kind of change.

The English would have had to acknowledge that pagan Indians, rather than their own Christian monarch, could legally own large tracts of land, even when they did not farm it intensively. But the English could not change their ideas about political power and "proper" land use, and since they soon became numerically dominant in the region, they had no reason to do so. The Indians, on the other hand, would have had to switch to plow farming and animal herding to coexist with the English. Both of those activities would have required new skills and a great deal of work for males, while keeping them from practicing the sharpshooting skills essential for hunter-warriors;[19] they would also have confined the hardworking females to a narrow, intensively domestic sphere that did not seem especially necessary. Sex roles are another value-laden area of life, striking deep into people's self-image, and they are extremely slow to change in a whole population. So the Eastern Shore tribesmen saw no valid reason to try to change their roles, as long as there was access to the estuaries for the Gingaskins or somewhere else "Indian" to move for the others.

With both sides having a rigid mindset, coexistence was not really possible. Competition, if not active conflict, was inevitable. What was *not* inevitable—and what did *not* happen—was the removal or dying-out of *all* the Indians. Their descendants are still there, all over the Eastern Shore.

Appendixes

Notes

Bibliography

Index

Appendix A

Indian Personal Names on the Virginia Eastern Shore

Helen C. Rountree

Key

N- = Northampton Co.; A- = Accomack Co.

D = Deeds; M = Minutes; O = Orders; W = Wills. Many seventeenth-century county record books have titles that are combinations of these.

r = recto, or right side; v = verso, or left side. Some seventeenth-century scribes gave each "page" two sides, usually front and back of a folio but occasionally left-and-right facing pages when the book was opened.

OCCOHANNOCK (in capitals) indicates membership in the paramount chiefdom of that name, rather than the individual tribe of that name.

NOTE: This list extends only up through the Gingaskin Reservation allotment of 1813, the exceptions beyond that being the few people who were listed in public documents as "Indian."

Name	Date	Tribe	Reference
Akomepen	1657	OCCOHANNOCK	N-DW 1657–66:5v
Alexander	1652–53	?	N-DW 4:141v, 170r
Amongos	1660s–70s	Metomkin	Many; see chap. 3
Andiaman	1652–55	Currituck	N-DW 4:51v, 225, 7:13
Andrew	1684	?	A-WD 1676–90: 402
Angood, Argoll	1683	?Gingaskin	N-O 11:253
Ann	1752	?	N-O 23:171, 186–87
Antony	1669	?	A-O 1666–70:181
Arthur	1669–90s?	?OCCOHANNOCK	Several; see chap. 3
Aruck/Richard	1667	Kegotank	A-O 1666–70:33v

Name	Date	Tribe	Reference
Assabe	1697	Occohannock	N-O 13:426
Atkinson, Robert	1682	?Occohannock	A-DWO 1678–82: 284
Awimbabe	1669	?Occohannock	A-DW 1664–71: 121
Awosseceucus: see Washeto			
Bagwell, Edward	1669–1709	?Occohannock	Several; see chap. 3
Baker, Betsey	1805–<35	Gingaskin	Several; see chap. 6
Baker, Thomas	1805–29	Gingaskin	Several; see chap. 6
Beavans, Mary	1794–1831	Gingaskin	Several; see chap. 6
Beavans, Susan	1812–<21	Gingaskin	Several; see chap. 6
Bess	1669	?Occohannock	A-O 1666–70:181
Bess	1673	?Gingaskin	N-O 9:220, 237
Betty	1684	?	A-WO 1682–97: 28v
Betty	1685	?	N-OW 12:176
Bingham, John	1813–31	Gingaskin	Several; see chap. 6
Bingham, Peggy	1813–53	Gingaskin	Several; see chap. 6
Bingham, Scarburgh	1760–93	Gingaskin	Several; see chap. 6
Bingham, Southy	1780–92	?Gingaskin	Several; see chap. 6
Blank Jant	1669	?Occohannock	A-DW 1664–71: 121
Blincks	1690	Metomkin	A-O 1690–97:2r
Bradford, Nicander	1667	?	A-O 1666–70:44v
Bundick	1677	Onancock	A-O 1676–78:96
Byan (Bian), Thomas	1645	?	N-DWO 2:242r
Carter, John	1813–<19	Gingaskin	Several; see chap. 6
Carter, Nancy	1812–<26	Gingaskin	Several; see chap. 6
Caus	1681	Occohannock	A-WDO 1678–82: 217
Charles	1663	?Gingaskin	N-O 8:183r
Charles	1712	?Occohannock	A-O 1710–14:34, 36
Charlton	1703	Occohannock	Several; see chap. 3

Name	Date	Tribe	Reference
Choratyswince	1658	?Occohannock	N-DW 1657–64:8v
Chotohoin/George	1667	Kegotqank	A-O 1666–70:33v
Collins, Betsy Sr.	1794–<46	Gingaskin	Several; see chap. 6
Collins, Betsy Jr.	1809–31	Gingaskin	Several; see chap. 6
Coraco	1651	Nandua	N-DW 4:168v
Cross, Charlton	1753	Gingaskin	N-O 24:28
Cross, Mary	1753	Gingaskin	N-O 24:28
Custis, Ann	1667	Metomkin	A-O 1666–70:40v
Custis, George	1667	Metomkin	A-O 1666–70:40v
Daniel	1728	?	N-DW 26:110
Daniel, John	1706–57(?)	Gingaskin	Several; see chap. 6
Darby	1669–78	?Occohannock	Several; see chap. 3
Debbedeavon: see Tapatiapon			
Drighouse, Ann	1813–29	Gingaskin	Several; see chap. 6
Drighouse, Betty	1812–<31	Gingaskin	Several; see chap. 6
Drighouse, Esther	1789	Gingaskin	N-O 31:285
Drighouse, Nathan	1813–<31	Gingaskin	Several; see chap. 6
Drummond, Major	1756	Gingaskin	N-O 24:355, 25:94
Ekeeks (Ihekecks)	1662–63	Onancock	Several; see chap. 3
Esmy Shichans	1621–36	Accomac	Several; see chap. 3
Ffeneca, Robert	1685	?	N-OW 12:176
Fisherman, Thomas	1731	?Gingaskin	N-O 19:62, 69
Francis, Ibby	1787–1835	Gingaskin	Several; see chap. 6
Francis, Tabby Press	1813–28	Gingaskin	Several; see chap. 6
Frank	1681	Gingaskin	N-O 11:147–48
Frank	1685	?	A-WO 1682–97: 102v
George	1672–79?	Occohannock	Several; see chap. 3
George Rawmush	1723	?Occohannock	A-O1719–24:68r
Gusman	1668–75	?Occohannock	Several; see chap. 3
Harry	1669–75?	?Occohannock	A-O 1666–70:181; W 1673–76:263
Harry	1684	?	A-WO 1682–97: 28v

Name	Date	Tribe	Reference
Hill, Dick	1667	?OCCOHANNOCK	A-O 1666–70:43
House, William	1813–31	Gingaskin	Several; see chap. 6
Ibbey	1732	Gingaskin	N-O 20:26
Indian Betty	1687	?	A-WD 1676–90: 455
Indian John	1725–31	?OCCOHANNOCK	A-O 1724–31:27r, 237
Jack	1666	?	N-DW 8:1
Jack	1667	?OCCOHANNOCK	A-O 1666–70:19v
Jack	1668–75	?	N-O 9:54, OW 10: 73
Jack	1669	?OCCOHANNOCK	A-O 1666–70:181
Jack (2 boys)	1684	?	A-WO 1682–97: 28v
Jackakick	1678	Chincoteague	A-WDO 1678–82: 53
Jack of Morocco	1655–71	?OCCOHANNOCK	Several; see chap. 3
James: see Wincewough			
Jeffery, Elizabeth	1731	Gingaskin	N-O 19:62, 69
Jeffery, Littleton	1812–24	Gingaskin	Several; see chap. 6
Jeffery, Mary	?1762–1812	Gingaskin	Several; see chap. 6
Jeffery, Solomon	1757–1815	Gingaskin	Several; see chap. 6
Jeffery, Sophia	1803–31+	Gingaskin	Several; see chap. 6
Jeffery, Stephen	1813	Gingaskin	Several; see chap. 6
Jeffery, Thomas	1813	Gingaskin	Several; see chap. 6
Jeffrey	1670–?1704	Gingaskin	Several; see chap. 6
Jenny	1686–94	?	Several; see chap. 3
Joan	1685	?	A-WO 1682–97:86
Joan	1692	?	N-OW 13:357
John	1651–?76	?	N-OW 4:34r, 10: 148
Johnaboy	1647	?	N-DWO 3:61a–r, 78a–r
John the Bowlmaker	1671	?OCCOHANNOCK	A-OW 1671–73:41

Name	Date	Tribe	Reference
Johnson	1672	?OCCOHANNOCK	Several; see chap. 3
Jones	1669	?OCCOHANNOCK	A-O 1666–70:181
King Robin	1677	?OCCOHANNOCK	A-O 1676–78:94, 101
King Tom	1649–50	Gingaskin	Several; see chap. 3
King Tom	1689	Gingaskin	N-OW 13:510–11
Kiptopeke	1621	OCCOHANNOCK	Smith 1986c [1624]:291
Kitt	1671–81	?Metomkin	Several; see chap. 3
Kokewiss	1663	OCCOHANNOCK	A-DW 1663–66:40v
Lin Stuchans: see Esmy Shichans			
Little Mannattark	1669	?OCCOHANNOCK	A-DW 1664–71:121
Major, William	1775	Gingaskin	Hungars Vestry Bk.:74
Manuel	1696	?	N-OW 13:352
Margaret	1687	?	A-WO 1682–97:216v
Marhesum	1657	OCCOHANNOCK	N-DW 1657–66:5v
Mary	1672–1703	OCCOHANNOCK	Several; see chap. 3
Mary	1684–97	?	N-OW 12:46, OW 13:435
Matahocus	1663–78	Onancock	Several; see chap. 3
Matom Apy	1664	OCCOHANNOCK	A-DW 1663–66:64v
Misseteage	1667	Occohannock	A-O 1676–79:80
Mister Peter	1660	Gingaskin	N-O 8:73v
Mister Thomas	1655	?OCCOHANNOCK	N-ODW 5:13v, 14r
Moll	1691	?	A-WO 1682–97:228r
Mongram, Peter	1685	?OCCOHANNOCK	A-WO 1682–97:75
Munatuck	1675	Kegotank	A-W 1673–76:314
Nan	1677	?	N-OW 10:191

Name	Date	Tribe	Reference
Nanny	1687	?	A-WO 1682–97: 216v
Ned	1669	?Occohannock	A-O 1666–70:181
Norris	1650–60	Occohannock	Several; see chap. 3
Nowchetrawen/ Monsatran	1663	Chesconnessex	A-DW 1663–66: 22, 53
Ochiawampe: see Wackawamp			
Oliver	1669	?Occohannock	A-O 1666–70:159
Oquoiock/Edward	1667	Kegotank	A-O 1666–70:33v
Parahokes/William	1658	?Occohannock	N-DW 1657–64:8v
Parker, George	1667	Onancock	A-O 1666–70:40v
Paul	1675	?Occohannock	A-W 1673–76:350
Peter	1697	?Occohannock	A-O 1697–1703:8r
Peter	1702	?Gingaskin	N-W 14:102
Philip	1719	?	N-W 1717–25:33
Picket	1702	?Occohannock	A-O 1697–1703: 131r
Pickpocket	1667	?Occohannock	A-O 1666–70:53
Pinato	1687	?Occohannock	A-WO 1682–97: 113r
Piney	1661–62	Machipongo	N-DW 1657–66: 74, O 8:120r
Press, Edmund	1790–1816	Gingaskin	Several; see chap. 6
Press, Molly	1813–26	Gingaskin	Several; see chap. 6
Protestant George	1701	?Occohannock	A-O 1697–1703: 122v
Quiemacketo	1657	Occohannock	N-DW 1657–66:5v
Quinney	1721	?Gingaskin	N-W 15:135
Revell, James	1667–80	Metomkin	Several; see chap. 3
Roapeto	1657	Occohannock	N-DW 1657–66:5v
Robert	1752	?	N-O 23:171, 186–87
Robin	1685	?	A-WO 1682–97: 86v

Name	Date	Tribe	Reference
Robin	1694	?	N-OW 13:301
Rozario, Philip	1714–52	?Gingaskin	Several; see chap. 6
Rozario, Philip (Jr.?)	1762	?Gingaskin	N-Min. 26:4
Sarah	1708	?	N-DW 1711–18: 59
Shoes, Dick	1670s	?Metomkin	Several; see chap. 3
Stephens, Molly	1828–60s	Gingaskin	Several; see chap. 6
Sunket, Brit	1766	Gingaskin	Several; see chap. 6
Tabby	1669	?OCCOHANNOCK	A-O 1666–70:181
Tapatiapon	1648–72	Nandua; OCCOHANNOCK	Several; see chap. 3
Thomas	1672	?OCCOHANNOCK	A-OW 1671–73: 117
Tom	1688–97	?	N-OW 12:356, 13: 435
Tom	1716	?	N-O 15:251
Tom	1728	?	N-O 18:326
Tonganaquato	1697	OCCOHANNOCK	N-OW 13:426
Uttomacoupars	1675	?OCCOHANNOCK	A-W 1673–76:263
Wackawamp	1643–57	Onancock; OCCOHANNOCK	Several; see chap. 3
Wamatahoke	1682	?OCCOHANNOCK	A-WDO 1678–82: 309
Washeto/Wasseta	1662–63	Onancock	N-DW 1657–66: 73; A-DW 1663– 66: passim
Watchesagon	1663	OCCOHANNOCK	A-DW 1663–66: 40v
Weanit	1680	?	A-WDO 1678–82: 181–82
Weeks/West, Wm.	1794–1827	Gingaskin	Several; see chap. 6
West, James	1813–31	Gingaskin	Several; see chap. 6
West, John	1707	Gingaskin	N-O 14:379
West, Mary	1812–14	Gingaskin	Several; see chap. 6

Name	Date	Tribe	Reference
West, Ned	1667	?Occohannock	A-O 1666–70:44–44v
West, Rachel	1812–15	Gingaskin	Several; see chap. 6
West, William	1749–50	?Gingaskin	N-O: 22:109 et passim
Wickepeason/ Humphrey	1667	Kegotank	A-O 1666–70:33v, 1671–73:130
Will	1669	?Occohannock	A-O 1666–70:181
Will	1701	?Occohannock	A-O 1697–1703: 122v
Wincewough/James	1667–78	Metomkin	Several; see chap. 3
Wise, James	1667	Onancock	A-O 1666–70:40v
Worakahon	1657	Occohannock	N-DW 1657–66:5v

Appendix B

Indian Personal Names on the Maryland Eastern Shore

Thomas E. Davidson

Key
AM = Archives of Maryland (Browne et al. 1883–1972)
D = Dorchester Land Records
DJ = Dorchester Judicials
SJ = Somerset Judicials
SL = Somerset Land Records
STax = Somerset Tax Lists
SR = Somerset (other) Records

Name	Date	Tribe/Community	Reference
Ababco	1669	Choptank	AM 2:195
Abraham	1742	Locust Neck	AM 28:261
Achquain/Dick	1722	Choptank	D 2:138
Agangh Queh Jensh	1727	Choptank	D 8:152
Ahatsawab	1683	Assateague	AM 17:193
Ahcatimousko	1704	Choptank	D 6:47
Ahcompatomack, Mr. William	1704	Choptank	D 6:47
Ahiewasuske	1704	Choptank	D 6:47
Ahighmante	1704	Choptank	D 6:47
Ahihestis	1722	Choptank	D 2:115
Ahiwassonsk	1722	Choptank	D 2:115
Ahquashow, Armstrong	1704	Choptank	D 6:47
Ahtatowin	1704	Choptank	D 6:47
Amannuasomus	1704	Choptank	D 6:47
Amaussenaugus	1723	Nanticoke	AM 25:419
Amekowarset	1704	Choptank	D 6:47

Name	Date	Tribe/Community	Reference
Amonugus	1668	Assateague	AM 15:170
Amsimus	1727	Choptank	D 8:152
Anatchom	1669	Wicomis	AM 2:195
Annachohill	1688	Nanticoke	AM 8:10
Annaheakows	1704	Choptank	D 6:47
Anna Mosey	1722	Choptank	D 2:116
Annatoughquan	1693	Nanticoke	AM 8:533
Anthony	1742	Unknown	AM 28:264
Anthony	1713	Chicone Nanticoke	AM 33:311
Aquasuskquanonsk	1722	Choptank	D 2:115
Arquankanah	1726	Choptank	D 8:142
Arquasuckanak	1726	Choptank	D 8:141
Ashinnak	1687	Nanticoke	AM 5:556
Ashquash	1693	Nanticoke	AM 8:533
Ashquash, Jeremy	1742	Chicone Nanticoke	AM 28:269
Ashquash, Molly	1757	Chicone Nanticoke	AM 31:353
Ashquash, Moses	1757	Chicone Nanticoke	AM 31:354
Ashquash, Nancy	1757	Chicone Nanticoke	AM 31:353
Ashquash, Uncle Abraham	1742	Chicone Nanticoke	AM 28:269
Ashquash, William	1721	Chicone Nanticoke	AM 35:369
Asoto	1692	Choptank	D 5:37
A Such Marsh	1722	Choptank	D 2:116
Atatowin	1722	Choptank	D 2:115
Athie	1722	Choptank	D 2:116
Atsquanch	1704	Choptank	D 6:47
Attahous	1722	Choptank	D 2:116
Attawease, George	1704	Choptank	D 6:47
Atuckqueawatow/ Tom Bishop	1722	Choptank	D 2:115
Bastobello	1742	Assateague/Pocomoke	AM 28:274
Ben	1722	Choptank	D 2:115
Benjamin	1727	Choptank	D 8:152
Best	1724	Unknown	STax 1724

Name	Date	Tribe/Community	Reference
Betty Caco	1722	Ababco Choptank	D 2:115
Bishop, Abraham	1754	Locust Neck	AM 31:40
Bishop, Anne	1758	Locust Neck	AM 31:298
Bishop, Betty	1727	Choptank	D 8:152
Bishop, Mary	1758	Locust Neck	AM 31:298
Bishop, Sarah	1754	Locust Neck	AM 31:45
Cahonke, Nannee	1726	Choptank	D 8:141
Canab	1683	Unknown	AM 17:225
Catani	1683	Unknown	AM 17:225
Ceazor	1724	Unknown	STax 1724
Cha Cha	1683	Unknown	AM 17:225
Chaquanouske	1704	Choptank	D 6:47
Chinah/James	1722	Choptank	D 2:138
Chincoricos	1677	Nanticoke	AM 15:145
Chinehopper, John	1742	Chicone Nanticoke	AM 28:274
Chinnigh/Jeme	1722	Choptank	D 2:115
Chinopah	1687	Nanticoke	AM 5:555
Chowhan (Choroho)	1683	Copanno?	SJ 1683–84:1,16
Cohonk	1722	Choptank	D 2:116
Cohonk, Anne	1757	Chicone	AM 31:353
Cohonk, Nancy	1757	Chicone	AM 31:353
Cohonk, Sarah	1757	Chicone	AM 31:353
Conig	1722	Choptank	D 2:116
Coponk (Cohonk), James	1754	Locust Neck	AM 31:30
Coponk (Cohonk), William	1754	Locust Neck	AM 31:30
Costin, John	1735	Unknown	STax 1735
Cotah	1687	Nanticoke	AM 5:555
Coursey, Dixon	1742	Chicone Nanticoke	AM 28:265
Coursey, Henry	1704	Nanticoke	AM 26:42
Coursey, John	1742	Chicone Nanticoke	AM 28:274
Coursey, Tom	1713	Nanticoke	AM 29:228
Coyahouse	1722	Choptank	D 2:116
Daniel/Wasseunge	1696	Pocomoke	AM 20:424

Name	Date	Tribe/Community	Reference
Dewaqua	1683	Unknown	AM 17:225
Dick	1726	Choptank	D 8:141
Edmond	1722	Pocomoke	AM 25:392
Eenamicho	1687	Pocomoke	AM 5:558
Gaiquefro	1722	Choptank	D 2:138
George	1722	Choptank	D 2:116
George, Old Mr.	1722	Choptank	D 2:138
Gin Nack	1725	Choptank	D 8:83
Ginney	1727	Choptank	D 8:152
Hamatoh	1687	Nanticoke	AM 5:556
Hanney	1727	Choptank	D 8:152
Hatsawap	1669	Choptank	AM 2:196
Heaack	1727	Choptank	D 8:161
Heerworhous	1722	Choptank	D 2:116
Henry, Ester	1798	Locust Neck	D 14HD:527
Hewetuck	1727	Choptank	D 8:152
Highwassuk	1727	Choptank	D 8:161
Hill, Tom	1742	Indian River	AM 28:582
Hockcommough/Samson	1722	Choptank	D 2:115
Hood, Robin	1727	Choptank	D 6:152
Hucktawcon	1707	Indian River	AM 26:442
Hyewoussouss	1727	Choptank	D 8:152
Imanaugh Cow/ Tom Cohonk	1722	Choptank	D 2:115
Isaac, Sam	1742	Chicone	AM 28:263
Jack, Cutiwilson	1690	Choptank	DJ 1690–92:193
James, Richard	1688	Monie	SR IKL(1688)
Jamme	1754	Locust Neck	AM 31:45
Janous Sanous	1692	Choptank	D 5:37
John, Captain	1742	Broad Creek	AM 28:268
John, Little	1727	Choptank	D 8:142
John, Mister	1727	Choptank	D 8:152
John, Robin	1728	Pocomoke	SJ 127–30:154

Name	Date	Tribe/Community	Reference
Joshua	1742	Chicone	AM 28:270
Joshua, Thomas	1758	Locust Neck	AM 31:298
Katuckcuweitick	1668	Manokin	SJ B1:116
Keepscow	1704	Choptank	D 6:47
Kehowh	1704	Choptank	D 6:47
Kenctagkcon	1707	Indian River	AM 26:442
King, James	1736	Unknown	STax 1736
Knosulm	1722	Assateague	AM 25:392
Lolloway	1724	Unknown	SJ 1722–24:189
Machacopah	1706	Pocomoke	SJ 1705–7:245
Machanousks	1722	Choptank	D 2:115
Mackismat (Matcha)	1683	Wicomico	SJ 1683–84:1,16
Macknouse	1722	Choptank	D 2:138
Mahchasowes	1704	Choptank	D 6:47
Malla Commousk	1725	Choptank	D 8:83
Manassen	1686	Assateague	AM 5:479
Mary, Indian	1759	Unknown	D 16:242
Matchoutown	1707	Indian River	AM 26:442
Maticamous	1722	Choptank	D 2:138
Matopank	1692	Choptank	D 5:37
Matta Commousk	1725	Choptank	D 8:84
Mechasusa	1748	Choptank	AM 28:424
Mochocommonsk	1722	Choptank	D 2:116
Monk, Jamy	1722	Choptank	D 2:116
Monk, Peter	1742	Chicone	AM 28:262
Monk, William	1722	Choptank	AM 25:329
Monoconson	1718	Assateague	AM 33:232
Mulberry	1742	Locust Neck	AM 28:261
Mulberry, Henry	1798	Locust Neck	D 14HD:527
Mulberry, Mary	1798	Locust Neck	D 14HD:527
Munk, James	1722	Choptank	D 2:138
Nacowetok	1727	Choptank	D 8:152
Nandum, Robert	1742	Pocomoke/Assateague	AM 28:269

Name	Date	Tribe/Community	Reference
Nehakeash	1704	Choptank	D 6:47
Nehatuckwis	1727	Choptank	D 8:161
Netaughwougton	1693	Choptank	AM 8:526
Newman, Henry	1750	Unknown	STax 1750
Newman, Isaac	1750	Unknown	STax 1750
Newnon, John	1748	Choptank	AM 28:424
Nicodepeto	1685	Nanticoke	AM 17:460
Noockyousk	1704	Hatsawap Choptank	D 6:47
Nowseawatowousk	1722	Choptank	D 2:115
Nuckeapanouske	1704	Choptank	D 6:47
Ohkeapattam	1704	Choptank	D 6:47
Ohocheknotah	1704	Choptank	D 6:47
Omapatoe	1687	Nanticoke	AM 5:555
Onnechacoughson	1677	Nanticoke	AM 15:145
Oupetoh (Ohopperoon)	1677	Nanticoke	AM 15:145
Ousawosson	1677	Nanticoke	AM 15:145
Overfeen, Sam	1727	Choptank	D 8:152
Owens, Thomas	1754	Locust Neck	AM 31:45
Pa Canabb	1683	Unknown	AM 17:225
Paccahounk	1722	Choptank	D 2:138
Pacowassamuck	1727	Choptank	D 8:152
Pama Wohusk	1725	Choptank	D 8:83
Panquas	1693	Nanticoke	AM 8:432
Panquash, Sam	1742	Chicone	AM 28:263
Paschach hoisi	1722	Choptank	D 2:116
Pasimmons, Jemmy	1742	Locust Neck	AM 28:260
Paskacowousk	1722	Choptank	D 2:115
Passemeacol	1687	Nanticoke	AM 5:555
Patasuske	1704	Tequassino Choptank	D 6:47
Patchyouske	1704	Hatsawap Choptank	D 6:47
Patrick	1727	Choptank	D 8:152
Pattasahook, Jacob	1742	Chicone	AM 28:262
Peake, Jeremy	1742	Assateague/Pocomoke	AM 28:274

Name	Date	Tribe/Community	Reference
Pemetasusk	1722	Hatsawap Choptank	D 2:115
Pequsatum	1704	Choptank	D 6:47
Perrecohos	1727	Choptank	D 8:152
Perretohas	1727	Choptank	D 8:152
Petowousk	1722	Choptank	D 2:115
Petty	1727	Choptank	D 8:152
Pike, John	1754	Locust Neck	AM 31:45
Pincher, Ann	1755	Broad Creek	SL B: 111
Pincher, James	1755	Broad Creek	SL B: 111
Pincher, Mary	1758	Locust Neck	AM 31:298
Pocateyhouse, George	1757	Chicone Nanticoke	AM 31:352
Pohosse	1683	Unknown	AM 17:225
Poh Poh Caquis	1683	Assateague	AM 17:225
Pomotahmow/ Harry Corwin	1722	Choptank	D 2:115
Ponas Quash	1692	Choptank	D 5:37
Ponasque	1692	Choptank	D 5:37
Popscoe	1727	Choptank	D 8:152
Potkess/Esq. John	1722	Choptank	D 2:115
Pregotos	1722	Choptank	D 2:116
Presillah	1754	Locust Neck	AM 31:45
Prince, Amey	1758	Locust Neck	AM 31:298
Prince, Naomi	1758	Locust Neck	AM 31:298
Puckham, John	1681	Monie	SR IKL(1682)
Puminapus	1704	Choptank	D 6:47
Pushshecks	1704	Choptank	D 6:47
Puttyousemous	1704	Choptank	D 6:47
Quash, John	1748	Choptank	AM 28:424
Quinackin	1677	Pocomoke	SJ 1727–30:154
Quitam, John	1748	Choptank	AM 28:424
Rassekettham	1713	Nanticoke	AM 29:228
Robert, Mr.	1681	Nanticoke	AM 17:33
Robin	1705	Indian River	AM 26:442

Name	Date	Tribe/Community	Reference
Robin	1715	Unknown	SJ 1715–17:75
Robin, Young	1741	Indian River	SL 19:224
Robin, son of Young Robin	1741	Indian River	SL 19:225
Rokahomp (Rokahaum), George	1742	Assateague/Pocomoke	AM 28:274
Roseawaahous	1722	Choptank	D 2:116
Sam, Hopping	1742	Locust Neck	AM 28:274
Samson	1686	Nanticoke	AM 5:475
Samson Cuchop	1727	Choptank	D 8:152
Sarah	1727	Choptank	D 8:152
Scouweto	1727	Choptank	D 8:161
Signm	1727	Choptank	D 8:152
Signunco	1727	Choptank	D 8:152
Simon	1742	Broad Creek	AM 28:270
Six Pence	1726	Choptank	D 8:141
Sixpence, Henry	1799	Locust Neck	D 14HD:527
Smallhominy, Jemmy	1742	Locust Neck	AM 28:260
Sonan/James	1688	Nanticoke	AM 8:10
Squash, John	1757	Chicone	AM 31:353
Tallowin	1726	Choptank	D 8:141
Tatain	1725	Choptank	D 8:84
Tatowino	1722	Choptank	D 2:138
Teaamoush	1722	Choptank	D 2:116
Teawatutusk	1722	Choptank	D 2:138
Tense	1704	Choptank	D 6:47
Tequassino	1669	Choptank	AM 2:196
Terraquett (Terrakill), George	1742	Pocomoke	AM 28:269
Thom	1687	Pocomoke	AM 5:558
Tikehouse, Old Tom	1704	Choptank	D 6:47
Tobe, Tom	1757	Chicone	AM 31:35
Tobia	1722	Choptank	D 2:138
Toby, Long	1770	Chicone Nanticoke	D 24:23

Name	Date	Tribe/Community	Reference
Tockowsk Towcosk	1704	Choptank	D 6:47
Tom, Harry Will	1690	Choptank	DJ 1690–92:171
Tomaneake/George	1722	Choptank	D 2:115
Tontawing	1722	Choptank	D 2:116
Toungacon	1707	Indian River	AM 26:442
Toychoy	1722	Choptank	D 2:116
Travers, Richard	1759	"Somerset Indian"	D 16:242
Unnarokassimon	1668	Nanticoke	AM 5:29
Wacowester	1722	Choptank	D 2:116
Wampatown	1704	Choptank	D 6:47
Wannucha	1687	Nanticoke	AM 5:555
Wannucha	1687	Pocomoke	AM 5:558
Wasanous	1692	Choptank	D 5:37
Wasattnaham	1683	Unknown	AM 17:225
Waspason/ Harry Waspason	1707	Indian River	AM 26:442
Watsawasco	1727	Choptank	D 8:161
Wattenan	1687	Nanticoke	AM 5:556
Weachoweto	1727	Choptank	D 8:161
Weanchum	1726	Choptank	D 8:141
Weantennousk	1704	Choptank	D 6:47
Weapatowin	1722	Choptank	D 2:115
Wechateack	1722	Choptank	D 2:138
Wecompese	1704	Choptank	S 6:47
Weenakaman	1683	Unknown	AM 17:225
Weesanush	1727	Choptank	D 8:152
Wehack Cash	1725	Choptank	D 8:83
Wicampo	1727	Choptank	D 8:152
Wicampo, Janney	1727	Choptank	D 8:152
Wiesk	1727	Choptank	D 8:152
Will (servant)	1702	Unknown	SJ 1702–5:52
William, Mr.	1722	Choptank	D 2:138
Williams, John	1757	Locust Neck	AM 31:354

Name	Date	Tribe/Community	Reference
Winogaco, son of Ababco	1701	Choptank	D 5:214
Wittonka (Wittonguis), John	1742	Assateague/Pocomoke	AM 28:274
Woakas	1722	Choptank	D 2:116
Wojhaneik	1722	Choptank	D 2:116
Woodchop	1722	Choptank	D 2:116
Woodenhoocke	1704	Choptank	D 6:47
Worwouch/Isaac	1722	Choptank	D 2:138
Woscoerfixpe	1727	Choptank	D 8:161
Wotscow Wetow/ Benny Claber	1722	Choptank	D 2:115
Wottocwacough	1677	Nanticoke	AM 15:145
Wouss	1727	Choptank	D 8:152
Wyranfconmickonous	1705	Indian River	AM 26:442
Yehock	1683	Unknown	AM 17:225
Yeopachton/Abraham	1722	Choptank	D 2:138

Appendix C

Major Useful Wild Plants of the Eastern Shore of Maryland and Virginia

Helen C. Rountree

The edible plant list, which is the bulk of this appendix, was compiled in three stages. (1) I made a master list of edible plants of eastern North America, using Fernald and Kinsey 1958, Angier 1974, and Peterson 1978, and included which plant parts are used at which seasons. (I excluded mosses, lichens, and mushrooms for the time being.) Fernald and Kinsey discussed many plants which they had not tried themselves and which do not appear in the other two later sources; I have not included those species in the list below. (2) I added specific local data to the master list, using: for Maryland, Brown and Brown 1972 and 1984, Shreve et al. 1969 [1910] (woody plants only), and Sipple 1978 (aquatic plants only); for Maryland and Virginia Eastern Shore, Tatnall 1946; for Virginia, Harvill 1970, Harvill et al. 1992, James 1969, Massey 1961; for North Carolina, Beal 1977 (aquatic plants only) and Radford et al. 1968. Several authors comment on which plants are nonnative to their states (e.g., most clovers [*Trifolium* spp.] are Eurasian, and the common sunflower [*Helianthus annuus*] and the Jerusalem artichoke [*Helianthus tuberosus*] are North American but not native east of the Appalachians). (3) From this detailed three-state master file, I then extracted plants that are both native to and located on the Eastern Shore of Virginia and Maryland, still relying at times on Radford et al. 1968 for fruiting times when Brown and Brown 1984 omitted them and on Beal 1977 for salinity tolerance data.

The medicinal list is shorter and much more tentative. I found the seventeenth-century Virginia and Maryland records to be of very limited help, an idea seconded in the probing article by Merrill and Feest (1975). So I relied heavily upon surviving ethnobotanical knowledge among twentieth-century Cherokee, Iroquois, Mohegan, and Delaware traditionalists (Fenton 1942, Hamel and Chiltoskey 1975, Herrick 1995, Tantaquidgeon 1928 and 1972), supplemented by the 1940 Virginia fieldwork of Speck et al. among the Rappahannocks (published in 1942) and the Pamunkeys (still in manuscript in the Speck Papers). My selection of plants for this appendix is based upon the reasonably safe assumption that a native plant used as a herbal remedy by two or more of these geographically distant twentieth-century groups may well have been widely used by historical Eastern Woodlands peoples, including the Eastern Shore tribes. Since I have had to go geographically far afield in compiling a plausible medicinal plant list of any length, I have been careful to say in each entry whether or not there is documentary evidence for Chesapeake region Indians using the plant. As with the edible plants, I have listed only plants native to the Virginia-Maryland coastal plain. (My major dissatisfaction with Cherokee, Iroquois, Mohegan, and Delaware herbal medicines is that they are not based upon a coastal plain environment, so that I had to eliminate many of the native plants they used from my list.) And needless to say, I cannot vouch for the efficacy of any of the remedies; in fact, some of the plants are highly poisonous and should not be tinkered with by amateurs.

PART 1: Plant Listings by Ecological Zone, Uses, and Season (for common names, details of use, and frequency on Eastern Shore, see Part 2)

I. Saltwater Marsh

A. STARCHY FOODS

Phragmites australis (rootstocks)	Reed	JFM . . . . . SOND
" " (seeds)		. . . . SON .
Polygonum prolificum (roots)	Proliferous knotweed	. . . . . JJASON .
Scirpus robustus	Salt-marsh bulrush	JFM . . JJASOND

B. VEGETABLES

Atriplex patula	Spearscale	. . . . MJJA . . . .
Phragmites australis (shoots)	Reed	. . MAM . . . .
Polygonum prolificum (leaves)	Proliferous knotweed	. . MAM . . . .
Salicornia bigelovii, europaea	(Glassworts)	. . MAMJJASON .
Suaeda linearis	Tall sea blite	. . MAMJJA . . . .

II. Brackish Marsh (including salty-brackish and fresh-brackish)

A. STARCHY FOODS

Amaranthus cannabinus (seeds)	Water hemp	. . . . . JASON .
Echinochloa walteri	(a Barnyard grass)	. . . . . . ASO . .

Phragmites australis (rootstocks)	Reed	JFM . . . . . SOND
" " (seeds)		. . MAM. . . . . .
Sagittaria falcata, graminea	(Arrowheads)	JFM . . . . . SOND
Scirpus robustus	Salt-marsh bulrush	JFM . . JJASOND
S. validus (pollen)	Great bulrush	. . . . MJJ . . . . .
" " (seeds)		. . . . SON .
" " (rootstocks)		JFM . . JJASOND
Typha angustifolia (pollen)	Narrow-leaved cattail	. . . . MJ. . . . . .
" " (rootstocks)		JFMAMJJASOND
Zizania aquatica	Wild rice	. . . . MJJASO . .

B. VEGETABLES

Amaranthus cannabinus (leaves)	Water hemp	. . MAMJJASON .
Atriplex patula	Spearscale	. . . . . JJA. . . . .
Phragmites australis (shoots)	Reed	. . MAM
Salicornia bigelovii, europaea	(Glassworts)	. . MAMJJASON .
Scirpus validus (shoots)	Great bulrush	. . MAM. . . . . .
Suaeda linearis	Tall sea blite	. . MAMJJA. . . .
Typha angustifolia (shoots, stalks)	Narrow-leaved cattail	. . . AM. . . . . . .
" " (sprouts from roots)		JFM . . . . . . OND

III. Freshwater marsh

A. STARCHY FOODS

Echinochloa walteri	(a Barnyard grass)	. . . . ASO . .
Glyceria obtusa, pallida, septentrionalis, striata	(Manna grasses)	. . MAMJJAS . . .
Nuphar advena/luteum (seeds)	Spatterdock	. . . . . . JASON .
" " (roots)		JFM . . . . ASOND
Nymphaea odorata (seeds)	Water lily	. . . . SON .
Orontium aquaticum (seeds)	Golden club	. . . . . . JASON .
" " (roots)		JFM . . . . ASOND
Peltandra virginica (roots)	Arrow arum	JFMAMJJASOND
Phragmites australis (rootstocks)	Reed	JFM . . . . . SOND
" " (seeds)		. . MAM. . . . . .
Polygonum hydropiperoides (roots)	Mild water pepper	. . . . . JJASON .
Pontederia cordata (seeds)	Pickerelweed	. . . . . JJASON .
Sagittaria falcata, graminea, latifolia, subulata	(Arrowheads)	JFM . . . . . SOND

Scirpus validus (pollen)	Great bulrush	. . . . MJJ . . . . .
" " (seeds)		. . . . SON .
" " (rootstocks)		JFM . . JJASOND
Sparganium americanum, eurycarpum	(Bur reeds)	JFM . . . . . SOND
Typha angustifolia (pollen)	Narrow-leaved cattail	. . . . MJ . . . . . .
" " (rootstocks)		JFMAMJJASOND
Zizania aquatica	Wild rice	. . . . MJJASO . .

B. VEGETABLES

Acorus calamus	Sweet flag	. . MAM . . . .
Impatiens capensis (shoots)	Jewelweed	. . MAM . . . .
" " (leaves)		. . . . . JJA . . . .
Nymphaea odorata (buds)	Water lily	. . MAMJJA . . . .
Polygonum hydropiperoides (leaves)	Mild water pepper	. . MAMJJA . . . .
Pontederia cordata (leaves)	Pickerelweed	. . . . . JJA . . . .
Rhexia mariana, virginica (leaves, roots)	(Meadow beauties)	. . . . . JJA . . . .
Scirpus validus (shoots)	Great bulrush	. . MAM . . . .
Sium suave	Water parsnip	JFM . . . . . SOND
Stachys hispida, hyssopifolia	(Hedge nettles)	JFM . . . . . SOND
Typha angustifolia (shoots, stalks)	Narrow-leaved cattail	. . . AM . . . .
" " (sprouts from roots)		JFM . . . . . . OND

C. MEDICINALS

Acorus calamus	Sweet flag
Alisma subcordatum	Common water plantain
Cicuta maculata	Cowbane
Impatiens capensis	Jewelweed
Iris versicolor	Blue flag

IV. Swamp (including both swamps and low woods)

A. STARCHY FOODS

Arisaema triphyllum	Jack-in-the-pulpit	JFM . . . . . SOND
Glyceria obtusa, pallida, septentrionalis, striata	(Manna grasses)	. . MAMJJAS . . .
Helianthus angustifolius, gigantaeus	(Sunflowers)	. . . . . . JASO . .
Peltandra virginica	Arrow arum	JFMAMJJASOND

Phragmites australis (rootstocks)	Reed	JFM . . . . SOND
" " (seeds)		. . . . SON
Polygonum punctatum, hydropiperoides (roots)	(Knotweeds)	. . . . . JJASON .
Quercus alba, nigra, palustris, phellos	(Oaks)	. . . . SON .
Rumex verticillatus	Water dock	. . . MJJ . . . . .
Symplocarpus foetidus	Skunk cabbage	JFM . . . . SOND
Verbena hastata	Blue vervain	. . . . . .ASON .

B. VEGETABLES

Aralia spinosa	Prickly ash	. .MAM. . . . . . .
Caltha palustris	Marsh marigold	. .MAM. . . . . . .
Impatiens capensis (shoots)	Jewelweed	. .MAM. . . . . . .
" " (leaves)		. . . . . JJA. . . .
Polygonum punctatum, hydropiperoides (leaves)	(Knotweeds)	. .MAMJJA. . . .
Rosa palustris (petals)	Swamp rose	. . . . . JJA. . . .
Sium suave	Water parsnip	JFM . . . . SOND
Smilax laurifolia	Bamboo (briar)	. .MAMJJA. . . .
Viola brittoniana, cucullata (Violets)		. .MAM. . . . . . .
Vitis rotundifolia, vulpina (leaves)	Muscadine, Frost grape	. . . . MJ. . . . . .

C. FRUIT

Amelanchier canadensis	Juneberry	. . . . MJ. . . . . .
Gaylussacia baccata	Black huckleberry	. . . . . .JA. . . .
Pyrus arbutifolia	Red chokeberry	. . . . SON .
Rosa palustris (hips)	Swamp rose	. . . . SO . .
Rubus hispidus	Swamp blackberry	. . . . . JJ. . . . .
Sambucus canadensis	Elderberry	. . . . . .JA. . . .
Vaccinium fuscatum, corymbosum	(Blueberries)	. . . . . JJA. . . .
Viburnum nudum	Possum haw	. . . . . .JAS . . .
Vitis rotundifolia, vulpina	Muscadine, Frost grape	. . . . . .ASO . .

D. MEDICINALS

Acer rubrum	Red maple
Alnus serrulata	Smooth alder
Aralia spinosa	Prickly ash
Arisaema triphyllum	Jack-in-the-pulpit
Aster novae-angliae	New England aster

Cicuta maculata	Cowbane	
Clematis virginiana	Virgin's bower	
Eupatorium perfoliatum	Boneset	
Impatiens capensis	Jewelweed	
Lindera benzoin	Spicebush	
Rubus hispidus	Swamp blackberry	
Sambucus canadensis	Elderberry	
Veratrum viride	White hellebore	

V. Waste Ground (disturbed soil, including fields under cultivation)

A. STARCHY FOODS

Cyperus esculentus	Chufa	JFMAMJJASOND
Impomoea pandurata	Wild potato vine	JFM . . . . . SOND
Polygonum erectum, pennsylvanicum (roots)	(Knotweeds)	. . . . . JJASON .
Smilax glauca (roots)	Saw brier	JFMAMJJASOND
Sporobolus vaginiflorus	Poverty grass	. . . . SO . .
Verbena hastata	Blue vervain	. . . . . . .ASON .

B. VEGETABLES

Allium canadense	Wild onion	JFMAMJJASOND
Asclepias syriaca (shoots)	Common milkweed	. .MAM. . . . . . .
" " (flower buds)		. . . . . JJA. . . .
Erectites hieracifolia	Fireweed	. . . . . JJA. . . .
Galium aparine	Cleavers	. .MAM. . . . . . .
Oenothera biennis, fruticosa, laciniata, tetragona (leaves)	(Evening primroses)	. .MA . . . .
" " (first-year roots)		JF . . . . . . .OND
Plantago rugelii, virginica	(Plantains)	. .MAMJJA. . . .
Polygonum erectum, pennsylvanicum (leaves)	(Knotweeds)	. .MAMJJA. . . .
Rosa carolina (petals)	Wild rose	. . . . . JJA. . . .
Smilax glauca (leaves)	Saw brier	. .MAMJJA. . . .
Veronica peregrina	Purslane speedwell	. . . .MJJA. . . .

C. FRUIT

Diospyros virginiana	Persimmon	. . . . .SO . .
Fragaria virginiana	Common strawberry	. . . . MJJ . . . . .

Passiflora incarnata	Passion flower	. . . . .JASO . .
Prunus americana, serotina	Wild plum, Wild cherry	. . . . . .JA. . . . .
Rosa carolina (hips)	Wild rose	. . . . . .ASO . .
Rubus flagellaris	Dewberry	. . . . MJJ . . . . .

D. MEDICINALS

Asclepias syriaca	Common milkweed
A. tuberosa	Pleurisy root
Baptisia tinctoria	Wild indigo
Ceanothus americanus	New Jersey tea
Diospyros virginiana	Persimmon
Gnaphalium obtusifolium	Rabbit tobacco
Lobelia inflata	Indian tobacco
Oenotheria biennis	Common evening primrose
Phytolacca americana	Pokeweed
Plantago rugelii	Broad-leaved plantain
Prunus serotina	Wild cherry
Rhus glabra, typhina	Smooth, Staghorn sumac
Rubus flagellaris	Dewberry
Sassafras albidum	Sassafras
Triosteum perfoliatum	Horse gentian

VI. Old Fields (fields fallow one or two years)

A. STARCHY FOODS

Helianthus giganteus	Tall sunflower	. . . . . JASO . .
Ipomoea pandurata	Wild potato vine	JFM . . . . . SOND
Opuntia humifusa (seeds)	Prickly pear cactus	. . . . . .ASO . .
Smilax bona-nox, glauca (roots)	(Briers)	JFMAMJJASOND

B. VEGETABLES

Asclepias syriaca (leaves)	Common milkweed	. . MAM. . . . . . .
" " (flower buds)		. . . . . JJA. . . .
Oenothera biennis, fruticosa, laciniata, tetragona (leaves)	(Evening primroses)	. . MA . . . .
" " (first-year roots)		JF . . . . OND

Opuntia humifusa (pads)	Prickly pear cactus	..MAMJJA....
Plantago rugelii, virginica	(Plantains)	..MAMJJA....
Pteridium aquilinum	Bracken	..MAM......
Rubus argutus, cuneifolius (shoots)	(Blackberries)	..MAM......
Smilax bona-nox, glauca (leaves)	(Briers)	..MAMJJA....
Veronica officinalis, peregrina	(Speedwells)	....MJJA....
Viola pedata	Bird's-foot violet	..MAM......

C. FRUIT

Diospyros virginiana	Persimmon	........SO..
Fragaria virginiana	Common strawberry	....MJJ.....
Opuntia humifusa (fruit)	Prickly pear cactus	.......ASO..
Passiflora incarnata	Passion flower	......JASO..
Prunus americana, serotina	Wild plum, Wild cherry	......JA....
Pyrus angustifolia	Wild crab apple	.......AS...
Rubus argutus, cuneifolius, flagellaris, occidentalis	(Black-, Dewberries)	....MJJ.....
Sambucus canadensis	Elderberry	......JA....
Viburnum prunifolium	Black haw	........SO..

D. MEDICINALS

Aletris farinosa	Colic root
Apocynum cannabinum	Indian hemp
Asclepias syriaca	Common milkweed
A. tuberosa	Pleurisy root
Aster novae-angliae	New England aster
Baptisia tinctoria	Wild indigo
Ceanothus americanus	New Jersey tea
Cicuta maculata	Cowbane
Diospyros virginiana	Persimmon
Eupatorium perfoliatum	Boneset
Euphorbia corollata, ipecacuanhae	Flowering spurge, Wild ipecac
Gnaphalium obtusifolium	Rabbit tobacco
Hedeoma pulegioides	Pennyroyal
Juniperus virginiana	Red cedar
Lobelia inflata	Indian tobacco

Monarda fistulosa, punctata	Wild bergamot, Horse mint	
Oenothera biennis	Common evening primrose	
Phytolacca americana	Pokeweed	
Plantago rugelii	Broad-leaved plantain	
Polygala verticillata	Whorled milkwort	
Potentilla simplex, canadensis	Old field, Common cinquefoil	
Prunus serotina	Wild cherry	
Rhus copallina	Dwarf sumac	
R. glabra, typhina	Smooth, Staghorn sumac	
Rubus argutus, cuneifolius, flagellaris, occidentalis	(Blackberries, Raspberries)	
Sambucus canadensis	Elderberry	
Sassafras albidum	Sassafras	
Veratrum viride	White hellebore	

VII. Thickets (fields fallow three to seven years)

A. STARCHY FOODS

Amphicarpa bracteata	Hog peanut	JFM . . . . . SOND
Apios americana	Groundnut	JFMAMJJASOND
Castanea pumila	Chinquapin	. . . . SO . .
Helianthus giganteus	Tall sunflower	. . . . . . JASO . .
Ipomoea pandurata	Wild potato vine	JFM . . . . . SOND
Smilax bona-nox, glauca, rotundifolia (roots)	(Briers)	JFMAMJJASOND

B. VEGETABLES

Comandra umbellata (fruit)	Bastard toadflax	. . . . . . J . . . . .
Galium aparine	Cleavers	. . MAM . . . .
Polygonum scandens	(a Knotweed)	. . MAMJJA . . . .
Rosa palustris (petals)	Swamp rose	. . . . . JJA . . . .
Rubus argutus, cuneifolius, hispidus (shoots)	(Blackberries)	. . MAM . . . .
Smilax bona-nox, glauca, herbacea, rotundifolia (leaves)	(Briers)	. . MAMJJA . . . .

Viola brittoniana	Coast violet	. . MAM . . . .
Vitis aestivalis, labrusca, rotundifolia, vulpina (leaves)	(Grapes)	. . . . MJ . . . . . .

C. FRUIT

Crataegus crus-galli	Cockspur thorn	. . . . SO . .
Diospyros virginiana	Persimmon	. . . . SO . .
Gaultheria procumbens	Wintergreen	. . . . SON .
Passiflora incarnata	Passion flower	. . . . .JASO . .
Prunus americana, angustifolia, serotina	(Wild plums, cherry)	. . . . MJJA . . . .
Pyrus arbutifolia, angustifolia, coronaria	(Chokeberries, Crab apples)	. . . . . . .ASON .
Rosa palustris (hips)	Swamp rose	. . . . SO . .
Rubus argutus, cuneifolius, flagellaris, hispidus, occidentalis	(Blackberries, etc.)	. . . . MJJ . . . . .
Sambucus canadensis	Elderberry	. . . . . . .JA . . . .
Vaccinium fuscatum, staminium, vacillans	(Blueberries)	. . . . . JJA . . . .
Viburnum prunifolium	Black haw	. . . . SO . .
Vitis aestivalis, labrusca, rotundifolia, vulpina	(Grapes)	. . . . . . .ASO . .

D. MEDICINALS

Alnus serrulata	Smooth alder
Apocynum cannabinum	Indian hemp
Aralia racemosa	Spikenard
Ceanothus americanus	New Jersey tea
Celastrus scandens	Bittersweet
Diospyros virginiana	Persimmon
Eupatorium purpureum	Boneset
Gaultheria procumbens	Wintergreen
Juniperus virginiana	Red cedar
Lobelia inflata	Indian tobacco
Potentilla simplex	Old-field cinquefoil
Prunus serotina	Wild cherry
Rhus copallina	Dwarf sumac
R. glabra, typhina	Smooth, Staghorn sumac
Rubus argutus, cuneifolius, flagellaris, hispidus, occidentalis	(Blackberries, Raspberries)
Sambucus canadensis	Elderberry

Sassafras albidum	Sassafras	
Smilax herbacea	Carrion flower	
Triosteum perfoliatum	Horse gentian	
Veratrum viride	White hellebore	

VIII. Pine Woods (pure stands or woods with pines dominant)

A. STARCHY FOODS

Helianthus angustifolius	Narrow-leaved sunflower	. . . . . . .ASO . .
Smilax bona-nox (roots)	(a Brier)	JFMAMJJASOND

B. VEGETABLES

Rosa carolina (petals)	Wild rose	. . . . . JJA . . . .
Smilax bona-nox (leaves)	(a Brier)	. .MAMJJA . . . .

C. FRUIT

Diospyros virginiana	Persimmon	. . . . .SO . .
Gaultheria procumbens	Wintergreen	. . . . .SON .
Mitchella repens	Partridge berry	JFM . . JJASOND
Prunus americana	Wild plum	. . . . . .JA . . . .
Rosa carolina (hips)	Wild rose	. . . . . .ASO . .
Rubus hispidus	Swamp blackberry	. . . . . JJ . . . . .
Vaccinium fuscatum, corymbosum	(Blueberries)	. . . . . JJA . . . .

D. MEDICINALS

Aristolochia serpentaria	Virginia snakeroot
Chimaphila maculata	Spotted wintergreen
Diospyros virginiana	Persimmon
Gaultheria procumbens	Wintergreen
Mitchella repens	Partridge berry
Rubus hispidus	Swamp blackberry

IX. Open Woods (woods with partial clearings or natural savanna)

A. STARCHY FOODS

Carya cordiformis, glabra, ovata, tomentosa	(Hickories)	. . . . .O . .
Castanea dentata, pumila	Chestnut, Chinquapin	. . . . .SO . .
Helianthus giganteus	Tall sunflower	. . . . . .JASO . .
Juglans nigra	Black walnut	. . . . .O . .

Opuntia humifusa (seeds)	Prickly pear cactus	. . . . . . .ASO . .
Quercus alba, coccinea, falcata, marilandica, stellata, velutina, virginiana	(Oaks)	. . . . SON .
Smilax bona-nox, glauca, rotundifolia (roots)	(Briers)	JFMAMJJASOND

B. VEGETABLES

Allium canadense	Wild onion	JFMAMJJASOND
Aralia spinosa	Prickly ash	. .MAM. . . . . . .
Asclepias syriaca (leaves)	Common milkweed	. .MAM. . . . . . .
" " (flower buds)		. . . . JJA. . . .
Comandra umbellata (fruit)	Bastard toadflax	. . . . . .J. . . .
Epigaea repens	Trailing arbutus	. .MAM. . . . . . .
Opuntia humifusa (pads)	Prickly pear cactus	. .MAMJJA. . . .
Pteridium aquilinum	Bracken	. .MAM. . . . . . .
Rosa carolina (petals)	Wild rose	. . . . JJA. . . .
Rubus argutus (shoots)	Blackberry	. .MAM. . . . . . .
Smilax bona-nox, glauca, herbacea, rotundifolia (leaves)	(Briers)	. .MAMJJA. . . .
Veronica officinalis	Common speedwell	. . . .MJJA. . . .
Viola brittoniana, lanceolata, primulifolia, sagittata (leaves)	(Violets)	. .MAM. . . . . . .

C. FRUIT

Crataegus crus-galli	Cockspur thorn	. . . . SO . .
Diospyros virginiana	Persimmon	. . . . SO . .
Gaultheria procumbens	Wintergreen	. . . . SON .
Gaylussacia frondosa	Dangleberry	. . . . . JJA. . . .
Mitchella repens	Partridge berry	JFM . . JJASOND
Opuntia humifusa (fruit)	Prickly pear cactus	. . . . . . .ASO . .
Prunus americana, serotina	Wild plum, Wild cherry	. . . . . .JA. . . .
Rosa carolina (hips)	Wild rose	. . . . . . .ASO . .
Rubus argutus, flagellaris, occidentalis	(Blackberries)	. . . .MJJ . . . . .
Vaccinium pallidum, stamineum, vacillans	(Blueberries)	. . . . JJA. . . .

D. MEDICINALS

Anemone virginiana	Thimbleweed
Aralia nudicaulis	Wild sarsaparilla
A. spinosa	Prickly ash

Aristolochia serpentaria	Virginia snakeroot
Asclepias syriaca	Common milkweed
Baptisia tinctoria	Wild indigo
Castanea dentata	Chestnut
Ceanothus americanus	New Jersey tea
Clematis virginiana	Virgin's bower
Cornus florida	Flowering dogwood
Diospyros virginiana	Persimmon
Eupatorium purpureum	Wide-leaved joe-pye weed
E. rugosum	White snakeroot
Euphorbia corollata	Flowering spurge
Gaultheria procumbens	Wintergreen
Gnaphalium obtusifolium	Rabbit tobacco
Hamamelis virginiana	Witch hazel
Hedeoma pulegioides	Pennyroyal
Hieracium venosum	Hawkweed
Iris verna	Dwarf iris
Lobelia inflata	Indian tobacco
Mitchella repens	Partridge berry
Monarda fistulosa	Wild bergamot
Potentilla simplex	Old-field cinquefoil
Prunus serotina	Wild cherry
Quercus velutina	Black oak
Rhus copallina	Dwarf sumac
R. glabra, typhina	Smooth, Staghorn sumac
Rubus argutus, flagellaris, occidentalis	(Blackberries, Raspberries)
Sassafras albidum	Sassafras
Smilax herbacea	Carrion flower
Triosteum perfolium	Horse gentian

X. Mixed Deciduous Forest (dense, moist, mature forest, including oak-hickory, oak-gum, and oak-pine subtypes)

A. STARCHY FOODS

Amphicarpa bracteata	Hog peanut	JFM . . ... SOND
Apios americana	Groundnut	JFMAMJJASOND

Arisaema triphyllum	Jack-in-the-pulpit	JFM . . . . . SOND
Carya cordiformis, glabra, ovata, tomentosa	(Hickories)	. . . . O . .
Castanea dentata	Chestnut	. . . . SO . .
Fagus grandifolia	American beech	. . . . SO . .
Juglans nigra	Black walnut	. . . . O . .
Polygonatum biflorum	Dwarf Solomon's seal	JFMAMJJASOND
Quercus alba, coccinea, falcata, stellata, velutina, virginiana	(Oaks)	. . . . SON .
Smilax glauca, rotundifolia (roots)	Saw, Green brier	JFMAMJJASOND
Symplocarpus foetidus	Skunk cabbage	JFM . . . . . SOND

B. VEGETABLES

Allium canadense	Wild onion	JFMAMJJASOND
Aralia spinosa	Prickly ash	. . MAM . . . .
Galium aparine	Cleavers	. . MAM . . . .
Impatiens capensis (shoots)	Jewelweed	. . MAM . . . .
" " (leaves)		. . . . . JJA . . . .
Medeola virginiana	Indian cucumber root	. . MAMJJASON .
Monotropa uniflora	Indian pipe	. . . . . JJA . . . .
Polygonatum biflorum	Dwarf Solomon's seal	JFMAMJJASOND
Smilax glauca, herbacea, rotundifolia (leaves)	(Briers)	. . MAMJJA . . . .
Tradescantia virginiana	Spiderwort	. . MAM . . . .
Viola affinis, lanceolata, palmata	(Violets)	. . MAM . . . .
Vitis aestivalis, labrusca (leaves)	Summer, Fox grape	. . . . MJ . . . . . .

C. FRUIT

Asimina triloba	Pawpaw	. . . . ASO . .
Crataegus uniflora	Dwarf thorn	. . . . ASO . .
Gaultheria procumbens	Wintergreen	. . . . SON .
Gaylussacia baccata	Black huckleberry	. . . . . . JA . . . .
Mitchella repens	Partridge berry	JFM . . JJASOND
Podophyllum peltatum	May apple	. . . . MJ . . . . . .
Pyrus arbutifolia	Red chokeberry	. . . . SON .
Rubus flagellaris, occidentalis	Dewberry, Black raspberry	. . . . MJJ . . . . .

Vaccinium fuscatum, corymbosum, staminium, vacillans	(Blueberries)	. . . . . JJA. . . .
Viburnum prunifolium	Black haw	. . . . SO . .
Vitis aestivalis, labrusca	Summer, Fox grape	. . . . SO . .

D. MEDICINALS

Acer rubrum	Red cedar
Aletris farinosa	Colic root
Aralia spinosa	Prickly ash
Arisaema triphyllum	Jack-in-the-pulpit
Aristolochia serpentaria	Virginia snakeroot
Asarum canadense	Wild ginger
Castanea dentata	Chestnut
Ceanothus americanus	New Jersey tea
Chimaphila maculata	Spotted wintergreen
Cornus florida	Flowering dogwood
Cypripedium calceolus	Small yellow lady slipper
Epigaea repens	Trailing arbutus
Euonymus americauns, atropurpureus	Strawberry bush, Wahoo
Eupatorum rugosum	White snakeroot
Gaultheria procumbens	Wintergreen
Hamamelis virginiana	Witch hazel
Impatiens capensis	Jewelweed
Lindera benzoin	Spicebush
Mitchella repens	Partridge berry
Panax quinquefolius	Ginseng
Podophyllum peltatum	Mayapple
Polygonatum biflorum	Large Solomon's seal
Quercus velutina	Black oak
Rubus flagellaris, occidentalis	Dewberry, Wild black raspberry
Sanguinaria canadensis	Bloodroot
Ulmus rubra	Slippery elm

PART 2: Plant Listings by Genus or Species

Acer rubrum (Red maple): bark decoctions used for eye ailments (Cherokees, Iroquois, but not documented for Chesapeake region). Common on Maryland Eastern Shore, less so to south.

Acorus calamus (Sweet flag): young shoots, partially grown flower stems eaten raw (spring). (Wild-foods enthusiasts can also candy the gingery rootstocks.) Medicinal: root tea used to relieve sore throat (Cherokees, Iroquois, but not documented for Chesapeake region); used in tonic (Mohegans, Rappahannocks); used in remedies for digestive problems (Delawares, Rappahannocks). Found in Accomack Co., common to northward.

Aletris farinosa (Star grass, Colic root): tea of the whole plant used for various "female troubles" (Cherokees, Rappahannocks). Frequent.

Alisma subcordatum (Common water plantain) [used by Cherokees; *A. plantago-aquatica,* used by Iroquois, does not occur in our region]: poultices of leaves for skin ailments, bruises, back pains (Cherokees, Iroquois, but not documented for Chesapeake region). Common, though absent in Accomack Co.

Allium canadense (Wild onion): bulbs eaten raw or cooked (all year). Frequent. Indians on the western shore of Virginia did not eat this plant.

Alnus serrulata (Smooth alder) [used by Cherokees; *A. incana,* used by Iroquois, does not occur in our region]: bark tea used as blood tonic in spring (Cherokees, Iroquois); twig tea of this [used by Cherokees] or alders in general [used by Mohegans] rubbed on for sprains, bruises, swellings, aches (neither use documented for Chesapeake region). Common.

Amaranthus cannabinus (Water hemp): Seeds dried and ground to flour (fall and early winter); tender stalks and leaves raw or boiled (spring through fall). Frequent on Virginia Eastern Shore.

Amelanchier canadensis (Common serviceberry): sweet but insipid fruit, raw, dried, or better when cooked (early summer). Occurs in Accomack Co., frequent northward.

Amphicarpa bracteata (Hog peanut): somewhat dry subterranean fruits boiled (late fall through early spring). Frequent. Field mice hoard large quantities of these, which the Indians took; the Omaha Indians replaced them with an equal amount of corn (Fernald and Kinsey 1953: 257).

Anemone virginiana (Thimbleweed): root tea for whooping cough or tuberculosis (Cherokees, Iroquois, but not documented for Chesapeake region). Rare.

Apios americana (Groundnut or Wild peanut): tubers better when cooked (all year, best in late summer through spring when starchier). Frequent.

Apocynum cannabinum (Indian hemp): probably one of the plants used to make emetics by seventeenth-century Virginia Indians. Common.

Aralia nudicaulis (Wild sarsaparilla): used to make blood remedy or tonic (Cherokees, Iroquois, Mohegans, Delawares, but not documented for Chesapeake region). Rare on the Eastern Shore.

Aralia racemosa (Spikenard): roots used in remedies for cuts, coughs, and weak muscles (Cherokees, Iroquois, but not documented in Chesapeake region). Rare on the Maryland Eastern Shore, absent to south.

Aralia spinosa (Hercules club, Prickly ash): young leaves (before thorns harden) boiled (spring). Medicinal: roots used in salve for sores and boils (Cherokees, Rappahannocks, and Pamunkeys). Common south of Virginia line, fairly common north of it.

Arisaema triphyllum (or *atrorubens*) (Jack-in-the-pulpit or Indian turnip): roots sliced, dried thoroughly, then eaten or ground to flour (fall through early spring). Medicinal: root used in remedies for bronchial colds, also in liniment for pains (Cherokees, Iroquois, Mohegans [liniment only], but not documented in Chesapeake region); crushed plant in poultice for bruises, swellings (Iroquois, Rappahannocks). Occurring in Accomack Co., common to northward.

Aristolochia serpentaria (Virginia snakeroot): mashed roots used for snake-bite, and leaf tea as remedy for chills (Cherokees, Mohegans [bites only], Rappahannocks). Rare, and absent south of Virginia line.

Asarum canadense (Wild ginger): root used for fever (Cherokees, Iroquois, but not documented in Chesapeake region); root used in remedy for coughs (Cherokees, Iroquois, and Rappahannocks). Common on Maryland Eastern Shore, absent south of Virginia line.

Asclepias syriaca (Common milkweed): young shoots and top leaves (spring) and flower buds (summer) boiled in several waters. Medicinal: milk used to remove warts (Cherokees, Iroqouis, and Rappahannocks). Common.

Asclepias tuberosa (Pleurisy root): used to cure pleurisy (Cherokees, Delawares, but not documented for Chesapeake region). Common.

Asimina triloba (Pawpaw): large, sweet fruit eaten raw or cooked (late summer to early fall). Occurs in Accomack Co., infrequent to northward.

Aster novae-angliae (New England aster): roots and leaves of this and other asters used for fevers (Cherokees, Iroquois, but not documented in Chesapeake region). Common on Maryland Eastern Shore, absent south of Virginia line.

Atriplex patula (Spearscale): leaves raw or boiled (summer). Common.

Baptisia tinctoria (Wild indigo): root tea washed on cuts, wounds, inflammations (Cherokees, Mohegans, Delawares, but not documented in Chesapeake region). Common.

Caltha palustris (Cowslip or Marsh marigold): young leaves boiled in two or three changes of water (spring). Found in Accomack Co., frequent to northward.

Carya spp. (Hickories): nuts (fall). *C. cordiformis* (Bitternut hickory), *C. gla-*

bra (Pignut hickory), *C. ovata* (Shagbark hickory), and *C. tomentosa* (Mockernut hickory) are all frequent in northern Maryland Eastern Shore, tapering off to southward; *C. cordiformis* and *C. ovata* do not occur south of Virginia line.

Castanea spp. (Chestnuts): nuts (fall). Medicinal: *C. dentata* leaf tea (sometimes with other ingredients) for coughs (Cherokees, Mohegans, but not documented for Chesapeake region). *C. dentata* (Chestnut) is occasional, especially in north; *C. pumila* (Chinquapin) is fairly common on Maryland Eastern Shore.

Ceanothus americanus (New Jersey tea): roots used in remedy for bowel complaints (Cherokees, Iroqouis, but not documented in Chesapeake region). Occasional, north of Virginia line.

Celastrus scandens (Bittersweet): used in wash for ulcers and sores (Cherokees, Delawares, but not documented in Chesapeake region). Common.

Chimaphila maculata (Spotted wintergreen) and *C. umbellata* (Pipsissewa, Prince's pine): former, used by Cherokees, and latter, used by Iroquois and Rappahannocks, have roots used to combat internal problems such as cancer; Cherokees and Iroquois also used roots in remedies for rheumatism. Common.

Cicuta maculata (Hemlock, Spotted cowbane): widely known by Eastern Woodlands peoples (including the Accomacs in 1621; see chap. 2) to be extremely poisonous; Iroquois used it for committing suicide, also using root or whole plant in poultice for sprains, joint pains, lameness, etc. Common.

Clematis virginiana (Virgin's bower): used for kidney trouble (Cherokees, Iroquois, but not documented in Chesapeake region). Common on Maryland Eastern Shore, absent south of Virginia line.

Comandra umbellata (Bastard toadflax): fruit is small but sweet when nearly ripe (summer). Common south to Virginia line, but not found farther south.

Cornus florida (Flowering dogwood): tea from bark of root as tonic and blood purifier (Cherokees, Delawares, and Rappahannocks). Common.

Crataegus spp. (Hawthorns): pulpy fruit with pectin, better cooked or dried (fall). *C. crus-galli* (Cockspur thorn) is increasingly common from Accomack Co. northward, *C. uniflora* (Dwarf thorn) from Virginia line northward.

Cyperus esculentus (Chufa): nutty and slightly sweetish tubers eaten raw, boiled, dried and ground to flour (all year). Common.

Cypripedium calceolus (Small yellow lady slipper): roots used in remedy for nervousness (Cherokees, Iroquois, but not documented in Chesapeake region). Occasional.

Diospyros virginiana (Persimmon): large but fibrous fruit raw, cooked, or dried (fall). Medicinal: bark used in remedy for sore throat and "thrash" (or "thrush," i.e., sore mouth) (Cherokees, Rappahannocks). Common.

Echinochloa walteri (a Barnyard grass): seeds ground to flour (midsummer through fall). Common.

Epigaea repens (Trailing arbutus or Mayflower): flower tubes eaten raw (early spring). Medicinal: various parts used in kidney medicines (Cherokees, Iroquois, but not documented in Chesapeake region). Formerly frequent (now uncommon) south to Talbot Co., phasing out by Northampton Co.

Erechtites hieracifolia (Fireweed): young leaves raw or cooked (summer). Common.

Euonymus americanus (Strawberry bush) and *E. atropurpureus* (Wahoo, Burning bush): Cherokees used the former, Mohegans the latter, in tonic (not documented in Chesapeake region). *E. americanus* is fairly common on the Eastern Shore, *E. atropurpureus* absent.

Eupatorium perfoliatum (Boneset): used in remedies for fever (Cherokees, Iroquois, Mohegans, Delawares, but not documented in Chesapeake region) and in tonics (Iroquois, Mohegans, Rappahannocks). Common.

Eupatorium purpureum (Wide-leaved joe-pye weed): root used in kidney remedies (Cherokees, Iroquois, but not documented in Chesapeake region). Common, though absent in Northampton Co.

Eupatorum rugosum (White snakeroot): plant used in urinary tract disorders (the Iroquois believed that a man's sleeping with a menstruating woman could give him such a malady), and root or whole plant used to make tonic (Cherokees, Iroquois, but not documented in Chesapeake region). Frequent in northernmost part of Shore.

Euphorbia corollata (Flowering spurge) and *E. ipecacuanhae* (Wild ipecac): probably two plants that John Clayton said the seventeenth-century Virginia Indians used as emetics, *E. corollata* being more frequently used. Common on Maryland Eastern Shore, absent south of Virginia line.

Fagus grandifolia (American beech): nuts (fall). Frequent.

Fragaria virginiana (Common strawberry): small but very flavorful fruit fresh or cooked (summer). Common.

Galium aparine (Cleavers): young leaves and shoots boiled (spring). Common on Maryland Eastern Shore, less so to southward.

Gaultheria procumbens (Teaberry or Wintergreen): juicy, wintergreen-tasting berries fresh or cooked (late summer). Medicinal: used in kidney remedies (Iroquois, Mohegans, Delawares, but not documented for Chesapeake region). Found in Accomack Co., frequent in Worcester, Wicomico, Caroline Cos.

Gaylussacia spp. (Huckleberries): fruit raw or cooked (summer); some Indians added it to stews (Angier 1974: 40). *G. baccata* (Black huckleberry) is common throughout, *G. frondosa* (Dangleberry) mainly in north.

Glyceria spp. (Manna grasses): seeds ground for flour (summer). *G. obtusa, G. pallida, G. septentrionalis* (Floating manna grass), and *G. striata* (Nerved manna grass) are frequent to common on the Eastern Shore, though *G. obtusa* and *G. septentrionalis* do not occur in Northampton Co. and *G. pallida* is not found in Accomack Co.

Gnaphalium obtusifolium (Cudweed, Everlasting, Rabbit tobacco): probably a plant that John Clayton said seventeenth-century Virginia Indians used on wounds; leaves smoked for asthma and roots used in remedy for colds and chills (Cherokees, Rappahannocks). Common.

Hamamelis virginiana (Witch hazel): leaf tea for colds, bark as ingredient in remedy for tuberculosis (Cherokees, Iroquois, but not documented in Chesapeake region); leaf or twig tea for sores, bruises, etc. (Cherokee, Mohegan, but not documented for Chesapeake region). Common.

Hedeoma pulegioides (Pennyroyal): used in fever remedy (Cherokees, Iroquois, but not documented in Chesapeake region), for menstrual difficulties (Cherokees, Rappahannocks), and to warm up body (or stomach) when chilled (Iroquois, Mohegans; Delawares and Pamunkeys [specifically for stomach pains]). Frequent on Maryland Eastern Shore, absent south of Virginia line.

Helianthus spp. (Sunflowers): seeds raw or ground for flour (late summer through fall). *H. angustifolius* (Narrow-leaved sunflower) and *H. giganteus* (Tall sunflower) are frequent on Maryland Eastern Shore; only *H. angustifolius* occurs on Virginia Shore, in Northampton Co.

Hieracium venosum (Hawkweed, Rabbit's ear): various parts of this and other *Hieracium* species to combat diarrhea (Cherokees, Iroquois, and Rappahannocks). Common.

Impatiens capensis (Jewelweed or Spotted touch-me-not): young shoots (early spring) and leaves (summer) boiled; leaves cooked in two changes of water. Medicinal: juice applied to relieve poison ivy, and stems or other parts used to ease difficult childbirth (Cherokees, Iroquois, but not documented in Chesapeake region). Common.

Ipomoea pandurata (Man-of-the-earth or Wild sweet potato vine): slightly bitter roots boiled or baked (fall through early spring when well filled with starch). Frequent.

Iris verna (Dwarf iris): probably one of the plants that John Clayton said seventeenth-century Virginia Indians used as emetic. Common.

Iris versicolor (Blue flag): root tea as general cure (Iroquois, Rappahannocks), or in poultice for pain (Mohawks, Mohegans, but not documented for Chesapeake region). Common, especially north of Virginia line.

Juglans nigra (Black walnut): nuts (fall). Frequent in northern Maryland Eastern Shore, tapering off to southward.

Juniperus virginiana (Red cedar): ingredient in cold remedy (Cherokees, Iroquois, but not documented in Chesapeake region, though Rappahannocks used it to alleviate asthma). Common.

Lindera benzoin (Spicebush): probably a plant that John Clayton said seventeenth-century Virginia Indians used for emetic; twig tea taken for colds, and bark of twig tea used to make measles erupt (Cherokees, Iroquois, but not documented in Chesapeake region). Common, though absent in Northampton Co.

Lobelia inflata (Indian tobacco): smoke or drink in tea to break tobacco habit; roots used to relieve sore legs, also as emetic (all used by Cherokees, Iroquois, but none of these uses documented for Chesapeake region). Common, though absent in Northampton Co.

Medeola virginiana (Indian cucumber root): crisp, cucumber-tasting tuber eaten raw (spring through fall). Common in north, infrequent in south, absent in Accomack Co.

Mitchella repens (Partridge berry or Two-eyed berry): dry, seedy, tasteless berries eaten raw (fall through early spring). Medicinal: root tea for various problems with female organs (Cherokees, Iroquois Delawares, but not documented in Chesapeake region). Common.

Monarda fistulosa (Wild bergamot) and *M. punctata* (Horse mint): plant tea for fever (Cherokees, Iroquois, Delawares, but not documented in Chesapeake region. *M. punctata* is common; *M. fistulosa* is frequent north of Virginia line.

Monotropa uniflora (Indian pipe): whole plant boiled and then roasted (summer). Frequent south to Virginia line, then found only in Northampton Co.

Nuphar advena/luteum (Cow lily): seeds parched, winnowed and ground for flour (late summer to fall), roots cooked like potatoes or dried and ground for flour (fall through early spring). Common on Maryland Eastern Shore; also occurs in Accomack Co. Beavers and muskrats hoard these roots in their dens, which some Woodland Indians then robbed (Angier 1974: 254).

Nymphaea odorata (Water lily): seeds parched, winnowed and ground for flour (fall); young unopened leaves and flower buds boiled (spring, summer). Occurs in Accomack Co., frequently in Maryland counties.

Oenothera spp. (Evening primroses): young leaves (early spring) peeled and eaten raw or cooked; also roots of first-year plants peeled and boiled in two changes of water (late fall through early spring). Medicinal: *O. biennis* roots used to combat piles (Cherokees, Iroquois, but not documented in Chesapeake region). *O. biennis* (Common evening primrose) and *O. laciniata* (Cut-leaf evening primrose) are common to frequent, *O. fruticosa* (Narrow-leaf sundrops) is common south to Accomack Co., and *O. tetragona* (Common sundrops) is common on Maryland Eastern Shore, especially to northward.

Opuntia humifusa (Prickly pear or Indian fig): seeds ground for flour (late summer through fall); tender, rather sweet, dethorned pads peeled, sliced, and boiled or roasted (spring through early summer); fruit eaten raw (late summer to fall). Common south of Delaware line.

Orontium aquaticum (Golden club): seeds dried, then ground for flour or boiled in several water and served like peas (late summer through fall); roots sliced, dried, ground for flour (fall through early spring). Frequent on Maryland Eastern Shore.

Panax quinquefolius (Ginseng): used to combat vertigo or dizziness (Cherokees, Iroquois), and with other ingredients in tonics and panaceas (Iroquois, Mohegans, Delawares; neither use documented in Chesapeake region). Once common in uplands of Maryland Eastern Shore, now nearly extinct due to overcollection for export market.

Passiflora incarnata (Passion flower or Maypop): mildly sweet but not very nutritious hen's-egg-sized fruit fresh or cooked (late summer to early fall). Occurs on Virginia Eastern Shore, only in Wicomico Co., Maryland. Virginia Algonquian name was *maracock*.

Peltandra virginica (Arrow arum): roots sliced, dried or slow-baked for twenty-four hours, then ground for flour or boiled in several waters (best in fall through early spring, when filled with starch; Powhatans used it mainly in late spring and early summer). Occurs in Accomack Co., frequently in Maryland counties. Very large roots, probably the main species that Indians called *tuckahoe*. Spring berries, which Virginia Powhatans called *ocoughtamnis*, can be used like capers.

Phragmites australis (Reed): rootstocks raw or roasted or boiled (fall through early spring); seeds dried and ground to flour (fall); shoots and partly unfolded leaves boiled (early spring). Common southward to Dorchester Co, less so from there.

Phytolacca americana (Pokeweed): seventeenth-century Virginia Indians used it as emetic (which it definitely is, being poisonous); twentieth-century Cherokees, Iroquois, Delawares, Rappahannocks, and Pamunkeys used various parts on skin ailments ranging from bruises to unidentified lumps, while Cherokees, Delawares, and Pamunkeys used various parts to treat rheumatism. Common.

Plantago spp. (Plantains): young leaves eaten raw or boiled (spring and summer). Medicinal: *P. rugelii* used in dressings for cuts, burns, etc. (Cherokees and

Mohegans [using nonnative *P. major* in twentieth century], Iroquois, not documented in Chesapeake region). *P. rugelii* (Broad-leaved plantain) and *P. virginica* (Dwarf or Hoary plantain) are frequent to common.

Podophyllum peltatum (Mayapple): fully ripe fruit raw or cooked (strongly cathartic when green) (late spring). Medicinal: root tea as laxative, also as tonic (Cherokees [laxative only], Iroquois, Delawares, but not documented in Chesapeake region). Common on Maryland Eastern Shore, less so to southward.

Polygala verticillata (Whorled milkwort): plant tea for diarrhea (Cherokees, Iroquois, but not documented in Chesapeake region). Common on Maryland Eastern Shore, absent south of Virginia line.

Polygonatum biflorum (Large Solomon's seal): rootstocks cooked like potatoes (all year); young shoots eaten raw or boiled (early spring). Medicinal: roots used in remedies for skin ailments (Cherokees, Rappahannocks). Common on Maryland Eastern Shore, absent south of Virginia line.

Polygonum spp. (Knotweed, Water peppers): rootstock raw, boiled, or best when roasted (summer through fall); young leaves eaten raw or boiled (spring). *Polygonum erectum* (a Knotweed), *P. pennsylvanicum* (Pennsylvania smartweed), *P. prolificum* (Proliferous knotweed), and *P. punctatum* (Water smartweed) are common to frequent throughout; *P. hydropiperoides* (Mild water pepper) is common north of Northampton Co.; and *P. scandens* (a Knotweed) is common north of Virginia line.

Pontederia cordata (Pickerelweed): seeds eaten fresh, dried, or roasted and ground to flour (late summer–fall); young leaves before fully unfurled eaten raw or boiled (early summer). Common.

Potentilla simplex (Old-field cinquefoil) and *P. canadensis* (Common cinquefoil): roots of former used by Cherokees, of latter by Iroquois, to combat diarrhea (Cherokees, Iroquois, but not documented in Chesapeake region). *P. simplex* is common except in Accomack, where it is absent; *P. canadensis* is common on Maryland Eastern Shore, absent south of Virginia line.

Prunus spp. (Wild cherries and plums): fruit fresh or cooked (late summer to early fall). Medicinal: *P. serotina* bark used in cough remedies and blood-purifying tonics (Cherokees, Iroquois, Mohegans [tonic only], Delawares, both Virginia groups); bark also used to make wash for sores and burns (Cherokees, Iroquois, but not documented in Chesapeake region). *P. serotina* (Wild cherry) is common; *P. americana* (Wild plum) is frequent at least south to Delaware line and occurs down to Accomack Co.; and *P. angustifolia* (Chickasaw plum) is fairly frequent on Maryland Eastern Shore.

Pteridium aquilinum (Bracken): unfurled shoots (early spring) raw or cooked (eat sparingly, for it has an enzyme that attacks vitamin B_1). Common south to Virginia line, less so to south.

Pyrus (Sorbus or Aronia) arbutifolia (Red chokeberry): juicy fruit contains pectin, eaten raw or cooked (early fall). Common.

Pyrus (Malus) angustifolia (Wild crab) and *P. coronaria* (Wild crab apple): tart fruit raw or cooked (early fall). *P. angustifolia* is infrequent; *P. coronaria* is frequent on northern Maryland Eastern Shore, tapering off to southward.

Quercus spp. (Oaks): acorns are shelled, then leached in various ways, and then roasted or ground for flour (fall); those of *Q. virginiana* are so sweet as to need no leaching. Medicinal: bark of *Q. velutina* in tea for hoarseness (Cherokees, Delawares) and sore throat (Iroquois)(not documented in Chesapeake region). *Q. alba* (White oak) is abundant on the Eastern Shore; *Q. coccinea* (Scarlet oak), *Q. falcata* (Spanish oak), *Q. nigra* (Water oak), *Q. palustris* (Pin or Swamp oak), *Q. phellos* (Willow oak), and *Q. stellata* (Post oak) are common; *Q. velutina* (Black oak) is frequent though less so to south; *Q. marilandica* (Black jack oak) is frequent north of Virginia line but absent to south; and *Q. virginiana* (Live oak) occurs only in Northampton Co.

Rhexia mariana (Maryland meadow beauty) and *R. virginica* (Virginia meadow beauty): tender leaves raw or boiled (summer), tubers eaten raw (summer). Common south to Worcester Co., rare south of Virginia line.

Rhus copallina (Dwarf or Winged Sumac), *R. glabra* (Smooth or Common sumac) and *R. typhina* (Staghorn sumac): bark or roots used for skin ailments like sunburn, cuts, etc. (Cherokees, Iroquois, Delawares; Rappahannocks used it for "various complaints"). All three are frequent to common on Maryland Eastern Shore; *R. copallina* is common on Virginia Eastern Shore, *R. glabra* is in Accomack Co. but not Northampton Co., and *R. typhina* does not occur south of Virginia line.

Rosa spp. (Roses): petals eaten raw in salads or can be boiled for flavor (summer); vitamin C–rich hips with applelike flavor boiled (fall through winter). *R. carolina* (Wild or Swamp rose) and *R. palustris* (Swamp rose) are frequent.

Rubus spp. (Blackberries, Raspberries): vitamin C–rich fruit raw, cooked, or dried (summer); young shoots of blackberries (*R. argutus*, *R. cuneifolius*, and *R. hispidus*) can also be eaten raw (spring). Medicinal: Rappahannocks used available species to combat dysentery (Cherokees preferred *R. idaeus*, *occidentalis*, and *odoratus*, Delawares *R. allegheniensis*, Iroquois *R. alleghenensis* and *odoratus*, and Mohegans *R. hispidus*); *R. occidentalis* also used in emetics (Cherokees, Iroquois, but not documented in Chesapeake region). *R. argutus* (Blackberry) is frequent on Virginia Eastern Shore but not northward; *R. cuneifolius* (Sand blackberry) is frequent southward from Delaware line; *R. flagellaris* (Dewberry) and *R. occidentalis* (Wild black raspberry) are common; *R. hispidus* (Swamp blackberry) is found in Accomack Co., common to northward.

Rumex verticillatus (Swamp dock): seeds cleaned and ground for flour (late spring). Frequent.

Sagittaria spp. (Arrowheads): tubers eaten raw, better when cooked like potatoes (midsummer through early spring). *S. falcata* (Scythe-fruited arrowhead) is found south of Caroline Co., Md., with increasing frequency to south; *S. graminea* (Grass-leaved arrowhead) is frequent as far south as Delaware-Maryland line; *S. latifolia* (Wapato or Duck potato: produces the largest tubers) occurs in Accomack Co. and is common to north; *S. subulata* (Dwarf arrowhead) is frequent south to Wicomico Co.

Salicornia bigelovii (Dwarf saltwort) and *S. europaea* (Slender glasswort): stems and branches are fleshy and salty, best when eaten raw (spring through fall). Common.

Sambucus canadensis (Elderberry): vitamin C–rich berries are rank when raw, better when cooked (late summer). Medicinal: used for emetic (Cherokees, Iroquois, Mohegans, but not documented in Chesapeake region); various parts are ingredient in remedies for cuts, burns, skin eruptions (Cherokees, Iroquois, Delawares, Rappahannocks); and flower tea for babies' colic (Iroquois, Mohegans, Delawares, but not documented for Chesapeake region). Common.

Sanguinaria canadensis (Bloodroot): roots used in remedies for coughs and ailing lungs, powdered and snuffed for catarrh, and used in poultice or wash for cuts, sores, etc. (Cherokees, Iroquois, but not documented in Chesapeake region); root tea for blood medicine (Iroquois, Mohegans, Delawares [for women only], but not documented for Chesapeake region). Infrequent, and absent in Northampton Co.

Sassafras albidum (Sassafras): root tea as blood purifier or spring tonic, and inner bark or pith tea as eyewash (Cherokees, Iroquois, Mohegans [tonic only], Delawares [tonic only], Rappahannocks). Common.

Scirpus robustus (Salt-marsh bulrush): tuberous enlargements on rootstocks are edible (fall through spring). Common.

Scirpus validus (Great bulrush): pollen (summer) and ground seeds (fall) used as flour; leading tips of rootstocks roasted like potatoes or dried and ground for flour (winter); young shoots and tender cores at bases of older shoots eaten raw or cooked (spring). Found from Accomack Co. northward, common on Maryland Eastern Shore.

Sium suave (Water parsnip): roots boiled (fall through early spring). Frequent southward to northern Accomack Co., then less common. Plant closely resembles the highly poisonous *Cicuta maculata* (which grows plentifully on the Eastern Shore).

Smilax spp. (Briers): young shoots, leaves, and tendrils eaten raw or boiled (spring and summer); roots of *S. bona-nox, S. glauca,* and *S. rotundifolia* produce gelatin substitute if dried, chopped, pounded, and strained (all year). Medicinal: *S. herbacea* used in remedies for rheumatism and stomach trouble (Cherokees, Iroquois, but not documented in Chesapeake region). *S. glauca* (Saw brier) and *S. rotundifolia* (Greenbrier) are common throughout; *S. bona-nox* (Bullbrier or Catbrier) is common south of Virginia line and infrequent north of it; *S. herbacea* (Carrion flower) is frequent on Maryland Eastern Shore; *S. laurifolia* ("Bamboo") is frequent from Delaware line southward.

Sparganium americanum (American burweed) and *S. eurycarpum* (Large burweed): tubers cooked like potatoes (fall through early spring). Both occur in Accomack Co., frequent on Maryland Eastern Shore.

Sporobolus vaginiflorus (Poverty grass): tiny seeds ground for flour (fall). Frequent.

Stachys spp. (Hedge nettles): tubers raw or cooked (fall). *S. hispida* (Rough hedge nettle) is common southward to Wicomico Co.; *S. hyssopifolia* (Hyssop hedge nettle) is infrequent southward to Delaware line.

Suaeda linearis (Tall sea blite): tender leaves and stems are very salty, useful to season stews (spring through late summer). Infrequently found south of Delaware line, but absent in Northampton Co.

Symplocarpus foetidus (Skunk cabbage): roots dried, ground for flour (fall through early spring). Common.

Tradescantia virginiana (Spiderwort): young leaves and stems eaten raw or boiled (spring). Frequent on Maryland Eastern Shore, especially in north.

Triosteum perfoliatum (Horse gentian): one of several plants that John Clayton said seventeenth-century Virginia Indians used as an emetic (bark of roots is known to have that property). Frequent on Maryland Eastern Shore, absent south of Virginia line.

Typha spp. (Cattails): pollen (early summer) used as flour; shoots (spring), stalks (spring), and sprouts from long rootstocks (late summer through winter) peeled and eaten raw or cooked; rootstocks (late fall through early spring) eaten raw, baked, roasted, or starch extracted from them by peeling, crushing in water, and removing fibers, and then soaking to let starch settle (or boil them and strain off starch). *T. angustifolia* (Narrow-leaved cattail) and *T. latifolia* (Common cattail) are both common.

Ulmus rubra (Slippery elm): inner bark used for eyewash (Cherokees, Iroquois, but not documented for Chesapeake region). Rare on Eastern Shore (or on whole coastal plain, for that matter).

Vaccinium spp. (Blueberries): fruit has pectin, good raw, cooked, or dried and used in pemmican (fall). *V. fuscatum* (Black highbush blueberry), *V. corymbosum* complex (Highbush blueberry), *V. staminium* (Deerberry), and *V. vacillans* (Low blueberry) are common to frequent, *V. pallidum* (Blueberry) less so.

Veratrum viride (White hellebore, Indian poke): possibly a plant that John Clayton said seventeenth-century Virginia Indians used for an emetic. Rare on Maryland Eastern Shore, absent south of Virginia line.

Verbena hastata (Blue vervain): seeds soaked in several waters, dried, ground (late summer through fall). Common southward to Wicomico Co.

Veronica spp. (Speedwells): bitter leaves and stems raw (late spring through summer). *V. officinalis* (Common speedwell) and *V. peregrina* (Purslane speedwell) are common in north, less so to south, and *V. officinalis* is not on Virginia Eastern Shore.

Viburnum spp. (Wild raisins): thin-pulped berries better cooked (late summer through fall). *V. nudum* (Possum haw) is common south to Wicomico Co., frequent to south; *V. prunifolium* (Black haw) is common.

Viola spp. (Violets): vitamin A and C–rich leaves eaten raw or boiled; leaves are also mucilaginous for thickening soups (spring and summer). *V. cucullata* (Blue marsh violet), *V. lanceolata* (Lance-leaf violet), and *V. primulifolia* (Primrose-leaf violet) are common, *V. pedata* (Bird's-foot violet) frequent; *V. brittoniana* (Coast violet) and *V. sagittata* (Arrow-leaf violet) are frequent in north, rare to southward; *V. affinis* (LeConte's violet) and *V. palmata* (Wood violet) are common south of Virginia line and rare in north of it.

Vitis spp. (Grapes): young leaves boiled (early summer); mildly sweet fruit with pectin before they are fully ripe, eaten fresh, cooked, or dried (fall). *V. aestivalis* (Summer grape), *V. labrusca* (Fox grape), *V. riparia* (Riverbank grape), *V. rotundifolia* (Muscadine grape), and *V. vulpina* (Frost grape) are all common, though *V. aestivalis* is less so to south and *V. riparia* has only become so since the early twentieth century.

Zizania aquatica (Wild rice): seeds parched while stirring constantly, husked by beating and winnowing, washed (to remove smoky taste), then boiled like rice or ground for flour (mid- to late summer). Found from Accomack Co. northward, common on Maryland Eastern Shore.

Appendix D

Fish and Shellfish Usable by the Indians of the Chesapeake Bay Region

Helen C. Rountree

Sources on fish and shellfish: Lippson and Lippson 1984, supplemented by Lippson 1973, Virginia Office of the Secretary of Commerce and Natural Resources 1977, Hoagman et al. 1973, Holdich and Lowery 1988. I have included only those species whose adult lengths are at least 10 in. (25 cm) in the case of fish and 5 in. (12.5 cm) in the case of shellfish. Items are listed by ecological zone and season.

I. Saltwater Zone

A. DEEP WATER

1. Fish

Acipenser brevirostrum (juveniles)	Shortnose sturgeon	JFMAMJJASOND
A. oxyrynchus (juveniles)	Atlantic sturgeon	JFMAMJJASOND
Anguilla rostrata	American eel	JFMAMJJASOND
Menticirrhus americanus	Southern kingfish	JFMAMJJASOND
M. saxatilis	Northern kingfish	JFMAMJJASOND
Paralichthys dentatus (adults)	Summer flounder	JFMAMJJASOND
Prionotus carolinus	Northern sea robin	JFMAMJJASOND
Pseudopleuronectes americanus (adults)	Winter flounder	JFMAMJJASOND
Scophthalmus aquosus	Windowpane	JFMAMJJASOND
Spheoroides maculatus	Northern puffer	JFMAMJJASOND
Trinectes maculatus	Hogchoker	JFMAMJJASOND
Urophycis chuss	Red hake	JFMAMJJASOND
U. regius	Spotted hake	JFMAMJJASOND

264

Acipenser brevirostrum (adults)	Shortnose sturgeon	. . MAM. . . . . . .
A. oxyrhynchus (adults)	Atlantic sturgeon	. . MAM. . . . . . .
Alosa aestivalis (adults)	Blueblack herring	. . MAM. . . . . . .
A. mediocris (adults)	Hickory shad	. . MAM. . . . . .
A. pseudoharengus (adults)	Alewife	. . MAM. . . . . . .
A. sapidissima (adults)	American shad	. . MAM. . . . . .
Aluterus schoepfi	Orange filefish	. . . . MJJASO . .
Archosargus probatocephalus	Sheepshead	. . . . MJJASO . .
Bairdiella chrysoura (adults)	Silver perch	. . . . MJJASO . .
Brevoortia tyrannus (adults)	Atlantic menhadden	. . . . MJJASO . .
Caranx crysos (adults)	Blue runner	. . . . MJJASO . .
C. hippos (adults)	Crevalle jack	. . . . MJJASO . .
Centropristes striatus (adults)	Black sea bass	. . . . MJJASO . .
Cynoscion nebulosus (adults)	Spotted sea trout	. . . . MJJASO . .
C. regalis (adults)	Weakfish	. . . . MJJASO . .
Euthynnus alletteratus	Little tunny	. . . . MJJASO . .
Leiostomus xanthurus (adults)	Spot	. . . . MJJASO . .
Micropogonias undulatus (adults)	Atlantic croaker	. . . . MJJASO . .
Monacanthus hispidus	Planehead filefish	. . . . MJJASO . .
Orthopristis chrysoptera	Pigfish	. . . . MJJASO . .
Pogonias cromis (adults)	Black drum	. . . . MJJASO . .
Pomatomus saltatrix (adults)	Bluefish	. . . . MJJASO . .
Rachycentron canadum	Cobia	. . . . MJJASO . .
Sciaenops oscellatus (adults)	Red drum	. . . . MJJASO . .
Sarda sarda	Bonito	. . . . MJJASO . .
Selene vomer (adults)	Lookdown	. . . . MJJASO . .
Stenotomus chrysops	Scup, porgy	. . . . MJJASO . .
Tautoga onitis	Tautog, blackfish	. . . . MJJASO . .
Trachinotus carolinus (adults)	Florida pompano	. . . . MJJASO . .
Morone americana (adults)	White perch	JFMA . . . . . . ND
M. saxatilis (adults)	Striped bass	JFMA . . . . . . ND

2. Shellfish

Busycon canaliculatum	Channeled whelk	JFMAMJJASOND
B. carica	Knobbed whelk	JFMAMJJASOND
Crassostrea virginica	American oyster	JFMAMJJASOND
Callinectes sapidus	Blue crab	JFMA . . . . . . ND

B. SHALLOW WATER (OPEN WATER)

1. Fish

Anguilla rostrata	American eel	JFMAMJJASOND
Scophthalmus aquosus	Windowpane	JFMAMJJASOND
Trinectes maculatus	Hogchoker	JFMAMJJASOND
Alosa aestivalis (adults)	Blueblack herring	..MAM.......
A. mediocris (adults)	Hickory shad	..MAM.......
A. pseudoharengus (adults)	Alewife	..MAM.......
A. sapidissima (adults)	American shad	..MAM.......
Bairdiella chrysoura (juveniles)	Silver perch	....MJJASO..
Brevoortia tyrannus (juveniles)	Atlantic menhadden	....MJJASO..
Caranx crysos (juveniles)	Blue runner	....MJJASO..
C. hippos (juveniles)	Crevalle jack	....MJJASO..
Centropristes striatus (juveniles)	Black sea bass	....MJJASO..
Cynoscion nebulosus (juveniles)	Spotted sea trout	....MJJASO..
C. regalis (juveniles)	Weakfish	....MJJASO..
Leiostomus xanthurus (juveniles)	Spot	....MJJASO..
Micropogonias undulatus (juveniles)	Atlantic croaker	....MJJASO..
Mugil cephalus	Striped mullet	....MJJASO..
M. curema	White mullet	....MJJASO..
Paralichthys dentatus (juveniles)	Summer flounder	....MJJASO..
Peprilus alepidotus	Harvestfish	....MJJASO..
P. triacanthus	Butterfish	....MJJASO..
Pogonias cromis (juveniles)	Black drum	....MJJASO..
Pomatomus saltatrix (juveniles)	Bluefish	....MJJASO..
Pseudopleuronectes americanus (juvenile)	Winter flounder	....MJJASO..
Sciaenops oscellatus (juveniles)	Red drum	....MJJASO..
Selene vomer (juveniles)	Lookdown	....MJJASO..
Trachinotus carolinus (juveniles)	Florida pompano	....MJJASO..
Alosa aestivalis (juveniles)	Blueblack herring	........SON.

A. mediocris (juveniles)	Hickory shad	. . . . SON .
A. pseudoharengus (juveniles)	Alewife	. . . . SON .
A. sapidissima (juveniles)	American shad	. . . . SON .

2. Shellfish

Busycon canaliculatum	Channeled whelk	JFMAMJJASOND
B. carica	Knobbed whelk	JFMAMJJASOND
Crassostrea virginica	American oyster	JFMAMJJASOND
Mercenaria mercenaria	Quahog, hard clam	JFMAMJJASOND
Mya arenaria	Soft clam, manninose	JFMAMJJASOND
Mytilus edulis	Blue mussel	JFMAMJJASOND
Callinectes sapidus	Blue crab	. . . . MJJASO . .

II. Saltier Brackish Water Zone

A. DEEPEST WATER ONLY

1. Fish

Prionotus carolinus	Northern sea robin	JFMAMJJASOND
Spheoroides maculatus	Northern puffer	JFMAMJJASOND
Acipenser brevirostrum (adults)	Shortnose sturgeon	. . MAM. . . . . . .
A. oxyrhynchus (adults)	Atlantic sturgeon	. . MAM. . . . . . .
Aluterus schoepfi	Orange filefish	. . . . MJJASO . .
Centropristes striatus	Black sea bass	. . . . MJJASO . .
Euthynnus alletteratus	Little tunny	. . . . MJJASO . .
Rachycentron canadum	Cobia	. . . . MJJASO . .
Sarda sarda	Bonito	. . . . MJJASO . .
Urophycis chuss	Red hake	. . . . MJJASO . .
U. regius	Spotted hake	. . . . MJJASO . .
Lepomis gibbosus	Pumpkinseed	JFMA . . . . . . ND
L. macrochirus	Bluegill	JFMA . . . . . . ND
Morone americana (adults)	White perch	JFMA . . . . . ND
M. saxatilis (adults)	Striped bass	JFMA . . . . . . ND

2. Shellfish

Callinectes sapidus	Blue crab	JFMA . . . . . . ND

B. VARIOUS DEPTHS (OPEN WATER)

1. Fish

Acipenser brevirostrum (juveniles)	Snortnose sturgeon	JFMAMJJASOND

A. oxyrynchus (juveniles)	Atlantic sturgeon	JFMAMJJASOND
Anguilla rostrata	American eel	JFMAMJJASOND
Trinectes maculatus	Hogchoker	JFMAMJJASOND
Alosa aestivalis (adults)	Blueblack herring	..MAM.......
A. mediocris (adults)	Hickory shad	..MAM.......
A. pseudoharengus (adults)	Alewife	..MAM.......
A. sapidissima (adults)	American shad	..MAM.......
Pseudopleuronectes americanus (adults)	Winter flounder	..MAM.......
Alosa aestivalis (juveniles)	Blueblack herring	....MJJASO..
A. mediocris (juveniles)	Hickory shad	....MJJASO..
A. pseudoharengus (juveniles)	Alewife	....MJJASO..
A. sapidissima (juveniles)	American shad	....MJJASO..
Bairdiella chrysoura (juveniles)	Silver perch	....MJJASO..
Brevoortia tyrannus (juveniles)	Atlantic menhadden	....MJJASO..
Caranx crysos (juveniles)	Blue runner	....MJJASO..
C. hippos (juveniles)	Crevalle jack	....MJJASO..
Centropristes striatus (juveniles)	Black sea bass	....MJJASO..
Cynoscion nebulosus (juveniles)	Spotted sea trout	....MJJASO..
C. regalis (juveniles)	Weakfish	....MJJASO..
Leiostomus xanthurus (juveniles)	Spot	....MJJASO..
Lepomis gibbosus	Pumpkinseed	....MJJASO..
L. macrochirus	Bluegill	....MJJASO..
Micropogonias undulatus (juveniles)	Atlantic croaker	....MJJASO..
Morone americana (adults)	White perch	....MJJASO..
M. saxatilis (adults)	Striped bass	....MJJASO..
Mugil cephalus	Striped mullet	....MJJASO..
M. curema	White mullet	....MJJASO..
Paralichthys dentatus (juveniles)	Summer flounder	....MJJASO..
Peprilus alepidotus	Harvestfish	....MJJASO..
P. triacanthus	Butterfish	....MJJASO..
Pogonias cromis (juveniles)	Black drum	....MJJASO..
Pomatomus saltatrix (juveniles)	Bluefish	....MJJASO..

Pseuopleuronectes americanus (juveniles)	Winter flounder	. . . . MJJASO . .
Sciaenops oscellatus (juveniles)	Red drum	. . . . MJJASO . .
Selene vomer (juveniles)	Lookdown	. . . . MJJASO . .
Trachinotus carolinus (juveniles)	Florida pompano	. . . . MJJASO . .
Alosa aestivalis (juveniles)	Blueblack herring	. . . . SON .
A. mediocris (juveniles)	Hickory shad	. . . . SON .
A. pseudoharengus (juveniles)	Alewife	. . . . SON .
A. sapidissima (juveniles)	American shad	. . . . SON .
Morone americana (adults)	White perch	JF . . . JJASOND
M. saxatilis (adults)	Striped bass	JF . . . JJASOND
Perca flavescens (adults)	Yellow perch	JF . . . JJASOND

2. Shellfish

Crassostrea virginica	American oyster	JFMAMJJASOND
Cyrtopleura costata	Angel wing	JFMAMJJASOND
Mercenaria mercenaria	Quahog, hard clam	JFMAMJJASOND
Mya arenaria	Soft clam, manninose	JFMAMJJASOND
Callinectes sapidus	Blue crab	. . . . MJJASO . .

III. Fresher Brackish Water Zone

A. DEEPEST WATER ONLY
1. Fish

Ictalurus punctatus	Channel catfish	JFMAMJJASOND
Spheoroides maculatus	Northern puffer	JFMAMJJASOND
Acipenser brevirostrum (adults)	Shortnose sturgeon	. . MAM . . . .
A. oxyrhynchus (adults)	Atlantic sturgeon	. . MAM . . . .
Lepomis gibbosus	Pumpkinseed	JFMA . . . . . . ND
L. macrochirus	Bluegill	JFMA . . . . . . ND

2. Shellfish

Callinectes sapidus	Blue crab	JFMA . . . . . . ND

B. VARIOUS DEPTHS (OPEN WATER)
1. Fish

Acipenser brevirostrum (juveniles)	Shortnose sturgeon	JFMAMJJASOND

A. oxyrynchus (juveniles)	Atlantic sturgeon	JFMAMJJASOND
Esox americanus	Redfin pickerel	JFMAMJJASOND
E. niger	Chain pickerel	JFMAMJJASOND
Lepisosteus osseus	Longnose gar	JFMAMJJASOND
Micropterus dolomieui	Smallmouth bass	JFMAMJJASOND
M. salmoides	Largemouth bass	JFMAMJJASOND
Trinectes maculatus	Hogchoker	JFMAMJJASOND
Alosa aestivalis (adults)	Blueblack herring	..MAM.......
A. mediocris (adults)	Hickory shad	..MAM.......
A. pseudoharengus (adults)	Alewife	..MAM.......
A. sapidissima (adults)	American shad	..MAM.......
Brevoortia tyrannus (juveniles)	Atlantic menhadden	..MAM.......
Morone americana (adults)	White perch	..MAM.......
M. saxatilis (adults)	Striped bass	..MAM.......
Alosa aestivalis (juveniles)	Blueblack herring	....MJJASO..
A. mediocris (juveniles)	Hickory shad	....MJJASO..
A. pseudoharengus (juveniles)	Alewife	....MJJASO..
A. sapidissima (juveniles)	American shad	....MJJASO..
Bairdiella chrysoura (juveniles)	Silver perch	....MJJASO..
Cynoscion nebulosus (juveniles)	Spotted sea trout	....MJJASO..
C. regalis (juveniles)	Weakfish	....MJJASO..
Leisostomus xanthurus (juveniles)	Spot	....MJJASO..
Lepomis gibbosus	Pumpkinseed	....MJJASO..
L. macrochirus	Bluegill	....MJJASO..
Micropogonias undulatus (juveniles)	Atlantic croaker	....MJJASO..
Morone americana (juveniles)	White perch	....MJJASO..
M. saxatilis (juveniles)	Striped bass	....MJJASO..
Mugil cephalus	Striped mullet	....MJJASO..
M. curema	White mullet	....MJJASO..
Paralichthys dentatus (juveniles)	Summer flounder	....MJJASO..
Peprilus alepidotus	Harvestfish	....MJJASO..
P. triacanthus	Butterfish	....MJJASO..
Pomatomus saltatrix (juveniles)	Bluefish	....MJJASO..

Pseudopleuronectes americanus (juv.)	Winter flounder	. . . . MJJASO . .
Dorosoma cepedianum	Gizzard shad	JF . . . JJASOND
D. petenense	Threadfin shad	JF . . . JJASOND
Ictalurus catus	White catfish	JF . . . JJASOND
I. nebulosus	Brown bullhead	JF . . . JJASOND
Perca flavescens	Yellow perch	JF . . . JJASOND

2. Shellfish

Callinectes sapidus	Blue crab	. . . . MJJASO . .
Cambarus diogenes	Burrowing crayfish	JFMAMJJASOND
Orconectes limosus	Coastal plains river crayfish	JFMAMJJASOND

IV. Freshwater Zone

A. DEEPEST WATER ONLY
1. Fish

Ictalurus punctatus	Channel catfish	JFMAMJJASOND
Acipenser brevirostrum (adults)	Shortnose sturgeon	. . MAM . . . .
A. oxyrhynchus (adults)	Atlantic sturgeon	. . MAM . . . .
Lepomis gibbosus	Pumpkinseed	JFMA . . . . . . ND
L. macrochirus	Bluegill	JFMA . . . . . . ND

2. Shellfish

| *Callinectes sapidus* (males) | Blue crab | JFMA . . . . . . ND |

B. VARIOUS DEPTHS (OPEN WATER)
1. Fish

Acipenser brevirostrum (juveniles)	Shortnose sturgeon	JFMAMJJASOND
A. oxyrynchus (juveniles)	Atlantic sturgeon	JFMAMJJASOND
Anguilla rostrata	American eel	JFMAMJJASOND
Dorosoma cepedianum	Gizzard shad	JFMAMJJASOND
D. petenense	Threadfin shad	JFMAMJJASOND
Esox americanus	Redfin pickerel	JFMAMJJASOND
E. niger	Chain pickerel	JFMAMJJASOND
Ictalurus catus	White catfish	JFMAMJJASOND
I. nebulosus	Brown bullhead	JFMAMJJASOND
Lepisosteus osseus	Longnose gar	JFMAMJJASOND

Micropterus dolomieui	Smallmouth bass	JFMAMJJASOND
M. salmoides	Largemouth bass	JFMAMJJASOND
Pomoxis annularis	White crappie	JFMAMJJASOND
P. nigromaculatus	Black crappie	JFMAMJJASOND
Trinectes maculatus	Hogchoker	JFMAMJJASOND
Alosa aestivalis (adults)	Blueblack herring	. .MAM. . . . . .
A. mediocris (adults)	Hickory shad	. .MAM. . . . . .
A. pseudoharengus (adults)	Alewife	. .MAM. . . . . .
A. sapidissima (adults)	American shad	. .MAM. . . . . .
Morone americana (adults)	White perch	. .MAM. . . . . .
M. saxatilis (adults)	Striped bass	. .MAM. . . . . .
Perca flavescens (adults)	Yellow perch	. .MAM. . . . . .
Alosa aestivalis (juveniles)	Blueblack herring	. . . .MJJASO . .
A. mediocris (juveniles)	Hickory shad	. . . .MJJASO . .
A. pseudoharengus (juveniles)	Alewife	. . . .MJJASO . .
A. sapidissima (juveniles)	American shad	. . . .MJJASO . .
Brevoortia tyrannus (juveniles)	Atlantic menhadden	. . . .MJJASO . .
Leiostomus xanthurus (juveniles)	Spot	. . . .MJJASO . .
Lepomis gibbosus	Pumpkinseed	. . . .MJJASO . .
L. macrochirus	Bluegill	. . . .MJJASO . .
Micropogonias undulatus (juveniles)	Atlantic croaker	. . . .MJJASO . .

2. Shellfish

Anodonta spp.	Freshwater mussels	JFMAMJJASOND
Cambarus diogenes	Burrowing crayfish	JFMAMJJASOND
Lampsilis spp.	Freshwater mussels	JFMAMJJASOND
Orconectes limosus	Coastal plains river crayfish	JFMAMJJASOND

V. Saltwater Marsh Zone

A. SHELLFISH

Geukensia demissa	Atlantic ribbed mussel	JFMAMJJASOND
Littorina irrorata	Marsh periwinkle	JFMAMJJASOND

VI. Brackish Marsh Zone

A. SHELLFISH

Geukensia demissa	Atlantic ribbed mussel	JFMAMJJASOND
Littorina irrorata	Marsh periwinkle	JFMAMJJASOND

VII. Freshwater Marsh Zone

A. SHELLFISH

Anodonta spp.	Freshwater mussels	JFMAMJJASOND
Lampsilis spp.	Freshwater mussels	JFMAMJJASOND

Notes

One. The Native People's World

1. Northampton Co., Va.: Cobb and Smith 1989; Kent Co., Md.: White 1982.
2. Lamb 1963.
3. USGS topographic maps, 7.5–minute series.
4. Donna M. E. Ware, personal communication 1994.
5. Rountree, personal observation; my appreciation to the staff at Jamestown Settlement and the Mariners' Museum for helping me to try out their canoes.
6. Smith 1986b [1612]: 171.
7. Cobb and Smith 1989, R. Hall 1970 and 1973, Hutton et al. 1963, Matthews and Hall 1966, Matthews and Reybold 1966, Reybold 1971, and E. White 1982. There is currently no soil survey for Accomack County.
8. We are assuming that the Indians had a definite say in where their reservations were located in the historic period.
9. No one at this writing has reconstructed what the salinities of the streams were in A.D. 1600. The salinity zones given here are the modern ones, whose boundaries are undoubtedly farther upstream than they were four centuries ago. The correlations, river by river, run:

Pocomoke River (over seventy-five miles long):
Reservations: Askiminikansen and Queponqua, located across from each other near Whiton on Wicomico Co. line; Parahocon (Dividing Creek) on far-up creek of that name, just above Whiteburg.
Prime soil: only extensive waterfront patch on whole river is where Askiminikansen and Queponqua were located; other patches are on lower reaches of Nassawango and Dividing Creeks.
Salinity of waters: salty in fall and salty-brackish in spring at mouth; becomes fresh-brackish just below where Virginia-Maryland line heads east overland; becomes fresh above Rehobeth at top of eastward bend there.
Edible emergent plants: arrow arum above where Virginia-Maryland line heads east overland; cow lilies from just above Rehobeth; duck potatoes well up Dividing and Nassawango Creeks. All limited by presence of swamp forest.
Anadromous fish spawning: striped bass throughout river; shad and herring above Snow Hill.
Big Annemessex River:
Reservations: none.
Prime soil: none near river.
Salinity of waters: salty-brackish throughout, though mouth is salty in fall.
Edible emergent plants: none.
Anadromous fish spawning: striped bass in upper reaches.
Manokin River:
Reservations: Manokin, near head of river.
Prime soils: along most of waterfront, especially higher up.

Salinity of waters: salty-brackish all year at mouth, becoming fresh-brackish at junction with Kings Creek.

Edible emergent plants: arrow arum above U.S. 13 bridge; wild rice from Princess Anne upward.

Anadromous fish spawning: striped bass along nearly whole river; shad and herring far upriver.

Wicomico River (about thirty-five miles long):

Reservations: Tundotank near modern Salisbury; Cottingham's Creek.

Prime soils: some along lower reaches of Wicomico Creek.

Salinity of waters: salty-brackish until narrowing just below Wicomico Creek, then fresh-brackish to 2½ miles below Salisbury, then fresh.

Edible emergent plants: arrow arum above Whitehaven; wild rice from seven miles below Salisbury upward and on Wicomico Creek from just below Allen; duck potatoes 2½ miles below Salisbury; cow lilies from several miles above Salisbury upward and on Wicomico Creek from just below Allen.

Anadromous fish spawning: striped bass from just below Whitehaven upward; shad and herring above near Trinity.

Nanticoke River (about seventy miles long, with big meanders):

Reservations: Chicone between lower Chicone and Marshyhope Creeks, Puckamee across the river; Broad Creek, on creek of that name (in Delaware).

Prime soils: almost all above U.S. Rt. 50 bridge; large patch above the bridge on west and between lower Chicone and Marshyhope Creeks; also some in upper reaches of Quantico Creek.

Salinity of waters: salty-brackish at mouth, becoming fresh-brackish about four miles below U.S. 50 bridge at Vienna and fresh near junction with Broad Creek. Quantico and Rewastico Creeks become fresh-brackish about three miles above mouths; Marshyhope Creek becomes fresh about two miles up.

Edible emergent plants: arrow arum, duck potatoes, and cow lilies from about one mile above Vienna upward; wild rice in same area, with greatest abundance near Broad Creek (Scott 1991: 111). In Quantico Creek, wild rice along its length, arrow arum in upper reaches to swamp forest line; in Marshyhope Creek, band of several edible emergents along banks.

Anadromous fish spawning: striped bass from just above Tyaskin Creek upward; shad and herring from just below Marshyhope Creek upward in river and in headwaters of Rewastico and Quantico Creeks.

Transquaking and Chicamacomico Rivers (about twenty-five miles long):

Reservations: none.

Prime soils: many small patches along upper reaches.

Salinity of waters: salty-brackish at mouth, soon turning to fresh-brackish and becoming fresh in headwaters.

Edible emergent plants: cow lilies, arrow arum, and duck potatoes in upper reaches.

Choptank River (about sixty-five miles long):

Reservations: Choptank (later Locust Neck), from modern Cambridge to Warwick River.

Prime soils: major patch on east side from above Cambridge to Hunting Creek; less to west or above that creek; some patches at meanders of Tuckahoe Creek.

Salinity of waters: salty-brackish except in spring below Cambridge, then fresh-brackish year-round above and fresh above Denton; tributaries often have fresh water at heads, obscured by swamp forest. Tuckahoe Creek becomes fresh above Md. Rt. 328 bridge.

Edible emergent plants: wild rice above Marsh Creek; some arrow arum above Hunting Creek; cow lilies from Rt. 331 bridge (east of Easton) upward; duck potatoes only at Watts Creek above Denton. Best broad-leaved emergents today are in meanders of Tuckahoe Creek below Hillsboro.

Anadromous fish spawning: striped bass from just above Cambridge upward; shad and herring above junction with Tuckahoe Creek, in both creek and river.
Tred Avon, Miles, Wye Rivers:
Reservations: none.
Prime soils: limited amount along most of lengths.
Salinity of waters: salty-brackish most of year (fresh-brackish in spring), with some freshwater at head of Tred Avon.
Edible emergent plants: arrow arum at head of Tred Avon.
Chester River (about forty-five miles long):
Reservations: none; "Ozinies" (later Wicomiss) shown on John Smith map far upriver but not located archaeologically yet.
Prime soils: very little except near Fryingpan Point and opposite Crumptown.
Salinity of waters: nearly fresh-brackish most of year (salty-brackish in fall), becoming so year-round above Chestertown, and fresh two miles below Millington.
Edible emergent plants: arrow arum at head of Corsica River; that and wild rice from just below Southeast Creek; duck potatoes near Chestertown; cow lilies from two miles below Millington upward.
Anadromous fish spawning: striped bass beginning above Corsica River; shad and herring in far upper reaches.
Sassafras River (about twenty miles long):
Reservations: none; "Tockwogh" shown on John Smith map far upriver but not located archaeologically yet.
Prime soils: moderately large patches on point above Freeman Creek and above Dyer Creek.
Salinity of waters: mouth is fresh-brackish in fall, fresh otherwise; freshwater from just above mouth upward.
Edible emergent plants: small amounts of arrow arum, duck potatoes and other arrowheads, cow lilies, and wild rice.
Anadromous fish spawning: striped bass throughout river.
Sources: Soils: Cobb and Smith 1989; Hall 1970 and 1973; Hutton et al. 1963; Hutton et al. 1964; Matthews and Hall 1966; Matthews and Reybold 1966; Reybold 1971; White 1982. Salinities: National Wetlands Inventory 1986; Lippson 1973: 7; and to a lesser extent Lippson and Lippson 1984. Plants: National Wetlands Inventory 1986 (Virginia) and Sipple 1978 (Maryland). Fish: Lippson 1973: 29, 37.
10. Deal 1981: 2.
11. James River Project 1950: 260.
12. Brown and Brown 1984: xxii.
13. Rountree, personal observation.
14. Scott 1991: 101–2, 73.
15. John Pory in Smith 1986c [1624]: 291.
16. Salty water in Chesapeake Bay: up the Chesapeake to the mouth of Occohannock Creek; from there to the neck between Manokin and Big Annemessex Rivers the water is salty-brackish in the spring and salty in the fall. Year-round salty-brackish water: up to Meekins Neck in spring and up to north side of Chester River's mouth in fall. Fresh-brackish (oligohaline) water: up to mouth of Fairlee Creek (below Sassafras River) in spring and up to Susquehanna River's mouth in fall. Our definitions of salinity follow Lippson 1973: 6; salty water has more than 18 parts per thousand of salt, salty-brackish water has 10–18 ppt, fresh-brackish (oligohaline) water has 1–10 ppt, and fresh water has less than 1 ppt. Placement of boundaries: Lippson 1973: 7, which shows a map each for spring and fall. The boundaries are based upon research done in the 1960s and early 1970s, in a fairly narrow range of time; the boundaries now may be somewhat different.

17. Virginia Legislative Petitions, Northampton Co., Mar. 17, 1842. The petition states that oysters were entirely gone from Occohannock, Hungars, and Old Plantation Creeks, but a few were left in Nassawaddox Creek; the oysters in Cherrystone Creek were still abundant but in danger of being depleted by overharvesting.

18. Rountree's almost nightly personal observation in Hampton; James River Project 1950: 249.

19. James River Project 1950: 251 (otters), 249 (raccoons); Scott 1991: 75 (raccoons).

20. Geologist Gerald Johnson (personal communication [to Rountree], 1996) feels that the location of the "salt plug" has changed in the last four centuries in rivers like the Nanticoke, whose valleys are not seriously inundated by seawater, but not in larger, much-flooded valleys like that of the lower James.

21. Rountree 1996. The appendix originally compiled for this article (omitted in the published version) formed the basis for Appendixes C and D of this volume.

22. Smith 1986b [1612]: 150.

23. John Pory, in Smith 1986c [1624]: 291; Smith 1986b [1612]: 162–63; Strachey 1953 [1612]: 80. Not all Powhatan scholars agree with this estimate; Turner (1976: 187) feels that corn may have provided 75 percent or more of the Powhatans' annual calorie intake, and that "at least 80%, and perhaps over 90%, of subsistence needs were met through agriculture and fishing" (ibid.: 188).

24. Sipple 1978, which plots the occurrence of marsh plants in general; the comparison between Eastern Shore and western shore is ours.

25. James River Project 1950: 239, 258.

26. Thomas et al. state that deer are most plentiful in "poorly drained to swampy woods," but their chart (1975: 48) distinguishes only between such woods and "well drained woods" and "transitional areas." Deer do prefer less-than-mature woods, especially in the winter, because of the greater ground cover that screens them from predators (ibid.: 47). However, the optimum deer country has vegetation that produces large amounts of nuts, seeds, and berries and also shrubs for camouflage (James River Project 1950: 271). The nuts and some of the seeds would come from deciduous forest cover, and the other seeds and the berries would come from plants that favor open areas that are being overgrown (see subsequent ecozones). Thus the open woods, when its tall stands are mixed deciduous forest, are extremely attractive to deer.

27. James River Project 1950: 202.

28. Turner 1976: 194.

29. Scott 1991: 92. Woodchucks may have been much less common—or not in the area at all—when little clearing was being done; they have benefited from clearing of fields for European-style agriculture (ibid.; James River Project 1950: 259).

30. Smith 1986b [1612]: 162; White 1910 [1634]: 40.

31. Chestnut plants still occur widely in the Chesapeake region, even though the blight causes most saplings to die back; we can therefore still trace the preblight incidence of chestnut trees in the region.

32. James River Project 1950: 270, 272; Scott 1991: 69.

33. Smith 1986b [1612]: 164.

34. James River Project 1950: 246, 255, 256. In the James River basin in 1950, bobcats were still common in the lowland swamps.

35. James River Project 1950: 254, 255.

36. Ibid.: 254; Scott 1991: 75.

37. Smith 1992: 275.

38. Dent 1995: 254; for *H. pusillum*, which came originally from the Midwest: Gardner 1994: 268, 275; as Indian cultigens: B. Smith 1994.

39. Griffith 1980.

40. Custer 1989: 316; Thomas 1977.

41. Hughes 1980: 49–52.

42. Potter 1993: 137.

43. Hughes 1980: 213; Davidson 1993: 147–49.

44. Turner 1993: 86. Late Woodland pottery from the Arlington site in Northampton County, Va., mainly consists of Townsend wares, but there are some sherds present there that are probably imported examples of Roanoke simple-stamped ware (Keith T. Egloff, personal communication 1994).

45. Custer 1989: 300.

46. Hutchinson, Calloway, and Bryant 1964; Custer 1989: 327.

47. The continual use of storage pits at Chicone during the latter part of the Late Woodland period is a trait not generally paralleled on the western shore, where aboveground storage seems to have been the rule (Potter 1993: 170–72). Until more extensive excavations have been carried out at Chicone and at other Late Woodland sites on the Eastern Shore, it is impossible to say whether storage pits are a typical feature of the latter part of the Late Woodland period there or not.

48. Hutchinson, Calloway, and Bryant 1964: 16. One of us (Davidson) observed the Potomac Creek material during an examination of excavated Chicone artifacts housed in the Delaware State Museum, Dover.

49. Davidson, Hughes, and McNamara 1985: 45–46.

50. Seventeenth-century historical accounts mention a "Nanticoke Fort" at the Chicone site, a fortified settlement at Tockwogh on the Sassafras River at the northern end of the Eastern Shore, and "forts" within the territories of the Choptank and the Pocomoke/Assateague Indians in modern Dorchester and Worcester Counties.

51. Potter 1993: 122–23.

52. Rountree and Turner forthcoming.

53. Chase n.d.

54. Anthropologists define a secondary burial as one in which the body is allowed to rot away to bones, and then the bones are collected and placed elsewhere.

55. Ubelaker 1993: 58.

56. Chase n.d.: 12.

57. Wall, Israel, and Otter 1988: 20; Custer and Griffith 1986: 46.

58. Chase n.d.: 12.

59. Custer and Griffith 1986: 56.

60. Potter 1993: 149–50.

61. Custer and Griffith 1986: 56.

62. Ibid.: 54–55.

63. Turner 1986: 24–25.

64. Ibid.: 25.

65. Turner 1992: 118.

66. Boyd and Boyd 1992: 261–62 and table 1.

67. Lucketti et al. 1994: 293–94.

68. Browne et al. 1883–1972: 3:403. In 1660 the Piscataways told the English that "long a goe there came a King from the Easterne Shoare who Comanded over all the Indians now inhabiting within the bounds of this Province (nameing every towne severally) and also over the Patawomecks and Sasquehannoughs, whome for that he Did as it were embrace and cover them all they called Vttapoingassinem . . . the Governm't descended for thirteene Generacons without interrupcon untill Kittamaqunnds tyme."

69. Custer 1989: 311; Custer et al. 1986: 32.

70. Custer 1989: 350.

71. Historical sources on the Eastern Shore are John Smith's description of his 1608 ex-

plorations of the region in Smith 1986b [1612]: 224–26 and Smith 1986c [1624]: 163–65, 171, and John Pory's 1621 account, in Smith 1986c [1624]: 289. Otherwise we must use ethnographic analogy with the western shore Algonquian-speakers of Virginia and Maryland. Two modern cultural descriptions of those people are Rountree 1989 for Virginia and Clark and Rountree 1993 for Maryland; the major early seventeenth-century sources are, for Virginia, Smith 1986a [1608], 1986b [1612], and 1986c [1624]; Strachey 1953 [1612]; Spelman 1910 [1613?]; for Maryland, A. White 1910 [1634], Anonymous 1910 [1635], and Jesuit Letters 1910 [1634 onward].

72. Smith's map of the Chesapeake region (Smith n.d. [1608]) shows a scrupulous recording of even small hamlets by name, but town names such as Nassawaddox and Onancock, occupied by native people under their own town chiefs in the mid-seventeenth century, are absent.

73. Virginia: Smith n.d. [1608]; John Pory in Smith 1986c [1624]: 289; supplemented by town names from the Virginia land patents (Nugent 1934) and the records of Northampton and Accomack Counties. Maryland: Smith n.d. [1608], supplemented by Browne et al. 1883–1972.

74. Anthropologists use the term *chief* to mean a moderately powerful, usually hereditary leader of a district; such leaders who dominate multiple districts are *paramount chiefs*. We do not use the term *chief* in the casual, derogatory sense that so offends Native Americans in the western United States. We prefer the term *chief*, as anthropologists use it, to the commoner but misleading English terms *king, queen,* or *emperor*, which we use only within quotation marks.

75. Smith 1986b [1612]: 225.

76. Smith 1986c [1624]: 165.

77. Different: Smith 1986b [1612]: 150. Unintelligible: Smith 1986c [1624]: 171: "it chanced one of them could speak the language of Powhatan."

78. Speck 1927. Ives Goddard (1978: 73) has firmly identified the Nanticoke and Choptank languages as Algonquian.

79. Sources from Virginia (centered upon James River valley): Smith 1986b [1612]: 161; Strachey 1953 [1612]: 77; Archer 1969b [1607]: 103. Source for both colonies: Smith n.d.

80. Va.: Smith 1986b [1612]: 162; Strachey 1953 [1612]: 113; Archer 1969b [1607]: 104; Percy 1969 [1608?]: 145; White 1969 [1608?]: 150.

81. "Countrey Villages": Anonymous 1910 [1635]: 86. Va.: Smith 1986b [1612]: 151, 162; Strachey 1953 [1612]: 77, 78, 119; Clayton 1968 [1687]: 434–35. Md.: Smith 1986c [1624]: 105; Stephenson, Ferguson, and Ferguson 1963.

82. Va.: Smith 1986a [1608]: 37, 39, 51; Smith 1986b [1612]: 206; Archer 1969 [1607]: 86; Archer 1969b [1607]: 103; Spelman 1910 [1613?]: cvi.

83. Rountree 1989: 29.

84. Va.: summarized (with illustrations) in Rountree 1989: 60–65; Smith 1986b [1612]: 161–62, 164, 245; Strachey 1953 [1612]: 78–79, 82–83, 115, 129; Spelman 1910 [1613?]: cvi–cvii, cxii; Archer 1969b [1607]: 103; Norwood 1947 [1649]: 35, 42 (which may involve Kegotank Indians or the people just north of them); Pargellis 1969: 232; Clayton 1968 [1687]: 435; Banister 1970: 40, 186, 321, 326, 360, 372, 380, 383; Beverley 1947 [1705]: 174–76, 182, 184, 220. Md.: Anonymous 1910 [1635]: 73, 85, 86, 87; Browne et al. 1883–1972: 4:373; Jesuit Letters 1910: 131; White 1910 [1634]: 43–44.

85. The medium-sized houses in the Indian Village at Jamestown Settlement, which have the addition of plastic film between the two layers of mats to give them greater permanence as museum exhibits, can be kept at about 60°F by a moderate-sized central fire when the outside temperature is in the thirties (Rountree, personal observation, and the accounts of Jamestown Settlement staff).

86. Va.: Smith 1986b [1612]: 163–64; Strachey 1953 [1612]: 81–82; description of Powhatan fish weirs: Rountree 1989: 35–38. Md.: little was recorded, but the natives' rights to hunt and fish were specifically protected by treaty later in the seventeenth century.

87. Va.: Smith 1986a [1608]: 59; Smith 1986b [1612]: 155, 164–65; Strachey 1953 [1612]: 82, 83–84, 125; Purchas 1617: 954 margin; Banister 1970: 42–43, 385–86; Kingsbury 1906–35: 3:438, 557; Clayton 1965 [1687]: 34–35. Md.: Anonymous 1910 [1635]: 86.

88. Norwood 1947 [1649]: 39. The account may be about the Kegotank or else the people just north of them. Norwood himself said he did not fully grasp the principle of the snare, but it was set in such a way that when a deer nibbled at the bait, which was on a pole, a leather thong would snatch its hind feet and hoist it up, helpless.

89. Mary C. Rountree, personal communication 1994.

90. Va.: Smith 1986b [1612]: 158, 162; Strachey 1953 [1612]: 79, 118; Spelman 1910 [1613?]: cxi–cxii; Percy 1969 [1608]: 134; Beverley 1947 [1705]: 230. Md.: Anonymous 1910 [1635]: 84.

91. Turner 1976: 194.

92. Radford, Ahles, and Bell 1968: 88.

93. Bruce Smith (1994: 106–7) states that it is difficult archaeologically to distinguish between "encouraged/quasi-cultivated" crops and truly "cultivated" crops, and between the latter and truly "domesticated" crops. That is true in midwestern river bottoms, where plants recolonize annually after spring floods; but shifting cultivation of nonflooded grounds, as in the Chesapeake region, probably means that people assisted the dispersal of seeds.

94. James River Project 1950: 258, 261, 271, 273, 258, 246; Scott 1991: 57, 92.

95. Scarecrows: documented only for Carolina Algonquians: Hariot 1972 [1590]: 68, in which the age and sex of the children are not mentioned. Target practice: conclusion independently arrived at by Rountree (in writing this chapter) and by the Indian Village interpreters at Jamestown Settlement (personal communications, 1994).

96. Va.: Smith 1986b [1612]: 153–54; Strachey 1953 [1612]: 122.

97. Jesuit Letters 1910: 129; Smith 1986b [1612]: 159.

98. Va.: Rountree 1989: 46.

99. The division of work that we consider normal—male: food/income production away from home versus female: domestic work close to home—is an outcome of the development of intensive agriculture such as plow farming; for an explanation of this process, see Martin and Voorhees 1975: 290ff.

100. For a detailed account of Indian travel in the Eastern Woodlands, see Rountree 1993b. Our sources describing canoes are entirely from Virginia: Smith 1986b [1612]: 163; Strachey 1953 [1612]: 81–82; Spelman 1910 [1613?]: cxiv; Percy 1969 [1608?]: 134. Lawson 1967 [1709]: 91; Norwood 1947 [1649]: 31. The standing position certainly would allow more force in poling, since the strength of the legs could be used to the full. The alternative, as both authors have learned from experience at Jamestown Settlement and the Mariners Museum, is to kneel on the canoe's bottom and strain with the arms and back.

101. Va.: for a modern overview, see Rountree 1989: 129–30, and Ubelaker 1993; Smith 1986b [1612]: 168; Strachey 1953 [1612]: 111, 113; Archer 1969b [1607]: 104; Pargellis 1959: 233; Beverley 1947 [1705]: 217. English people of that time were almost continually ailing: their diet was poor in fruits and vegetables for most of the year, they were extremely reluctant to bathe (many bathed about once a year, which helped make skin diseases very common), and their villages, towns, and cities were often densely packed and lacked even elementary sanitation. See, for instance, Bridenbaugh 1968: chaps. 3–4.

102. Donna Boyd, personal communication (to Rountree) 1994.

103. Archer 1969a [1607]: 94. Percy (1969 [1608?]: 142) remembered the man as being

"about" 160, or 80 years old; however, Archer describes the counting method by which Captain Newport checked the man's age.

104. Va.: Smith 1986b [1612]: 160; Strachey 1953 [1612]: 71; Archer 1969b [1607]: 103; Spelman 1910 [1613?]: cxiii; Purchas 1617: 954; Pargellis 1959: 230. Md.: Anonymous 1910 [1635]: 83; White 1910 [1634]: 42. For an overview of the region, see Ubelaker 1993, esp. p. 72.

105. Va.: Smith 1986a [1608]: 73; Smith 1986b [1612]: 154, 160–61, 163; Strachey 1953 [1612]: 71–74, 114, 122; Archer 1969a [1607]: 92; Archer 1969b [1607]: 102–3; Percy 1969 [1608?]: 136–37, 142, 147; White 1969 [1608?]: 147; Strachey 1964 [1610]: 89; Durand de Dauphiné 1934 [1687]: 152; Banister 1970: 374; Beverley 1947 [1705]: 162. Md.: Anonymous 1910 [1635]: 87–88; White 1910 [1634]: 42–43.

106. Oiling one's skin for warmth really does work, as long-distance swimmers in cold water can attest. Bear grease has been found effective as well by the Indian Village staff at Jamestown Settlement.

107. Marriage: Pory in Smith 1986c [1624]: 291. In general, Va.: Rountree 1989: 92; Md.: Cissna 1986: 81; Seib-Toup n.d.

108. Va.: Archer 1969b [1607]: 103; Strachey 1953 [1612]: 61, 64–65, 84, 112–13, 116, 123; Spelman 1910 [1613?]: cvii, cxi; Purchas 1614: 768; Hamor 1957 [1615]: 41–42; Durand de Dauphiné 1934 [1687]: 153–54; Pargellis 1959: 234. Md.: Anonymous 1910 [1635]: 85–86.

109. Va.: Clayton 1968 [1687]: 434; Pargellis 1959: 241 (both of these late accounts may include Indians beyond the Powhatans). Md.: Anonymous 1910 [1635]: 87.

110. Va.: Smith 1986b [1612]: 162; Strachey 1953 [1612]: 114. Md.: Anonymous 1910 [1635]: 85.

111. Spelman 1910 [1613?]: cxii.

112. Va.: Smith 1986b [1612]: 162; Strachey 1953 [1612]: 113–14; Beverley 1947 [1705]: 170; Spelman 1910 [1613?]: cix. Md.: Anonymous 1910 [1635]: 85; Jesuit Letters 1910: 126.

113. Strachey 1953 [1612]: 56.

114. Va.: Smith 1986b [1612]: 171–72; Strachey 1953 [1612]: 89, 96, 98–99; Spelman 1910 [1613?]: cv–cvi; White 1969 [1608?]: 147–49; Purchas 1617: 952, 955; Pargellis 1959: 234–35; Banister 1970: 380–81; Beverley 1947 [1705]: 164, 207–9. Md.: Anonymous 1910 [1635]: 85.

115. John Pory in Smith 1986c [1624]: 291.

116. Va.: Smith 1986a [1608]: 59; Smith 1986b [1612]: 169–71; Strachey 1953 [1612]: 88, 95–98; Percy 1921–22 [1612]: 277–78; Whitaker 1964 [1611]: 498–99; Purchas 1617: 954–55; Smith 1986c [1624]: 149–50; Pargellis 1959: 232–33; Banister 1970: 378; Beverley 1947 [1705]: 164, 212, 217–18. Md.: Jesuit Letters 1910: 126, 130; 1678 mention of councillors gathering bones of the dead: Browne et al. 1883–1972: 15:185.

117. All sources from Va.: autonomy: Smith 1986b [1612]: 172, 266; Strachey 1953 [1612]: 101; Purchas 1617: 952, 955. Creation: Strachey 1953 [1612]: 89, 102; Purchas 1614: 767; Purchas 1617: 954–55.

118. Va.: Smith 1986b [1612]: 169; Strachey 1953 [1612]: 88–89; Spelman 1910 [1613?]: cv; Purchas 1614: 765; Purchas 1617: 955; Smith 1986c [1624]: 122; Banister 1970: 378; Beverley 1947 [1705]: 198, 200–213. Md.: Anonymous 1910 [1635]: 88; White 1910 [1634]: 44–45.

119. Va.: Smith 1986b [1612]: 170–71: Strachey 1953 [1612]: 97–98; Percy 1969 [1608?]: 143, 145–46; Pargellis 1959: 235; Banister 1970: 377–78; Beverley 1947 [1705]: 210, 213.

120. Va.: Smith 1986b [1612]: 169–70, 173–74; Strachey 1953 [1612]: 62, 88–89, 95; Spelman 1910 [1613?]: cv; Percy 1921–22 [1612]: 272; Pargellis 1959: 235; Beverley 1947

[1705]: 196–98. Md.: White 1910 [1634]: 45. Pocomokes and Assateagues: Browne et al. 1883–1972: 5:480.

121. Va.: Smith 1986b [1612]: 169, 262; Strachey 1953 [1612]: 95; Spelman 1910 [1613?]: cx. Md.: Stephenson, Ferguson, and Ferguson 1963; Ubelaker 1974.

122. Va.: Smith 1986b [1612]: 172; Strachey 1953 [1612]: 100, 102–3; Archer 1969b [1607]: 104; White 1969 [1608?]: 150; Purchas 1617: 955.

123. Va.: Smith 1986b [1612]: 160–61, 174; Strachey 1953 [1612]: 65, 71–72, 78; Smith 1986c [1624]: 151; Spelman 1910 [1613?]: cxiii; Norwood 1947 [1649]: 31–37. Md.: Anonymous 1910 [1635]: 84–85; Jesuit Letters 1910: 125.

124. Tribute: Rountree 1989: 109–11. Eastern Shore: Smith 1986a [1608]: 69; Beverley 1947 [1705]: 227–28. Nanticokes: Smith 1986c [1624]: 168.

125. Smith 1986a [1608]: 51 and 1986b [1612]: 173 (Powhatan); Norwood 1947 [1649]: 35 (Kegotank). The Kegotank chief's bed apparently lay along the side of the house; John Smith's accounts indicate that Powhatan's bed lay across the house's end.

126. Greeting: Va.: Archer 1969a [1607]: 84; Smith 1986a [1608]: 65; Percy 1969 [1608?]: 135; Smith 1986b [1612]: 167–68; Strachey 1953 [1612]: 84–85. Md.: Anonymous 1910 [1635]: 73, 87; Fleet 1876 [1631–32]: 25; Jesuit Letters 1910: 125. Feasting: Va.: Smith 1986a [1608]: 65–69; Smith 1986c [1624]: 148, 150; Hamor 1957 [1615]: 43, 45–46. Wives: Va.: Archer 1969b [1607]: 104; Strachey 1953 [1612]: 61; Spelman 1910 [1613?]: cvii–cviii; Smith 1986c [1624]: 128. Sentinels: Smith 1986b [1612]: 173; Strachey 1953 [1612]: 59.

127. Terms: Va.: Smith 1986b [1612]: 174; Strachey 1953 [1612]: 56, 59. Md.: Anonymous 1910 [1635]: 84. For a modern comparison of Virginia Indian chiefs with chiefs in other parts of the world, see Rountree 1993a. Cognates in Nanticoke and Piscataway: Paul Cissna, personal communication (to Rountree) 1991. Addressing: Strachey 1953 [1612]: 56.

128. Power: Rountree 1989: 146–48 and 1993a. Crimes: Va.: Smith 1986b [1612]: 160, 174–75; Strachey 1953 [1612]: 60, 76; Spelman 1910 [1613?]: cx–cxi. Md.: Anonymous 1910 [1635]: 87.

129. Va.: Smith 1986b [1612]: 174, 247. Md.: Anonymous 1910 [1635]: 84; Browne et al. 1883–1972: 3:403, 454, 482.

130. Va.: Strachey 1953 [1612]: 46, 63, 65, 67, 69; Argall 1904–6 [1613]: 93; Pory in Smith 1986c [1624]: 291. Md.: Browne et al. 1883–1972: 3:454; Calvert 1910 [1638]: 158–59; Jesuit Letters 1910: 136; Pory in Smith 1986c [1624]: 289.

131. Smith 1986c [1624]: 291; Esmy Shichans's name comes from Nugent 1934: 30, 75.

132. Councils: Va.: Clayton 1968 [1687]: 435. Md.: Anonymous 1910 [1635]: 84, 87; White 1910 [1634]: 44. Terms: Norwood 1947 [1649]: 36. Va.: Hening 1809–23: 2:34; Palmer 1875–93: 1:22. Md.: Anonymous 1910 [1635]: 84; Browne et al. 1883–1972: 3:453, 15:291. Hierarchy: Md.: Browne et al. 1883–1972: 3:453, 15:291. White (1910 [1634]: 45) calls the Patuxent temple a *matchacomico*, which may reflect where council meetings were held among those people. Speaker: Md.: Browne et al. 1883–1972: 5:65, 15:185.

133. Alliances: Va.: Strachey 1953 [1612]: 56–57. Md.: Browne et al. 1883–1972: 3:403. For a modern summary of goods traded through the Eastern Woodlands in general, see Rountree 1993b: 44–49. Beads: Va.: Smith 1986a [1608]: 69; Banister 1970: 322–23, 373; Beverley 1947 [1705]: 167–69, 227–28. Md.: Anonymous 1910 [1635]: 89. In December 1622 Virginia colonist John Martin wrote that the western shore Powhatans were receiving corn from both the Eastern Shore and "from the Southward" (probably the Chowan River and Carolina Sounds areas, since the Nansemonds and others in Southside Virginia were under English attack), to the amount of "fiue tymes more then they sett them selues" (Kingsbury 1906–35: 3:705). East-west trade for food was not recorded before that time; it is likely that the Accomacs and Occohannocks were helping to supply the deficit caused by English occupation of the prime farmlands in the James River valley.

134. Once in a while roanoke was even used in a case between two Englishmen, with no Indians involved (e.g., Northampton Co., Deeds, Wills, Orders, etc. 3:17v). 1681: Browne et al. 1883–1972: 15:372.

135. Accomac-Powhatan: John Pory in Smith 1986c [1624]: 291. Accomac-Patuxent: ibid.: 290. Ozinies: Anonymous 1910 [1635]: 88. Massawomecks: Smith 1986b [1612]: 230–31. Rountree (1993b: 32) was the first to suggest a connection between geographical extent of the fear and the nature of the canoes.

136. Va.: much of the cause for the Powhatan concept of manliness, in Rountree 1989: chap. 4; Spelman 1910 [1613?]: cxiv. Md.: Anonymous 1910 [1635]: 88–89; Browne et al. 1883–1972: 3:501; Jones 1963 [1699]: 95; Pory in Smith 1986c [1624]: 290; White 1910 [1634]: 43.

137. War captains: Va.: Strachey 1953 [1612]: 69; Smith 1986c [1624]: 127; Bland et al. 1911 [1651]: 9; Banister 1970: 354; Beverley 1947 [1705]: 149, 226. Md.: Anonymous 1910 [1635]: 73, 84. Weapons: Va.: Smith 1986b [1612]: 163–64; Strachey 1953 [1612]: 108–9; Spelman 1910 [1613?]: cxiii; Archer 1969b [1607]: 103; Percy 1969 [1608?]: 140; Banister 1970: 382; Hamor 1957 [1615]: 39. Md.: Anonymous 1910 [1635]: 86; White 1910 [1634]: 43. Striking and finishing: Va.: Smith 1986a [1608]: 87; Smith 1986b [1612]: 136, 163, 167; Strachey 1953 [1612]: 109; Spelman 1910 [1613?]: cxiv; Percy 1969 [1608?]: 138; Beverley 1947 [1705]: 196–97. Md.: Anonymous 1910 [1635]: 86. Speed and camouflage: Va.: Smith 1986b [1612]: 166; Strachey 1953 [1612]: 109; Spelman 1910 [1613?]: cxiii–cxiv; Archer 1969b [1607]: 103. Torture: Va.: Smith 1986b [1612]: 175; Strachey 1953 [1612]: 60, 85–86; White 1969 [1608?]: 150; Percy 1921–22 [1612]: 263. Md.: Browne et al. 1883–1972: 3:501; Jesuit Letters 1910: 128. Trophies: Smith 1986b [1612]: 161, 175; Strachey 1953 [1612]: 44, 74; Clayton 1965 [1687]: 23 and 1968 [1687]: 436.

Two. The First Century with Virginia

1. Rountree's dissertation (1973) explores this hypothesis in depth.

2. Wroth 1970: 82–83, 90 (Verrazzano's account is so vague that it is hard to tell where he was at any time; the one place he did stop was probably New York harbor); Lewis and Loomie 1953: 13 (translation of 1559 original); Quinn 1974: 190; James River Project 1950: 252.

3. Lewis and Loomie 1953 (p. 56 for post-1572 visits); Gradie 1987 and 1993; Rountree 1990: 15–20.

4. Quinn 1955: 244–46, 257–58; Quinn 1984; Quinn 1974: 255 and chap. 17; Quinn 1984; Quinn 1985: 42, 345–53; Rountree 1990: 20ff.

5. Strachey 1953 [1612]: 68, 104–5. For detailed assessments of the paramount chiefdom's development and possible reasons for it, see Turner 1976 and 1993, and Rountree and Turner 1994 and n.d.

6. Smith 1986a [1608]: 69.

7. Canner 1904–6 [1603]; Quinn 1974: chap. 16; Smith 1986a [1608]: 51; Wingfield 1969 [1608]: 227.

8. Smith 1986b [1612]: 225.

9. Expeditions: Smith 1986b [1612]: 224–25. Geography: Smith 1986c [1624]: 163. The major secondary sources on this and subsequent parts of the seventeenth-century Indian-English relations are: Deal 1993; Rountree 1990: chaps. 2–6. Major secondary sources on English society in the same place and period are: Deal 1993; Breen and Innes 1980; Perry 1990; Ames 1940; Whitelaw 1968 [1951]. Wise 1967 [1911] is comprehensive but much less carefully researched. Interpreters: Thomas Savage was still living with Powhatan in 1608, and Henry Spelman began his term with Powhatan in summer 1609.

10. Argall 1904–6 [1613]; Rolfe 1848 [1616]: 106, 110; Perry 1990: 15–16; Kingsbury 1906–35: 4:515.

11. Smith 1986c [1624]: 291 (conspiracy), 264–65 (renegade Chickahominies).

12. Poison: Thomas Wieboldt and Donna Ware, personal communication via Martha McCartney, 1985. Plot: Kingsbury 1906–35: 3:556, 4:10. The Eastern Shore ruler was never named, but the only person fitting that paramount position was Esmy Shichans.

13. Smith 1986c [1624]: 288–91.

14. Perry 1990: chap. 1. Wise (1911: 29) wrote, without evidence, that it started in 1619.

15. Deal (1993: 14–15, 24) came to the same conclusion after reading the original records.

16. Company purchase: Kingsbury 1906–35: 3:304 (Dale); ibid., 1:349, 3:99–101, 585, McIlwaine 1979 [1924]: 148, and Smith 1986c [1624]: 288 (secretary's land). Saltworks: Perry 1990: 19–20, based upon Virginia Company Records in Kingsbury 1906–35. Savage and Yeardley: cited in a deposition of 1668: Northampton Co., Orders 9:49. The actual patents came later: Nugent 1934: 96 (Argoll Yeardley, 1638), 35, 75 (widow Hannah Savage, 1635), 524 (renewal by son John, 1664, specifying 9,000 acres). Wise (1911: 29) wrote, without evidence, that when John Pory visited the Delmarva Peninsula in 1621, Savage was already living there. Headright claimants: Kingsbury 1906–35: 3:100–101, 107–8, 359–62; summarized in Perry 1990: 18.

17. 1622: Kingsbury 1906–35: 3:697 (commission); McIlwaine 1924: 11; Smith 1986c [1624]: 311. 1623: Kingsbury 1906–35: 4:275–76.

18. Nugent 1934: 7ff., 46; Perry 1990: 25–26.

19. McIlwaine 1924: 116.

20. Deal 1993: 12; we agree, for the Northampton and Accomack County records say next to nothing about furs in connection with Indians.

21. Trade: McIlwaine 1979 [1924]: 48, 50; Min. Coun., *Va. Mag.* 25 (1917): 345; McIlwaine 1979 [1924]: 104, 193. Glass: McIlwaine 1924: 165 (which speaks only of bottles, not of arrowheads; however, green glass arrowheads have been found archaeologically in seventeenth-century sites at several locales in Virginia); Hening 1809–23: 1:167 (1631); Nugent 1934: 23, 35 (1635).

22. Source of visits is a 1668 deposition: Northampton Co., Orders 9:49. Payment: Northampton Co., Orders, Wills, and Deeds 1:76 (transcribed version, pp. 55–56; Ames 1954: 57).

23. Local claims: Nugent 1934: 27 (Stone), 77 (Winley), 96 (Argall); Northampton Co., Orders, Deeds, and Wills 2:17v (Ames 1973: 33). We agree in part with Deal (1993: 15), who discusses Yeardley's victory, but we find no evidence for Deal's assertion that William Stone caused the Indian town to be moved off "his" land. Promise: McIlwaine 1924: 478.

24. The two bayside towns had Bojac fine sandy loam, while Gingaskin had Bojac sandy loam; both are "warm," easy to till, and moderately good for corn (Cobb and Smith 1989).

25. Nugent 1934: 150.

26. Court case: Northampton Co., Orders, Deeds, and Wills 2:28v (Ames 1973: 56). Patent: Nugent 1977: 211; this patent supposedly renewed an earlier one, now lost, issued in 1641.

27. Northampton Co., Orders, Deeds, and Wills, 2:89r–90v (Ames 1973: 179–80) (commander of force); Deal 1993: 16. Taylor died in 1646, and in his inventory the Indian goods consisted of only one "old Indyan matt," showing that he was not an Indian trader (Northampton Co., Deeds, Wills, and Orders 3:78v).

28. Northampton Co., Orders, Deeds, and Wills, 2:124v, 142v (Ames 1973: 235, 265).

29. Northampton Co., Deeds, Wills, and Orders 3:203r, Orders 8:73v.

30. Beverley 1947 [1705]: 232.

31. Northampton Co., Deeds, Wills, and Orders 2:156r (Ames 1973: 289); Deal 1993: 17.

32. 1638: Northampton Co., Orders, Wills, and Deeds 1:129 (transcribed version, pp. 95–96; Ames 1954: 100). 1642: Northampton Co., Deeds, Wills, and Orders 2:91v (Ames 1973: 181). Savage: Northampton Co., Orders, Wills, and Deeds 1:203 (transcribed version, p. 153; Ames 1954: 159). The cattle, of course, were European ones left free to roam. Book: Northampton Co., Orders, Wills, and Deeds 1:151 (transcribed version, p. 115; Ames 1954: 120). There is no indication of what language was described or what book it was, unfortunately. The famous *A Key into the Language of America* by Roger Williams did not come out until 1643. Northampton Co., Deeds, Wills, and Orders 3:61a-r, 67v, 78a-r (Johnaboy); the thief was William Hinman, husband of the Sarah Hinman who was publicly ridiculed on suspicion of sleeping with an Indian about that same time.

33. Northampton Co., Deeds, Wills, and Orders 3:113r (gun); Norwood 1947 [1649]: 40; Deal 1993: 34 (two colonies).

34. Northampton Co., Deeds, Wills, etc. 1657–66:5v.

35. Taking a new name following a great deed or a major change in status was standard practice among the Powhatans of the western shore of Virginia (Rountree 1989: 80).

36. Accomack Co., Orders, Wills, etc. 1671–73:143, 150; Wills 1673–76: 33.

37. Accomack Co., Orders 1703–9:8r (she was executrix for her deceased son, Charlton).

38. Northampton Co., Orders 8:8v.

39. Northampton Co., Orders, Deeds, and Wills 2:194v, 206r (Ames 1973: 359, 360, 383; Taylor), 208v (Ames 1973: 386; Andrews); Hening 1809–23: 1:293 (spies).

40. Hening 1809–23: 1:323–326 (treaty); Northampton Co., Deeds, Wills, and Orders 3:207r (proclamation, saying in general terms that the "Laughing King's Indians" should not be molested; in 1649 several laws were passed improving upon the 1646 treaty [Billings 1975: 63–66, 68], but they seem not to have been applied to the Eastern Shore); Orders, Wills, etc. 10:203 (gun); Commissioners Appointed under the Great Seale of England for the Virginia Affairs 1896 [1677] (treaty).

41. Kulikoff 1986: 218ff. and Perry 1990: 141 (occupations, stores); Clemens 1980: 90–91 (imports).

42. Clemens 1980: 82 (acreage, crops); Carr, Menard, and Walsh 1991: xvi–xvii and Main 1982: 75 (fields).

43. Main 1982: 140, 141 (borrowing the word *dribbled* from Henry Glassie's *Folk Housing in Middle Virginia* [1975]), 153.

44. Sobel 1987: 100–102 and Main 1982: chap. 4 (sleeping), 190–91 (cooking). Forks did not become common tableware among the New England English until the 1770s (James Deetz, In *Small Things Forgotten* [1972], p. 123, cited in Main 1982: 60n). Beverley 1947 [1705]: 182 (Indian spoons).

45. Main 1982: 153.

46. Ibid.: 62–67; Morgan 1975: 136–40.

47. Eastern Shore mortality seems to have been as high as on the western shore, though documents on the former are sparse (Deal 1993: 97).

48. Carr, Menard, and Walsh 1991: 16–18; Kulikoff 1986: 168ff.; Carr and Walsh 1977; Rutman and Rutman 1979. "*Ménage* family" is Rountree's term.

49. Sobel 1987: 110; Kulikoff 1986.

50. Main 1982: 181 (field work); Kulikoff 1986: 178, 183; Main 1982: 112 (freed from labor) and 194 (servants); Rountree 1989: 89 (Indian women).

51. Kulikoff 1986: 295ff (servility); Main 1982: 112ff. (abuses).

52. Perry 1990: 72ff., 105ff. The Northampton and Accomack court records have many cases of people being charged by their neighbors—or in the eighteenth century by a grand jury chosen to ferret out offenses—with misdemeanors such as slander, swearing, bastard bearing, and fornication.

53. Autonomy: Rountree 1993a, 1990: 133, 151. Alcohol: Rountree 1993c: 202–3.

54. Hening 1809–23: 2:13–14 (1660); Northampton Co., Deeds, Wills, etc. 8:19v (1667), Orders 9:48v (1668).

55. No law was ever passed that legalized Englishmen's claiming land pending Indians' desertion of it. The closest thing to a precedent is two 1657 colonial council orders in which English people were granted the Wiccocomico and Chiskiack reservations after the Indians "deserted" (McIlwaine 1979 [1924]: 506). As Rountree has shown (1990: 116–17, 120–21), English claimants sometimes waited half a century or more for the Indians to leave; the impatient ones pushed the Indians off the land. The idea underlying the custom was that Indians, not being Christians or Englishmen, did not really "own" the land, hence the necessity for Indians to patent their lands.

56. McIlwaine 1979 [1924]: 353, 369, 381. Time of survey: mentioned in patent of 1680.

57. Northampton Co., Orders 11:57, 63–64, 69, 97; Nugent 1977: 211–12. The total damages, in trees cut down "on both sides ye Indians Corne field," amounted to 300–400 fence logs and seven "boards timber trees with other logg timber borne away wch are up in ye woods" (ibid.: 108).

58. Ibid.: 259–60 (stag), 160 (Warren).

59. Northampton Co., Deeds, Wills, and Orders 3:135a–v, 166v (Nandua), 223v (Craddock), 226r and Deeds, Wills, etc. 4:35v (Occohannock), 4:90r (Onancock), 125v and 174v (Pungoteague); Accomack Co., Deeds and Wills 1663–66:22, 39v, 53 (Chesconnessex).

60. Billings 1975: 72–73 (1652); Hening 1809–23: 1:391 (1654), 396 and 467–68 (1656), 471 (1658 repassing); Deal 1993: 19.

61. Northampton Co., Deeds, Wills, etc. 4:225r (both 1652 cases), Orders, Deeds, Wills, etc. 5:134v (1653).

62. Nugent 1934: 406 (identifying creek); Northampton Co., Orders 8:88v (man paying gun), 88r (Onancocks selling).

63. Accomack Co., Deeds and Wills 1663–66:40v–41r, 57v, 64v (Onancock), 74v (Wachapreague), 45r (Matahocus), Orders, Wills, etc. 1671–73:63 (1672).

64. Beverley 1947 [1705]: 232; Sainsbury et al. 1860–1926: 15:425.

65. Accomack Co., Wills, etc. 1692–1715, pt. 1:311, 357, 496, pt. 2:4, 11, 165, 226, 370, 396, Deeds, Wills, etc. 1715–29, pt. 1:43, 128, 209, 315, 372, 399, 454, 479, 509, 543, pt. 2:92, 145. There are more references to Indian bowls, a tray, a mat (in 1747), and especially baskets up through the 1750s (Accomack Co. Will Books through 1757), by which time these probably came from New England in the then-active Atlantic coastal trade (Miles Barnes, personal communication 1995).

66. W. Perry 1870: 301; Accomack Co., Orders 1710–14:34v and r, 36r (Charles), Orders 1719–24:68r (George Rawmush), Orders 1724–31:27r, 237.

67. Summarized in J. Perry 1990: 210–12 and Deal 1993: 31.

68. 1649: Northampton Co., Deeds, Wills, etc. 4:22r, 12v (Andrews, Dutch), Deeds, Wills, and Orders 3:166v, 174v–175r, 179r, and Orders, Deeds, Wills, etc. 5:135v (Clawson).

69. Northampton Co., Deeds, Wills, and Orders 3:207r (governor), 217v–217r, 219r, 219v (county).

70. Northampton Co., Deeds, Wills, and Orders 3:226r, Deeds, Wills, etc. 4:40v, 40r (raid), 36v–37r, 37v (militia).

71. Northampton Co., Orders 6:27r; Browne et al. 1883–1972, 3:379–81.

72. Northampton Co., Orders 8:117v; Accomack Co., Deeds and Wills 1663–66:42v–44.

73. Ibid.: 44v, Deeds and Wills 1664–71:3v.

74. Accomack Co., Deeds and Wills 1663–66:92v (Assateague), Orders 1666–70:47r–47v (1667), 63v (1668), 55v and 67 (Acquintankee).

75. Accomack Co., Wills 1673–76:335, 350; Northampton Co., Orders and Wills 13:89.

76. Tuchman 1978: xviii.

77. Northampton Co., Deeds, Wills, and Orders 3:61a–r, Orders 8:137r, Orders and Wills 13:352 (vague problem); Accomack Co., Orders, Wills, etc. 1671–73:117, Orders 1676–78:101 (vague problem), 96, 94, 101 (nonappearance).

78. Accomack Co., Deeds and Wills 1663–66:38v, Orders 1666–70:194, Orders, Wills, etc. 1671–73:41; Northampton Co., Wills, etc. 14:102.

79. Hening 1809–23: 1:518; Northampton Co., Orders 8:73v, 120r.

80. Northampton Co., Orders, Deeds, Wills, etc. 5:13v, 14r, Orders 8:101v; Hening 1809–23: 1:391, 470.

81. Northampton Co., Deeds, Wills, and Orders 3:121v, 203v.

82. Northampton Co., Orders, Deeds, Wills, etc. 5:13v, 14r, Orders 8 (1657–64): 28v, 55v, 183r, 186r; Accomack Co., Orders 1666–70:15r, 16v, 19–20, 27r, Orders 1676–78: 133 (1678), Wills, Deeds, Orders 1678–82:241, 323.

83. Northampton Co., Deeds, Wills, etc. 4:141v, 170r. (Alexander), 5:18r, 55v (Metomkin and Machipongo), Orders 8:93v (Tapatiapon); Accomack Co., Orders, Wills, etc. 1671–73:146–47 (1672), Wills, etc., Orders 1682–97:103v (1687).

84. Northampton Co., Orders 8:72r; Accomack Co., Wills, Deeds, Orders 1678–82: 278–79; Northampton Co., Orders and Wills 13:54.

85. Indians stealing: Northampton Co., Deeds, Wills, etc. 4:102v, Orders and Wills 13: 510–511; Accomack Co., Orders 1678–82:96. English stealing: Accomack Co., Wills 1673–76:285, Wills, etc., Orders 1682–97:189v, Orders 1690–97:2r, Orders 1703–9:8r. Theft and beating: Northampton Co., Orders 9:40r; Accomack Co., Wills 1673–76:263. Wherry: Northampton Co., Deeds, Wills, etc. 4:51v. Stockings: Northampton Co., Deeds, Wills, etc. 4:168v. Weir: Accomack Co., Wills, Deeds, Orders 1678–82:284 (the Indian, Robert Atkinson, may have been a detribalized member of one of the Occohannock groups). Debt, trespass, cabins, hunting, hogs: Accomack Co., Wills, etc., Orders 1682–97:75, 167r–168v; Northampton Co., Deeds, Wills, and Orders 3:212v, Orders 11:147–48, Orders, Deeds, Wills, etc. 5:151v.

86. Accomack Co., Orders 1666–70:53.

87. Break-in: Northampton Co., Orders 11:253 (the man, Argoll Angood, was perhaps a detribalized Gingaskin). English beating Indians: Accomack Co., Wills 1673–76:314 (accusation unproved), Wills, Deeds, Orders 1678–82:53, 217, Orders 1697–1703:122v, 145v (accusation by "Protestant George" against free mulatto John Odrygus [Driggus]). Misseteage: Accomack Co., Orders 1676–78:80 and 85. Threat: Northampton Co., Deeds, Wills, etc. 4:226v. Indians beating English: Northampton Co., Deeds, Wills, etc. 4:168r, Accomack Co., Deeds and Wills 1663–66:54v, 55. Killing: Accomack Co., Wills, Deeds, Orders 1678–82:181–82.

88. Northampton Co., Deeds, Wills, etc. 4:87v and Orders 9:82r; Deeds, Wills, and Orders 3:148v–148r. The party, consisting of the wife, four Indians, and five Englishmen, had consumed a gallon of brandy. The deponent found the wife and her lover in bed the next morning, for he went snooping through the house. He woke the wife, demanding "whether she was sensible when she had drank a cup of drink," to which, badly hung over, she replied, "Why do you ask?" He told her she had "played a very mad part to go to bed with a man and leave all the doors open [unlocked]." "What man?" she asked. He pointed to the inert male form beside her, at which point she exclaimed, "What a rogue was that, I will scold with him for it!" So much for contrition. The deponent remonstrated with the wife about her affair on subsequent occasions, when her suspicious husband was away. Then one day the deponent, the wife, and the lover were all sitting on a mat in her dooryard when she and her lover "fell a tickling" of each other. He claimed that in putting a hand behind him to get up, he accidentally seized the lover in the most sensitive place (recorded in gutter English), at which the wife laughed and said "that it was the key of her lock." The logistics of the seizure,

while supposedly struggling to stand up, are a little dubious. So, for that matter, is the disinterestedness of the deponent.

89. Affairs with husband's permission (easily gained), reported for the Powhatans: Rountree 1989: 91–92. Children of affairs remaining with mother: analogy with widespread Woodland Indian custom, in Rountree 1993b: 41–42.

90. Northampton Co., Deeds, Wills, and Orders 3:48r, 63r–67r. Deal (1993: 41–42) identifies the one woman, recipient of a scurrilous poem, as Sarah Hinman; she in turn received a "scandalous" speech from yet another Englishwoman to the effect that three English women had been sleeping with Indians (Northampton Co., Deeds, Wills, and Orders 3:77v). Widow: Northampton Co., Orders and Wills 13:427. Trial of Jenny: McIlwaine 1925–66: 1:320 and Accomack Co., Deeds, Wills, etc. 1692–1715:108–9 and Orders 1690–97:135v–135r.

91. Accomack Co., Orders and Wills 1671–73: 23, 51–52, 115, and Loose Papers, Packet no. 11, cited in Deal 1993: 44n (1671); Accomack Co., Wills, Deeds, Orders 1678–82:276 (1681).

92. Accomack Co., Wills, Deeds, Orders 1678–82:13.

93. Accomack Co., Wills, etc., Orders 1682–97:67v, Orders 1697–1703:8r, 73r, 131r.

94. Northampton Co., Deeds, Wills, and Orders 3:78v, 151v, Orders 9:33v, 99r, 11:13, Deeds, Wills, etc. 11:6, 91, Deeds and Wills 12:126; Accomack Co., Orders 1666–70:123, Orders, Wills, etc. 1671–73:70, Orders 1676–78:49, Wills, etc., Orders 1682–97:215r, and many later entries (see note 65).

95. Northampton Co., Orders 8:169v–170r, 11:11–12, 29; Accomack Co., Orders 1666–70:27v. The only surviving record of an Indian being hired actually to build a weir comes from Norfolk County.

96. Billings 1975: 69; Hening 1809–23, 2:274–75; Accomack Co., Orders 1666–70: 142–43, Orders 1676–78:76; Northampton Co., Wills, etc. 14:214.

97. Northampton Co., Deeds, Wills, and Orders 3:138r, 183r, Deeds, Wills, etc. 4:9v, 34r, 140r.

98. Deal 1993: 89.

99. Tithe lists: Northampton Co., Orders 9:54, Orders, Wills, etc. 10:73, 75, 148, 191, and Accomack Co., Wills 1673–76:196. Bess: Northampton Co., Orders 9:220, 237. One Indian on a 1675 tithe list was not from Virginia: Gusman (probably a variant of the Portuguese Guzman; Accomack Co., Orders 1666–70:62v) represented steady flow of nonwhites into Virginia by way of Spanish territories (Deal 1993: 187). Several other free nonwhite surnames became established on the Virginia Eastern Shore thereafter: Driggus (from Rodriguez) and Cisco (from Francisco). Dick: Accomack Co., Orders 1676–78:131.

100. Accomack Co., Orders 1666–70:33v, 35, 40v–41, 43, 44r–44v, 159, 181, 194.

101. Briceland 1987: chap. 11; Merrell 1989: 28ff., esp. 36–37; J. Martin 1994: 308.

102. Deal 1993: 52 (superiority and "sacrifice"), citing Spelman 1910 [1613]: cv–cvi. Smallpox: Northampton Co., Deeds and Wills 8:19v (smallpox). We agree with Deal (p. 52n) that Wise's statement (1969 [1911]: 63–64) about the Indians being decimated by smallpox is entirely without foundation.

103. Accomack Co., Orders 1666–70:196 (John), Deeds and Wills 1664–71:166 and Deal 1993: 39 (Scarburgh).

104. Ages adjudged: Accomack Co., Wills, etc., Orders 1682–97:28v, 47r, 51r, 61v, 86r, 86v, 102v; Northampton Co., Orders and Wills 12:46, 176, 217, 356. Some of them, as well as some new names, also appear in wills and estates, sometimes specifically listed as slaves: Northampton Co., Orders and Wills 12:418, 13:301, 357, 435; Accomack Co., Wills and Deeds 1676–90:402v, 455, Wills, etc., Orders 1682–97:228r. Africans: Main 1982: chap. 3; Williamson 1980: 35, 38.

105. Accomack Co., Wills, etc., Orders 1682–97:216v. Neither slave was adjudged for age in court.

106. Northampton Co., Orders 8:68r, 117v; Accomack Co., Deeds and Wills 1663–66: 79, 94.

107. Runaways: Northampton Co., Deeds, Wills, etc. 4:93r (1652), 217r (1654), 53v (around 1655), Orders, Deeds, Wills, etc. 5:113r (around 1655); Accomack Co., Orders, Wills, etc. 1671–73:130 (1672), Wills, Deeds, Orders 1678–82:309 (1682); Northampton Co., Orders and Wills 12:313, 322 (1687). Servant-catchers: Northampton Co., Deeds, Wills, etc. 4:53v (1651), Accomack Co., Wills, Deeds, Orders 1678–82:309 (1682), Northampton Co., Orders and Wills 12:185 (1686).

108. Accomack Co., Orders 1666–70:35, Orders and Wills 1671–73:115, 119, Wills 1673–76:221, 249, 264, 296, Orders 1676–78:54–55, Wills, Deeds, Orders 1678–82:39.

109. Ibid.: 266, 271, 281, 291, 295–96.

110. Accomack Co., Wills 1673–76:296, Wills, Deeds, Orders 1678–82:281, 289, 291.

111. Angood, Atkinson, and Mongram only appear once each in the records: Northampton Co., Orders 11:253; Accomack Co., Wills, Deeds, Orders 1678–82:284, Wills, etc., Orders 1682–97:75. Bagwell: Accomack Co., Deeds and Wills 1664–71:121, Orders 1697–1703:45r, 48r, 49v, 55v, 58r, 62v, Wills, etc. 1692–1715:376.

112. Northampton Co., Orders and Wills 13:510–11.

113. Cf. a Nanzatico case of 1704 (Rountree 1990:154).

114. Deal 1993:22.

115. Mariner 1996:36–37, 42, 176.

116. Runaway: Accomack Co., Wills, Deeds, Orders 1678–82:309. Free blacks: Deal 1993: see especially pt. 2. The evidence that some people stayed lies in the appearance of free blacks in the Order Books of Northampton County throughout the eighteenth century.

Three. The First Century with Maryland

1. Argall 1904–6 [1613]; Fausz 1990:44–45.
2. Somerset Co., Judicial Records 1670–71:12.
3. Kingsbury 1906–35:4:275.
4. Browne et al. 1883–1972:1:42, 307.
5. Ibid.: 3:67–68.
6. Plantagenet 1947 [1648].
7. Hening 1809–23:1:219.
8. Anonymous 1947 [1655]: 5.
9. Hening 1809–23:1:525.
10. Browne et al. 1883–1972:4:214.
11. Ibid.: 5:190.
12. Marye 1938:147.
13. Ibid.: 150.
14. Marye 1939:53–54.
15. Browne et al. 1883–1972:3:74.
16. Ibid.: 3:129.
17. Alliance with Susquehannocks: Jennings 1982. Clawson: Browne et al. 1883–1972: 3:430–31. Bateman: Maryland Testamentary Proceedings, lib. 1E, fol. 82.
18. Browne et al. 1883–1972:3:129.
19. Ibid.: 3:191.
20. Torrence 1979:486.
21. Browne et al. 1883–1972:4:209–10.
22. Ibid.: 3:450.
23. Maryland Testamentary Proceedings, lib. 3, fol. 23.
24. Norwood 1947 [1650].

25. Marye 1937.

26. Browne et al. 1883–1972: 25:256.

27. Ibid.: 32:210–11.

28. Ibid.: 3:452.

29. Rountree 1993a.

30. Somerset Co., Judicial Records 1670–71:8. Gillett said in 1670 that "about fourteen years since I was trading in Manokin River from Rappahannock with one William Cook who was my interpreter when he had me a mile or two in the river he left me in the sloop and went by land and sent an Indian two days after for me and the sloop to come up, and I asked why he sent for me so far up the river he said that we must come up to the Trading Branch or else we could not have any trade with them."

31. Browne et al. 1883–1972: 15:213.

32. Ibid.: 5:479.

33. Ibid.: 3:379–80.

34. Ibid.: 5:480.

35. Ibid.: 15:142.

36. Goddard 1978: 223.

37. Feest 1978: 240.

38. Goddard 1978: 215.

39. Marye 1938: 150–51.

40. For an account of the complex commercial and military interaction between the Dutch, the Delawares, the Iroquois, the Susquehannocks, and the Maryland colony in the mid-seventeenth century, see Jennings 1982: 216–41.

41. McMahon 1831: 168.

42. Laws of 1669, chap. 1, quoted in McAllister 1962: 4–5.

43. Browne et al. 1883–1972: 5:452.

44. "A considerable quantity of matchcoats" was "to come to the said emperor from persons settled upon land in Nanticoke and places adjacent according as people usually give him at seating where the Emperor claims som perogative" (Somerset Co., Judicial Records L [reverse: 1675–77]: 52–55).

45. Somerset Co., Judicial Records 1670–71:12.

46. Browne et al. 1883–1972: 15:213.

47. Mowbray and Mowbray 1981: 109. This was "Genney Plantation"; Edmondson had a license from the proprietary government to "trade and traffic with the Indians for Beavor and Roanoke" (Browne et al. 1883–1972: 3:555).

48. Browne et al.: 51:71–72.

49. Torrence 1979: 471–72, quoting Provincial Patents 9:468, 6:302.

50. Somerset Co., Land Records, 06:425; Provincial Patents 9:14.

51. Torrence 1979: 471

52. Somerset County, Judicial Records B1 (1665–68): 116. In 1667, for example, two colonists stole corn stored by the chief of the Manokin at Manokin town.

53. Browne et al. 1883–1972: 3:450.

54. Ibid.: 3:452.

55. Marye 1939: 53.

56. Browne et al. 1883–1972: 5:29.

57. Ibid.: 5:136.

58. Ibid.: 5:29ff. There is evidence that a treaty between Maryland and the Nanticokes was proposed in 1642, but no such treaty has survived in the Maryland records.

59. The legislative act that created the Choptank reservation notes that the Indians "are in danger to be cut off and destroyed by the Wiccomesses and their Confederates the Matwhas Indians" (Laws of 1669, chap. 1, quoted in McAllister 1962: 4).

60. Sometimes the Indians extended their belief that wild resources were free for the taking to straying English livestock as well. In 1689 colonists living in the vicinity of Askiminikansen Indian Town complained about the Indians' hunting activities to the Somerset County court, stating that "Your Petitioners . . . some very near and some farther from the Indian town . . . are very much damnified by the Indians our hogs and horses and other cattle being daily killed and destroyed by them, not only in their own town but likewise out of it."

The petition went on to cite as evidence of the Indians' transgressions the fact that some of the colonists' hogs came home "with arrows in their sides" (Somerset Co., Judicial Records, Sept. 1689–Nov. 1690:33).

61. Browne et al. 1883–1972: 5:480.

62. Ibid.: 31:356.

63. Jennings 1982.

64. Browne et al. 1883–1972: 5:269.

65. Ibid.: 3:489.

66. Davidson 1982.

67. The reservation at Broad Creek was not created until 1711.

68. Browne et al. 1883–1972: 33:22.

69. Ibid.: 17:95; Somerset Co., Judicial Records L (prefix: 1683): 1, 16.

70. Maryland Provincial Patents BC and GS 23:438.

71. Browne et al. 1883–1972: 32:210–11.

72. In 1690 English settler William Joyles went to "the Indian town called Rotkawawkin" looking for a lost horse. He encountered no Indians there but did "find his mare shot by some of the Indians." This suggests that by 1690 Rotkawawkin had no permanent Indian inhabitants but was still an Indian hunting territory used by the Wicomicos of Tundotank Indian Town just across the river (Somerset Co., Judicial Records, Sept. 1689–Nov. 1690:164).

73. Somerset Co., Judicial Records L (reverse: 1675–77):75, 80.

74. Rountree 1989: 29.

75. Browne et al. 1883–1972: 22:200, 29:10.

76. Ibid.: 8:532–36.

77. Ibid.: 8:526, 532.

78. Ibid.: 8:533.

79. Ibid.: 8:535.

80. Ibid.: 19:521.

81. Ibid.: 23:456.

82. Ibid.: 8:532–36.

83. Ibid.: 25:255; Somerset Co., Judicial Records 1670–71:216.

84. Browne et al. 1883–1972: 17:230.

85. Ibid.: 17:369.

86. The Choptank reservation included the headwaters of the Transquaking or "Tresquakin" River, and one of the Choptank bands had been called the "Trasquakin" in 1659. In 1683 Ababco had been referred to as "emperor" of the "Tresquique." Hatsawap is the name used by the English for another of the three bands or tribes of the Choptank Indians (ibid.: 2:196, 3:363).

87. Ibid.: 8:532.

88. In 1683 a Choptank chief, when discussing raids on his people by the "Sinniquos" (Senecas?), stated that "the Delaware Bay Indians were the instruments to bring them upon them" (ibid.: 17:77).

89. Ibid.: 8:532–36.

90. 1678 roster: Assateague, Pocomoke, Yingoteague, Nuswattax, Annemessex, Aquintica, Morumsco (ibid.: 15:213–15). 1686 roster: Pocomoke, Assateague, Annemessex, Manoakin, Nasswattex, and Aquintica; the Assateagues included the Assateagues proper plus

Transquakin, Choptico, Moteawaughkin, Quequashkecasquick, Hatsawap, Wachetak, Maraughquaick, and Manaskson (ibid.: 5:479–80).

91. Ibid.: 5:525.

92. Although the provincial records give the thief's name as Edward Hammond, this was almost certainly Edmund Hammond, who had a plantation just across the Pocomoke River from Askiminikansen. This plantation was on land that was probably part of the Queponqua Indian town.

93. Browne et al. 1883–1972: 5:480.

94. Ibid.: 5:520.

95. Somerset Co., Judicial Record, Sept. 1689–Nov. 1690:33.

96. Browne et al. 1883–1972: 23:289.

Four. The Maryland Reservations after 1700

1. Carr 1988.

2. In 1697 Maryland's governor commented that it was very difficult to determine the size of the colony's Indian population, noting that "the Eastern Shore Indians Remove very often to Virginia and Pennsylvania" (Browne et al. 1883–1972: 25:256).

3. Dorchester Co., Land Records Old 2:115, 116, 138, quoted in McAllister 1962: 37–46.

4. Browne et al. 1883–1972: 25:256.

5. Murray, quoted in Speck 1927: 40.

6. William Becket, quoted in Perry 1878a: 36.

7. Somerset Co., Judicial Records, Sept. 1689–Nov. 1690: 40. In 1726 a complaint by the Pocomoke and Assateague Indians of the Askiminikansen reservation refers to Englishmen entering their "towns" against their will (Browne et al. 1883–1972: 25:457).

8. Browne et al. 1883–1972: 26:445.

9. Maryland Provincial Patents EE 6:32, 33.

10. Somerset Co., Land Records O 20:224, 225.

11. Browne et al. 1883–1972: 28:263.

12. The Broad Creek reservation was in the same approximate location as the Nanticoke town of Kuskarawaok, shown on John Smith's 1608 map of the Chesapeake Bay (Hutchinson 1961: 3); see fig. 4.1.

13. Especially after 1720, there is evidence for the long-term or even permanent relocation of Indians as individuals or families from one tribal area to another. Members of the Cohonk and Asquash families moved from the Nanticoke town of Chicone to the Choptank reservation; the Bishops, a Choptank family, were listed as living at Chicone in the 1750s, and Peter Monk, an Indian River man, lived at Chicone as early as 1742 and by 1757 was contending for leadership of the Nanticoke tribe.

14. William Vans Murray, quoted in Speck 1927: 40.

15. Dorchester Co., Judicial Records 1690–92:110, 159; Somerset Co., Judicial Records 1727–30:154.

16. Browne et al. 1883–1972: 13:204, 23:251.

17. Other Indian interpreters included Montague (Browne et al. 1883–1972: 17:187), Thom (ibid.: 5:558), William Monk (ibid.: 25:392–93), and Edmond (ibid.: 25:392).

18. W. Perry 1878b: 212.

19. Ibid.: 218, 229.

20. W. Perry 1878a: 36.

21. A 1695 Maryland law specified that "Negroes, Indians and Mulattos" should not be included in parish records (Browne et al. 1883–1972: 38:39).

22. Torrence 1979: 143, 399.

23. Quoted in Speck 1927: 41.

24. Heckewelder 1881: 92.

25. Ibid.: 29:228.

26. In 1726 the "queen" of the Ababco Choptanks was Betty Caco, "Daughter and heir of Winnecaco," and the "queen" of the "Hatchswamp" Choptanks was Pemetasusk, "Daughter and heir of Patchyosk." The last ruler of the Tequassino Choptanks was "queen" Patasuske (Dorchester Co., Land Records Old 8:141, Old 6:87, quoted in McAllister 1962: 29, 63).

27. Murray, quoted in Speck 1927: 40.

28. Dorchester Co., Land Records Old 6:47, 87, quoted in McAllister 1962.

29. Norwood 1947 [1649]: 42.

30. Browne et al. 1883–1972: 31:43.

31. As far as the Eastern Shore is concerned, the 1654 Maryland law against selling guns to the Indians seems to have been a dead letter from the start, since guns remained available from the Dutch and the Virginia English. However, there was one prosecution in Somerset County in 1675 for selling ammunition to the Indians. This occurred during a period of heightened English-Indian tension. The Somerset authorities probably hoped to discourage Indian attacks not by depriving the Indians of their guns, which would have infuriated the still powerful Nanticokes, but by keeping the Indians' ammunition stocks low enough to discourage the use of guns for anything but hunting. Somerset Co., Judicial Records L [reverse: 1675–77]: 37.

32. Browne et al. 1883–1972: 15:13, 2:479.

33. In 1690 Harry Will Tom came to the house of colonist Edmond Brannock and found several Englishmen drinking there. He began drinking with them and at some point was sent to another nearby plantation on an errand. On the way he fell asleep and lost the "stillard [steelyard] and can" that Brannock had loaned him. At that point, "John Brannock distrained of the Indian one gun, a certain quantity of peake, and one match coat" (Dorchester Co., Judicial Records 1690–92:171).

34. Dorchester Co., Judicial Records 1690–92:193.

35. Browne et al. 1883–1972: 38:148, 8:533.

36. Encroachment: Browne et al. 1883–1972: 25:364, 34:362. Fences: 26:443, 35:369; Somerset Co., Judicial Records 1707–11:96, 131, 1727–30:154, 222.

37. Browne et al. 1883–1972: 8:350, 17:77. In 1681 George Kent reported seeing a hundred hogs at Chicone (ibid.: 15:360).

38. Somerset County probate inventories copied in Worcester Co. Records JW 15 (1688–1742): 5 (1695). The earliest reference to these bowls being used in Somerset County dates to 1688 (Somerset Co., Judicial Records AW [1687–89]: 62); the last reference dates to 1726 (Somerset Co., Inventories EB 15 [1725–91]: 36). During the period 1695–1715, 7 percent of all surviving Somerset County probate inventories mention "Indian bowls." Colonoware: Henry 1992.

39. Beverley 1947 [1705]: 176.

40. For example, the same 1734 Somerset County property description mentions both a "negro house" and an "Indian cabin" (Land Records AZ: 168).

41. Murray, quoted in Speck 1927: 41.

42. Somerset Co., Judicial Records AB (1705–7): 246–47, 254, 257, 316.

43. Provincial Court Judgments PL 1:242.

44. Spelman 1910 [1613?]: cv.

45. Beverley 1947 [1705]: 227–28; copied, with additions, from Banister 1970: 322–23, 370.

46. Even as late as the 1750s the matchcoat was so typical an article of Eastern Shore Indian dress that the mere wearing of such a garment suggested an Indian identity to observers. An advertisement in the *Maryland Gazette*, dated May 21, 1752, concerns a slave who

had escaped from a Somerset County planter. This individual was described as "a tall thin Mulatto Slave, looks very much like an Indian, and will endeavor to pass for such when it suits him." The advertisement went on to say that "it is imagined he is making upwards to get among the Back Indians, having with him an Indian Match Coat" (*Maryland Gazette*, May 21, 1752, on microfilm in the Maryland Hall of Records).

47. Brasser 1978: 201 (fig. 4).

48. Goddard 1978: 218 (fig. 3).

49. Somerset Co., Judicial Records 1701–2:102–3.

50. Maryland Eastern Shore Indians were accused of several murders and/or kidnappings during the seventeenth century (Browne et al. 1883–1972: 2:195, 478, 480, 5:475–76, 8:18–19, 15:142–45, 147, 17:224–225).

51. Ibid.: 25:150.

52. Somerset Co., Judicial Records 1722–24:289, 1727–30:154, 184.

53. Letter from Maryland governor John Seymour, 1707, printed in Dielman 1921: 357.

54. Somerset Co., Judicial Records 1727–30:154.

55. Browne et al. 1883–1972: 25:390–391.

56. Ibid.: 33:111.

57. Ibid., 113.

58. Ibid.: 38:104–5.

59. Somerset Co., Judicial Records 1750:178.

60. The Servants and Slaves Act of 1717, which forbade "Negroes and Mulattoes" to marry "any White Person," did not extend the ban on interracial marriage to Indians (Browne et al. 1883–1972: 33:112). With regard to the tax status of Eastern Shore Indians, white heads of households and heads of households identified as "Indians" in the Somerset County tax lists were not assessed poll taxes for any female household members. By contrast, free black and free mulatto heads of household listed in those same tax lists were assessed taxes for female household members, as was specified in Maryland law (Somerset Co., Tax Lists 1735, 1736, 1750).

61. Browne et al. 1883–1972: 20:225.

62. Ibid.: 23:456.

63. Dorchester Co., Land Records Old 6:6, 3, Old 5:214, all quoted in McAllister 1962: 11, 13, 16.

64. Dorchester Co., Land Records Old 6:6.

65. Ibid., Old 5:37, quoted in McAllister 1962: 6.

66. Dorchester Co., Land Records Old 5:32, 45.

67. Ibid., Old 6:47, quoted in McAllister 1962: 21.

68. Browne et al. 1883–1972: 33:311–12, 34:252.

69. Dorchester Co., Land Records, Old 2:97.

70. Mowbray and Mowbray 1981: 109.

71. Maryland Laws of 1723, chap. 18, quoted in McAllister 1962: 51–55.

72. Browne et al. 1883–1972: 23:456.

73. Dorchester Co., Land Records, Old 5:32, 45.

74. Browne et al. 1883–1972: 5:556, 7:38–39, 8:18–19, 13:204, 17:399.

75. Somerset Co., Probate Inventories, EB 14:299–303.

76. Browne et al. 1883–1972: 26:442.

77. Ibid.: 26:442.

78. Ibid.: 25:364.

79. Ibid.: 29:229.

80. Kent 1984: 105.

81. Dorchester Co., Land Records, Old 2:45, 52.

82. Browne et al. 1883–1972: 35:368–70.

83. Dorchester Co., Land Records, Old 15:259, quoted in McAllister 1962: 34.

84. Dorchester Co., Land Records, Old 24:9.

85. Circa 1755 John Steptoe cut enough timber to "Build two Sea Vessels" on the Chicone reservation (Dorchester Co., Land Records Old 24:15). Steptoe claimed to have bought the timber from the Nanticokes, but it is likely that much timber was taken from Chicone without the Indians' permission. Certainly the Choptanks at Locust Neck complained about extensive illegal timber cutting during the 1750s (Browne et al. 1883–1972: 31:40–46).

86. The manor created in 1753 at Chicone was not the tract of land named Nanticoke Manor, a preexisting proprietary manor located on the Nanticoke River south of Chicone which was just one of many tracts set aside for use by the Calvert family (Dorchester Co., Land Records NH5-8 [1785–86]: 245).

87. Ibid.: 23.

88. Somerset Co., Judicial Records 1696–98:15, 55.

89. Torrence 1979: 473; Provincial Patents 9:469.

90. Provincial Patents, n.s., B:277–78.

91. Somerset Co., Wills, EB 5:176.

92. In 1676 John Parker was a servant in the household of Francis Jenkins (Somerset Co., Judicial Records L [reverse: 1675–77]: 81).

93. The Parkers repeatedly claimed parts of Askiminikansen as theirs (Proprietary Rent Rolls, Somerset Co., 1707:159, 174, 175), cut down boundary trees and cleared Indian land (Browne et al. 1883–1972: 22:295, 25:73, 244), burned Indian fences, and on one occasion assaulted a Pocomoke man named Robin John (Somerset Co., Judicial Records 1727–30: 154, 222).

94. Somerset Co., Land Records O–10-CD:812. In this document, dating to 1712, the property is described as including within its boundaries "an Indian Fort now standing remote from any landing."

95. Browne et al. 1883–1972: 25:392, 457.

96. Somerset Co., Judicial Records 1727–30:154.

97. Browne et al. 1883–1972: 19:319, 20:501.

98. Kent 1984: 72.

99. Somerset Co., Judicial Records AB (1705–7): 150.

100. Browne et al. 1883–1972: 29:211.

101. Ibid.: 42:573.

102. Ibid.: 28:257–58.

103. Ibid.: 28:263.

104. Ibid.: 28:264.

105. Ibid.: 28:260–69.

106. Ibid.: 28:269.

107. Ibid.: 28:268.

108. Ibid.: 28:582–91.

109. Ibid.: 35:370.

110. The earliest reference to a Nanticoke Indian with the surname Coursey dates to 1704, when Henry Coursey pawned a belt of peak and complained about not being paid its full value. Another member of the Coursey family, Tom Coursey, appears to have been an ally of Panquash in his successful 1713 attempt to regain political control of the Nanticokes from the "emperor" Ashquash (ibid.: 26:42, 29:228).

111. Somerset Co., Land Records O-20:224, 225.

112. Worcester Co., Land Records A:475.

113. Anonymous 1837 [1746].

114. Brown et al. 1883–1972: 28:268.

115. Worcester Co., Land Records B:311.

116. Somerset Co., Land Records B:111.
117. Browne et al. 1883–1972: 28:338.
118. Ibid.: 32:25.
119. Dorchester Co., Land Records Old 8:152, quoted in McAllister 1962: 58; Browne et al. 1883–1972: 31:30.
120. Browne et al. 1883–1972: 31:298–99, 352–55.
121. Ibid.: 31:355–57.
122. Ibid.: 32:209–11.
123. Maryland Laws of 1768, quoted in McAllister 1962: 72–75.
124. Eddis 1969: 59–60.
125. Browne et al. 1883–1972: 71:148.
126. Speck 1927.
127. Maryland Laws of 1798, chap. 82, quoted in McAllister 1962: 100–108.
128. There is an 1837 reference to "Thomas Joshua's Lot," which suggests he was still alive in that year (Dorchester Co., Chancery Court Decrees, no. 11240 [unrecorded, filed in Maryland Hall of Records, Annapolis]).
129. Dorchester Co., Land Records Old 2:115, quoted in McAllister 1962: 46.
130. Browne et al. 1883–1972: 31:84.
131. Dorchester Co., Land Records 2HD:604–17.
132. Ibid.: 472, 563.
133. Ibid. 12HD:298, 14HD:312, 15HD:248.
134. U.S. Census of 1800, Population Schedules, Dorchester Co.
135. Dorchester Co., Land Records 14ER:494.
136. Brackett 1889: 33–34.
137. Davidson 1985: 156; Somerset Co., Land Records O-7 (1683): 31.
138. Somerset Co., Tax Lists 1735, 1736, 1748, 1750.
139. At that time in Maryland, manumission by will was not valid, and the only legal way to give a slave freedom was by a deed that had to be recorded in the county land records. The Somerset Land Records contain very few manumissions until after the Revolutionary War, and none of these persons could be James Scokem.
140. Porter 1979.

Five. Virginia's Gingaskin Reservation after 1700

1. Kulikoff 1986; Main 1982: 260–61 and chap. 6; Sobel 1978: 24ff., 64.
2. Main 1982: 128ff. (quarters), 135 (furnishings); analogy to hamlets is ours.
3. Clemens 1980: chap. 5; Hast 1979: 34 (crops); Deal 1981: 3 (tobacco); Main 1982: 73–74, 77–78, 183 (crafts), 74–75 (fields), 76 (nutrition).
4. Northampton Co., Wills, etc. 15:135 (Quinney), Orders 14:214 (Jeffery).
5. Northampton Co., Orders 24:28 (Cross), 355 (repeated 25:94), 400, 22:127 (Drummond), and Wills and Inventories 22:479 (Daniel), Deeds, Wills, etc. 19:309 (Rozario), Minutes 27:54 (Sunket).
6. Northampton Co., Wills, etc. 14:379 (West), Orders 20:26 (Press).
7. Northampton Co., Orders 20:102 (in which a white female Beavans had a mulatto bastard in 1734), 22:345, Minutes 28:225, 240, Marriage Register 1 (1706–1852) (Beavans); other names: ibid. A common variant of Beavans today in Northampton County is Bibbins.
8. Northampton Co., Deeds, Wills, etc. 19:300, 303; Wills, etc. 15:14, 101, 151, 156, 204, 213.
9. Northampton Co., Deeds, Wills, etc. 19:309 (indenture), Orders 15:160 (acknowl-

edgment), 201–2, Wills, etc. 15:33, Orders 18:140, 186, 19:51, 77, 23:143, Minutes 26:4.

10. Northampton Co., Orders 25:230, Minutes 26:4 (Scarburgh Bingham), 29:278 (Southy Bingham), 27:466 (Press); Hungars Parish Vestry Book, 54 (boarding).

11. Northampton Co., Orders 20:26, 35 (Ibbey-Press), 22:109, 112, 127–28, 145, 175, 197, 354 (Daniel-West); other Daniel suits: Orders 22:297, 312–13, 331 (against William Press), 24:400, 406, 25:113, 116, 259 (against Solomon Jeffery). No reason is given in the records why John Daniel was collecting a debt from West; he may have represented the tribe, or he and his family may have been letting West use their portion of Gingaskin farm-land. Later disputes: Orders 25:165, Minutes 26:35, 27:197, 29:167, 252. Prosecutions by non-Indians: ibid. 26:41, 27:294, 394, 28:235, Orders 24:28.

12. Northampton Co., Orders 15:86, Deeds and Wills 1711–18:33–34 (patent), Orders 24:474 (road; "from the bay side County Road to the Indian Road"—except that the bay-side road runs through, not around, the old reservation).

13. Hening 1809–23: 8:414–15.

14. Ibid.: 661; McIlwaine 1915: 13:14; Hungars Parish Vestry Book, 33, 34, 41.

15. Doris Adler, personal communication (to Rountree), 1994. Gingaskin descendants are not hard to identify genealogically, given the recent date of the reservation's demise. How-ever, most of those living on the Eastern Shore remain extremely reluctant to talk about their Indian ancestry with whites (including Rountree) for fear of being identified with the all-too-common—and quite erroneous—stereotype of Indians as mean, lazy drunks.

16. Hast 1979: chaps. 2, 7; pp. 34, 135 emphasize the shore's vulnerability to raids. The statement about isolation during bad weather is still partially true.

17. Berlin 1983: xix, xxi; Raboteau 1983: 208–9; Sobel 1987: 5n.

18. Deal 1988: 279. See that source and also Deal 1993 for a more comprehensive view of free blacks on the Virginia Eastern Shore.

19. Northampton Co., Orders 17:192, McIlwaine 1915: 5:369 (1722–23), 9:73 (1758). Only three anti–free black petitions, other than the ones of 1831, reached Richmond from any of the other counties with higher percentages of free blacks in their populations: Isle of Wight complained in 1809 about free-running hogs, suspecting that most were owned by free blacks; it also demanded tougher laws to control all blacks in 1817 (Commonwealth of Virginia, Legislative Petitions, Isle of Wight Co., Dec. 19, 1809, Dec. 9, 1817). King William complained about stealing by both free and enslaved blacks (ibid., King William Co., Jan. 6, 1847).

20. Commonwealth of Virginia, Legislative Petitions: various counties in the piedmont and coastal plain. Northampton's are dated Dec. 6, 1831, and Feb. 23, 1839; Nansemond's is dated Feb. 2, 1833.

21. Hening 1809–23: 2:267 (1668), 3:87 (1691), 251, 298, 459 (1705), 12:184 (1785), 4:133 (voting). Quadroons are one-fourth African, three-fourths European in ancestry; oc-toroons are one-eighth African, seven-eighths European in ancestry.

22. For a list of persons emancipated between 1782 and 1865 in Northampton County, see Latimer 1994.

23. Hening 1809–23: 11:39–40 (manumission); Kulikoff 1986: 305 (mini–civil war). Liberal period: Russell 1913: 56ff.; Berlin 1974: chaps. 1–3; Jordan 1968: chaps. 9–10; Sobel 1987: 197ff. Mariner 1979 (Methodism); Jordan 1968: 391 (Haitians). Berlin 1974: 92 (expulsion law; for debates surrounding law's passage, see Russell 1913: 65ff.); Jordan 1968: 348 (other states). Certificates: Shepherd 1835: 1:238 (1793), 2:417–18 (1803), 3:274 (firearms; also Northampton Co., Orders 35:253), 124 (reading). Berlin 1974: 185–86 (colonization movements); Jordan 1968: 553ff., who calls colonization movements "a compelling fantasy" on the part of whites; Russell 1913: 152ff. and Berlin 1974: 146–48 (white friends), 331 (insecurity), 94ff. (labor laws)

24. Northampton County, Order and Minute Books, passim. Criminal cases: Orders 31 (1787–89): 63, 33 (1796–1800): 392, 34 (1801–7): 361; 35 (1808–16): 30, 106–7. 1792 plot: Orders 32 (1789–95): 212; Palmer 1875: 5:540, 542, 547; Barnes 1988: 37–39; Jordan (1968: 122) wrote that the only such free black incitement to rebellion he found was in South Carolina, so this one must be added to it. Robbery and rape: Orders 33 (1796–1800): 264–65, 355. White women having mulatto children: Minutes 1761–65:66, Minutes 1777–83:237, Orders 34 (1801–7): 92, 252. Free blacks in suits: Orders 33 (1796–1800): 182, 235, 247–48, 365, 377, 431, 34 (1801–7): 516, 35 (1808–16): 60. Women fighting: Orders 34 (1801–7): 236–39, 35 (1808–16): 4–5. Woman (Esther Collins) living on former reservation land: Deeds 27:227. "Dealing with slave": Orders 34 (1801–7): 433. Some of the names that appear in the free black community of Northampton County from at least the mid-eighteenth century onward are Becket, Carter, Collins, Driggus (formerly Rodriguez), Sisco (formerly Francisco), Stephens, and Webb.

25. Klein 1967: 235 (population); Berlin 1974: 3 and Russell 1913: 40–41, 51 (origins); Deal 1993, also Breen and Innes 1980 (families).

26. Hening 1809–23: 3:87; Jordan 1968: 124; Russell 1913: 51; Hast 1969.

27. Williamson 1980; Main 1982: 127.

28. Northampton Co., Wills, Deeds, etc. 26:110, Orders 18:326. In 1752 two Indians with Christian names only claimed their freedom (legal basis unspecified), but the court ruled that "they have no leave to prosecute for their Freedom" (ibid., 23:171, 186–87).

29. Deal 1993; Klein 1967: 228; see also Russell 1913: 18ff.

30. Klein 1967: 242.

31. Berlin 1974: 3–4, 57–58. Berlin generalizes from Maryland, the one mid-Atlantic colony where a census was taken in the middle of the eighteenth century. In 1755, 2 percent of Maryland's population were free African Americans. Eighty percent of the free blacks were mulattoes, and 50 percent were under the age of sixteen; 90 percent of the under-sixteens were mulattoes, indicating recent miscegenation was a major source of mulattoes.

32. Berlin 1974: 218–19 (occupations); Sobel 1978: 24ff., 64 (time).

33. Berlin 1974: 224–26.

34. Berlin 1974: 232–33 (refusals); Kulikoff 1986: 166 (patriarchy).

35. Sobel 1987: 100–102.

36. Berlin 1974: 269ff. (close ties), 271, 273ff. (distancing), 251 (settlement); Kulikoff 1986: 346 (family ties).

37. Kulikoff 1986: 217ff., 229.

38. Berlin 1974: 260, also Kulikoff 1986: 180 and Sobel 1987: 44ff. (men); Kulikoff 1986: 218ff., 229 (women); Berlin 1974: 299 and Raboteau 1983: 202–5 (churches).

39. Berlin 1974: 261; see also Sobel 1987: 150; Williamson 1980: 35, 37, 42; Kulikoff 1986: 386–87. For an overview of miscegenation in pre–Civil War Virginia, see Johnston 1970.

40. Berlin 1974: 264–68 (liaisons). One local historian believes that some modern Eastern Shore whites' very conservative racial attitudes derive from their male ancestors' probable clandestine liaisons. When blood relationship to members of the black community is uncertain but likely, then anything leading to miscegenation could also lead to incest (Rountree, field notes 1994).

41. Cassell 1972; Hast 1979: 143, 136.

42. Ibid.: 136ff.

43. Nansemond: Commonwealth of Virginia, Legislative Petitions, Nansemond Co., May 21, 1783, Nov. 11, 1784, Nov. 16, 1785. Northampton: ibid., Northampton Co., May 27, 1782, May 23, 1783, June 12, 1784.

44. Commonwealth of Virginia, Legislative Petitions, Northampton Co., Nov. 26, 1784.

45. The petition was deemed "reasonable," but no text of a resulting law exists. North-

ampton Co., Orders 30:210, 246–47 (commissions); report dated Jan. 1785, in loose papers in courthouse (courtesy of Jean Mihalyka); Orders 32:193 (prosecution). The Langs in the county at that time were free blacks.

46. Commonwealth of Virginia, Legislative Petitions, Northampton Co., Oct. 26, 1787 (Savage), Oct. 10, 1787 (landowners).

47. Hening 1809–23: 13:551; Northampton Co., Orders 32:283 (appointment), 447 (replacement); Palmer 1875: 6:649.

48. Northampton Co., Orders 31:173, 32:284, 317 (Edmund Press), 295, 302 (Scarburgh Bingham), 31:285 (Esther Drighouse; there are two Betty Drighouses and two Nathan Drighouses whose lives overlapped, and the relationship among them is not wholly certain), 34:444, 454 (Polly Press).

49. Shepherd 1835: 1:238 (1793), 2:417–18 (1803). For an overview, see Berlin 1974: 92ff. and Jordan 1968: chap. 11. Ira Berlin questions how large a percentage of the free black population actually complied with the registration law at any given time (1974: 328–29).

50. Northampton Co., Orders 32:354, 358.

51. Schreiner-Yantis 1971: N–1.

52. Northampton Co., Orders 35:281–82.

53. Commonwealth of Virginia, Legislative Petitions, Northampton Co., Dec. 2, 1812. The signers were Ibby (Mrs. John) Francis, Edmund Press, Molly (Mrs. Samuel) Beavans, Betty Drighouse, Susan (Mrs. John) Beavans, Molly Jeffery, Rachel West, Polly West, Nanny (Mrs. James) Carter, Littleton Jeffery, and Betsy Collins (one of two, possibly Mrs. Mac Collins).

54. Enclosed with petition of Dec. 2, 1812.

55. Commonwealth of Virginia, Acts of Assembly 1812–13: 117–18.

56. Northampton Co., Orders 35:395, 412, 416–17 (report); loose papers in courthouse (courtesy of Jean Mihalyka); expenses copied into Deeds 26:184–85.

57. Edmund Press (parcel no. 25): Northampton Co., Deeds 26:238, Orders 36:27. Solomon Jeffery (parcel no. 23): Deeds 26:142–43, Orders 35:444. Rachel and Molly West (parcels no. 6 and 5): Deeds 26:76–78, Orders 35:409. William West/Weeks (parcel no. 2): Deeds 26:315–16. James West (parcel no. 3): Deeds 26:212, 248, Orders 35:518, 358.

58. William House (parcel no. 11): Northampton Co., Deeds 26:165–66, 29:191–92. House was probably the son of Susanna Press, daughter of an earlier Edmund, who married William House (Sr.) in 1788. Tabby Francis (parcel no. 24): Deeds 29:8–9, 27–28, 35:191–92, Orders 38:247, 279. Tabby Press had married Thomas Francis in 1796.

59. Northampton Co., Orders 38:60, 37:304 (registration), 35:491 (Rachel West), 493, 36:400 (James West), 38:99, 128, 149–50, 186 (Nancy Jeffery), 345 (George Press), 347, 349, 360, 373 (descendants), 452 (young Press; identity of his father is uncertain, but his mother's name was Vianna Press), 57 (young Drighouse).

60. Northampton Co., Deeds 28:222–23 (Weeks, 1826), 27:262–63 (West, 1822), 370–71 (Francis, 1823), 455 and Orders 37:73 (Jeffery mortgage, 1823), Orders 37:83, 196, Wills 37:60–62 (Jeffery estate, 1824), Deeds 28:18–19 (Collins, 1824), 180 (House, 1826), Deeds 29:35–36 (1829; Charles Pool was literate, one of the few Gingaskin connections to be so), 112–13 (Francis, 1830), Orders 38:34, 53, Wills 37:350 (Press, 1826).

61. Littleton Jeffery died in 1824, leaving two children as heirs to the reservation land he still owned. The daughter, Bethany, chose Gingaskin allottee Nathan Drighouse as her guardian in 1826, probably in order to get legal permission for her marriage to Luke Trower that same day. Early in 1831 Elizabeth Baker, orphan of allottee Thomas Baker, chose Nathan Drighouse as her guardian, and Luke Trower stood as Drighouse's security. Mac Collins, free black husband of allottee Betsy Shepherd Collins, was chosen as guardian the same day by Surany Collins; he and Drighouse stood as security for each other, and Surany and a young (non-Indian) Littleton Jeffery married each other two days later. In 1829 Caroline Press,

daughter of allottee Molly Press, chose William Stephens as her guardian, with John Beavans, a Gingaskin allottee's husband, acting as security; Molly and William were married the same day (Northampton Co., Orders 38:37, and Marriage Register 1 [Trower; the court assigned Severn Wickes as her brother John's guardian]; Orders 38:244 [Francis], 337 [Press], 524 [Baker]).

62. Berlin 1974: 188.

63. C. Hall 1963: 74, citing the Richmond *Inquirer* of Nov. 11, 1831 (mass meeting); Commonwealth of Virginia, Legislative Petitions, Northampton Co., Dec. 6, 1831, and Acts of Assembly 1831–32: 23 (Northampton law); Acts of Assembly 1832–33: 51 ("mixed").

64. Nancy Carter, married to free black man James Carter, had her own allotment and all but three acres of another one, inherited before 1819 from John Carter (presumably a relative). After she died in 1826, her widower sold the rest of the John Carter tract, but he held onto Nancy's original allotment until November 1831. Then he sold out, keeping a life interest in his house and one and a half acres (John Carter [parcel no. 10]: Northampton Co., Deeds 27:8, 28:300–301; Nancy Carter [parcel no. 7]: Deeds 29:217). Betsy Shepherd Collins (Betsy Collins the younger, Mrs. Mac Collins since 1809) sold out in November 1831, retaining a life interest in the house and two acres of land (parcel no. 13: Deeds 28:18–19, 30:427). Molly Press Beavans (Mrs. Samuel Beavans since 1797) had been able to keep her land mortgage-free, but she and her husband unloaded it in November 1831 (parcel no. 19: Deeds 29:285, Orders 39:104). Susan Beavans (Mrs. John Beavans) died before 1821, when her widower sold one acre from her allotment. He and later his heirs managed to keep the land free of liens until November 1831, when the land was sold away (parcel no. 9: Deeds 27:130, Orders 36:400, 39:221, 253). John Bingham and then his heirs held onto his portion of the Indian land until November 1831, when the heirs sold out (parcel no. 21: Deeds 29:239, Orders 39:46). Betty Drighouse (Mrs. Nathan Drighouse Jr. from 1810; probably a sister of John Bingham, for her daughter was one of John's heirs) was dead by 1831, and her daughter, another Betty Drighouse (Mrs. Isaiah Carter since 1823), sold the land away in November 1831 (parcel no. 17: Deeds 26:80–81, 29:220, 281, Orders 35:414, 39:102). William Drighouse (heir of allottee Nathan Sr.) was dead by 1831. His heir, Nathan (presumably his son, and married to Polly Bingham, another heir of John Bingham), sold the land in November 1831 (parcel no. 18: Deeds 29:282).

Two more Gingaskins had mortgaged their allotments, and in November 1831 they suddenly redeemed their land and sold it. Betsy Collins (the elder; probably born a Jeffery; Mrs. John Collins from 1803, Mrs. Robert Powell since before 1822) had mortgaged her own plot in 1822, and in November 1831 she paid off her debt and sold her original parcel (parcel no. 15: Deeds 27:275, 29:231, 235–36, Orders 39:23). Ann Drighouse (Mrs. Charles Pool from 1820 until his death sometime after 1829) was one of John Bingham's heirs who sold out in 1831; she mortgaged her own plot in 1829 and then redeemed it and sold out in November 1831 (parcel no. 16: Deeds 29:35–36, 220–21, 222).

Five more Gingaskin allotments were sold after court cases that got the heirs to agree to sell; three of the cases originated in November 1831. Thomas Baker, who married a Gingaskin Beavans as his second wife and died in 1829, was an allottee in his own right and also inherited the allotment of his first wife, Betsy Bingham Baker (married in 1805, dead by 1825). In mid-November 1831 the eldest son sued the other heirs, winning a decree within only three days that ordered the sale of all of the father's allotment and part of the mother's; they sold the rest of their mother's allotment at the same time (Thomas Baker [parcel no. 27] and Betsy Bingham Baker [parcel no. 1]: Deeds 29:233, 374, Orders 38:362, 363, 39:15, 17–18, 26, 27). Littleton Jeffery died in 1824 with his land intact. His heirs held onto it until November 1831, when they found themselves in a court case to determine the division of the land; naturally, there was no division, but rather a sale (parcel no. 20: Deeds 29:339–340, Orders 39:18, 23, 153). Molly Fisherman Press, widow since before 1813 of Littleton Press, died herself in 1826, leaving her allotment to several children. Three of them sold her land in early November 1831, but they had to sue their two youngest siblings before the sale could be legal, which sale occurred a year later (parcel no. 22: Deeds 29:218–219, 341–342, Orders 39:27). Thomas Jeffery's allotment was held jointly by heirs until in 1828 Bethany Jeffery Trower and her free black husband Luke sued the other heirs about a division. After three years of continuances of the case, the heirs suddenly agreed to sell out in mid-November 1831. Luke and Bethany Trower had sold their interest in the land a week previously, apparently illegally, and they had to resell it along with the other heirs (parcel no. 14: Deeds 29: 223, 230, 232, Orders 38:169–70, 185, 233, 299, 331, 417, 39:21, 23, 37).

65. Northampton Co., Orders 39:15 (allottees Betty Drighouse and Ann Drighouse Pool, heirs of John Carter, Molly Fisherman Press, one or more of the Jefferys), 28 (road), Deeds 29:609–10 (West).

66. Sophia Jeffery (parcel no. 8; Stephen Jeffery, parcel no. 4): Northampton Co., Deeds 26:278–79, 29:228–29, 33:29–30, Orders 39:15. Peggy Bingham (parcel no. 12): Deeds 27:273, 30:151–52, 35:70 (Francis purchase), 36:100–101 (1860 sale).

67. Ebby Baker (parcel no. 26): Northampton Co., Deeds 30:307–8, 558, 589–90, 33:151–52.

68. Marzone 1855.

69. Northampton Co., Orders 39:18–19, 39, 52, 475, 40:336.

70. Some of them appear in Latimer 1992.

71. Upshur 1901–2: 92.

72. U.S. Bureau of the Census: Schedules for 1850; Northampton Co., Deeds 35:180, 548–49. The 1840 schedule shows George Stephens living with a woman (probably his wife) a bit older than Molly's 1813 birthdate would indicate, and a girl aged 10–24 years old. No Stephens household appears in the 1860 schedules.

73. Weslager 1983.

74. U.S. Census 1790 and 1800, Population Schedules.

75. John Leeds Bozman, writing in the 1820s, stated that the few surviving Maryland Eastern Shore Indians were "intermixed with negro blood" (Bozman 1837: 1:115). Scharf believed that the last Indians of the Maryland Eastern Shore had "intermarried with negroes" and disappeared as a separate racial group before the Civil War (Scharf 1879: 1:428).

76. Davidson 1982: 82.

77. For example, a woman named Alsy Quash was a free black inhabitant of the region in 1830 (U.S. Census 1830, Dorchester Co., Md.).

78. Porter 1979.

79. Mooney 1928: 5–6.

80. Mooney 1907: 144, 152.

81. Because we have not done in-depth genealogical and historical research on the immediate ancestors of these modern people, we are unable to comment upon their claimed descent from the historic tribes or their claim for unbroken social cohesion among their ancestors (i.e., the continued existence of *tribes*, even when the reservations were gone).

Six. Geography, Ecology, and the Eastern Shore Tribes

1. In 1993 one of us wrote that in order to understand Native Americans in history, the disciplines of "history and anthropology (all four subfields) plus sociology, psychology, geography, and ecology" should be put to use (Rountree 1993d: 228). In writing this volume, we agreed that geography and ecology stood out as explanatory factors when we began to compare regions.

2. We are aware that compiling data for that kind of precise description—plants that are both edible and native—requires either a botanical specialist's coming into the project or the

ethnohistorian's investing a great deal of time in learning the subject. We are fortunate that one of us (Rountree) became curious about native, usable plants in 1987 and began making detailed files for the whole mid-Atlantic region, trying to understand the foraging that underlay a major part of Indian life there. One by-product of her study (Rountree forthcoming) is a much more detailed grasp of what Indian women's lives were like.

3. Carneiro 1978, 1987.

4. Rountree and Turner n.d.; Potter 1993: 150–68; Turner 1976, 1993.

5. Smith 1986a [1608]: 69.

6. Goddard 1978: 73.

7. Davidson 1993: 139.

8. Smith 1986b [1612]: 225.

9. Davidson 1993: 146–47.

10. The one exception we have found comes from 1677, when some Chicconeses ("Checonesseck") from the North brought manninoses (soft-shelled clams, *Mya arenaria*), presumably dried ones, to trade with the Nanticokes for peak (Browne et al. 1883–1972: 15:146).

11. Shells going westward: Smith 1986a [1608]: 69. Copper: no direct mention, but the metal did not occur east of the fall line. Puccoon: the only direct mention comes from 1681, when Nanzaticos from the Rappahannock River are recorded as taking it to the Nanticokes (Browne et al. 1883–1972: 15:372). Today puccoon (*Lithospermum caroliniense*) occurs only in Sussex Co., Va., formerly Nottoway Indian territory, and in southeastern South Carolina.

12. Turner 1993: pp. 84–86 and fig. 3.2.

13. Hughes 1980: 205–13.

14. Rountree 1990: chap. 5.

15. Commissioners Appointed under the Great Seale of England for the Virginia Affairs 1896 [1677]: 291 (civil rights), 290 ("Neighbour Indians").

16. Browne et al. 1883–1972: 2:25 (1666), 5:29 (1668), 8:318, 319, 321 (1692), 532 (1693), 15:170 (1668), 213 (1678), 25:87, 89 (1700), 28:582, 585, 587, 590 (1742).

17. Browne et al. 1883–1972: 33:113.

18. Hening 1803–23: 3:298; Browne et al. 1883–1972: 33:111.

19. John Banister wrote in the late seventeenth century that no Indian male felt fully clothed without "their gun on their shoulder, & their shot-bag by their side" (Banister 1970: 382).

Bibliography

Abbott, R. Tucker. 1974. *American Seashells*. 2d ed. New York: Van Nostrand.

Accomack County, Va. 1668 to present. County records. Housed in the courthouse in Accomack, Va.; copies in the Library of Virginia, Richmond.

Ames, Susie May. 1940. *Studies of the Virginia Eastern Shore in the Seventeenth Century*. Richmond: Dietz Press.

Ames, Susie May, ed. 1954. *County Court Records of Accomack-Northampton, Virginia, 1632–1640*. Washington, D.C.: American Historical Association.

———. 1973. *County Court Records of Accomack-Northampton, Virginia, 1640–1645*. Charlottesville: Univ. Press of Virginia.

Angier, Bradford. 1974. *Field Guide to Edible Wild Plants*. Harrisburg, Pa.: Stackpole Books.

Anonymous. 1837 [1746]. Observations in Several Voyages to Maryland and Virginia. Reprinted in the *Farmers Register*, vol. 3.

———. 1910 [1635]. A Relation of Maryland, 1635. In *Narratives of Early Maryland, 1633–1684*. Ed. Clayton Colman Hall. New York: Charles Scribner's Sons. Pp. 70–112. Rept. 1967; also rept. 1984 in Maryland Hall of Records 350th Anniversary Document Series.

———. 1947 [1610]. A *True Declaration of the Estate of the Colonie in Virginia* . . . . In *Tracts and Other Papers*. Ed. Peter Force. New York: Peter Smith. Vol. 3, no. 1.

———. 1947 [1655]. *Virginia and Maryland, or the Lord Baltimore's Printed Case, Uncased and Answered*. In *Tracts and Other Papers*. Ed. Peter Force. New York: Peter Smith. Vol. 2, no. 9.

Archer, Gabriel. 1969a [1607]. Relatyon of the Discovery of Our River. In *The Jamestown Voyages under the First Charter*. Ed. Philip L. Barbour. Cambridge: Hakluyt Society. Ser. 2, vol. 136. Pp. 84–98.

———. 1969b [1607; authorship uncertain]. Description of the People. In *The Jamestown Voyages under the First Charter*. Ed. Philip L. Barbour. Cambridge: Hakluyt Society. Ser. 2, vol. 136. Pp. 102–104.

Argall, Samuel. 1904–6 [1613]. A Letter of Sir Samuel Argall Touching His Voyage to Virginia, and Actions There: Written to Master Nicholas Hawes. In *Hakluytus Posthumus or Purchas His Pilgrimes*. Ed. Samuel Purchas. Glasgow: James MacLehose and Sons. 19:90–95.

Banister, John. 1970. *John Banister and His Natural History of Virginia, 1678–1692*. Ed. Joseph and Nesta Ewan. Urbana: Univ. of Illinois Press.

Barnes, Alton Brooks Parker. 1988. *Petersburg to Pungoteague*, vol. 1, *The Eastern Shore Militiamen before the Civil War, 1776–1858*. N.p.: Lee Howard.

Beal, Ernest O. 1977. *A Manual of Marsh and Aquatic Vascular Plants of North Carolina with Habitat Data*. Raleigh: North Carolina Agricultural Experiment Station, Technical Bulletin no. 247.

Berlin, Ira. 1974. *Slaves without Masters: The Free Negro in the Antebellum South*. New York: Pantheon Books.

——. 1983. Introduction. In *Slavery and Freedom in the Age of the American Revolution*. Ed. Ira Berlin and Ronald Hoffman. Charlottesville: Univ. Press of Virginia. Pp. xv–xxvii.

Beverley, Robert. 1947 [1705]. *The History and Present State of Virginia*. Ed. Louis B. Wright. Chapel Hill: Univ. of North Carolina Press.

Billings, Warren M. 1975. Some Acts Not in Hening's Statutes: The Acts of Assembly, April 1652, November 1652, and July 1653. *Virginia Magazine of History and Biography* 83:22–76.

Bland, Edward, Abraham Wood, Sackford Brewster, and Elias Pennant. 1911 [1651]. The Discovery of New Brittaine, Began August 27, Anno Dom. 1650.... In *Narratives of Early Carolina, 1650–1708*. Ed. Alexander S. Salley, Jr. New York: Charles Scribner's Sons. Pp. 5–19.

Boyd, Donna C., and C. Clifford Boyd. 1992. Late Woodland Mortuary Variability in Virginia. In *Middle and Late Woodland Research in Virginia: A Synthesis*. Ed. Theodore R. Reinhart and Mary Ellen N. Hodges. Archaeological Society of Virginia Special Publication no. 29. Pp. 249–76.

Bozman, John Leeds. 1837. *The History of Maryland*. 2 vols. Baltimore.

Brackett, Jeffrey R. 1889. *The Negro in Maryland*. Baltimore: Johns Hopkins Univ. Press.

Brasser, T. J. 1978. Mahican. In *Handbook of North American Indians*, vol. 15 (Northeast). Ed. Bruce G. Trigger. Washington, D.C.: Smithsonian Institution Press. Pp. 198–212.

Breen, T. H., and Stephen Innes. 1980. *"Myne Owne Ground": Race and Freedom on Virginia's Eastern Shore, 1640–1676*. New York: Oxford Univ. Press.

Briceland, Alan Vance. 1987. *Westward from Virginia: The Exploration of the Virginia-Carolina Frontier, 1650–1710*. Charlottesville: Univ. Press of Virginia.

Bridenbaugh, Carl. 1967. *Vexed and Troubled Englishmen, 1590–1642*. New York: Oxford Univ. Press.

Brown, Alexander. 1898. *The First Republic in America*. Boston.

Brown, Melvin L., and Russell G. Brown. 1972. *Woody Plants of Maryland*. Baltimore: Port City Press.

——. 1984. *Herbaceous Plants of Maryland*. Baltimore: Port City Press.

Browne, William Hand, et al., eds. 1883–1972. *The Archives of Maryland*. 72 vols. Baltimore: Maryland Historical Society.

Calvert Family Papers. Somerset County Rent Roll. MS 174, Enoch Pratt Free Library, Baltimore.

Calvert, Leonard. 1910 [1638.] Letter of Governor Leonard Calvert to Lord Baltimore, 1638. In *Narratives of Early Maryland, 1633–1684*. Ed. Clayton Colman Hall. New York: Charles Scribner's Sons. Pp. 150–59.

Canner, Thomas. 1904–6 [1603]. A Relation of the Voyage Made to Virginia in the *Elizabeth* of London . . . in the Yeere 1603. In *Hakluytus Posthumus or Purchas His Pilgrimes*. Ed. Samuel Purchas. Glasgow: James MacLehose and Sons. 18:329–35.

Carneiro, Robert L. 1978. Political Expansion as an Expression of the Principle of Competitive Exclusion. In *Origins of the State: The Anthropology of Political Evolution*. Ed. Ronald Cohen and Elman R. Service. Philadelphia: Institute for the Study of Human Issues. Pp. 205–23.

———. 1987. Further Reflections on Resource Concentration and Its Role in the Rise of the State. In *Studies in the Neolithic and Urban Revolutions*. Ed. Linda Manzanilla. Oxford: BAR International Series 349. Pp. 245–60.

Carr, Lois Green. 1988. Diversification in the Colonial Chesapeake: Somerset County, Maryland, in Comparative Perspective. In *Colonial Chesapeake Society*. Ed. Lois Green Carr, Philip D. Morgan, and Jean B. Russo. Chapel Hill: Univ. of North Carolina Press. Pp. 342–88.

Carr, Lois Green, and Lorena Walsh. 1977. Planter's Wife: The Experience of White Women in Seventeenth-Century Maryland. *William and Mary Quarterly*, 3d ser., 34:542–71.

Carr, Lois Green, Russell R. Menard, and Lorena S. Walsh. 1991. *Robert Cole's World: Agriculture and Society in Early Maryland*. Chapel Hill: Univ. of North Carolina Press.

Cassell, Frank A. 1972. Slaves of the Chesapeake Bay Area and the War of 1812. *Journal of Negro History* 57:144–55.

Chase, Joan W. N.d. Analysis of Skeletal Material from the Thomas Site 18CA88. 1990 report filed with Maryland Historical Trust, Crownsville, Md.

Cissna, Paul B. 1986. The Piscataway Indians of Southern Maryland: An Ethnohistory from Pre-European Contact to the Present. Ph.D. diss., American Univ.

Clark, Wayne E., and Helen C. Rountree. 1993. The Powhatans and the Maryland Mainland. In *Powhatan Foreign Relations, 1500–1722*. Ed. Helen C. Rountree. Charlottesville: Univ. Press of Virginia. Pp. 112–35.

Clayton, John. 1965 [1687]. The Aborigines of the Country: Letter to Dr. Nehemiah Grew. In *The Reverend John Clayton*. Ed. Edmund Berkeley and Dorothy S. Berkeley. Charlottesville: Univ. Press of Virginia. Pp. 21–39.

———. 1968 [1687]. Another Account of Virginia. Ed. Edmund Berkeley and Dorothy S. Berkeley. *Virginia Magazine of History and Biography* 76:415–36.

Clemens, Paul G. E. 1980. *The Atlantic Economy and Colonial Maryland's Eastern Shore: From Tobacco to Grain*. Ithaca: Cornell Univ. Press.

Cobb, Philip R., and David W. Smith. 1989. *Soil Survey of Northampton County, Virginia*. Washington, D.C.: U.S. Department of Agriculture.

Commissioners Appointed under the Great Seale of England for the Virginia Affairs. 1896 [1677]. Articles of Peace between the Most Mighty Prince . . . Charles the II . . . And the Severall Indian Kings and Queens &c . . . the 29th Day of May: 1677. *Virginia Magazine of History and Biography* 14:289–96.

Cope, Walter. 1969 [1607]. Letter to Lord Salisbury. In *The Jamestown Voyages under the First Charter*. Ed. Philip L. Barbour. Cambridge: Hakluyt Society. Ser. 2, vol. 103. Pp. 108–10.

Custer, Jay F. 1989. *Prehistoric Cultures of the Delmarva Peninsula: An Archaeological Study*. Newark: Univ. of Delaware Press.

Custer, Jay F., and Daniel R. Griffith. 1986. Late Woodland Cultures of the Middle and Lower Delmarva Peninsula. In *Late Woodland Cultures of the Middle Atlantic Region*. Ed. Jay F. Custer. Newark: Univ. of Delaware Press. Pp. 29–57.

Custer, Jay F., Patricia A. Jehle, H. Henry Ward, Scot C. Watson, and Claire Mensack. 1986. Archaeological Investigations at the Arrowhead Farm Complex, Kent County, Maryland. *Maryland Archaeology* 22(2):20–32.

Davidson, Thomas E. 1982. Historically Attested Indian Villages of the Lower Delmarva. *Maryland Archaeology* 18(1):1–8.

———. 1985. Free Blacks in Old Somerset County, 1745–1755. *Maryland Historical Magazine* 80:151–56.

———. 1993. Relations between the Powhatans and the Eastern Shore. In *Powhatan Foreign Relations, 1500–1722*. Ed. Helen C. Rountree. Charlottesville: Univ. Press of Virginia. Pp. 136–53.

Davidson, Thomas E., Richard Hughes, and Joseph McNamara. 1985. Where Are the Indian Towns? Archaeology, Ethnohistory, and Manifestations of Contact on Maryland's Eastern Shore. *Journal of Middle Atlantic Archaeology* 1: 43–50.

Deal, Joseph Douglas, III. 1988. A Constricted World: Free Blacks on Virginia's Eastern Shore, 1680–1750. In *Colonial Chesapeake Society*. Ed. Lois Green Carr, Philip D. Morgan, and Jean B. Russo. Chapel Hill: Univ. of North Carolina Press. Pp. 275–305.

———. 1993. *Race and Class in Colonial Virginia: Indians, Englishmen, and Africans on the Eastern Shore during the Seventeenth Century*. New York: Garland.

Dent, Richard J., Jr. 1995. *Chesapeake Prehistory: Old Traditions, New Directions*. New York: Plenum Press.

Dielman, Louis H., ed. 1921. Unpublished Provincial Records. Ed. Louis H. Dielman. *Maryland Historical Magazine* 16:354–69.

Dorchester County, Maryland. 1669 to present. Court Records. Housed in the Maryland Hall of Records, Annapolis; copies in the courthouse in Cambridge, Md.

Durand de Dauphiné. 1934 [1687]. *A Huguenot Exile in Virginia . . . from the Hague Edition of 1687*. New York: Press of the Pioneers.

Eddis, William. 1969. *Letters from America*. Ed. Aubrey C. Land. Cambridge: Harvard Univ. Press.

Fausz, J. Frederick. 1990. "An Abundance of Blood Shed on Both Sides": England's First Indian War, 1609–1614. *Virginia Magazine of History and Biography* 98:3–56.

Feest, Christian F. 1978. The Nanticoke and Neighboring Tribes. In *Handbook of North American Indians*, vol. 15 (Northeast). Ed. Bruce G. Trigger. Washington, D.C.: Smithsonian Institution Press. Pp. 240–52.

Fenton, William N. 1942. Contacts between Iroquois Herbalism and Colonial Medicine. Bureau of American Ethnology, *Annual Report for 1941*:503–26.

Fernald, Merritt Lyndon, and Alfred C. Kinsey. 1958. *Edible Wild Plants of Eastern North America*. Rev. ed. New York: Harper and Row.

Fleet, Henry. 1876 [1631–32]. A Brief Journal of a Voyage Made in the Bark *Virginia*, to Virginia and Other Parts of the Continent of America. In *The Founders of Maryland*. Ed. Edward D. Neill. Albany: Joel Munsell. Pp. 19–37.

Gardner, Paul S. 1994. Carbonized Plant Remains. In *Paspahegh Archaeology: Data Recovery Investigations of Site 44JC308 at the Governor's Land at Two Rivers, James City County, Virginia*. Ed. Mary Ellen N. Hodges and Charles T. Hodges. Williamsburg, Va.: James River Institute for Archaeology, Inc. Pp. 267–78.

Goddard, Ives. 1978a. Eastern Algonquian Languages. In *Handbook of North American Indians*, vol. 15 (Northeast). Ed. Bruce G. Trigger. Washington, D.C.: Smithsonian Institution Press. Pp. 70–77.

———. 1978b. Delaware. In *Handbook of North American Indians*, vol. 15 (Northeast). Ed. Bruce G. Trigger. Washington, D.C.: Smithsonian Institution Press. Pp. 213–39.

Gradie, Charlotte M. 1988. Spanish Jesuits in Virginia: The Mission That Failed. *Virginia Magazine of History and Biography* 96:131–56.

———. 1993. The Powhatans in the Context of the Spanish Empire. In *Powhatan Foreign Relations, 1500–1722*. Ed. Helen C. Rountree. Charlottesville: Univ. Press of Virginia. Pp. 154–72.

Griffith, Daniel R. 1980. Townsend Ceramics and the Late Woodland in Southern Delaware. *Maryland HIstorical Magazine* 75:23–41.

Hall, Claude H. 1963. *Abel Parker Upshur: Conservative Virginian, 1790–1844*. Madison: State Historical Society of Wisconsin.

Hall, Richard L. 1970. *Soil Survey of Wicomico County, Maryland*. Washington, D.C.: U.S. Department of Agriculture.

———. 1973. *Soil Survey of Worcester County, Maryland*. Washington, D.C.: U.S. Department of Agriculture.

Hamel, Paul B., and Mary U. Chiltoskey. 1975. *Cherokee Plants: Their Uses — A 400 Year History*. Sylva, N.C.: Herald.

Hamor, Ralph. 1957 [1615]. *A True Discourse of the Present State of Virginia*. Richmond: Virginia State Library.

Hariot, Thomas. 1972 [1590]. *A Briefe and True Report of the New Found Land of Virginia*. New York: Dover.

Harvill, A. M., Jr. 1970. *Spring Flora of Virginia*. Parsons, W.Va.: privately printed.

Harvill, A. M., Jr., Ted R. Bradley, Charles E. Stevens, Thomas F. Wieboldt, Donna M. E. Ware, and Douglas W. Ogle. 1992. *Atlas of the Virginia Flora*. 3d ed. Burkeville, Va.: Virginia Botanical Associates.

Hast, Adele. 1969. The Legal Status of the Negro in Virginia, 1705–1765. *Journal of Negro History* 54:217–39.

———. 1979. *Loyalism in Revolutionary Virginia: The Norfolk Area and the Eastern Shore*. Ann Arbor, Mich.: U.M.I. Research Press.

Heckewelder, John G. E. 1881 [1819]. *An Account of the History, Manners, and Customs of the Indian Nations Who Once Inhabited Pennsylvania and the Neighboring States*. Philadelphia: Historical Society of Pennsylvania.

Hening, William Waller, comp. 1809–23. *The Statutes at Large.* 13 vols. New York: R. and W. and G. Bartow.

Henry, Susan L. 1992. *Physical, Spatial, and Temporal Dimensions of Colono Ware in the Chesapeake, 1600–1800.* Columbia: Univ. of South Carolina Press.

Herrick, James W. 1995. *Iroquois Medical Botany.* Syracuse: Syracuse Univ. Press.

Hoagman, Walter J., John V. Merriner, Richard St. Pierre, and Woodrow L. Wilson. 1973. *Biology and Management of River Herring and Shad in Virginia.* Completion Report 1970–73. Gloucester Point: Virginia Institute of Marine Science.

Holdich, D. M., and R. S. Lowery, eds. 1988. *Freshwater Crayfish: Biology, Management, and Exploitation.* Portland, Oreg.: Timber Press.

Hughes, Richard. 1980. *A Preliminary Cultural and Environmental Overview of the Prehistory of Maryland's Lower Eastern Shore Based upon a Survey of Selected Artifact Collections.* Annapolis: Maryland Historical Trust, Manuscript Series, no. 26.

Hungars Parish, Northampton Co., Va. 1753–82. Vestry Book. In Library of Virginia.

Hutchinson, H. 1961. Indian Reservations of the Maryland Provincial Assembly on the Middle Delmarva. *Archaeolog* 13(2):1–5.

Hutchinson, H., W. H. Calloway, and C. Bryant. 1964. Report on the Chicone Site #1 (18-DO-11) and Chicone Site #2 (18-DO-10). *Archaeolog* 16 (1): 14–17.

Hutton, F. Z., Sr., A. P. Faust, R. Feuer, H. R. Frantz, T. J. Gladwin, A. H. Kodess, and T. E. McCuen. 1963. *Soil Survey of Dorchester County, Maryland.* Washington, D.C.: U.S. Department of Agriculture.

Hutton, F. Z., Sr., A. P. Faust, F. J. Gladwin, A. H. Kodess, J. E. McCuen, and William Y. Reybold III. 1964. *Soil Survey of Caroline County, Maryland.* Washington, D.C.: U.S. Department of Agriculture.

Jackson, Luther Porter. 1970. *Free Negro Land and Property Holding in Virginia, 1830–1860.* New York: Russell and Russell.

James, Frederick Charles. 1969. *The Woody Flora of Virginia.* Ph.D. diss., Univ. of North Carolina.

James River Project Committee. 1950 *The James River Basin, Past, Present, and Future.* Richmond: Virginia Academy of Science.

Jennings, Francis. 1982. Indians and Frontiers in Seventeenth Century Maryland. In *Early Maryland in a Wider World.* Ed. David B. Quinn. Detroit: Wayne State Univ. Press. Pp. 216–41.

Jesuit Letters. 1910 [various years, 1634 onward]. Extracts from the Annual Letters of the English Province. In *Narratives of Early Maryland, 1633–1684.* Ed. Clayton Colman Hall. New York: Charles Scribner's Sons. Pp. 118–44.

Johnston, James Hugo. 1970. *Race Relations in Virginia and Miscegenation in the South, 1667–1860.* Amherst: Univ. of Massachusetts Press.

Jones, Hugh. 1963 [1699]. Maryland in 1699: A Letter from the Reverend Hugh Jones. *Chronicles of St. Mary's* 11:98–95.

Jordan, Winthrop D. 1968. *White over Black: American Attitudes toward the Negro, 1550–1812.* Chapel Hill: Univ. of North Carolina Press.

Kent, Barry C. 1984. *Susquehanna's Indians*. Harrisburg: Pennsylvania Historical and Museums Commission, Anthropological Series no. 6.

Kingsbury, Susan Myra, comp. 1906–35. *Records of the Virginia Company of London*. 4 vols. Washington, D.C.: Library of Congress.

Klein, Herbert S. 1967. *Slavery in the Americas: A Comparative Study of Virginia and Cuba*. Chicago: Univ. of Chicago Press.

Kulikoff, Alan. 1986. *Tobacco and Slaves: The Development of Southern Cultures in the Chesapeake, 1680–1800*. Chapel Hill: Univ. of North Carolina Press.

Lamb, H. H. 1963. On the Nature of Certain Climatic Epochs Which Differed from the Modern (1900–1939) Normal. In *Changes of Climate: Proceedings of the Rome Symposium*. Paris: UNESCO. Pp. 125–50.

Latimer, Frances Bibbins. 1992. *The Register of Free Negroes, Northampton County, Virginia, 1853–1861*. Bowie, Md.: Heritage Books.

———. 1994. *Instruments of Freedom: Deeds and Wills of Emancipation, Northampton County, Virginia, 1782 to 1864*. Bowie, Md.: Heritage Books.

Lewis, Clifford M., and Albert J. Loomie. 1953. *The Spanish Jesuit Mission in Virginia, 1570–1572*. Chapel Hill: Univ. of North Carolina Press.

Lippson, Alice Jane, ed. 1973. *The Chesapeake Bay in Maryland: An Atlas of Natural Resources*. Baltimore: Johns Hopkins Univ. Press.

Lippson, Alice Jane, and Robert L. Lippson. 1984. *Life in the Chesapeake Bay*. Baltimore: Johns Hopkins Univ. Press.

Lucketti, Nicholas M., Mary Ellen M. Hodges, Charles T. Hodges, and 11 contributors. 1994. Summary and Discussion. In *Paspahegh Archaeology: Data Recovery Investigations of Site 44JC308 at the Governor's Land at Two Rivers, James City County, Virginia*. Ed. Mary Ellen N. Hodges and Charles T. Hodges. Williamsburg, Va.: James River Institute for Archaeology, Inc. Pp. 291–97.

Main, Gloria L. 1982. *Tobacco Colony: Life in Early Maryland, 1650–1720*. Princeton, N.J.: Princeton Univ. Press.

Mariner, Kirk. 1979. *Revival's Children: A Religious History of Virginia's Eastern Shore*. Salisbury, Md.: Peninsula Press.

———. 1996. *Once Upon an Island: The History of Chincoteague*. New Church, Va.: Miona Publications.

Martin, Joel W. 1994. Southeastern Indians and the English Trade in Skins and Slaves. In *The Forgotten Centuries: Indians and Europeans in the American South, 1521–1704*. Ed. Charles Hudson and Carmen Chaves Tesser. Athens: Univ. of Georgia Press. Pp. 304–24.

Martin, M. Kay, and Barbara Voorhees. 1975. *Female of the Species*. New York: Columbia Univ. Press.

Marye, William B. 1936a. Indian Paths of the Delmarva Peninsula. *Bulletin of the Archaeological Society of Delaware* 1(3):5–22.

———. 1936b. Indian Paths of the Delmarva Peninsula. *Bulletin of the Archaeological Society of Delaware* 2(4):5–27.

———. 1937. Indian Paths of the Delmarva Peninsula. *Bulletin of the Archaeological Society of Delaware* 2(5):1–37.

———. 1938a. Indian Paths of the Delmarva Peninsula. *Bulletin of the Archaeological Society of Delaware* 2(6):4–11.

———. 1938b. The Wicomiss Indians of Maryland. *American Antiquity* 4:146–52.

———. 1939a. The Wicomiss Indians of Maryland, Part II. *American Antiquity* 5:51–55.

———. 1939a. Indian Towns of the Southeastern Part of Sussex County. *Bulletin of the Archaeological Society of Delaware* 3(2):18–25.

———. 1940. Indian Towns of the Southeastern Part of Sussex County. *Bulletin of the Archaeological Society of Delaware* 3(3):21–28.

Maryland, State of. Testamentary Proceedings. Housed in the Maryland Hall of Records, Annapolis.

Marzone, William. 1855. Map and Profile of Experimental Survey . . . of the New York and Norfolk Airline Railway. 8 parts. Copy at Virginia Department of Historical Resources, Richmond.

Massey, A. B. 1961. *Virginia Flora: An Annotated Catalog of Plant Taxa Recorded as Occuring [sic] in Virginia.* Blacksburg: Virginia Agricultural Experiment Station, Technical Bulletin no. 155.

Matthews, Earle D., and Richard L. Hall. 1966. *Soil Survey of Somerset County, Maryland.* Washington, D.C.: U.S. Department of Agriculture.

Matthews, Earle D., and William U. Reybold III. 1966. *Soil Survey of Queen Annes County, Maryland.* Washington, D.C.: U.S. Department of Agriculture.

McAllister, J. A. 1962. *Indian Lands of Dorchester County, Maryland.* Cambridge, Md.: privately printed.

McIlwaine, H. R., comp. 1915. *Journal of the House of Burgesses.* 13 vols. Richmond: Virginia State Library.

———. 1925–66. *Executive Journals of the Council of Colonial Virginia.* 6 vols. Richmond: Virginia State Library.

———. 1979 [1924]. *Minutes of the Council and General Court of Virginia, 1622– 1632, 1670–1676.* 2d ed. Richmond: Virginia State Library.

McMahon, John V. L. 1831. *Historical View of the Government of Maryland from Its Colonization to the Present Day,* vol. 1. Baltimore.

Merrell, James H. 1989. *The Indians' New World: Catawbas and Their Neighbors from European Contact through the Era of Removal.* Chapel Hill: Univ. of North Carolina Press.

Merrill, William L., and Christian F. Feest. 1975. An Exchange of Botanical Information in the Early Contact Situation: Wisakon of the Southeastern Indians. *Economic Botany* 29:171–184.

Mooney, James. 1907. The Powhatan Confederacy Past and Present. *American Anthropologist* 9:129–52.

———. 1928. The Aboriginal Population of America North of Mexico. *Smithsonian Miscellaneous Collections* 80 (7). Washington, D.C.: Smithsonian Institution.

Mowbray, Calvin W., and Mary I. Mowbray. 1981. *The Early Settlers of Dorchester County and Their Lands.* N.p.: privately printed.

National Wetlands Inventory. 1986. *Atlas of National Wetlands Inventory Maps, Chesapeake Bay.* 4 vols. Newton Corner, Mass.: National Wetlands Inventory, Region 5, U.S. Fish and Wildlife Service.

Northampton County, Va. 1634 to present. County Records. Housed in the courthouse in Eastville, Va.; copies in the Library of Virginia, Richmond. (The first two volumes also are transcribed in Ames 1954 and 1973.)

Norwood, Col. 1947 [1649]. A Voyage to Virginia by Col. Norwood. In *Tracts and Other Papers*. Ed. Peter Force. New York: Peter Smith. Vol. 3, no. 10.

Nugent, Nell Marion. 1934. *Cavaliers and Pioneers: Abstracts of Virginia Land Patents and Grants, 1623–1800*. Vol. 1. Richmond: Dietz Press.

Palmer, William P., et al., comps. 1875–93. *Calendar of Virginia State Papers and Other Manuscripts, 1652–1781*. 11 vols. Richmond.

Pargellis, Stanley, ed. 1959. The Indians of Virginia. *William and Mary Quarterly*, 3d ser., 16:228–53.

Percy, George. 1921–22 [1612]. A Trewe Relacyon. *Tyler's Quarterly* 3:259–82.

———. 1969 [1608?]. Observations Gathered Out of a Discourse of the Plantation of the Southern Colonie in Virginia by the English, 1606. In *The Jamestown Voyages under the First Charter*. Ed. Philip L. Barbour. Cambridge: Hakluyt Society. Ser. 2, vol. 136, pp. 129–46. Also printed in *New American World: A Documentary History of North America to 1612*. Ed. David B. Quinn. 5 vols. New York: Arno Press. 5:266–74.

Perry, James R. 1990. *The Formation of a Society on Virginia's Eastern Shore, 1615–1655*. Chapel Hill: Univ. of North Carolina Press.

Perry, William Stevens. 1870. *Papers Relating to the History of the Church in Virginia, A.D. 1650–1776*. N.p.: Privately printed.

———. 1878a. *Papers Relating to the History of the Church in Colonial Delaware*. N.p.: Privately printed.

———. 1878b. *Papers Relating to the History of the Church in Colonial Maryland*. N.p.: Privately printed.

Peterson, Lee. 1978. *A Field Guide to Edible Wild Plants of Eastern and Central North America*. Boston: Houghton Mifflin.

Plantagenet, Beauchamp. 1947 [1648]. A Description of the Province of New Albion. In *Tracts and Other Papers*. Ed. Peter Force. New York: Peter Smith. Vol. 2, no. 7.

Porter, Frank W., III. 1979. Strategies for Survival: The Nanticokes in a Hostile World. *Ethnohistory* 26:325–45.

Potter, Stephen R. 1993. *Commoners, Tribute, and Chiefs: The Development of Algonquian Culture in the Potomac Valley*. Charlottesville: Univ. Press of Virginia.

Purchas, Samuel. 1614. *Purchas His Pilgrimage*. 2d ed. London.

———. 1617. *Purchas His Pilgrimage*. 3d ed. London.

Quinn, David Beers. 1974. *England and the Discovery of America*. New York: Knopf.

———. 1984. *The Lost Colonists and Their Probable Fate*. Raleigh: North Carolina Department of Cultural Resources.

———. 1985. *Set Fair for Roanoke: Voyages and Colonies, 1584–1606*. Chapel Hill: Univ. of North Carolina Press.

Quinn, David Beers, ed. 1955. *The Roanoke Voyages, 1585–1590*. Cambridge: Hakluyt Society. Ser. 2, vol. 104.

Raboteau, Albert J. 1983. The Slave Church in the Era of the American Revolution. In *Slavery and Freedom in the Age of the American Revolution*. Ed. Ira Berlin and Ronald Hoffman. Charlottesville: Univ. Press of Virginia. Pp. 193–213.

Radford, Albert E., Harry E. Ahles, and C. Ritchie Bell. 1968. *Manual of the Vascular Flora of the Carolinas*. Chapel Hill: Univ. of North Carolina Press.

Reybold, William U., III. 1971. *Soil Survey of Talbot County, Maryland*. Washington, D.C.: U.S. Department of Agriculture.

Richter, Daniel K. 1992. *The Ordeal of the Longhouse : The Peoples of the Iroquois League in the Era of European Colonization*. Chapel Hill: Univ. of North Carolina Press.

Rolfe, John. 1848 [1616]. Virginia in 1616. *Virginia Historical Register* 1 (3).

Rountree, Helen C. 1973. Indian Land Loss in Virginia: A Prototype of Federal Indian Policy. Ph.D. diss., Univ. of Wisconsin-Milwaukee.

———. 1989. *The Powhatan Indians of Virginia: Their Traditional Culture*. Norman: Univ. of Oklahoma Press.

———. 1990. *Pocahontas's People: The Powhatan Indians of Virginia through Four Centuries*. Norman: Univ. of Oklahoma Press.

———. 1992. Powhatan Priests and English Rectors: Worldviews and Congregations in Conflict. *American Indian Quarterly* 16:485–500.

———. 1993a. Who Were the Powhatans and Did They Have a Unified "Foreign Policy?" In *Powhatan Foreign Relations, 1500–1722*. Ed. Helen C. Rountree. Charlottesville: Univ. Press of Virginia. Pp. 1–19.

———. 1993b. The Powhatans and Other Woodland Indians as Travelers. In *Powhatan Foreign Relations, 1500–1722*. Ed. Helen C. Rountree. Charlottesville: Univ. Press of Virginia. Pp. 20–52.

———. 1993c. The Powhatans and the English: A Case of Multiple Conflicting Agendas. In *Powhatan Foreign Relations, 1500–1722*. Ed. Helen C. Rountree. Charlottesville: Univ. Press of Virginia. Pp. 173–205.

———. 1993d. Summary and Implications. In *Powhatan Foreign Relations, 1500–1722*. Ed. Helen C. Rountree. Charlottesville: Univ. Press of Virginia. 206–28.

———. Forthcoming. Powhatan Indian Women: The People Captain John Smith Barely Saw. Presidential address to American Society for Ethnohistory (November 1994), to be published in *Ethnohistory*.

———. 1996. A Guide to the Late Woodland Indians' Use of Ecological Zones in the Chesapeake Region. *The Chesopiean, a Journal of Archaeology* 34 (2–3).

Rountree, Helen C., and E. Randolph Turner III. 1994. On the Fringe of the Southeast: The Powhatan Paramount Chiefdom in Virginia. In *The Forgotten Centuries: Europeans and Indians in the American South, 1513–1704*. Ed. Charles Hudson and Carmen Chaves Tesser. Athens: Univ. of Georgia Press. Pp. 355–72.

———. Forthcoming. The Evolution of the Powhatan Paramount Chiefdom in Virginia. In *Chiefdoms and Chieftaincy: An Integration of Archaeological, Ethnohistorical, and Ethnographic Approaches*. Ed. Elsa M. Redmond. Gainesville: Univ. Presses of Florida.

Russell, John H. 1913. *The Free Negro in Virginia, 1619–1865*. Baltimore: Johns Hopkins Studies in Historical and Political Sciences. Ser. 31, no. 3.

Rutman, Darrett B., and Anita H. Rutman. 1979. "Now-Wives and Sons-in-
Law": Parental Death in a Seventeenth-Century Virginia County. In *The Ches-
apeake in the Seventeenth Century: Essays on Anglo-American Society*. Ed.
Thad W. Tate and David L. Ammerman. Chapel Hill: Univ. of North Carolina
Press. Pp. 153–82.

Sainsbury, Noel, J. W. Fortescue, and Cecil Headham, comps. 1860–1926. *Calendar of State Papers, Colonial Series*. 60 vols. London: Longman, Green and
Roberts.

Scharf, James Thomas. 1879. *History of Maryland from Earliest Times to the
Present Day*. 3 vols. Baltimore.

Schreiner-Yantis, Nettie. 1971. *A Supplement to the 1810 Census of Virginia*.
Springfield, Va.: privately published.

Scott, Jane. 1991. *Between Ocean and Bay: A Natural History of Delmarva*. Cen-
treville, Md.: Tidewater Publishers.

Seib-Toup, Rebecca. N.d. Descent, Kinship, and Residency. 1991 MS on file, Piscataway Recognition Project, Accokeek, Md.

Shepherd, Samuel, comp. 1835. *The Statutes at Large of Virginia . . . Being a
Continuation of Hening*. 3 vols. Richmond: privately printed.

Shreve, Forrest, M. A. Chrysler, Frederick H. Blodgett, and F. W. Wesley. 1969
[1910]. *The Plant Life of Maryland*. New York and Codicote, Herts.: Verlag
von J. Cramer. [Orig. pub. by Johns Hopkins Univ. Press.]

Sipple, William S. 1978. *An Atlas of Vascular Plant Species Distribution Maps for
Tidewater Maryland*. Annapolis: Maryland Department of Natural Resources,
Wetland Publication no. 1.

Smith, Bruce D. 1992. *Rivers of Change*. Washington, D.C.: Smithsonian Institution Press.

Smith, John. 1986a. *A True Relation*. In *The Complete Works of Captain John
Smith (1580–1631)*. Ed. Philip Barbour. 3 vols. Chapel Hill: Univ. of North
Carolina Press. 1:3–118.

———. 1986b. A Map of Virginia. [Including "The Proceedings of the English Colonie," compiled from various texts by William Simmond.] In *The Complete
Works of Captain John Smith (1580–1631)*. Ed. Philip Barbour. 3 vols. Chapel Hill: Univ. of North Carolina Press. 1:119–90.

———. 1986c. *The Generall Historie of Virginia, New England, and the Summer
Isles, 1624*. In *The Complete Works of Captain John Smith (1580–1631)*.
Ed. Philip Barbour. 3 vols. Chapel Hill: Univ. of North Carolina Press. 2:25–
488.

———. n.d. Virginia Discouered and Described by Captyn John Smith, 1606. [Map,
in various editions, including 1612.]

Sobel, Mechal. 1987. *The World They Made Together: Black and White Values in
Eighteenth-Century Virginia*. Princeton, N.J.: Princeton Univ. Press.

Somerset County, Md. 1665 to present. Court Records. Housed in the Maryland
Hall of Records, Annapolis; copies in the courthouse in Princess Anne, Md.

Speck, Frank G. N.d. Papers. Housed in the American Philosophical Society Library, Philadelphia.

———. 1927. The Nanticoke and Conoy Indians, with a Review of Linguistic Material from Manuscript and Living Sources: An Historical Study. *Papers of the Historical Society of Delaware*, n.s., vol. 1.

Speck, Frank G., Royal B. Hassrick, and Edmund S. Carpenter. 1942. Rappahannock Herbals, Folk-lore, and Science of Cures. *Proceedings of the Delaware County Institute of Science* 10:7–55.

Spelman, Henry. 1910 [1613?]. Relation of Virginea. In *The Travels and Works of Captain John Smith*. Ed. Edward Arber and A. G. Bradley. New York: Burt Franklin. Pp. ci–cxiv.

Stephenson, Robert L., Alice L. L. Ferguson, and Henry G. Ferguson. 1963. *The Accokeek Creek Site: A Middle Atlantic Seaboard Culture Sequence*. Anthropological Papers, no. 20. Ann Arbor: Univ. of Michigan.

Strachey, William. 1953 [1612]. *The Historie of Travell into Virginia Britania*. Ed. Louis B. Wright and Virginia Freund. Cambridge: Hakluyt Society. Ser. 2, vol. 103.

———. 1964 [1610]. A True Reportory of the Wreck and Redemption of Sir Thomas Gates . . . . In *A Voyage to Virginia in 1609, Two Narratives*. Ed. Louis B. Wright. Charlottesville: Univ. Press of Virginia. Also published in *New American World: A Documentary History of North America to 1612*. Ed. David B. Quinn. New York: Arno Press. Pp. 288–301.

Tantaquidgeon, Gladys. 1928. Mohegan Medicinal Practices, Weather-Lore, and Superstition. Washington, D.C.: *43d Annual Report*, Bureau of American Ethnology, pp. 264–79.

———. 1972. *Folk Medicine of the Delawares and Related Algonkian Indians*. Harrisburg: Pennsylvania Historical and Museum Commission, Anthropological Series 3.

Tatnall, Robert R. 1946. *Flora of Delaware and the Eastern Shore*. [N.p.]: Society of Natural History of Delaware.

Thomas, Ronald A. 1977. Radiocarbon Dates of the Woodland Period from the Delmarva Peninsula. *Bulletin of the Archaeological Society of Delaware* 11: 49–57.

Torrence, Clayton. 1979 [1935]. *Old Somerset on the Eastern Shore of Maryland: A Study in Foundations and Founders*. Baltimore: Regional Publishing Co.

Tuchman, Barbara. 1978. *A Distant Mirror: The Calamitous Fourteenth Century*. New York: Knopf.

Turner, E. Randolph, III. 1976. An Archaeological and Ethnohistorical Study on the Evolution of Rank Societies in the Virginia Coastal Plain. Ph.D. diss., Pennsylvania State Univ.

———. 1986. Difficulties in the Archaeological Identification of Chiefdoms as Seen in the Virginia Coastal Plain during the Late Woodland and Early Historic Periods. In *Late Woodland Cultures of the Middle Atlantic Region*. Ed. Jay F. Custer. Newark: Univ. of Delaware Press. Pp. 19–28.

———. 1992. The Virginia Coastal Plain during the Late Woodland Period. In *Middle and Late Woodland Research in Virginia: A Synthesis*. Ed. Theodore R. Reinhart and Mary Ellen N. Hodges. Archaeological Society of Virginia Special Publication no. 29. Pp. 97–136.

———. 1993. Native American Protohistoric Interactions in the Powhatan Core

Area. In *Powhatan Foreign Relations, 1500–1722*. Ed. Helen C. Rountree. Charlottesville: Univ. Press of Virginia. Pp. 76–93.

Ubelaker, Douglas H. 1974. *Reconstruction of Demographic Profiles from Ossuary Skeletal Samples: A Case Study from the Tidewater Potomac*. Smithsonian Contributions to Anthropology 18. Washington, D.C.

———. 1993. Human Biology of Virginia Indians. In *Powhatan Foreign Relations, 1500–1722*. Ed. Helen C. Rountree. Charlottesville: Univ. Press of Virginia. Pp. 53–75.

United States Bureau of the Census. 1830. *Fifth Census: or Enumeration of the Inhabitants of the United States, 1830*. Washington, D.C.

———. 1840. *Sixth Census, 1840*. Washington, D.C.

———. 1850. *Compendium of Enumeration: Seventh Census of the United States*. Washington, D.C.

Upshur, Thomas T. 1901–2. Eastern Shore History: An Address Delivered at Accomack Courthouse on June 19, 1900, Being the Occasion of the Dedication of the New Courthouse at That Place. *Virginia Magazine of History and Biography* 9:89–99.

Virginia, Commonwealth of. *The Acts of Assembly*. Richmond: printed session by session since 1809.

———. Legislative Petitions. Housed in the Library of Virginia, Richmond.

Virginia Office of the Secretary of Commerce and Resources. 1977. *Proposals for Coastal Resources Management in Virginia*. Richmond.

Wall, Robert, Stephen Israel, and Edward Otter. 1988. Potts 1 Lower Site: A Late Woodland Component on the Lower Wicomico Creek, Wicomico County, Maryland. *Maryland Archaeology* 24(2):1–26.

Weslager, C. A. 1983. *The Nanticoke Indians: Past and Present*. Newark: Univ. of Delaware Press.

Whitaker, Alexander. 1964 [1611]. Letter to Raleigh Croshaw. In *The Genesis of the United States*. Ed. Alexander Brown. New York: Russell and Russell (orig. pub. 1898). Pp. 497–500.

White, Fr. Andrew. 1910 [1634]. A Briefe Relation of the Voyage unto Maryland. In *Narratives of Early Maryland, 1633–1684*. Ed. Clayton Colman Hall. New York: Charles Scribner's Sons. Pp. 29–45.

White, Edgar. 1982. *Soil Survey of Kent County, Maryland*. Washington, D.C.: U.S. Department of Agriculture.

White, William. 1969 [1608?]. Fragments Published before 1614. In *The Jamestown Voyages under the First Charter*. Ed. Philip L. Barbour. Cambridge: Hakluyt Society. Ser. 2, vol. 136. Pp. 147–50.

Whitelaw, Ralph T. 1968 [1951]. *Virginia's Eastern Shore: A History of Northampton and Accomack Counties*. 2 vols. Gloucester, Mass.: Peter Smith.

Williamson, Joel. 1980. *New People: Miscegenation and Mulattoes in the United States*. New York: Free Press.

Wise, Jennings Cropper. 1967 [1911]. *Ye Kingdome of Accawmacke or the Eastern Shore of Virginia in the Seventeenth Century*. Baltimore: Regional Publishing Co.

Worcester County, Md. 1742 to present. Court Records. Housed in the Maryland Hall of Records, Annapolis; copies in the courthouse in Snow Hill, Md.

Wroth, Lawrence C. 1970. *The Voyages of Giovanni da Verrazzano, 1524–1528.* New Haven: Yale Univ. Press.

Wynn, Peter. 1969 [1608]. Letter of November 16, 1608. In *The Jamestown Voyages under the First Charter.* Ed. Philip L. Barbour. Cambridge: Hakluyt Society. Ser. 2, vol. 136:245–46.

Index

Page numbers for illustrations are in italics.

975.2
ROU

PER

Rountree, Helen C.,
Eastern Shore Indians
Virginia and Maryland

stain
noted
2/19 Anne